ENGAGING THE ENEMY

ENGAGING THE ENEMY

ORGANIZATION THEORY AND SOVIET

MILITARY INNOVATION, 1955–1991

Kimberly Marten Zisk

PRINCETON UNIVERSITY PRESS   PRINCETON, NEW JERSEY

Library of Congress Cataloging-in-Publication Data

Zisk, Kimberly Marten
Engaging the enemy : organization theory and Soviet
military innovation, 1955–1991 / Kimberly Marten Zisk.
p.   cm.
Includes bibliographical references and index.
ISBN 0-691-06982-4
1. Military doctrine—Soviet Union. I. Title.
UA770.Z54   1993
355.02′0947—dc20   92-33250   CIP

This book has been composed in Laser Sabon

Princeton University Press books are printed
on acid-free paper and meet the guidelines
for permanence and durability of the Committee
on Production Guidelines for Book Longevity
of the Council on Library Resources

Printed in the United States of America

10   9   8   7   6   5   4   3   2   1

To My Husband, Matt

Contents

Acknowledgments

MY RESEARCH was assisted by a grant from the Joint Committee on Soviet Studies of the Social Science Research Council and the American Council of Learned Societies, with funds provided by the U.S. Department of State. Research travel grants were provided by the Berkeley-Stanford Program in Soviet Studies, the Stanford Center on Conflict and Negotiation, and the Institute for the Study of World Politics. Research travel was also assisted by the (then-) Soviet Academy of Sciences USA and Canada Institute. Additional research funding was provided by the MacArthur Foundation Summer Fellowship of the Stanford University Center for International Security and Arms Control (CISAC). Completion of the project was made possible by an extended sojourn at CISAC, and by a summer appointment at the Mershon Center of the Ohio State University. I am especially grateful to John Lewis and William Perry, then-co-Directors of CISAC, and to Charles F. Hermann, Director of the Mershon Center, for their generous support.

A great many people helped me as I worked to shape the ideas underlying this book. Others gave me welcome advice in my attempts to communicate and defend those ideas. Many generously shared source materials with me. Back when this book was becoming a doctoral dissertation at Stanford University, I was blessed with an unusually active and supportive graduate committee: Alexander Dallin, Nina Halpern, and Scott Sagan; and my graduate advisor and mentor, David Holloway. Others who provided valuable advice at that time include Lynn Eden, Raymond Garthoff, and Alexander George.

As revisions began to emerge, many of these individuals continued to read new versions of the manuscript and to provide me with useful criticism. Significant portions of the book manuscript-in-progress were also read and critiqued by Matthew Evangelista, Harry Gelman, Jonathan Haslam, Robert Jervis, Condoleezza Rice, Jack Snyder, and Marc Trachtenberg, among others. My arguments in the chapter on Soviet reactions to the Schlesinger Doctrine were honed by the comments I received at a 1991 seminar at Stanford sponsored by the Nuclear History Program (NHP), arranged by G. Allen Greb. Versions of other chapters were presented at the American Political Science Association annual meetings in 1989 and 1990, and benefitted from comments received there. The entire manuscript was aided by its presentation at the 1991 NHP Third Study and Review Conference in Ebenhausen, Germany, led by Uwe Nerlich. Jack Snyder and Stephen Peter Rosen provided final critical reviews. I am also grateful for the extensive and supportive work of Malcolm DeBevoise and Bill Laznovsky at Princeton University Press.

The book is stronger because of the suggestions I have received from all of these people.

At a personal level, I am indebted to my parents and parents-in-law for their support and advice through these years of research and writing. My greatest debt is to my husband and soulmate, Matt. At a mundane level, he has given me countless hours of assistance with the high-tech world of word processing and typesetting, and the low-tech world of proofreading. Much more important, he has given me endless understanding, encouragement, and love. He has helped me to keep things in perspective, and thus this book is dedicated to him.

ENGAGING THE ENEMY

Introduction

MANY POLITICAL SCIENTISTS have recently become interested in the study of military organizations and the development of military doctrine. Most work in this area has argued that military organizations suffer from dysfunctional organizational biases. Military organizations are seen to be primarily bureaucratic actors, focused on domestic battles for resources and autonomy from civilian control. Military organizations are believed to value their own prestige and organizational stability and predictability above all else. This is thought to distort officers' views of the objective strategic situation that their state faces.[1] Barry R. Posen in particular concludes from this perspective that military organizations resist innovation in doctrine, and remain wedded to doctrines that have become routine. He posits that military organizations are likely to innovate only when they or their close allies suffer obvious defeat on the battlefield, or when they are forced to adopt new doctrines by civilians who intervene in the military decision-making process.[2] Most scholars whose work falls within this perspective believe that civilian intrusion into the military doctrine formulation process is considered a challenge to military autonomy, and therefore leads to pitched bureaucratic battles.

This book explores and challenges these common propositions. Its theoretical framework recognizes that military officers, like members of other organizations, often prefer to maintain policies that have been worked out in the past, and often resist efforts to introduce innovative thinking into the organizational decision-making process. It also recognizes that military officers try to protect and expand their budgetary resources and the autonomy of the military institution from civilian control. However, I argue that a more complex set of arguments from organization theory should be used to provide a better understanding of how military organizations respond to the idea of change.[3] I do not accept the thesis that organizational resistance to change and forceful civilian intervention into the decision-making process alone are sufficient to explain the development of military doctrine over time. Three additional variables are necessary for a complete explanation.

First, I argue that professional military officers are attuned to changes occurring in the military doctrines and force postures of their potential future enemies. Officers are often concerned not only about their own institutional interests in domestic politics, but also about the protection of state security interests from foreign threats. When military officers no-

tice that a change in their adversary's doctrine for future war has potential significant ramifications for the conduct of that war, they are likely
to reexamine their own doctrinal precepts to determine whether they are
still adequate. If current doctrine is found to be inadequate, innovation in
doctrine can result without civilian interference into military affairs. Innovation in one state's military doctrine can therefore lead to a reactive
innovation in the doctrine of its potential future opponent. When military
officers' views about the hostility of potential future enemies and about
the need for adequate future war preparation are brought into the equation, doctrinal innovation within the military organization is no longer an
anomaly.

For the purposes of this book, "doctrinal innovation" will be defined
as a major change in how military planners conceptualize and prepare for
future war. In particular, it involves a reconceptualization of what sorts
of military tasks need to be performed in wartime, or major alterations in
how existing tasks are performed.[4] Civilian leaders may propose doctrinal innovations, and may in fact believe that such innovations have
been implemented through their own policy decisions. However, according to my definition, innovations have only been realized when they are
reflected in the actual war plans and preparations of military commanders. Examples of innovation discussed in this book include significant de-
partures from previous military thinking and planning on questions such
as whether war will be nuclear or conventional, whether nuclear war will
be total or limited, and whether initial preparations for war must be offensive or defensive.[5] I define "reactive innovation" as a major change in
thinking about and preparation for future war that occurs because of a
change in war thinking or preparation made by a potential opponent.
The reactive innovation may, but need not, mirror the opponent's innovation. This definition, which recognizes that innovation in one state may
copy innovation in another state, is consistent with the definitions of
many political scientists who have studied innovation: a policy innovation occurs when a new idea is adopted by an organization or a state, and
followed by policy action, no matter how long the idea has been present
in the world, and no matter how many other states have adopted the
policy beforehand.[6]

Second, I argue that not all military officers from a particular institution act according to a simple, conservative calculation of that institution's organizational interests. Instead, officers are individuals who bring
unique political and personal considerations, as well as organizational
considerations, into policy debates. Some individuals are more inclined
than others to propose or accept innovative ideas. Receptivity to innovation may depend on such factors as age, length of service, educational
experience, and psychological predisposition. Not all individuals in any

institution value stability and predictability above all else. Some individuals value change.

Individuals with different perspectives on policy form a community of experts on national security issues. In some cases, this community includes civilian defense experts as well as members of the military institution. The decisions made by national security organizations about doctrine will reflect the interplay of a community of individuals, reacting to a changing environment. As this community of individuals reacts to the environment, innovation can be introduced into an organization that otherwise would seem to value conservative, incremental policy-making. Some individuals act as innovation entrepreneurs.

Third, I argue that civilian intervention into military doctrine formulation can take several forms, and that various forms of intervention are accompanied by varying degrees of bureaucratic infighting and interorganizational hostility. When civilian leaders decide that they want to encourage innovation in military doctrine in ways that are inimical to the interests of the military institution, they can choose among various political strategies to accomplish their goals. They may decide to try to force particular policy changes on the military, and this can result in a pitched bureaucratic battle and strained civil-military relations. If time is of the essence in the eyes of these civilians, they may not have a choice other than conflict; they may decide that they need immediate change in the behavior of the military organization. However, if they have time to experiment, then they may decide instead to try to broaden the defense policy community. They may force military officers merely to interact with and listen to civilian experts who have alternative viewpoints on doctrinal issues, rather than forcing officers to accept particular predetermined policies. By broadening the defense policy community, civilians can build coalitions with reformist segments of the officer corps, and thus gain political power through the persuasive power of ideas.

Thus civilian intervention into doctrinal decision-making does not have to be characterized by the pure conflict of bureaucratic interest groups. In fact, in cases where the military organization controls the diffusion of information that is necessary to plan and execute doctrinal innovation, bureaucratic conflict is detrimental to civilian policymakers. Only by building coalitions within the organization can such civilians obtain the information they need to make policy and verify its implementation.

The addition of these three new arguments about the development of doctrine leads to the conclusion that the timing and content of military doctrine innovations are a result of the interaction of international and domestic political factors, of foreign doctrine changes and of domestic civilians' political strategies.[7] The need for clear theoretical delineation of the effects of international and domestic stimuli on foreign and military policies of states is now widely accepted in the international relations literature. Sometimes, this problem is posed in terms of testing various levels of international relations analysis against each other. The question then asked is whether elegant international system-level theories, such as those presented by Kenneth N. Waltz or other balance-of-power theorists, best explain the motives of foreign policy decisionmakers, or whether bureaucratic and organizational politics theories such as Graham T. Allison's describe those motives better.[8] This levels-of-analysis testing approach can help to demonstrate the relative power of various political science theories.

However, I argue that security policymakers, both military and civilian, do not choose between being state actors oriented toward finding the best solutions to international problems, or being bureaucratic actors oriented toward preserving the health of their organizations. They are both, and both orientations, along with their unique characteristics as individuals, go into their choice of policies.[9]

There is no question that military officers tend to see challenges to state security through a lens provided by their organization. The organization provides them with a social construction of reality that differs from the constructions of those outside the organization. Yet that organizational lens does not always blind them to foreign challenges to their state's security. It may color or even distort their views; yet it is not accurate to portray that lens as only pointing inward, at the domestic scene. As the empirical case studies presented here demonstrate, in periods of low civil-military conflict, militaries spend a great deal of time analyzing the impact of doctrinal innovations made by their potential future enemies. Furthermore, the lens of each individual in the organization is slightly different from the lenses of all the others. It is not surprising that some officers are more attuned to issues of organizational stability, while others concentrate on international problems. It is thus impossible to achieve a complete picture of officers' views on military doctrine if they are portrayed simply as monochromatic bureaucratic actors who merely use foreign threats as excuses for their inherent organizational policy preferences.

Several recent studies of foreign policy decision-making recognize that policymakers have a combination of external balancing and internal bureaucratic and political motives, and turn to political structures or strategies to explain how these motives are expressed in policy.[10] This book is an attempt to apply the insights from these synthesizing works to a different policy area and a different body of theoretical literature. The question asked is not whether doctrinal thinking and policy are a result of reaction to the international arena or of domestic politics, but rather how the combination of the two processes leads to policy outcomes.

Analysis of this interplay can contribute to the building of foreign policy theory, theory that bridges the gap between international relations and comparative politics. The in-depth study of one state over time can be particularly useful, especially if during that time the state undergoes demonstrable changes in its domestic bureaucratic power structure. Such an example fits well the requirements of Alexander George's method for structured, focused, comparative case studies: extraneous variables (such as national strategic culture, geography, and major changes in the international balance of power) are held constant, while the impact of one independent variable—the domestic political situation—on policy can be traced.[11]

This book examines the development of military doctrine in the Soviet Union during the post-Stalin era.[12] It takes as its case studies Soviet reactions to the three major changes in doctrine for future war in Europe that were adopted by the United States or the North Atlantic Treaty Organization (NATO) during the Cold War era: the American and NATO adoption of the Flexible Response doctrine in the 1960s; the American adoption of the Schlesinger Doctrine in 1974; and the combination of the American adoption of the AirLand Battle doctrine and the NATO adoption of the Follow-on Forces Attack (FOFA) doctrine in the early 1980s.

This set of cases was chosen because of its completeness; every major change in Western doctrine for future war in Europe from the mid-1950s through the end of the Cold War is examined as a possible stimulus for Soviet doctrinal innovation. But it has an additional important property: in each case, the conditions of Soviet domestic politics and civil-military relations were different. In the first case, at the time that the United States first adopted the Flexible Response policy in 1961, the Soviet military was already engaged in a bitter bureaucratic struggle with Communist Party First Secretary Nikita Khrushchev about the content of Soviet military doctrine and about the distribution of resources between the civilian and military sectors of the economy. The foreign stimulus hit at a time when the Soviet military was already busy defending its autonomy from civilian interference in a different direction. In the second case, when the United States adopted the Schlesinger Doctrine, Soviet civil-military relations were calm, and General Secretary Leonid Brezhnev appeared to be willing to give the military all the resources and doctrinal policy autonomy that it demanded. The military appears to have been free to react to the foreign stimulus as it saw fit. In the final case, as U.S. and NATO leaders shifted toward the adoption of deep-strike doctrines that were intended to match perceived Soviet doctrinal strengths in Europe, the Soviet Union was in the midst of budgetary and foreign policy crises that would eventually lead to reconsideration of the resource share and policy role of the Soviet military institution. Most important, Soviet General Secretary (and later, President) Mikhail Gorbachev supported the entrance of a new set of actors—civilian national security experts—into the doctrinal policy community, to act as a counter to the voices of military officers. This community changed in the midst of the Soviet reaction, and therefore it should not be surprising that the reaction itself was altered as well.

The development of Soviet military doctrine over time is interesting both from a practical perspective, and from a theoretical perspective. At the practical, policy level, it remains important to understand the Soviet military institution and military policy-making. The military institutions that eventually coalesce from the ruins of the Soviet state are likely to carry significant portions of the Soviet military's institutional culture into the future. In the uncertain future of post–Soviet East-Central Europe, the remnants of the Soviet military officer corps will remain potentially influential players in both domestic politics and security policy issues. The Russian state in particular will still have a huge arsenal of military power at its disposal, and could reemerge in future decades as a military powerhouse. It is therefore vital to understand what stimulated change in Soviet military policy, and how foreign developments and the varying character of civil-military relations interacted to create either stagnancy or innovation in Soviet military doctrine. The issue of military doctrines in Europe is far from being settled, even though the competition between NATO and the former Warsaw Pact has faded. It is not clear whether the security situation in Europe will be more stable or less so in the post–Cold War world;[13] undoubtedly the remnants of the Soviet military will play a role in determining that outcome.

The Soviet case is also interesting for two theoretical reasons. First, the Soviet military is an important example of a general staff military planning system. General staffs are structured in ways that discourage interservice rivalry; they stand in sharp contrast to the United States Joint Chiefs of Staff (JCS) system. Whereas the American military is structured so that representatives of each service branch (the Army, the Air Force, and the Navy) compete with each other in the top-level decision-making process, general staff representatives are encouraged to lose their distinctive service identities early in their careers, and to make policy arguments based on national security interests as a whole. In the Soviet case, the General Staff's tools for promoting interservice cooperation included a holistic staff culture, as well as integrative structures and promotion policies.[14]

This difference in the two systems is not always obvious to those who are not Sovietologists. It can have an impact on the theoretical approach that American scholars take to the question of military doctrine decision-making. If the American JCS example is taken as the norm for theory development, then the incidence of bureaucratic conflict and infighting will be expected to be quite high. Officers at the very top of the military planning process have their attention constantly directed toward domestic battles over resources and missions.[15] If a general staff system is taken as the norm for theory development, then organizational and bureaucratic concerns might be seen to play a lesser role in military officers' preferences; officers' concerns about state security will receive more attention. Military officers are less likely to focus on internal resource competition, and more likely to focus on meeting foreign threats to state security, when interservice rivalry is not a constituent part of their daily lives. Theories developed for militaries with general staff systems may not describe the policy-making process in the United States as well as JCS-based theories do; but many powerful states now have or did have general staff systems (including France, historical Prussia, interwar Germany, Israel, and the People's Republic of China).

The second major reason that these particular Soviet cases are interesting from a theoretical perspective is that they provide a decades-long example of one state's concern about a continuing international military competition. While other enemies (such as China) waxed and waned in importance in Soviet eyes during this time, NATO and the United States remained the primary probable future military opponent for over forty years. Analysis of whether or not the development of U.S. and NATO doctrine acted as a stimulus on Soviet doctrine development allows us to draw conclusions about whether or not international "doctrine races" exist.

Reactive innovations in doctrine are likely to feed off of each other. Each side wants to protect and enhance its ability to fight the kind of war it believes is likely. Often, when one side believes that its innovation enhances its own security, the other side perceives the innovation as something which threatens its security. When the second side reacts to that threat with an innovation of its own, a new, and probably threatening, strategic situation will be perceived by the side which innovated first. The end result is a competition in doctrines, where one innovation provokes another ad infinitum. Arms competitions (sometimes called "arms races"), especially the one between the Soviet Union and the United States, have been rigorously studied; theories have been developed about how domestic and/or international factors aggravate or ameliorate them.[16] However, doctrinal competitions have not received this attention.

The study of the Soviet case over time can help analysts to understand the role of doctrinal competition in perpetuating a competitive military relationship. At a broader level, it can help us to understand an often neglected factor which may need to be overcome if the Cold War is to be put permanently behind us. If it is indeed true, as most theorists argue, that militaries tend to prefer offensive doctrines that involve heavy resource investments, this suggests that doctrinal competitions may continue to spiral upward even as quantitative disarmament takes place. Decreases in weapons numbers alone may not lessen military competitions, if the weapons which remain are developed and deployed according to concepts which the other side finds threatening. As U.S. and NATO policymakers debate their future approach to security in Europe, they must take into account the likely reactions of the remnants of the Soviet military to Western doctrinal developments. Otherwise, we may be doomed to repeat the dangerous military competition of the Cold War era.

1

Military Organizations and Innovation

The Interests of Professional Officers

The major tendency in current studies of doctrine development is to portray military institutions as bureaucratic organizations that are sluggish and resistant to innovation. According to most scholars who study this topic, all organizations focus on maintaining standard operating procedures, and therefore tend to be conservative in their approach to problem solving. Militaries are thought to be like any other organization in this regard. Militaries are believed to innovate only when they are prodded by failure in the battlefield or by civilian intervention into military policy.[1] Furthermore, the doctrines preferred by military institutions are seen to be those which best serve military interests in bureaucratic battles over resources or organizational prestige.[2] Minor, "routine" innovations in existing military technology or tasks are valued by militaries, according to this perspective, because they guarantee an expanding military budget and the continued importance to the state of military expertise and the military instrument in international affairs; but innovation in the way that militaries think about war is not considered routine, and is in fact unexpected without civilian intervention.[3] When militaries do consider adopting doctrinal change, the policy results are expected to be incremental at best.[4] The overall picture drawn is of militaries as hidebound bureaucratic actors, inert unless pushed, and oriented above all toward domestic political competition and organizational predictability.[5]

Yet not all scholars who study military organizations as domestic bureaucratic actors agree that the military is inert and resistant to innovation, especially to innovation originating abroad. Those who study arms competitions often argue that desire for more resources and recognition makes militaries prone to reaction, and even overreaction, to innovative foreign developments in weaponry. Although these scholars do not specifically dispute the "merely routine innovation" hypothesis, their portrayal of militaries as the catalysts of an accelerating arms race indicates that it is major weapons innovations that they have in mind.[6]

A synthesis of these two incompatible positions on the bureaucratic character of militaries is possible only if the arguments of the first group of scholars are modified. Perhaps it is not that military officers are resistant to innovation in general, but merely to innovation that they believe will damage their bureaucratic and institutional interests.[7] Innovation per se is not an unexpected event in organizations.

In fact, the older theoretical literature on professional militaries as corporate institutions argues that senior military officers are inherently reactive to military developments occurring abroad. The basis for this reactivity is professional officers' own conceptions of the proper role of the military within the state. Top-level military officers in stable states are thought to see their own careers in terms of fulfilling an international security mission for the state, utilizing their unique corporate expertise.[8] Morris Janowitz confirmed that in the United States in the 1950s, this orientation toward mission performance separated the high-level, elite officers from the lower ranks of service personnel.[9]

The state assigns the military institution the primary duty of protection of the state from foreign menace. Therefore, senior officers in professional militaries will define their own career missions in reactive terms. The professional military officer's mindset is often hypothesized to include a "subjective professional bias" toward overestimating foreign threats and the likelihood of future war, and toward emphasizing the efficacy of large military forces in solving international problems.[10] Military service mission interests are thus likely to prod senior officers to react to innovations in their potential foreign enemies' plans for future war, if they believe that their own state's security interests are threatened as a result.

Since professional military institutions tend to focus on how to fight and win wars that may arise in the future, their definition of security "threat" is likely to differ somewhat from definitions used by political actors. Officers are less likely to focus on the issue of whether hostile political intentions are present in the foreign state; that question is left to political leaders to determine. Officers are more likely to be concerned with estimating the technical situation on future potential battlefields. A threat to state security, as defined by military officers, will be found in any foreign innovation that leaves the military less able to carry out its battle plans successfully.

This definition can include foreign innovations in technology. For example, the Soviet military discussed the need for change in Soviet air defense systems, to deal with the threat of Stealth and cruise missile technology that was demonstrated by U.S. and allied success in the 1991 war against Iraq.[11] What has been neglected in the theoretical literature on military innovation, however, is the fact that foreign doctrine shifts can be threatening, too. What matters to military planners is not only which weapons their adversaries plan to use, but how they plan to use them. Change in one state's plans for how to wage future war can threaten the likelihood of success for their adversaries' war plans. Thus, military officers will see a threat in any foreign doctrine shift that lowers their own future chances for achieving success in war.

Military officers may also react to a foreign doctrine innovation that significantly changes their future battle calculus, even if the foreign shift is not in and of itself a direct new threat to state security. After a foreign innovation has occurred, the state's existing doctrine may simply not defend state security interests as well as a new doctrine would. An example of this is presented in the case study in this book on the Soviet reaction to Flexible Response. In that case, the United States and NATO decided to avoid the use of nuclear weapons in future war for as long as possible. If the Soviet Union chose to use nuclear weapons first, then the West would immediately respond with nuclear weapons. This new Western doctrine did not make existing Soviet war plans unworkable. The Soviet military could have retained its doctrine of using nuclear weapons from the beginning of a conflict. However, if it had done so, it would have missed the opportunity to accomplish future war goals when its command and control systems and battlefield personnel were not hampered by radioactive contamination and electromagnetic interference from nuclear explosions. The change in Western doctrine meant that the old way for the Soviet military to accomplish its war goals was no longer the best way. There was thus an environmental stimulus to innovate for the sake of Soviet national security interests, even though the Western innovation in and of itself did not create a new threat.

Reaction to a foreign innovation does not always demand reactive innovation in doctrine; sometimes, a selective strengthening of an existing force posture or the addition of new combat technology may be all that officers deem necessary. The decision of whether or not to innovate depends on a complex mix of factors: perceptions of the foreign threat; perceptions of one's own strengths and weaknesses; and the existence of a personnel mix that allows a coalition to be built in favor of innovation. However, it makes sense that officers sometimes will determine that new threats can only be overcome by new doctrinal approaches. Officers' mindsets are not limited to bureaucratic concerns about policy continuity and institutional stability. Because officers are also genuinely concerned about maintaining national security in a changing and threatening international environment, they will sometimes perceive that reactive innovation in doctrine is necessary.

One factor influencing the calculus of whether or not innovation is a good idea is that military officers tend to see the health of their institution as a determining condition of the health of national security. Because military officers believe that their bureaucratic organization has been given the primary role of state defense, the officer as servant to the state and the officer as bureaucrat tend to coexist inside a single mindset. Innovation in doctrine is likely to be accepted most easily by the military institution when it is consistent with that institution's bureaucratic interests. This has two fundamental implications.

First, military organizations will resist innovative ideas that threaten their budgetary resource share or corporate autonomy. All bureaucratic organizations are interested in maintaining or expanding their share of state resources; professional institutions like the military are also interested in maintaining the corporate identity of their members. Among the elements of that corporate identity is the belief among officers that their expertise on military issues makes them uniquely qualified to make certain contributions to national security policy.[12] Potential innovation that threatens the military officer corps' definition of itself and its prerogatives will be resisted.

Second, military officers will react both to perceived threats to state security from abroad, and to perceived bureaucratic threats to the military organization from within the domestic policy-making system on doctrinal issues. Doctrinal innovations do not always have foreign roots; sometimes, political leaders have their own domestic-centered reasons for proposing changes in strategic policy. Often, these reasons are centered on cost-cutting efforts which would allow nonmilitary sectors of the economy to expand their budget share.[13] Senior officers must therefore be attuned to threats on doctrinal issues from two directions, both foreign and domestic.

If threats occur simultaneously on both fronts, the military is likely to respond to the domestic threat first (assuming that the "threats" from abroad are not considered immediate, i.e., war is not on the horizon). Since officers see their institution as the one final source of protection of their state from external enemies, they will identify a domestic bureaucratic threat as a threat to state security. Reaction to a foreign threat will do no good if that reaction is overridden by civilian policymakers who do not understand military realities. Therefore, if military officers are engaged in a bureaucratic battle over a doctrinal issue, the senior officers who are responsible for doctrine development are likely to try to contain the domestic threat first. Since that demands organizational coherence, reactive innovation to events occurring abroad will likely be a secondary concern. Attempts to innovate always create resistance inside the organization, so officers are unlikely to risk considering innovation when they are facing a domestic threat that demands corporate cohesion.

✳ Organization Theory and Innovation
-see bib.

The notion that militaries innovate on their own in reaction to changes in the international environment should not be surprising to those who study organization theory. Those who analyze organizations do not all agree that organizations always resist innovation. Many instead argue that organizations can be convinced to innovate when environmental stimuli indicate that the normal functioning of the organization is no longer satisfying organizational goals. An entire school of organization theory has developed around the idea that organizations compete for resources and survival in a Darwinian environment, and that only those organizations which adapt themselves to fit changing niches ultimately succeed.[14]

This ecological perspective is most directly useful for research on large populations of organizations, and thus is not directly applicable to studies of doctrinal competition between two states or coalitions. Its postulates were developed to describe the behavior of multiple business firms all competing for the same set of resources and markets. Nonetheless, this body of literature does call attention to an important insight: organizational innovation is often a result of pressure emanating from a competitive environment. All organizations exist in an environmental "domain," which is defined by the other organizations who act as their customers, competitors, and suppliers broadly defined.[15] The environment is a key variable in explaining organizational innovation, even when one is not dealing with a large population of organizations whose domains are identical. During the Cold War, the U.S. and Soviet militaries had overlapping domains as competitors, even though their primary suppliers and consumers were separate.[16]

As early as 1958, James G. March and Herbert A. Simon argued that organizational innovation was related to environmental pressure. March and Simon noted that organizations adopt their own internal criteria for measuring the qualitative level of their output. In other words, organizations keep tabs on their own performance. Each organization decides that some particular level of performance will define organizational satisfaction. When environmental clues indicate that the organization is not meeting its own criteria of satisfaction, this performance discrepancy can motivate innovation. Organizations innovate when they are dissatisfied with their own performance relative to the performance of their competitors.[17]

March and Simon pointed out that competition between organizations can stimulate one organization to become dissatisfied with its own outputs, and this in turn can stimulate innovation.[18] An example which March and Simon cite of such competitive pressure from the environment is the decline in a private corporation's relative market share. With a little extrapolation, it can be argued that when one state adopts a new doctrine which seems to improve its future war-fighting ability, and especially one which increases its military resources and technology, its competitor's military will be encouraged to examine its relative position in the competition, and to innovate if that relative position is no longer satisfactory.

More recently, March's work on environmental pressures and organizational innovation has led him to consider the relationship between incremental organizational procedures and innovative organizational outputs.[19] As noted above, much of the literature on innovation in military doctrine has been centered on the notion that organizations resist disruption of their standard operating procedures. Therefore, the argument goes, when change occurs it comes gradually and incrementally. Organizations do not usually adopt radical innovations.

The roots of this incrementalist argument are found in Charles Lindblom's work on how U.S. government administrators "muddle through" their policy directives. He noted that these organizational actors fail to make complete searches of possible policy choices when they are faced with the need to make a decision, and instead tend to consider only those policies which bear a strong resemblance to choices they have adopted in the past.[20]

March argues, however, that it is a mistake to think that incremental policy-making styles correlate with incremental policy outcomes. Routine processes for policy-making are endemic to organizations; organizational actors usually turn to their past experience with similar environmental situations to come up with policy alternatives. Their choices today are likely to look a lot like the choices they made in similar situations in the past. Nonetheless, this does not mean their choices of policy will look incremental in comparison with normal, workaday outputs. He writes: "Many of the most stable procedures in an organization are procedures for responding to economic, social, and political contexts. . . . If the environment changes rapidly, so will the responses of stable organizations; change driven by such shifts will be dramatic if shifts in the environment are large."[21]

March and Simon had made a related point about the relationship between incrementalist procedures and innovative policies in their early work on how organizations change in response to their competitors' actions. They suggested that organizations tend to "borrow" from the ideas of their competitors, instead of "inventing" new solutions to the problem of meeting organizational satisfaction criteria in a changing environment. Such borrowing decreases organizational risk. They also suggest that solutions will draw as much as possible on programs already stored in institutional memory.[22] March and Olsen have made the same argument more recently: "A repertoire of routines is . . . the basis for an institutional approach to novel situations. . . . [T]he most standard organizational response to novelty is to find a set of routines that can be used."[23]

In other words, according to this well-developed school of organization theory, organizations do use standard operating procedures and incremental searches for policy ideas. Yet in unusual circumstances, the outputs resulting from these incremental procedures will not be incremental.[24]

James N. Rosenau has applied these arguments about incremental procedures, innovative outcomes, and environmental change in his work on habit-driven actors in international environments. He argues that while all individuals, and thus all organizations (including states, state bureaucratic actors, and transnational groups), are driven by habits built up by their past experiences, those habits include the ways that actors respond to environmental change. Each actor has a certain style of responding to changes in the environment. There is no a priori reason to assume that all individuals or organizations respond to environmental change with a rigid refusal to alter their behavior in response to that change, even though each individual and organizational actor is likely to follow rigidly its own pattern of response (be it to stagnate or to learn by quantum leap).[25] The international environment is not stable; as it changes, successful actors change their policies, even though they are driven by standard operating procedures.

John D. Steinbruner, a scholar whose work has often been quoted in support of the notion of organizational incrementalism, actually makes a similar point to these.[26] His primary argument is that organizations do not engage in a rational, analytic search for solutions to problems. Instead, they operate in a cybernetic paradigm, where they will try to solve problems with the solutions they have at hand and have used in the past in a tried and true manner. However, he cautions against interpreting his paradigm to mean that organizations will only change gradually. He uses as a metaphor W. Ross Ashby's discussion of a "homeostatic device" which has two feedback loops. One loop tells the brain of the device that there is environmental variation within a certain defined interval; such variation causes the device to make minor adjustments in its operation. The example Steinbruner cites is of a cat sitting in front of a fire. When the cat's skin temperature becomes too hot, the cat will move slightly away from the fire; when the cat's skin temperature then falls too far, the cat will move back closer to the fire. Change in outputs provoked by stimuli within the "normal" range thus is in fact incremental. But the second loop in the machine tells the brain that a "state" change in the environment has taken place, that the environment is no longer operating within the normal range.[27] In our example, presumably if the fire turned out to be a conflagration that was in the process of burning the house down, the cat would not merely move back slightly, but would run away yowling. Such a response would be made to any threatening change in the cat's environment. The cat's policy-making style is still incremental, even though not all of its reactions to the environment fall within the bounds of incremental changes in response.

The argument made by this book is that an innovation in one state's military doctrine can be perceived by a competitor as what Steinbruner calls a "state" change in the environment. If one state's doctrinal innovation causes the other state's officer corps to believe that the likely environment for future war is significantly different from what it was earlier, reactive innovation is no longer an anomaly. The procedure and even the content of the reaction to that abnormal environmental stimulus are likely to bear a lot of resemblance to policies taken toward similar stimuli in the past. Therefore, once one threatening change in Western doctrine leads to an innovation in Soviet doctrine that neutralizes that threat, innovation in reaction to environmental threats becomes a behavior pattern for the Soviet military. Innovation in doctrine, defined as a significant deviation from the content of existing doctrinal policies, is not unexpected, even when standard operating procedures for dealing with foreign threats are followed.

It should be noted that the environment which organizations face will not be seen in its entirety, as some objective entity. Members of the organization perceive the environment selectively, and then place their own interpretations on what they perceive. The processes of perception and interpretation occur in a social environment, where common training and pressures for conformity endow an organization with common expectations about what sorts of data are likely to be found in the environment, and of what that set of data signifies. Organizations, like other social groups, adapt their perceptions and interpretations of the environment to their own models of what the environment should hold.[28] Organizations are likely to try to fit new data into their own existing worldview frameworks. They may be attuned to data that fits their preconceptions, and may ignore data that is anomalous.

A prime example of this phenomenon of organizational selection of environmental data and how to intepret it is found in national intelligence organizations.[29] In part this is because the interpretation of national intelligence data often reads like a John LeCarre novel, where no one is ever sure whether the environmental data found are real, or designed by the enemy for the analyst's own consumption. Analysts must develop rules for deciding whether information is genuine or merely a ruse.[30] But mostly this is because selective interpretation of the environment is necessary for analysts to develop coherence in their policy recommendations. As Lawrence Freedman argues in his study of U.S. intelligence organizations, "An intelligence estimator whose mind was equally open to all evidence and interpretations would not be very good at his job. He would be receiving information without processing it."[31] Obviously, national intelligence collection is a constituent component of the process military organizations use when deciding how to react to moves made by their opponents.

This means that military officers are likely to see the environment in a way similar to that of other officers in their organization. Theories of how professional military officers see the world tell us that they are likely to see an ominous coherence in the intentions and policies of their adversaries, and therefore to see numerous threats to their own state's security; they are also likely to look for environmental reasons why their own stocks of weapons and technology need to be upgraded or increased.

Yet as our questions about military officers' interpretations of the environment become more specific, the predictive value of this perspective declines. For example, will military organizations believe that their adversaries consistently develop more and newer threats to their own security, and therefore be overly attentive to potential doctrinal innovations from abroad? This would be logical in an organizational mindset which sees the enemy as crafty and unpredictable. Or will officers instead believe that their adversaries' threatening policies fall on a bounded path of development, and therefore be attuned only to those evolutionary changes which fit their pet notions of how the adversary fights war? This would be logical in an organizational mindset which sees the enemy as conservative, or as constrained by historical experience or outside political forces. Both of these possibilities fit within the framework of consistent organizational perceptions of what the environment holds. Without experiencing the environment of the particular organization we seek to analyze, we cannot know precisely how the environment will in fact be perceived. There is no reason to expect that all organizations, or even all military organizations, will approach the environment with identical mindsets, given differences in specific organizational cultures and histories.

This perspective on military mindsets is useful as a caution to the outside analyst, since it argues that as far as the actors are concerned, there is no such thing as an "objective" environment. Instead there are merely different ways of ordering environmental data that are inherently chaotic. Environmental threats to organizational health are defined by the organization, and not by the outside world. One of the tasks of historical case studies is to determine the parameters of the environmental perceptions that particular military organizations have had over time.

One additional task remains for organization theory before we can move on. We must decide how to reify military organizations. Are they unitary actors, or are they groups of individual actors?

Much of modern organization theory, especially that branch which studies individual organizational decisions, rather than the behavior of large populations of organizations, argues that neither organizations as a whole, nor individuals within them, pursue a single goal. In fact, goals pursued within organizations often conflict,[32] and the values of individual members of an organization do not always correspond to the goals of the organization as a whole.[33]

Perhaps the most useful way to think of organizations is as shifting coalitions of individual actors. March observed in his early work on business firms that organizational systems all contain conflictual interest groups; resources are allocated and policies produced through the building of political coalitions of these interest groups.[34] A variety of theorists from different perspectives share this concept of organizations as coalitions.[35] The executive leadership of the firm acts as a political broker between these interest groups, but does not make decisions alone at the top.

This argument leads to the conclusion that organizations are not single-minded. Even if it is correct that military organizations value the maintenance of stability, predictability, autonomy, and control over the environment, there is room for individuals to make their voices heard. Not all individuals or interest groups within organizations will hold equally dear those postulated conservative organizational goals.

Finally, it must be recognized that organizations do not always remain the same over time. Some changes in organization are so drastic that they leave the bounds not only of incremental policy outcomes, but of incremental operating procedures. Institutional change sometimes occurs in organizational policy styles. There must be some way of defining the difference between innovation driven by incremental organizational behavior, and "radical" change of the organization itself. Robert B. Albritton has usefully characterized this difference by specifying three components of organizational change: change in organizational concepts (an example relevant to military organizations might be how best to prepare for future war); change in organizational outcomes (an example might be the development of a new doctrine); and change in organizational technology, or the rules and procedures for dealing with policy.[36] It is this final variable which seems to define the boundary between innovation within the organization and radical change of the organization.

This boundary becomes important for the Soviet military during the Gorbachev era. As will be shown in the next chapter, during most of the post-Stalin era the Soviet military had fairly free reign over doctrinal decisions. The General Staff could develop routine operating procedures for dealing with strategic policy, and there is no reason to expect that those procedures changed over time. However, under Gorbachev civilian experts on international affairs were encouraged to become involved in doctrine and strategy discussions in the Soviet Union, and there is evidence that they had a hand in influencing the design of both declaratory and operational doctrine for war in Europe. This is a "radical" change, and not merely an innovation; it meant a basic alteration in the procedures followed for dealing with foreign threats. It should thus not be surprising that the content of Soviet doctrine for conventional war changed so drastically under Gorbachev's leadership. We would expect that radical organizational change would produce results even more innovative than those produced by stable organizations reacting to a changing environment.

The Defense Policy Community

In determining whether or not a particular military organization is likely to support a reactive innovation in doctrine, it is important to keep in mind the fact that military officers are individuals, not merely bureaucratic and organizational actors. Although they will probably share certain outlooks on doctrinal issues, they are unlikely to have identical policy preferences when a new problem appears. Different officers will have different ideas about how to react to a changed strategic environment, and about whether or not innovation is needed. Undoubtedly, in some cases these differences are well described as a competition between service divisions. This would be especially true for an organization such as the American military, which is headed by the JCS/service-rivalry system described in the introduction. But in the case of militaries with general staff systems, policy arguments should not necessarily be defined along service rivalry lines. Another analytic model is needed.

A more appropriate model for militaries not split by service rivalries is the "policy community" model, an off-shoot of organization theory. This model was developed as a way of describing the American federal bureaucracy, where policy ideas percolate fairly freely among and between upper-level, full-time government employees, part-time advisers to government bureaucracies, and academics with policy interests and influence links.[37] More recently, Nina P. Halpern has applied many of the insights of this model to the question of economic policy reform in the People's Republic of China, whose Marxist-Leninist party-dominated agenda bears more resemblance to the historical Soviet case.[38] Matthew Evangelista has recently also used a framework which combines policy communities theory and political coalition-building theory to present a plausible explanation for change toward moderation in Soviet arms control and security policy.[39]

The term "policy community" was developed to describe the influence that elite policy experts have over the range of ideas that are considered by policymakers. Those who have used the term to describe the American political system have stated that a policy community is defined by two characteristics: it is made up of people who have expertise in a certain policy area and are passionately concerned about policy outcomes in that area; and it is made up of people who interact with each other regularly to exchange ideas.[40] Because political access of expert groups to the policy agenda was traditionally more limited in the Soviet Union than in the United States, I will add a third element to this definition as it applies to comparative analysis across political systems: a group enters a policy community when it attains a certain degree of access to decisionmakers. If it is denied access and influence, the group may be a "latent" policy community or a latent segment of an existing policy community. A similar definition has been used in the international relations literature for the concept of "epistemic communities," which are essentially policy communities that bridge state boundaries and advise governments on international cooperation issues.[41] According to Peter M. Haas, an epistemic community is "a specific community of experts sharing a belief in a common set of cause-and-effect relationships as well as common values to which policies governing these relationships will be applied";[42] the success of the community depends on the bureaucratic power granted to it by various governments.[43]

The new element I have added to the definition of "policy community" becomes important in the Soviet Union under Gorbachev's leadership. On many policy issues, including international security, there were for many years groups of academic experts who interacted with each other regularly (at academic conferences, for example) and who preferred certain policy outcomes, but who did not have any real opportunity to influence those outcomes to any significant degree.[44] While their ideas were being formed in the years before they attained the status of policy actors, these experts were not members of the Soviet policy community in the way that nongovernmental experts in American think tanks, for example, are; they interacted among themselves, but not to any significant degree with the experts who were actually making policy. It is only in the past handful of years that Soviet policy think tanks have truly arisen.[45]

In this book, the concept of the Soviet defense policy community will be used to describe and explain military doctrine formulation from the Khrushchev era through the USSR's demise. The defense policy community label fits well the group of professional military officers who had primary responsibility for doctrine policy formulation from Stalin's death in 1953 through the late 1980s. The entrance of civilian experts into doctrinal debates in the mid- to late 1980s can be described as a qualitative expansion of that defense policy community. Earlier, General Staff military scientists constituted the interacting community of experts who were concerned about policy outcomes. Their expert recommendations had a decisive impact on the policies adopted by the top Soviet leadership. Under Gorbachev, civilian academic experts with different ideas about policy outcomes interacted with the old community in debates and exchanges of ideas. These interactions seem to have stimulated both change in the range of ideas considered by the General Staff, and change in the pattern of influence over top-level military policy-making. Both the ideas presented and the policy procedure followed are innovative.

Jack Walker argued that the supply of innovative ideas in a policy community increases in parallel with three factors: the level of autonomy of the community from outside political control (if community members fear political retribution, they are less likely to propose new ideas); the level of interchange within the community (the more the members communicate with each other, the more ideas circulate); and the level of competition between various segments of the community (when resources are scarce, each segment wants to produce the ideas that leaders consider the most interesting).[46] In the following chapter it will be seen that the level of the Soviet defense policy community's autonomy varied greatly depending on who was General Secretary of the Communist Party of the Soviet Union. However, a high degree of community interchange and competition is always expected in general staff systems. A significant number of high-level officers from varied backgrounds are constantly writing articles, giving conference papers, and holding roundtable discussions on policy issues. Furthermore, when a new, previously outside group joins the policy community, as some civilian academic experts have recently done, the levels of interchange and competition should increase, and the supply of innovative ideas should grow.

No matter who is in the community of experts, the process of gaining support for innovation is bound to be slow. According to policy communities theorist John Kingdon, the state's policy agenda, the list of problems which the state must solve, can change quickly in response to sudden changes in the environment. For example, a threatening innovation in a competing state's military doctrine should place the issue of military doctrine high on the agenda very quickly. However, the generation and acceptance of policy alternatives, or the proposal of solutions to problems on the agenda, will develop gradually over time.[47] Consensus among the relevant policy-making elite about the need for innovation and about what type of innovation to pursue must be achieved, and this is possible only after debate of various options. New ideas must percolate throughout the entire community of relevant policymakers.[48]

In any community, some members will be "policy entrepreneurs." These individuals will devote their organizational resources to advocating a particular idea, especially when a "policy window" opens—when an opportunity for agenda change presents itself. They can pick the ideas they advocate for a variety of reasons, from bureaucratic turf protection to self-fulfillment.[49] Once ideas are proposed by the entrepreneurs, the community will "evaluate them, argue with one another, marshal evidence and argument in support or opposition, persuade one another,

solve intellectual puzzles, and become entrapped in intellectual dilemmas."[50] The entrepreneur's job is to "soften up" the community, which,
like all organizations, is relatively resistant to the notion of change.[51]
Whether or not the entrepreneur succeeds will depend on the combination of persuasive power and organizational pressure that can be
marshalled against those who resist change.[52]

The likelihood of both the generation of new ideas, and their eventual
acceptance among the community as a whole, depends on the identity of
the involved decisionmakers. Different decisionmakers will be more or
less receptive to different ideas. Various ideas about change in doctrine
will have different levels of "salience"; that is, they will be received differently by people whose opinions differ.[53] The receptivity of the individual
to various ideas will be a result of a complex mix of factors, including
career interests, deep-seated beliefs in certain values or issue-areas, and
the context (both of the external environment and of the preexisting internal psychology of the individual) in which various ideas are presented to
that person. James Q. Wilson has argued that innovation is thus a
"chance appearance" in organizations, since whether or not an innovation is considered or accepted depends very heavily on the outlook of the
organization's executive leadership.[54] Lawrence Freedman has pointed
out that the definition of foreign military "threat" is itself subjective.
Whether or not a change in an opponent's military doctrine is interpreted
as a threat depends both on how policymakers view the characteristics of
that change, and on how they view their own military strengths and how
those strengths can be undermined.[55]

It makes sense that when newly empowered civilians enter the defense
policy community, the supply of innovative ideas on defense will increase. But in the absence of civilian intervention into doctrinal policy,
when is innovative thinking expected within the military?

It would be ideal if scholars could delineate exactly what various military officers have perceived about foreign doctrinal innovations, and then
trace exactly how those perceptions were reflected in their policy preferences and eventually in state policy decisions. Deborah Welch Larson has
defined a rigorous set of requirements for similar process-tracing efforts
in her work on American decisionmakers' reactions to Soviet policies
during the Cold War.[56] Unfortunately, such requirements are difficult to
meet when the subject is the development of Western policymakers' foreign policy opinions; they are impossible to meet when the subject is military policy opinions in a closed society such as the Soviet Union, for
which source material remains limited and fragmentary.[57] In addition, it
is extremely difficult for Western scholars to determine even what sorts of
alternative policies might have been considered within the Soviet national
security policy-making community, exactly who the relevant decision-

makers were, and what the various decisionmakers' opinions were on policy choices.

Nonetheless, a theoretical proposition can be derived from the policy communities literature which predicts a correlation between personnel turnover and innovation. Any significant turnover in top-level military personnel is bound to bring in new sets of saliences as it brings in people with new sets of opinions.[58] In part, this is merely a result of differences among individuals; no two groups of people are likely to have exactly the same balance of policy opinions. More important, however, is the fact that individual career interests develop around the set of opinions expressed during previous policy-making encounters. People who have built their careers around a particular type of thinking about military doctrine are unlikely to be overly receptive to innovative ideas; their reputations have been built around the old way of thinking, and they may have been granted organizational perquisites as a result. The established policy community is likely to reward those whose thinking remains within the dominant "paradigm" of the community; those who challenge the old way of thinking with innovative ideas must be willing to brave disapproval from the greater community.[59] Posen's argument about organizational inertia is thus at least partially correct; innovation within any organization is difficult to achieve.

Innovative thinking within the military is therefore likely to begin among individuals who have no established interests to protect, or who (for whatever individual psychological reasons) are able to overcome careerist interests and social pressure within the organization. Innovators can be newcomers to the organization, who have not yet internalized the organization's goal structure (i.e., "young turks"); or they can be oldtimers, who have already accomplished so much in their careers that they are willing to risk disapproval and loss. In his study of weapons innovation within the U.S. Navy, Vincent Davis discovered that innovators are likely to be passionate zealots, in the middle ranks, ranging in age from the early thirties to the mid-forties. He postulates that this group of people has been associated with the organization long enough to have an abiding affection for it, but not so long as to become cynical, and not so high in rank as to have to worry about the broader political implications of their ideas.[60]

Innovative thinking is likely to be institutionalized in policy only if innovative thinkers can back up their ideas with organizational power. As Stephen Peter Rosen has argued, this power includes control over personnel promotion within the military. Maverick thinkers within the military may introduce new ideas, but new ways of thinking will only thrive when the powerful interests standing behind the old ways of thinking are replaced, or when powerful old thinkers are convinced to join the innovators.[61] In his study of U.S. Navy innovation, Davis noted that most innovators tried first to get alliances built for their ideas among those of their own rank, and then went up the ranks to search for higher-level support.[62] Ultimately, if an innovative idea is to be accepted, it must have support within the very top levels of both the command and staff structures of the military. Those who are ultimately responsible for both planning and implementing future war strategies must support the innovative idea for it to take hold.

✳️ Theoretical Hypotheses

Postulates from the study of professional militaries, and from the literature on organizations and policy communities, can be used to formulate hypotheses about the timing and content of a state's reaction to doctrinal innovation by its potential enemies. While organization theory does not give us any clues as to the likely policy directions of innovations adopted by organizations, it does tell us that personnel changeover and the persuasion of powerful coalitions are important factors in the timing of innovations. Furthermore, the literature on professional militaries does tell us what sorts of innovations military officers are likely to prefer, even if receptivity and response to particular environmental stimuli depend on the organizational culture of the individual military institution.

>Hypothesis #1: [Military organizations are likely to develop innovative doctrines on their own, in the absence of civilian intervention, when they interpret a foreign doctrinal shift as a threat to the success of their current war plans.] Because senior professional military officers believe that their institution's primary role is to defend state security, their interests extend beyond a narrow bureaucratic focus. If enough powerful officers perceive that a foreign doctrinal change has changed the future battlefield, institutional support will be garnered for an innovative policy change. In other words, Posen's analysis of the sources of doctrinal innovation is incomplete. Militaries sometimes innovate on their own.

>Hypothesis #2: [Military officers will prefer innovations which augment military resources and autonomy.] Military officers want to preserve the health of their organization above all else, since without a healthy military organization they see no chance for the preservation of state security. Therefore, when the military is the sole repository of policy advice on security issues for the political leadership, and when the military has a great deal of power over doctrine decision-making, the state is likely to adopt a reaction which heightens, rather than lowers, the level of international military competition. Spirals of increasingly threatening doctrines

can result from this competition, and the outbreak of war can become more probable if each side believes that it must act first in a crisis to preserve its chances for victory.

> Hypothesis #3: [Military officers will react to domestic threats to their organizational health and autonomy first, before reacting to foreign threats to state security.] Bureaucratic infighting between military and civilian leaders may impede, at least temporarily, an effective reaction by the military institution to the adversary's threatening doctrinal shift, because military strategists are likely to see a domestic threat as demanding immediate attention in order to preserve the institution's ability to respond to foreign threats.] The decision of how to react to a foreign threat may involve acrimonious debate within the military, lessening military unity against the domestic foe. This acrimony will be avoided until after the domestic threat is contained. This is particularly likely if political leaders are attempting to change the boundaries of the military's authority over doctrinal policy-making issues in order to redirect budgetary resources. Therefore, the domestic power situation is an important factor influencing the timing of the military reaction.

> Hypothesis #4: [Policy innovations will be institutionalized slowly within the expert policy community; discussion and debate will permeate the community.] Changes in doctrinal thinking, whether proposed within the military alone or within a broader defense policy community, will not be immediate or spontaneous; instead, they will develop slowly as institutional interest can be garnered in favor of them. A perceived foreign threat may change the agenda immediately, but alternative innovative policies will develop slowly. Personnel shifts may be necessary if a new policy is to be implemented, and not merely declared. Therefore, a time-lag and a period of policy debate are expected in the reaction.

Such a hypothesis should not surprise anyone who has observed the process of political decision-making. Nonetheless, this process of debate within the policy community is often ignored in Western analyses of Soviet defense policy development. As was noted above, the Soviet military has often been portrayed as simply a bureaucratic actor, competing in debates with the Communist Party or along service division lines. A better description of Soviet defense policy idea development is provided by Franklyn Griffiths's "tendency analysis," where trends in thinking are seen to vary across interest groups and over time, and eventually to coalesce into policies.[63] Griffiths's approach has not usually been applied to the analysis of Soviet defense policy. This approach is implicit within the policy communities framework, and this hypothesis therefore challenges the assumption that Soviet doctrinal policy is only or primarily a result of struggle between bureaucracies or among services.

⟩Hypothesis #5: [An expansion of the policy community, to include different types of actors, can result in a new type of reactive innovation to a foreign doctrinal shift] Procedural change in organizational decision-making can lead to radical policy changes. In the Soviet case, civilian experts on security issues in the Gorbachev era did not share military officers' institutional biases; they did not seem to prefer strong military solutions to military problems. The state can choose to create a civilian community of experts to provide a viable alternative to military control of the defense policy agenda. This hypothesis has two subpoints.

⟫Hypothesis #5a: [If a variety of institutions, both military and civilian, compete with each other in presenting alternatives to the political leadership, there is a greater chance that the state will implement a conciliatory reactive innovation] Political leaders might prefer to try such a solution before committing additional resources to the military, in the belief that it may lower military requirements by lowering the level of international tension. The result can be a brake on doctrinal competition. When the policy community expands, there is hope that international military tensions can be lowered.[64]

⟩Hypothesis #5b: [Not all strategies of civilian intervention into doctrinal questions lead to strained civil-military relations and bureaucratic in-fighting] A qualitative expansion of the defense policy community is an alternative civilian intervention strategy, potentially more productive and less conflictual than a civil-military bureaucratic battle over doctrine innovation. New coalitions can be built across institutions which favor reform. So long as those coalitions survive, policy outcomes are not dependent on the purported conservative goals of the military organization.

These five hypotheses will be tested in the three case studies presented as chapters 3 through 5. There are two new basic theories which underlie these hypotheses, and which compete with the model presented early in this chapter of militaries as sluggish, parochial bureaucratic organizations. [First is the argument that innovation is not unexpected in most organizations, and that military organizations can and do innovate on their own without civilian intervention. Second is the argument that when civilians do choose to intervene in military policy, the strategy that they choose to use matters] [Each of the three cases I have selected is a "hard" case for one of these theories; in other words, each case has variables which would seem to fit well with the models I am challenging.]

⟩The case of the Soviet reaction to Flexible Response is a hard case for my first theory (that militaries innovate on their own), because all of the independent situational variables would indicate that the Soviet military should not make changes in its doctrine if my postulated key variable of international competition is meaningless. The existing approach to operations involved the integration of nuclear weapons into a ground force war plan that valued surprise, initiative, and offensive operations. The organizational needs of the military, for resources, autonomy, and control over a potential future battlefield, seemed to be well met by the new civilian leadership under General Secretary Leonid Brezhnev. There would be no reason to expect change, if the military acted as a parochial bureaucratic organization.

≻The case of the Soviet reaction to the Schlesinger Doctrine is a hard case for this first theory in the same way. The Soviet military had plans to use surprise, initiative, and massive offensive strategic nuclear strikes in the event that the other side seemed to be about to use strategic nuclear weapons first. There is no reason to expect that the military would want to change this doctrine, or even to discuss change, if it were only concerned with parochial organizational goals. In both cases, decisive, offensive action could be implemented by the Soviet military's use of massive nuclear options, regardless of what the West chose to do in future war.

≻The case of the Soviet reaction to FOFA and the AirLand Battle doctrine is not such a hard case for this first theory. Posen notes that the experience of a state's client states in war can be interpreted within the military as a vicarious learning experience, and can thereby act as a stimulus for innovation.[65] The experiences of the Soviet Union in World War II, of the Arab-Israeli War of 1973, and of the Vietnam War were directly relevant to the Western development of deep-strike emerging technology weapons and plans, and were in fact discussed as such by Soviet General Staff officers. Innovation in military planning was not unexpected.

However, this case is a hard case for my second basic theory: that a better alternative to acrimonious bureaucratic fights exists when civilians want to influence doctrine innovation. Military institutional interests were completely undercut by Gorbachev's doctrinal innovation plans— by movement away from offensive operations to solely defensive ones, by massive budget and troop cuts, and by loss of military institutional autonomy. Therefore, the standard theory would predict solid military outrage, hostility, and rebellion.

Gorbachev's threat to military autonomy certainly does mean that a very large segment of the senior military officer corps should have held these anti-Gorbachev positions, especially initially. Yet my theory suggests that this should not be an eternal or universal sentiment among the officer corps. An expansion of the defense policy community is qualitatively different from an attempt to change military doctrine by political force (for example, through replacement of the high command with cronies of the political leadership). Military officers may have to put up with the fact that their expertise is no longer the only input into doctrinal decision-making, but this type of civilian intervention into doctrinal formulation still recognizes that military officers' expertise is key. The unique mission of officers as servants to the state in preserving national security is not being denied; instead, new ideas about how to preserve security are being introduced into the officer corps in the hopes of building a reformist coalition in favor of those ideas inside the military.

I will thus have to demonstrate that parochial bureaucratic interests did not define the civil-military relationship on doctrinal issues in the Soviet Union at the end of the Gorbachev era. Perhaps one anecdotal indication that my theory will prove useful is the fact that the Soviet military did not line up behind the August 1991 coup attempt to unseat Gorbachev. Bitter conflict between officers and reformist civilian leaders did not define civil-military affairs, even as the Soviet state disintegrated.

2

Doctrinal Debate and Decision in the USSR

THE THEORIES developed in the previous chapter were constructed so as to be generalizable. They should apply to any professional military organization, structured as a general staff, that has responsibility for the development of the state's doctrine for future warfare. Given that the subject of this study is the reactions of the Soviet military to foreign innovations in doctrine, the next task is to demonstrate that the Soviet General Staff was in fact a professional organization which did indeed have a great deal of control over the formulation of doctrine. If it was not a professional organization, with a mission and a corporate identity, then we should not expect it to behave as a relatively cohesive policy community, focused on defense of the state from external threat. If it did not have primary responsibility for the development of military doctrine, then its preferences are not very important predictors of policy outcomes.

Soviet General Staff Service as a Profession

Burkart Holzner and John H. Marx have reviewed the sociological literature on definitions of the term "profession," and have distilled the following list of attributes that all professions have: "[A]n abstract, theoretical knowledge base; an esoteric, specialized, technical skill; a long training and socialization; strong professional subculture and ideology; lifelong commitment to a structured career; autonomy of action; a formal occupation association; control over training and legal licensing; and a code of ethics and/or a client-centered orientation—the service ideal."[1]

Traditionally, Soviet sources have not revealed much information about the professional attributes of the General Staff. The General Staff's duties and the requirements for membership were often stated in only the vaguest terms, which are subject to multiple interpretations. However, the 1990 Soviet military publication and analysis of a 1937 draft "Statute on the Service of the General Staff of the Worker-Peasant Red Army" goes a long way toward confirming that the General Staff was designed to be a professional body.[2]

According to this document, all General Staff officers must either be graduates of the General Staff Academy, or graduates from the command departments of other military academies. Those who fall into the latter category must have served on a military staff for at least one year, and must come in with excellent recommendations concerning their staff experience. All General Staff officers must have both significant command and staff experience, so that they understand both military planning and execution. Once admitted to the General Staff, officers retain their General Staff ranks for the rest of their service careers. The analysis of the document concludes with a statement about the "steadily growing role and responsibility of the General Staff in peace and in war as the basic operational organ of the Defense Ministry and the Supreme Command in construction, preparation, and operational utilization of the Armed Forces [and] in defense construction."[3]

Most of the attributes from Holzner and Marx's list appear in this description. Soviet General Staff officers had an abstract theoretical knowledge base from their previous field and academic work; they had esoteric, specialized technical command and planning skills; they most likely had a strong professional subculture and a lifelong commitment to their structured career, given that all of them underwent a similar training experience and maintained their General Staff identities until retirement; and they had both autonomy of action, and a likely orientation toward serving a client, since they served as the basic operational organ of the Defense Ministry and Supreme Command. (While the Defense Ministry in the Soviet Union was not a civilian client, even though the appointed Minister of Defense was sometimes a civilian, the Supreme Command did include the top civilian leadership of the state.) The General Staff had unique expertise and an exclusive corporate identity, and was therefore professional by design. We would expect General Staff officers to behave in accordance with the theories on military preferences set out in the previous chapter.

The General Staff and Doctrine

If we understand what professional military officers prefer in terms of doctrine, the next question to answer is how much power they wield over doctrine formulation. Official Soviet descriptions of the work of the General Staff indicate that it was quite powerful in matters of military policy. The clearest Soviet statements about who had what sort of responsibilities for military policy are found in articles in a variety of reference works put out by the Soviet military publishing house, *Voenizdat*. While the exact words used in these definitions of responsibility have varied slightly over time, their meanings have remained basically similar.

The most authoritative statement about what the Soviet General Staff did is probably the article entitled "General Staff" in the *Soviet Military*

Encyclopedia, written in 1976 by Gen. V. G. Kulikov, Chief of the General Staff. He stated:

> The General Staff comprehensively analyzes and evaluates the developing military-political situation, defines the development trends of the means of waging war [and] the capabilities for their use, [and] organizes the preparation of the Armed Forces and the implementation of necessary measures for guaranteeing their high combat readiness to repulse any possible aggression. An important place in the General Staff's activities is occupied by the further development of military theory. It leads military-scientific work, works up the most important [field] manuals and actual problems of Soviet military science, [and] introduces its achievements into the practice of operational and combat preparations of the troops and staffs.[4]

In turn, "military science," whose development is said to be one of the General Staff's chief responsibilities, is defined as "the system of knowledge about the character [and] laws of war, the preparation of the Armed Forces and the country for war, and the capabilities for waging it."[5]

These descriptions, while not mentioning the word "doctrine," actually give us a great deal of information about the role of the General Staff in that policy area. The General Staff is said to have responsibilities ranging from threat assessment and operational planning to combat theorizing and training. The official Soviet definition of the word "doctrine" gives special emphasis to some of the key activities mentioned in the description of the General Staff's work. According to the *Military Encyclopedic Dictionary* of the Soviet Union,

> Military Doctrine is the system of views in the state, adopted at a particular time, on the essence, goals, and possible character of a future war, on the preparation of the Armed Forces for it, and on the means of waging it. . . . Military Doctrine has two closely interconnected and interdependent aspects: the social-political and military-technical. The social-political aspect encompasses questions relating to the methodological, economic, social and legal foundations of the achievement of the goals of a possible future war. It is determining, and possesses the most stability, as it reflects the class essence and political goals of the state, which are relatively permanent over the long term. The military-technical aspect, in accordance with social-political goals, includes questions of immediate military construction, technical equipment of the military forces and their preparation, and the definition of the forms and means of carrying out by the Armed Forces of operations in the war as a whole.[6]

Sometimes this division of doctrine into "social-political" and "military-technical" aspects has been portrayed as a division of responsibility between the Communist Party or state leadership, on the one hand, and the General Staff, on the other. By this interpretation, it was the state leadership that controlled doctrinal decision-making, and the General Staff which offered technical input into that process based on its knowledge of military science. However, these official Soviet definitions and descriptions of the General Staff, of doctrine, and of military science tend to throw some doubt on that neat division of labor.

The General Staff was defined as an organization which "analyzes and evaluates the military-political situation," not merely the military-technical situation. "Military Politics" was defined as "a constituent part of the general politics of classes, states, parties, and other social-political institutions," and was thought to be reflected in doctrine, strategy, and the design and preparation of military organizations.[7] In other words, the General Staff analyzed and evaluated the social-political inputs into Soviet military doctrine, and not merely the military-technical inputs.

Further evidence of the range of influence of the General Staff on doctrine is provided by the observation that the two officially defined sides of military doctrine do not seem to be clearly distinguished from each other. The concept of the "methodological foundations" of the achievement of the goals of war does not seem clearly separated from the concept of "the definition of the forms and means" for carrying out war, especially when "military science" is the repository of knowledge about the character and laws of war. Certainly, the methodological foundations of war must be developed out of knowledge about the character and laws of war.[8]

What emerges is a picture of the General Staff as the primary source of military scientific and military technical information, and a vital source of military political information, which the state used when Soviet military doctrine was formulated and adopted. While "the state," traditionally defined as the leadership of the Communist Party, made doctrinal decisions, the General Staff provided the information upon which those decisions were based. Both Stephen M. Meyer and Condoleezza Rice argue that while the Soviet state may have had ultimate decision authority on military policy issues, the General Staff had the power to set the options considered by the state and to influence the direction that military policy decisions took. Information in this case is power. In that sense, real power over technical military policy, including military doctrine, rested to a significant extent with the General Staff, even if it was not the official top decision-making body in military affairs.[9]

Military policy in the Soviet Union was officially the purview of the Defense Council, a joint political-military state body charged with overseeing and coordinating all defense-related decision-making. Its membership over time has never been precisely revealed, but it is known that the General Secretary of the Communist Party was traditionally its chairman. Probably it also usually included the Defense Minister, the KGB Chief, the Foreign Minister, and perhaps others responsible for such things as military-industrial policy.[10] Some Western analysts, such as Ellen Jones, have portrayed the Defense Council as a powerful control mechanism for reviewing military development plans and the basic operational plan for state defense in the event of war.[11] But Condoleezza Rice has emphasized that the General Staff was still the major analytic arm of the Defense Council;[12] this means that the Defense Council would not have been capable of countering military plans with alternative sources of expertise. Even if the General Staff did not hold decision-making power, it controlled decision options.

Uri Ra'anan and Igor Lukes, who conducted a series of interviews with recent Soviet and East European defectors who held relatively high government positions, have gone even further in discounting the role of the Defense Council in the Brezhnev era. Three of their subjects said that the Soviet Defense Council had an insignificant role in peacetime (which contrasts with the powerful role played by Defense Councils in the East European Communist regimes), and that its powers were primarily invoked in times of crisis or war.[13] One respondent, a KGB officer who defected, claimed, "I had many friends in the Ministry of Defense, including a military journalist with *Red Star* [the daily newspaper of the Defense Ministry]. I asked them about the Defense Council and they said it meant nothing, a big zero. . . . It is really an artificial organization. . . . I never heard of any meetings of this body and I doubt if it did meet regularly."[14] This picture has been confirmed by a report of Gorbachev's remarks at the Supreme Soviet confirmation hearings for Defense Minister Dmitrii Yazov in July 1989. Gorbachev apparently said there that under Brezhnev the Defense Council had only "formal" duties, and authorized policies that had already been approved. He then spoke about his own efforts to change this situation: "I cannot say that [the Defense Council] has assumed this [leading] role yet. The process is very painful. So painful that I received word that the Chairman of the Defense Council [Gorbachev is referring to himself in the third person] was acting too vigorously. The marshals asked me to consider this."[15] In other words, the General Staff seems to have controlled the Defense Council, and in turn, peacetime military policy.

Yet these statements about the role of the General Staff during the Brezhnev era should not be taken as an indication that the General Staff has always had such power over doctrine. The level of the General Staff's real control over doctrine has in fact varied over time. For example, under Gorbachev a variety of civilian security-issue experts, not just military experts, were involved in doctrinal policy-making. Earlier, there were no civilian think tanks parallel to the RAND Corporation or the Brookings Institution; in addition, there were no civilian analysts in the Soviet Defense Ministry. In the mid- to late 1980s, that situation changed. Civilian analysts at the international relations institutes in Moscow, particularly the Institute of USA and Canada Studies (ISKAN), the Institute of World Economics and International Relations (IMEMO), and various organizations associated with the Soviet Peace Committee, in cooperation with reformers in the Foreign Ministry, educated themselves in military-technical questions and convinced a number of retired General Staff officers to give them technical military policy advice. Their ties with moderate reformers in the Soviet political leadership, along with their efforts to cooperate with General Staff representatives in making policy recommendations, loosened the General Staff's exclusive postwar hold over operational doctrine formulation. Some civilians gained both the information and the political savvy to institute a revolution in the organizational power structure which determined Soviet military policy. (This revolution is described in depth in chapter 5.)

While the particulars of this power shift are unprecedented, the relative power of the General Staff over military doctrine formulation has varied significantly in the past, especially before the mid-1950s. Soviet leaders have tended to recognize the need for a professionalized, expert military organization with its own knowledge store and staff culture; at the same time, they have feared that the army might usurp too much political power unless it remained clearly subordinate to the civilian leadership of the Communist Party. The question of who should control doctrine has tended to fall in the middle of this dilemma, since doctrine for future war involves by definition both military science issues and broader political and foreign policy questions.

Debate over whether or not a professional, powerful General Staff should be formed began with the creation of the Soviet state. During the first Soviet military reform era of 1924, when the Civil War was won and the future of the Soviet military institution was being debated, military theorists argued about whether a powerful General Staff was useful for clear leadership of the military affairs of the state, or dangerous as a means of usurping civilian control and leading to Bonapartism. At that time the Red Army Staff was split into three branches, so no military organ could effectively coordinate training, planning, and military construction for the future.

According to a recent Soviet article, current and future leaders of the Red Army Staff, including M. V. Frunze, M. N. Tukhachevskii, and B. M. Shaposhnikov, some of the best Soviet military minds of that era, wanted to establish a General Staff as "the fundamental working organ of the government for the defense of the country." They recognized that effective military planning had to be coordinated, and thought that top military scientists should be responsible for that coordination. Other military officers, including S. M. Budennyi (whom Timothy J. Colton has called an alcoholic "know-nothing"), argued against giving a General

Staff any "fixed functions," fearing that a General Staff dictatorship would arise.[16]

While this description of the debate may be the one preferred by General Staff officers in the 1980s, where the pro-General Staff heroes were on one side and the Stalinist know-nothings were on the other, the truth is somewhat more complex. It is quite clear that Frunze, for example, did indeed envision a large military-political role for the General Staff. It was to base its operational plans on a wide review of economic, political, and strategic potentials, and to be "not only the brain of the army—it should be the military brain of the whole Soviet state."[17] Yet it is also clear that B. M. Shaposhnikov, who is famed for his characterization of the General Staff as the "brain of the army," in fact meant by this that the General Staff should *only* be the brain of the army, and that its broader policy role should be contained. He spent a great deal of effort distinguishing the role of the Soviet General Staff from that of the German General Staff, which he thought had usurped too much power. He wrote that the Soviet General Staff should not have "authorship" over politics, since politics is the realm of other state actors who are specialists in drawing conclusions from political life. He wrote, "Clausewitz' exhortation should not be forgotten: that 'in any case politics is not obliged to do what military art decrees.' "[18] Specifically, war should be led by the state, and not by military organs.[19] The General Staff should be the brain of the army on operational concerns, but should not be responsible for political and economic war planning,[20] even though officers should be well enough schooled in economics and diplomacy to give good advice to other state actors about how operations would fit in with broader state goals.[21]

Both of these men are lionized as great Soviet military thinkers; yet they did not see eye to eye on the role of the General Staff in planning for future war (and thus, in controlling doctrine). It is therefore not surprising that civilian officials in the USSR also had different approaches to the question of the General Staff's autonomy, and that the level of independence of the General Staff in discussing and formulating doctrine varied over time. This variation is particularly well illustrated by the difference in the amount of control over doctrine granted to the military in the "golden age" of the 1920s and early 1930s, versus the repressive years from the late 1930s through Stalin's death in 1953.

The Golden Age: 1922 through 1936

After the successful conclusion of the Soviet Civil War in 1922, heated debates broke out within the Soviet military on almost every conceivable military policy issue. Many of these debates revolved around questions of doctrine. The participants in the debates included everyone from prerevolutionary tsarist officers (brought back into the Red Army as "experts"), to Bolshevik ideologues who had educated themselves in military history, but who lacked formal military training and gained battlefield or military leadership experience for the first time in the Civil War (the "reds"). Politics, personalities, and policy ideas all intermingled, and policy preferences tended to be cross-cutting. Established factions on certain issues broke down on others.

The "experts," whose most prominent member was probably Maj. Gen. A. A. Svechin, tended at first to argue for the establishment of a standing army guided by a traditional professional war-fighting doctrine; the "reds" (including M. V. Frunze, S. I. Gusev, K. E. Voroshilov, S. M. Budennyi, and M. N. Tukhachevskii) responded that a part standing/part territorial army would be more in line with Bolshevik ideology. They felt that a special revolutionary doctrine suited uniquely to the Soviet future had been developed during the Civil War. Leon Trotskii, the civilian revolutionary who was Commissar of War and Commissar of the Army and Navy until 1924, argued a middle ground; he favored a territorial militia with a professional military doctrine. The "reds" eventually won partially on this issue, by making a political alliance with Stalin and his cohorts in the military against Trotskii; and Frunze became the new Commissar of the Army and Navy. Yet while the Civil War experience influenced doctrinal development, the "reds" eventually accepted the need for a unified professional doctrine.[22]

Meanwhile, another set of doctrinal issues, intertwined with the first but without such clear lines of demarcation, was under consideration: the proper balance to be achieved between offensive and defensive planning and between attrition and maneuver warfare. These issues became especially important in the late 1920s and early 1930s, as a unified professional military doctrine was being established for the Red Army. These debates are difficult to chart because individuals changed their opinions over time, and because many of those who favored one type of operation over the other recognized that it would be foolish to concentrate only on one type of planning. However, the basic lines of the debate are well known. Svechin and Trotskii (an "expert" and a "red") were proponents of planning for a mainly defensive war, relying heavily on an attrition defense with the whole country participating in the defense effort. The offense was not eliminated from consideration, but was thought of as something that followed a successful strategic defense. Tukhachevskii, and his ally V. Triandafillov, in contrast developed a theory of deep offensive operations which relied on decisive mobile strike forces; they believed that against a good maneuver-strike offensive, no successful defense was possible. Frunze originally argued against Svechin's concentration on positional defense, but later seemed to accept a middle ground. (Frunze was apparently murdered through an unnecessary medical operation, ordered by Stalin, in 1925; once he was eliminated, the deep operations theorists consolidated their political power.)[23]

Col. Gen. V. N. Lobov, the most recent Chief of Staff of the Warsaw Treaty Organization before its disbanding in 1991, argued in 1989 that this period of Soviet history was characterized by the free exchange of opinions on doctrinal issues, untainted by dogmatism. He contrasted it with the Stalinist imposition that followed.[24] While Frunze's untimely death indicates that freedom of expression in these early years of Stalin's reign was not absolute, there was clearly a distinction between the level of creativity and independence in the discussions of this era, and those of the following decade and a half.

According to Albert Seaton, "the Red Army already belonged to Stalin" by July 1926, when Trotskii was removed from the Politburo.[25] Nonetheless, it is not clear how heavily Stalin interfered in the doctrinal debates of the time. Seaton claims that from the late 1920s on, Stalin "controlled senior military appointments, and approved or directed military theory, training, organization, equipment and deployment."[26] This may well be true, especially since Stalin does seem to bear responsibility for the death of Frunze. Yet doctrinal debates continued at a sufficiently high level into the mid-1930s to suggest that Stalin did not yet demand that the General Staff toe a single theoretical line. Many of Stalin's top military appointees, including K. E. Voroshilov, were considered ignorant and were therefore ignored by the rest of the General Staff with no apparent immediate negative consequences; and while Tukhachevskii would eventually be killed in Stalin's purges, Stalin apparently listened to his views on the need to mechanize forces in the modern world.[27] Further evidence of Stalin's self-restraint on doctrinal issues at this time is provided by the creation of a General Staff in 1935. Stalin allowed the establishment of a center of professional military expertise whose right to exist had been hotly debated for a decade.[28]

The Stalinist Repression

In 1936, the military command began to note that the morale of peasant recruits was declining because of the hardships caused in rural areas by Stalin's collectivization policies. There is some evidence that several of the officers were reaching out for coalitions with Stalin's opponents, including Nikolai Bukharin, who were more sympathetic to peasant economic and cultural needs. Stalin and his allies apparently began to fear that a military coup was possible.[29] By 1936, Stalin's show trials and blood purges of Party members and state officials were in high gear, although they had not yet reached the level of the senior military officer corps.

In May 1937 the political commissar system was suddenly restored. The commissars had operated in the early days of the Red Army, when the expertise of the former Tsarist military officers was needed but the "experts" were not trusted; this system had begun to atrophy by 1924, and had been completely abolished by 1934.[30] Its restoration meant that army officers were once more under the constant watchful eyes of people who reported to Stalin. Then in June 1937, Stalin's blood purge hit the Red Army high command. On June 9, Tukhachevskii and a group of his supporters were relieved of their commands; on the 11th, they were arrested on charges of treason; the next day they were condemned and executed.[31] By the fall of 1937, "all the brakes were released," and the entire Soviet officer corps was subjected to the purge. Entire staffs and commands disappeared.[32]

Stalin at this point gained total control over military policy. The vast majority of talented military theorists were killed, and as a result the Soviet Army faced Hitler's invasion of 1941 without adequate strategic or operational planning. Both Stalin personally, and the remainder of the General Staff, underestimated the likelihood of a surprise attack. As a result, defensive preparations on the Soviet borders were inadequate.[33] Yet by mid-1943 enough talented young officers had risen through the ranks, and Stalin was chastened enough by the horrible initial Soviet defeats, to allow the reestablishment of a role for creative military scientists and war planners. According to Colton, Stalin's "most astute generals, Zhukov and Vasilevskii included, learned how to nudge Stalin toward a decision without talking back to him."[34] As a result, Tukhachevskii's offensive and defensive doctrines for operations in depth came to be the centerpiece of Soviet efforts in World War II, even though Stalin had silenced those doctrines with Tukhachevskii's murder in 1937,[35] and had simultaneously eliminated the Strategy Department of the General Staff Academy (it was reestablished in 1940, too late to develop creative solutions to use against the Germans in 1941).[36]

Yet once the war was won, Stalin reasserted his control over military affairs. He insisted that his own view of the "permanently operating factors of war" was a sufficient basis for doctrine. These "factors" were in fact merely broad categories of military capability (including the quantity and quality of troops and equipment, the morale of the troops, the organizational capabilities of the military staff, and the stability of the rear); they provided little of real value for operational planning, but significantly restricted the issues the General Staff was allowed to consider. In particular, the General Staff was not allowed to discuss the role of the surprise German attack in the initial Soviet defeats in World War II.[37]

Stalin's most damaging move against both the morale and planning capabilities of the General Staff was his refusal to allow the military to consider the impact of atomic weapons on war planning.[38] As a result, from the very beginning of the Cold War era the Soviet military found itself in a position of lagging behind Western developments in military doctrine. In its initial consideration of atomic weapons in the 1950s, the General Staff had to cite Western military sources in order to discuss the biological, battlefield, and strategic effects of the bomb.

Post-Stalin Lessons

Following Stalin's death in 1953, the immediate direction of military policy in the future was unclear. But the General Staff did begin to consider, in conferences, press articles, and military exercises, the impact of nuclear weapons on war.[39] By 1955, Communist Party General Secretary Nikita Khrushchev had built an alliance with Minister of Defense and war hero Marshal Zhukov, allowing him to defeat Prime Minister Malenkov in the post-Stalin power struggle. Malenkov had argued that a minimum deterrent posture was sufficient in the nuclear age, and that Soviet resources should be concentrated on consumer goods. This would have meant limiting the role of the General Staff in doctrine development. Khrushchev defeated him by arguing that more attention had to be paid to improving Soviet defenses and expanding the Soviet military budget.[40] Khrushchev also aided military autonomy through his anti-Stalinist campaign, and by the time of the Twentieth Congress of the Soviet Communist Party in February 1956 (the event most associated with the ideological thaw of the Khrushchev era), "the authority of the professional commanders was largely free of political interference."[41]

As we shall see in the next chapter, Khrushchev's policies led to the reestablishment of independent thinking and will in the General Staff. When Khrushchev attempted, several years later, to change Soviet military doctrine for future nuclear war by fiat, he failed. He encountered heavy opposition from most General Staff officers, and seems to have had no real effect on operational planning.

The combination of the two very different initial eras of Soviet civil-military relations—the golden age of the 1920s and 1930s, and the repressive age of Stalin—seems to have left the General Staff with some rather contradictory lessons about its own proper role in doctrine formulation. On the one hand, officers could look back in time and find encouragement for holding open and freewheeling discussions on a wide variety of doctrinal questions. Discussions led to creativity and foresightedness. On the other hand, Soviet officers must have learned caution; a powerful civilian leader could crush those whose opinions he distrusted. Discussions led to potential political danger. These two eras held different lessons as well on how inventive Soviet military doctrine should be. On the one hand, the Soviet General Staff had an early history of combining its own military experience with that of the West, to develop independent doctrines that seemed to be properly suited to future threats to Soviet security. On the other hand, military planners later found themselves in a game of catch-up with Western military organizations. Western militaries had combined their World War II experience with extensive knowledge gained in field exercises and war-gaming based on the use of atomic weapons. The Soviet General Staff had not been allowed this experimentation, and was forced early on to obtain its information on how nuclear weapons affected planning from the experience of its potential future enemies.

As we shall see in the following chapters, these lessons from the history of Soviet military affairs seem to have had their impact on Soviet doctrine formulation ever since. There clearly were discussions and debates in the General Staff from the 1950s onward; General Staff officers came down on radically different sides of the same doctrinal issue. Thus the pattern of the golden age was somewhat restored in the post-Stalin era. The General Staff ceased to bow to the narrow will of political leaders. Yet the creativity and variety of debating positions, at least before the 1980s, did not come close to equaling that of the early period. For whatever reason, General Staff officers seemed to be more circumspect in their views. No one trumpeted the virtues of the defense over the offense, for example; and no one seemed to question the role or the value of the General Staff system in military planning.

Soviet doctrinal innovations of this time were not mere copies of their Western counterparts. The Soviet development of the conventional option in the 1970s, where conventional weapons alone were thought sufficient to win a war in Europe between nuclear-armed adversaries, was an original contribution to the East-West military competition. Yet innovation in Soviet military doctrine seemed only to come in response to Western doctrinal innovations. The basic direction of Soviet planning was stagnant, centered on the offensive half of the General Staff's World War II experience.

This peculiar combination of debate and conservatism within the Soviet military may be explained by the theoretical framework of the previous chapter. The General Staff held unchallenged influence over doctrinal decision-making. No outsiders entered the Soviet General Staff organization; control over candidate training and staff culture ensured continuity in personnel. (The one exception to organizational continuity was the perceived need in the 1960s to improve the technical and engineering training of cadres; this led to conflict between the technocrats and those who felt threatened by them.[42]) Stringent military control over the spread of military-technical information meant that civilians were unable to challenge the military's doctrinal hegemony.[43] The organization was thus free to do what all organizations tend to do: follow in the same path that they have cut for themselves, until some perceived external pressure convinces them to change course. Debate and discussion occurs among any group of experts; but the group of experts was not as diverse as it had been in an earlier era. While discussion permeated the defense policy community, and real innovation in doctrine did occur during this time, the discussion and innovation were limited in scope (particularly in terms of favoring the offense), and the community was limited in membership.

The Process of Doctrine Formulation

It seems fairly clear that doctrine formulation was controlled by the General Staff in between the Stalin and Gorbachev eras. Even when the General Staff did not control doctrinal decision-making in the Soviet Union, it was the key source of information and opinions on potential doctrinal choices. However, it is not clear exactly how the process of doctrine formulation proceeded within the General Staff. The contours of General Staff discussions about future doctrinal choices are presented in Soviet military publications. Several of these discussions will be examined in the following chapters. Nonetheless, we do not know for sure exactly who participated in General Staff discussions on doctrinal issues (presumably, debates in journals are a part of these discussions, but are not by themselves the whole discussion), nor do we understand precisely what the relationship was between discussion and decision. Soviet sources do not describe in any detail the process of doctrine change. This stands in stark contrast to the United States, where, for example, the U.S. Army commissions unclassified historical studies of its own doctrinal shifts.

There are some indications about which subgroups of officers would have taken an interest in doctrinal decisions. The General Staff's Main Intelligence Directorate (GRU) would most likely have provided most of the technical information available to General Staff officers on Western military developments. This might have been supplemented by information on Western political developments supplied by the independent state Committee on State Security (KGB), although that agency was traditionally considered a competitor of the GRU and might not have willingly shared all of its key information with the General Staff.[44] It is not known precisely through which channels information would have flowed from

GRU and/or KGB sources to the General Staff leadership. One major journal has presented information and analysis of Western military developments: *Zarubezhnoe Voennoe Obozrenie* (it was called *Voennyi Zarubezhnik* before 1973, and was at that time semiclassified). Presumably, this journal was not the only means of communicating intelligence data to the wider Soviet officer corps, but it does provide some indication of the sorts of Western doctrinal developments that were interesting to the General Staff at various times.

Several of the other General Staff directorates would presumably have been involved in discussions of doctrinal change and its practical consequences. These would include the Main Operations Directorate, the Organization and Mobilization Main Directorate, and most important, the Military Science Directorate. (In 1989 or 1990, the Military Science Directorate was eliminated; its functions were apparently subsumed under a new General Staff Center for Strategic and Operational Research.) Input would also be received from the Soviet General Staff Academy, which functioned not only as an educational institution, but as a basic center for military scientific work.[45] The Institute of Military History, established in 1966, might also have given advice about contemporary military science issues, based on its store of knowledge about past planning efforts.[46]

Discussion was carried out on the pages of the key Soviet military journals. These include the General Staff journal, *Voennaia Mysl'* (which was semiclassified, "Only for Generals, Admirals and Officers of the Soviet Army and Navy," until 1989); the military history journal, *Voenno-Istoricheskii Zhurnal*, which has often presented opinions about current military events using a relatively transparent "code" of historical discussion; and, to a lesser extent, *Kommunist Vooruzhennykh Sil*, the journal of the Main Political Directorate of the Defense Ministry. (The official functions of this latter journal included doctrinal inculcation of the officer corps, although the cases presented in the following chapters demonstrate that debate, and not mere inculcation, appeared on its pages.) Discussion might also have spilled over into the journals of the individual service branches, as well as onto the pages of the daily newspaper of the Defense Ministry, *Krasnaia Zvezda*. Occasionally, officers have written contentious articles on military-scientific topics in civilian newspapers and journals as well.

In addition to debates on the pages of journals, the Soviet General Staff frequently hosted conferences on military-scientific topics. An interesting comment on such conferences was provided by a colonel who specialized in military science, in 1971: "The common goal of conferences is, as is correct, not merely to discuss pressing questions of military art, but also to work out unified views on them, [and] to outline the most effective ways and means of realizing their conclusions in the practice of preparing troops."[47] This indicates that the purpose of these doctrinal discussions was not merely to test one's debating prowess, but to reach policy conclusions that had practical impact.

Some Soviet General Staff officers emphasized that doctrinal discussion had to be resolved, and that unity had to be achieved about what current doctrine should be. This theme appeared as early as 1921, in an article by M. V. Frunze on "Unified Military Doctrine and the Red Army."[48] Gen. Makhmut Gareev, former head of the Military Science Directorate of the General Staff, recently wrote of Frunze's beliefs (and probably, of his own agreement with those beliefs) that, "[B]old, far-reaching decisions must sometimes be taken contrary to opinion and to the fierce resistance of conservatively thinking persons, while decisions based on too great compromises and satisfying everyone, as a rule, are the weakest or are completely useless. For this reason, he [Frunze] was firm in taking decisions and in unswervingly carrying them out after the essence of the question had been brought out and the discussion completed."[49] According to Gareev, Frunze as Chief of Staff made sure that most important decisions were discussed and implemented *within weeks*, even in the absence of unanimous consent, and then spent whatever time was needed to justify them to doubters.[50]

This suggests that heated debate and discussion might have continued in the General Staff even after a policy decision had been made. It is not necessarily the case that a policy decision came only after consensus was reached. The span of a discussion (which can go on for years) may not indicate exactly when a policy was implemented. However, the presence of a heated debate about whether or not a doctrinal innovation is a good idea is probably an excellent indication that innovation was either under consideration or completed.

Outside observers need hard data—from exercises, new weapons development and deployment, etc.—to know whether or not an innovation has occurred. As David Alan Rosenberg has forcefully noted, there is often a disconnect between strategic ideas and declaratory strategy, and the actual operational strategy which appears in classified planning documents.[51] Nonetheless, material found in Soviet military journals is clearly directly related to policy decisions. In fact, the United States Army used unclassified Soviet military journals as its primary source of information for the training and operations of its Soviet-style "OPFOR," mock opposition force, troops at the National Training Center in Fort Irwin, California. It is against these OPFOR troops that elite U.S. Army brigades trained for Cold War battle.[52] Debates in military journals are the best means that outside observers have to discover which sort of doctrinal innovations were considered and implemented at which time in the General

Staff. They are the only means we have for trying to determine which factors provoked innovative developments in doctrine.

In the empirical chapters which follow, I will attempt to trace the Soviet reaction to three shifts in Western doctrine for future war in Europe. For each case, I will provide a summary of what Western scholars now know about each of the Western shifts, in order to establish an accurate baseline of what the international environment held for the General Staff. I will then try to determine what Soviet military officers perceived about each Western shift at the time that they occurred. This should assist the outside observer's efforts to understand the Soviet military's construct of its environment. I will then speculate about how the possibility of reactive innovation might have been received by Soviet officers who acted in accordance with theories about the interests of professional militaries. This will be followed by a description of General Staff debates about whether or not the Soviet Union should innovate in response to these Western shifts. Any hard data available about the quality and timing of a Soviet operational innovation will be included. Finally, I will attempt to assess the degree of control that the General Staff had over doctrinal decision-making at each time period. For the final case, where it is clear that Gorbachev and other moderate Soviet reformers attempted to change the boundaries of General Staff responsibility for doctrine, I will describe the strategies used and positions taken in doctrinal discussions among both military officers and civilians, and will speculate about the likelihood of long-term success in those Soviet doctrinal reform efforts.

3

Soviet Reactions to Flexible Response

A Clear Case of Reactivity

As the evidence presented below demonstrates, U.S. and NATO planning for the flexible use of conventional weapons against the Soviet Union in the European theater had a strong impact on Soviet military debates and Soviet military planning from the mid-1960s onward.

The doctrine of Flexible Response was officially adopted by the United States in 1961, and by NATO as a whole in 1967. However, these dates are not the ones which mark actual Western operational policy for the limited use of conventional weapons against a Soviet military threat in Europe. In reality, NATO military planners and politicians realized by the late 1950s that their declaratory doctrine of Massive Retaliation lacked credibility. This doctrine stated that large numbers of strategic nuclear weapons would be used against Soviet territory in the event of any Soviet military incursion in Western Europe. Many Western planners believed that this doctrine might tempt the Soviet Union to play a nibbling game, since it was unlikely that the alliance would agree to allow the use of nuclear weapons in response to small instances of hostile military activity by the Soviets. The Western perception of a credibility gap was strengthened by the series of threatening but minor military confrontations which the Soviet Union began in divided Berlin in 1958. In fact by the early 1960s, NATO operational plans included options for limited conventional-only weapons use in response to small-scale Soviet military threats in Europe.

At the same time, NATO outlays on conventional weapons deployments and troop levels never reached the level originally forseen by Flexible Response proponents. Both Western and Soviet observers agreed that while NATO leaders appeared to want to avoid the use of nuclear weapons for as long as possible, NATO commanders would face defeat by superior Soviet conventional forces in a matter of days (or perhaps even hours) in a major war, unless NATO battlefield and theater nuclear weapons were then used.

Thus from the early 1960s on the Soviet military faced a real change in NATO military operational planning, such that limited incursions would be met by limited means. Yet from the mid-1960s on it became clear that if war continued past a day or two, NATO nuclear weapons would likely be used. While some Western analysts have emphasized the ineffectiveness of Flexible Response as an alternative to nuclear warfare, and the continuity in NATO planning for theater nuclear operations,[1] this chapter presents the adoption of NATO flexible conventional planning in Europe as an innovation in Soviet eyes, one that played an important role in the U.S.-Soviet military competition.

Through the 1950s, Soviet military planning for future war in Europe was based on the use of nuclear weapons on the battlefield. Combined arms forces would have integrated nuclear weapons into their offensive operations as a matter of course. There is no evidence that the Soviet military entertained any concept of step-by-step escalation from conventional to nuclear use at that time. If nuclear weapons were seen to be useful for a particular military goal, then they would be used if they were available.

The Western adoption of flexible conventional force options in the late 1950s challenged the Soviet General Staff to rethink its approach to war. Commentary in the military press, especially by the mid-1960s, indicated that many Soviet officers felt a need to catch up to Western doctrinal concepts for future war in Europe. Exercise and weapons development and deployment data from the late 1960s and early 1970s indicate that these officers' concerns were in turn reflected in Soviet operational planning. It was at this point that the Soviet General Staff began to implement its infamous "conventional option," which was fully developed by the late 1970s: Soviet conventional weapons would be used to try to destroy NATO theater nuclear weapons before they could be used, and thus secure victory in European war for the Warsaw Pact without the use of nuclear weapons.

While the evidence presented in this chapter clearly shows that the Soviet General Staff recognized a shift in Western doctrine, that officers debated the significance of this shift and how to react to it, and that the conventional option reaction was well underway in the Soviet Union by the early 1970s, one anomaly appears in the record. Although the General Staff began talking about the significance of the Western shift in the 1950s, and while some passing mention of a need to react to that shift appeared in the early 1960s, the full-fledged military debate about Flexible Response did not emerge immediately. It emerged suddenly and in full force in 1963 and 1964. It appears that the explanation for this delay lies in Soviet domestic politics, specifically in the 1960–1964 confrontation between Soviet First Secretary Nikita Khrushchev and the Soviet General Staff.

Khrushchev tried to force his own doctrinal ideas on the Soviet General Staff in 1960, arguing that the outcome of all future world wars would be determined by strategic nuclear rockets, and that therefore Soviet combined arms planning and deployments should be sharply curtailed. The General Staff for the most part reacted with outrage to this suggestion. It would seem that by pointing to the Western shift, Soviet officers could have made an argument against Khrushchev for the need to retain significant conventional forces on the ground. Yet this argument does not seem to have been made, or at least it was not made publicly. Instead, Soviet officers argued that combined forces were still important for future nuclear war.

This anomaly is best explained by the organizational politics involved in doctrinal innovation. In order to argue that the Western doctrinal shift demanded change in Soviet operational planning, the General Staff would have to agree that its own existing doctrine, that of combined forces use on the *nuclear* battlefield, was no longer sufficient. Organizational agreement on the need for such innovation does not come easily to any organization, especially one dominated by those who have been in the organization for decades. Raising the issue of innovation in doctrine would likely have created deep fissures in the organization. And at this point in time, organizational unity in the General Staff was crucial if Khrushchev's "hare-brained scheming" was to be overcome. Thus, it makes sense that senior General Staff officers would have wanted to delay discussion of the implications of the Western shift until Khrushchev's challenge to their organizational autonomy was defeated.

Therefore, the argument of this chapter is that in this case, Soviet General Staff officers cared a great deal about changes in the international threat environment, and eventually changed Soviet military doctrine at an operational level in response to the Western changes. At the same time, Soviet domestic politics and the quality of civil-military relations affected the quality and timing of the eventual Soviet reaction.

The Western Strategy Shift

On January 12, 1954, the U.S. strategy of Massive Retaliation was officially announced by Secretary of State John Foster Dulles in a speech before the Council of Foreign Relations in New York. Dulles claimed that world Communism was attempting to overextend U.S. military resources by forcing the United States to plan for local emergencies everywhere. Involvement in local wars, such as the Korean conflict, would sooner or later exhaust the United States, leaving it without genuine security anywhere. The solution, he stated, was for the United States to retain the option of responding to aggression at the time of its own choosing, using atomic weapons. The threat of the use of nuclear weapons in retaliation for local incursions would deter aggression, and military budget resources could be conserved, since large conventional force outlays would no longer be necessary. The United States would thereby attain greater security at less cost.[2] The military planning for this strategy had already been instituted by the National Security Council in the fall of 1953. By December of that year, the U.S. Joint Chiefs of Staff intended to use tactical nuclear weapons to offset conventional deficiencies in the field whenever the use of nuclear weapons would be "militarily advantageous."[3] Also in December, a three-year defense program was adopted by the administration which reflected the New Look strategy.[4] By late 1954, it had apparently become the basis for NATO military policy as well; the Deputy NATO Supreme Commander, Field Marshal Montgomery, stated in November of that year that all Allied Supreme Command planning in Europe was based on the use of nuclear weapons.[5] The impact of Massive Retaliation on U.S. planning throughout the remainder of the 1950s was reflected in a sharp drop-off in the number of U.S. troops stationed in Europe, beginning in 1956.[6]

As soon as the strategy was announced in 1954, it received severe criticism from a variety of Western strategy experts who did not believe that sole reliance on nuclear weapons for deterrence was credible. Dulles felt obligated to publish a clarification of Eisenhower's policy in *Foreign Affairs* in April 1954; he emphasized that nuclear retaliation was not an automatic response to any aggression, and that, if conflict broke out, the U.S. retained a variety of options from which to choose. Dulles wrote in support of ambiguity in this article, saying that it was beneficial to leave the opponent guessing about which option would be chosen by the United States. Lawrence Freedman notes that this was in sharp contrast to the thrust of the basic Massive Retaliation document, NSC 162/2, which emphasized the clarity of the U.S. retaliation threat, not its ambiguity.[7]

This muddling of U.S. declaratory policy did not prevent the eruption of acrimonious debate throughout the Western strategic policy community on the proper role of nuclear weapons and nuclear threats in deterrence and defense policy. It is in these debates that the roots of the Flexible Response shift are found. By the mid-1950s, it was clear that the consensus in the community was shifting toward a belief in the need to be prepared for limited wars in Europe. Critics of Massive Retaliation believed that the threat of nuclear retaliation was not credible enough to deter limited conventional incursions. These critics thought that such aggression would be easier to prevent if the opponent believed that any attack on the West would be met in kind. Support was being garnered for the institutionalization of a conventional pause in Western war planning, where conventional force probes would be met with a conventional response, and nuclear weapons would only be used if this first response failed to stop the attack. There were variations within this type of thinking. For example, some argued that the pause should not be limited to conventional weapons, but instead to the battlefield, tactical level of nuclear weapons use, and that tactical nuclear weapons were separable from strategic nuclear weapons as a means of signalling the alliance's intentions during a conflict.[8]

The element of this shift which should have been particularly interesting to Soviet military planners was the fact that senior military officers in both the United States and in the NATO command objected to the idea that strategic nuclear weapons were a defense panacea. As early as 1956, U.S. Army Chief of Staff Gen. Maxwell Taylor wrote that nuclear weapons were unusable in European wars because of high population concentrations and the resulting likelihood of massive civilian deaths on the Western side alone.[9] While Taylor was prevented by the State Department from publishing this article, similar views on the desirability of avoiding nuclear weapons use of any kind were expressed by U.S. Army Gen. J. Lawton Collins in the April 1956 issue of *Foreign Affairs*. Taylor also had the opportunity to make his views known when he testified before the Senate Armed Services Committee in June. Many Army officers believed that the U.S. force structure was unbalanced because of its focus on nuclear (and particularly Air Force) weapons.[10]

In November 1956, U.S. Air Force Gen. Lauris Norstad became Supreme Allied Commander of NATO forces in Europe (SACEUR). He saw it as his mission to relieve NATO of reliance on Massive Retaliation, and to create a sufficient "shield" of ground forces to stave off a limited attack on Europe. While he did not see this shield as being made up of only conventional forces, he did endorse the concept of a pause before the full brunt of nuclear weapons would be brought to bear on the opponent.[11] In early 1957, Col. Richard G. Stilwell, Director of the Strategic Studies Group under the Supreme Headquarters for Allied Planning in Europe (SHAPE) Plans and Policy Division, submitted a study to SACEUR which concluded that the credibility of Massive Retaliation was deteriorating and that more flexibility in planning was needed. He suggested that a conventional forward defense should be the first stage of response, to be followed by tactical nuclear use. Norstad approved of this report, and used it to lobby for support of his pause concept among NATO political leaders.[12]

In April, the NATO doctrinal document used as the basis of Massive Retaliation operational planning, MC 48, was modified by a new document approved by the allies, MC 14/2. This document stated that strategic nuclear weapons use by NATO against limited Soviet incursions was not credible, and that NATO must be prepared to react to limited uses of force without immediate nuclear weapons employment (even though major war would certainly still be nuclear).[13] By June of that year, even Dulles had become a public advocate of increased flexibility in European force planning.[14] A major and respected private think tank source of strategic thinking about limited war was also developing at this time, at what would become the RAND Corporation.[15]

In late 1958, an additional reason arose for NATO to consider the question of how to react to limited Soviet incursions in Europe. On November 27, the Soviet government sent a note to the three other states then occupying Berlin (the United States, France, and Great Britain) and to the West German government in Bonn, demanding that a resolution to the division of Berlin be reached in six months. The note indicated that the Soviets would prefer to make Berlin a demilitarized "free city," independent from any state control. The Soviets implied that if this deadline were not met, they would act with East Germany to cut off Western access routes to Berlin. The note also contained an implied threat about the horrors of war.[16] While the Western powers reacted to this note with a decision to pursue diplomacy rather than military confrontation, military officers from the three Western occupiers began at this point to prepare contingency plans for limited military responses to possible Soviet military pressures in Berlin. A particularly significant role was played by a tripartite organization code-named LIVE OAK, which drew up conventional force use options for everything from limited probes to action at the battalion and division level.[17]

Almost immediately after taking office in 1961, U.S. President John F. Kennedy confronted renewed Soviet pressure in Berlin. This time the Soviet government sent an *aide memoire* to the West German government, once again with an implied threat of military action if an acceptable agreement on Berlin was not reached before September. In March, U.S. Ambassador to the USSR Llewellyn Thompson met with Khrushchev, and Khrushchev emphasized to him the importance of that memorandum.[18]

In response, Kennedy announced in a special message to Congress that the defense budget would be redirected toward the development of flexible options at the non-nuclear level, so that any aggression against the U.S. or its allies would face response at the level chosen by the enemy.[19] Throughout that spring and summer, Kennedy encouraged his NATO partners to undertake a conventional force build-up; on July 25, he announced the build-up of U.S. troops in Europe as a response to the crisis situation developing over Berlin.[20]

The U.S. Flexible Response doctrine was reflected in operational planning. New plans were drawn up for the use of American troops, including an offensive conventional "autobahn probe," designed to challenge Soviet troops in the event that road access to Berlin was cut off.[21] The content of doctrinal articles in official American military journals changed as well in 1961, as attention was focused on conventional, rather than nuclear, fighting in the theater.[22] And the U.S. Army Field Manual for the Armored Division, FM 17–100, was altered that year to acknowledge that nuclear war could involve non-nuclear environments (a backhanded way of admitting the possibility of a conventional pause).[23] By February 1962, the conventional pause concept and the existence of a range of possible war-fighting options at various levels (from conventional war through tactical nuclear weapons use to general nuclear warfare) was reflected in the main Army Field Manual, FM 100–5, "Operations."[24] Particularly interesting was the manual's new admonition that "force must be applied so as to minimize the risk that the conflict will expand to general war."[25]

Despite this early operational impact of the Flexible Response strategy, its effect on U.S. and NATO deployments policy was not sustained. U.S. troop commitments to Europe declined throughout the mid-1960s and into the early 1970s, as the Berlin crisis faded and the Vietnam conflict gained a higher priority in American military planning.[26] NATO as a whole was unable to reach agreement on ratifying Flexible Response as official alliance strategy until 1967. Domestic political battles in Great Britain and West Germany were a contributing cause of this delay, as was the French insistence on maintaining a nuclear-based national strategy (the withdrawal of France from the NATO joint command in 1966 was the necessary condition for approval of the strategy).[27] Even official approval of the strategy did not lead to a change in overall European defense expenditures; West European conventional defense spending actually declined throughout the remainder of the decade.[28]

Yet it is clear that at the operational planning level, Flexible Response was maintained. While low NATO force levels probably meant that Western forces could not hold out in a major war for more than a few days without using nuclear weapons, it was nonetheless now established in NATO policy that nuclear use would be delayed as long as possible. The hope was that this pause could give political leaders time to negotiate an end to military conflict, before a nuclear holocaust rained down on Europe.

Soviet Recognition of the Shift

Much of the Western debate in the 1950s occurred at the classified level, so it is not possible to determine exactly what Soviet policymakers knew about its extent and seriousness. However, it is quite clear that senior Soviet officers had access to information demonstrating that the debate was proceeding within Western military establishments. As early as 1956, Soviet military officers were introduced to Western strategic thinking that

was at odds with a pure Massive Retaliation outlook on future conflict in
Europe. *Voennyi Zarubezhnik*, the semiclassified[29] Soviet military journal which at that time[30] summarized and analyzed NATO military developments, reproduced, in Russian translation, several critical articles by
West European military thinkers. Some of these articles argued against a
wholly nuclear focus in European war-planning, and others presented
conventional war as an alternative to nuclear war in the European theater.[31] By 1958, the journal was reproducing American military journal
articles which stated that the U.S. Army was prepared for European war
which might begin on the conventional-only level.[32] In 1958, *Voennyi
Zarubezhnik* also included an accurate summary and analysis of U.S.
Army Chief of Staff Maxwell Taylor's statements about the need to prepare for limited and local war,[33] and in 1959, a review of Lt. Col. F.
Miksche's book, *La Faillite de la Strategie Atomique*, which implied that
NATO was searching for a new strategy to replace Massive Retaliation.[34]
In 1960, Maxwell Taylor's new book, *The Uncertain Trumpet*, was accu-
rately summarized as a major call for the United States to restructure its
limited war strategy;[35] within the year, a full Russian translation of the
book was put out by the Soviet military publishing house, *Voenizdat*,
along with translations of two other significant American books on limited war, Bernard Brodie's *Strategy in the Missile Age* and Robert
Osgood's *Limited War*.[36] Furthermore, the Chief of SHAPE's Historical
Section has written that "The existence of LIVE OAK, with its contingency
plans, chains of command for operations, and exercises of various coun-
termeasures, was certainly known to the Soviet Union and may have had
a deterring effect in preventing the Soviet Union from attempting to go
even farther in restricting access to West Berlin."[37]

Soviet Defense Minister Malinovskii, in a January 1960 public speech,
indicated that changes were occurring in the West, but expressed his res-
ervations:

> [I]n the West now they speak and write a lot about "limited nuclear war,"
> "tactical use of nuclear weapons," "a strategy of measured dosages," "strategy
> of deterrence," etc. etc. All these "theories" and, if one may say it, "strategies"
> testify to the terror of imperialists before the inevitable retribution which they
> may receive in the event of an attack on the countries of the socialist camp. In
> addition to this, such "theories" are preached for the soothing of the wide
> popular masses, so that under the cover of this smoke-screen the dark business
> can be created of preparation of a new world war.[38]

Public accusations by Soviet military leaders that the Western strategies
were not real manifestations of Western plans were common in these
years. Many articles in *Voennyi Zarubezhnik* at this time also contained
analyses which stated that the U.S. was planning only a surprise, massive

nuclear attack on the USSR as the beginning of general war.[39] Nonetheless, by late 1961, overviews of Western developments that appeared in the journal were focusing on the impact of Kennedy's policies on U.S. conventional war planning.[40] This trend was continued by articles appearing in several journals in 1962, including *Voennaia Mysl'*, the General Staff strategy journal that was at that time semiclassified.[41]

As will be discussed below, Soviet First Secretary Nikita Khrushchev might have had reasons for wanting to prevent the Soviet military from learning about this Western shift, or at least for wanting the military to believe that the Western shift was not real or serious. However, this review of the Soviet military press indicates that any efforts he made in that direction failed. Senior Soviet military officers clearly had the opportunity to learn exactly what was happening in Western strategy development from the mid-1950s through the early 1960s.

The Soviet Reaction

The failure of Western deployments to live up to operational planning goals should not have prevented a Soviet discussion of limited war doctrine in reaction to the shift in Western strategic thinking during the early 1960s. Operational doctrine, as outlined in U.S. Army and NATO Field Manuals, did change; and for a few years following the shift, U.S. deployments and budgetary priorities changed to reflect a new emphasis on ground force conventional defense in Europe. Furthermore, since new strategic thinking is often an indicator of the future direction of strategic planning (witness the Massive Retaliation decision, outlined above), Soviet military officers in their role as state defenders should have shown an interest in discussing the shift that began in the mid-1950s. It would have been imprudent for military strategists not to pay attention to their opponents' innovative military thinking until there was definite evidence of its impact on deployments; by then, they would have fallen behind in the future war planning competition.[42]

The 1960s is a particularly interesting decade in the history of the development of Soviet military thought, because Western scholars still do not agree in their analyses of how Soviet reactions to Flexible Response developed in this period. Some believe that there was no reaction, or at least that the reaction had no significant policy impact, and that Soviet planning for nuclear war in Europe endured, basically unchanged.[43] Others believe that a sea change occurred, and that beginning in 1966 Soviet military planning was designed to avoid nuclear escalation in Europe and to keep any future war limited.[44] Still others believe that while the Soviet military accepted the idea of a conventional pause in a European war at this time, the General Staff did not yet accept the idea of a fully conventional option.[45] While the evidence summarized below indicates that this latter view is closest to a true picture, an important element of the Soviet shift in strategic thinking is not covered by any of these sources: the level of debate and discussion within the Soviet military about whether or not conventional, limited force-planning for the European theater was wise.

Why Innovate?

Soviet military officers' reactions to the Flexible Response decision provide clear evidence in support of the hypothesis that when militaries perceive significant changes in their threat environment, they are likely to support innovation in their own state's policy to counter that change. Before the Western shift occurred, Soviet General Staff officers believed that a future ground war in Europe would inevitably be nuclear, and their writings give no evidence that a conventional pause concept or a limited war option was being considered. After the Western shift occurred, Soviet officers for the first time wrote that conventional, limited war had to be considered in Soviet operational doctrine. By the late 1960s, official Soviet military doctrine seemed indeed to have adopted a conventional pause concept as one contingency in planning for future war in Europe. Some officers (but not a majority) went so far as to state that a completely conventional war with a nuclear-armed adversary was possible. Many Soviet military writings stated that the duration of the conventional pause depended on U.S. and NATO willingness to avoid the use of nuclear weapons, reinforcing the notion that the Soviet shift was a reactive one.

It is not immediately obvious why the Soviet General Staff would be interested in matching Flexible Response with a conventional pause doctrinal innovation of its own. Soviet military officers before the early 1960s had reached an apparent consensus that while large numbers of conventional troops and weapons were important for future war, they would most effectively be used in conjunction with nuclear weapons. The military utility of these plans did not seem to be threatened by a NATO conventional pause; nuclear weapons in the battlefield would seem to be more effective in achieving victory over a conventional fighting force than would conventional weapons alone.

Civilian political leaders might have had diplomatic or moral qualms about using nuclear weapons against an adversary using conventional weapons. (Hypothetically, military leaders could share these moral doubts, but there is no evidence that a significant number of Soviet military officers viewed nuclear weapons use as morally suspect.) Yet in this case, there is no evidence that the push for Soviet doctrinal innovation came from civilian sources. As will be demonstrated below, civilian analysts and political leaders were publicly silent on the Soviet military's shift toward a conventional option. Meanwhile, a lively debate about the military utility of the shift occurred in the semiclassified and public Soviet military press. The shift seems to have occurred among military thinkers and planners, without civilian interference.

There is a very good reason why military leaders may have wanted to avoid nuclear use against NATO for as long as possible. The Soviet military had been obviously concerned since the early 1950s with the effects of nuclear weapons use on battlefield conditions. The Soviet General Staff seemed to have been fascinated with what the U.S. and NATO thought about use of nuclear weapons against troops. A 1950 Los Alamos Laboratory book on the effects of radioactivity on military personnel was excerpted;[46] U.S. Army classroom training and field exercises involving battlefield use of nuclear weapons were highlighted;[47] and special attention was given to what U.S. and West German strategists believed about how tactical nuclear weapons had changed the conduct of battle.[48] The General Staff understood that nuclear contamination of the battlefield limited the activity of troops,[49] and that electromagnetic pulses could interfere with battlefield command, control, and communications (C^3) efforts.[50] This would give them a strong incentive for wanting to delay NATO's use of nuclear weapons for as long as possible, so that Soviet battle plans could be fulfilled to whatever extent possible before the battlefield became uninhabitable and uncontrollable. It would also give them an incentive for destroying NATO theater nuclear weapons with their own conventional forces to whatever extent possible.

Western critics of Soviet strategy have sometimes noted that Soviet plans to destroy NATO nuclear weapons on the ground would probably have been fruitless; as soon as NATO leaders recognized that their nuclear weapons were being threatened, they would have an incentive to use them before they were lost entirely. Destroying nuclear weapons with conventional forces did not follow the conventional-only logic of Flexible Response.[51] Yet as the evidence presented below demonstrates, the Soviet General Staff did not seem to think at this time that NATO nuclear use could be avoided indefinitely. The consensus reached by 1973 seemed to be that NATO would use its nuclear forces in a matter of days anyway, in order to avoid defeat. Thus to Soviet General Staff officers, it probably would have seemed foolish to operate as if nuclear weapons would not enter the battlefield equation. If NATO theater nuclear forces were going to be used sooner or later anyway, it might indeed make sense for the Soviets to try to make them as useless as possible as soon as possible, and to try to accomplish as much as possible before they came into play.

Thus, the Soviet General Staff did have incentives, arising from its role as guarantor of state security, for reacting to the adoption of Flexible Response in a way that would allow it to use the conventional pause to its own maximum benefit. It was not so much that the Western doctrinal shift was threatening to current Soviet doctrinal positions, as that the old Soviet operational doctrine no longer served the military's battlefield interests. The international environment for future war had changed, and the Soviet military would have been at a disadvantage if it did not make doctrinal innovations to meet that change. There would have been no reason for the General Staff to innovate in the absence of the Western shift.

The General Staff Debate Begins

Throughout the mid- to late 1950s, articles appearing in *Voennaia Mysl'* focused on preparation for a nuclear ground war in Europe. It was argued that the experience of World War II was no longer sufficient for the understanding of military phenomena because of changes in military technology.[52] The specific recommendations given about how atomic battle should affect use of tanks, artillery, and infantry, and size and independence of units suggest that the Soviet military was not considering only Western planning for war, but also its own. Through 1959, there was much in-depth discussion of the correct use of tactical nuclear weapons in conjunction with Ground Forces operations; there did not seem to be any discussion of conventional-only Ground Forces operational planning.[53]

As will be discussed below, in the early 1960s Soviet military officers focused almost completely on the domestic bureaucratic struggle over Khrushchev's ideas about nuclear doctrine. During these years, the Western shift to Flexible Response and the problems of limited and conventional war did not receive much discussion within the Soviet military. The fact that external competition was given short shrift because of this debate is confirmed by Col. I. Korotkov, in a 1964 article. He first summarizes the Khrushchev-era debate over the role of "military science" (i.e., the opinions of professional military officers) in military doctrine development, and over Khrushchevian ideas about nuclear war. Then, he continues, "It should be recognized that our military thinking, while giving appropriate investigation to the problem of waging a nuclear-rocket war, has given insufficient attention to the investigation of limited (local) wars, although the imperialist powers more than once during post-war history have run to them to achieve their goals along a violent path. Only in the most recent time has this inadequacy been corrected."[54]

A relatively low level of interest in the Western changes was in evidence among Soviet military officers until after Khrushchev left office. Nonetheless, the first glimmer of real Soviet military interest in attaining the ability to respond in a limited way to a limited attack in Europe seems to have appeared in the first, 1962 edition of Marshal Sokolovskii's classic volume *Military Strategy*. While the vast majority of doctrinal statements in the book concentrated on strategic nuclear weapons and on responding to a surprise strategic nuclear attack on the Soviet homeland, there was one chapter on limited war. Most of the discussion on limited war referred to national liberation movement struggles in the periphery, but the book contains one paragraph on Europe that stands out:

> [The possibility] is not excluded that the FRG [the Federal Republic of Germany], either independently or together with other NATO members, can unleash a war of local character in Europe through a surprise attack on the GDR [the German Democratic Republic]. At the beginning of such a war, nuclear weapons might not even be utilized. Military activities in this case could, for example, begin with massed strikes of tactical aviation and rocket troops with the use of conventional ammunition over the whole territory of the GDR or other neighboring socialist countries, and with an invasion of huge tank groupings.[55]

This statement was repeated word for word in the 1963 and 1967 editions. Also in 1962, *Voennaia Mysl'* published suggestions from a couple of General Staff officers that the Soviet Union should pay attention to developments in Western military planning.[56]

The first explicit statement that "Soviet military science" (which, in the vocabulary of the Khrushchev era, meant "the professionals on the General Staff") believed that non-nuclear war could be waged in Europe appeared in the Main Political Administration journal in May 1963. Maj. D. Kazakov, in the journal's favored philosophical terminology, stated, "It must not slip from view that the imperialists, in terror before the inevitable powerful retaliatory nuclear rocket strike, can thrust on us one or another form of war without the use of nuclear weapons. And from this [arises] a practical conclusion: our Armed Forces should be prepared to give a reliable repulse also with conventional means of struggle, having nuclear rocket weapons at the highest level of readiness."[57] While the rest of the article focused on nuclear rocket war and the importance of surprise nuclear strikes in the opening phase of such hostilities, it is the one-paragraph departure from the norm that makes the article so significant. The majority of articles at that time in the Soviet military press which talked about the character of a future war with imperialism stuck with the conservative perspective: war with imperialism would inevitably be a world nuclear rocket war with a significant role for ground troops, and local war was not an acceptable concept to the Soviet outlook.[58]

In May 1963, a conference of military strategists was held in the Soviet Union to discuss a wide variety of issues relating to doctrinal development. Excerpts from many of the speeches made at this conference were published in the military historical journal in October of that year. It is clear that both the doctrinal clash with Khrushchev and the question of limited war and Flexible Response were discussed at the conference. Two speeches were especially noteworthy. Maj. Gen. A. A. Prokhorov, who was apparently the keynote speaker (his paper title was the same as the conference title, "The Essence and Content of Soviet Military Doctrine," and his speech was the first one after the opening remarks to be summarized in the article), said that the "central tenet" of Soviet military doctrine was that future war with imperialists would be a world nuclear war. But, he added, "At the same time, the possibility of waging local war is not excluded," and then said that this brought forth "root questions relating to the character of war, views on its forms and capabilities for waging it, and concrete questions of military construction."[59] In other words, Soviet military planning had to be altered to take into account the possibility of limited war–fighting. Col. V. Mochalov was said to have added that while NATO doctrine considered that future war would be a nuclear rocket war, "it does not exclude the possibility of waging local and limited war. Comrade Mochalov noted that views of the probable opponents on the character of future war should be considered by us in working out questions of armed struggle."[60]

This conference seems to have marked a turning point in Soviet analysis of Flexible Response and limited war in Europe. Debate on the issue had finally broken out. But the question was far from resolved. The publication of the conference summary was followed in quick succession by a number of articles in the military press which stressed the nuclear rocket aspect of a future war.[61] Many articles emphasized U.S. planning for nuclear weapons use in army operations,[62] rather than U.S. conventional weapons planning. Many articles mentioned tasks that the Soviet military had to accomplish in order to be prepared for the nuclear battlefield: the psychological indoctrination of troops,[63] the mastering of operations research techniques for nuclear ammunition allocation,[64] preparation for troop activity under radioactive contamination conditions,[65] and an increased attention to the problem of maneuver.[66]

But in 1964, the innovators began to emphasize their challenge to the old thinkers in the military press. Prominent among this group was Maj. Gen. S. Kozlov, who began to publish a series of articles on limited war planning. (He had been identified by Western analyst Roman Kolkowicz as a Khrushchev apologist for an article he wrote in 1961.[67] He was no Khrushchev apologist by 1964.) In the February issue of the semiclassified General Staff journal, Kozlov wrote, "While recognizing as a basis for the conclusions of military science that the most probable future war will be a world nuclear-rocket war, our doctrine, in complete conformity with the conclusions of military science, does not ignore other methods of waging war which may arise within the framework of a nuclear war as well as in a war in which nuclear weapons are not used."[68] At around the same time, Kozlov published another article in the MPA journal in which he suggested that military doctrine should conform to the recommendations of military science, and that one should not overestimate the nuclear capabilities of one's own country.[69] This last remark must have been intended as a pointed remark concerning Khrushchev's habit of nuclear bluffing. A few months later, Kozlov repeated his theme in yet another fashion. In the military history journal, he wrote an article about the mistakes made in planning for World War I, and especially on the overconfidence in the offense that arose because of the belief that the war would be short. Two sentences deserve to be highlighted: "It is necessary to emphasize especially the danger of underestimation, for military science and correspondingly for military doctrine, of 'limited' war"; and, concerning the miscalculation of how savage and long drawn-out the war would be, "Unfortunately, history repeats itself."[70] When combined with his other recent writings on doctrine, this article seems to be a plea for planning for limited war in Europe in the future, so that the brutality of total nuclear war could be avoided if at all possible. In fact, he ends the article by writing: "The dismal experience, repeated in significant measure in the second world war, should serve as a convincing lesson in contemporary conditions, when the character of a war can turn into a catastrophe before mistakes in science and doctrine that were assumed in relation to the war can be eliminated."[71]

Two years later, Kozlov apparently still felt the need to defend his approach to military strategy. In a *Voennaia Mysl'* article in 1966, he stated that during the Bolshevik Civil War and in the late 1920s and early 1930s, the Red Army was forced to incorporate foreign bourgeois concepts into its doctrine in order to prepare itself to win wars against the imperialists. Kozlov wrote that "the consideration of foreign opinions did not signify any form of borrowing."[72] The defensiveness of his tone, coupled with his earlier articles on the need to consider the possibility of limited war, suggests that he was not only referring to the historical time-periods involved, especially since the periods he chose are often cited as being the formative years of the unique socialist doctrinal outlook. He seems at this point to have been doing battle against those in the military who were reluctant to admit that Flexible Response, as a bourgeois doctrine, was worth emulating.

Kozlov was not the only General Staff officer who became interested in conventional war planning in 1964. The theme was apparently raised around the same time in a paper written by Maj. Gen. V. Reznichenko, which was summarized in the General Staff journal. According to Col. N.

Liutov, in a comment on Reznichenko's paper, "From everything that has been said, it follows that at the present time it is necessary to plan and accomplish combat training of troops in such a manner that exercises and tactical training are conducted not only in conditions where the sides employ nuclear weapons, but also when they are not used, under the constant threat of nuclear attack by the enemy."[73]

Threats to Military Autonomy

The delay of several years between the Western adoption of Flexible Response–type operational planning (in 1958 and 1959) and the beginning of real General Staff discussion of the likelihood and significance of a conventional phase in European war (which only began in earnest in 1963 and 1964) needs to be explained. Since the Soviet military obviously knew that the Western shift had occurred, it would have made sense that the discussion of how to respond should have evolved immediately.[74]

The most likely explanation for the delay lies in the fact that the early 1960s was an era of bitter domestic bureaucratic struggle over military doctrine in the Soviet Union. The major issue in this battle was First Secretary Nikita Khrushchev's heavy-handed intrusion into the military-technical aspects of defense planning. In January 1960, Khrushchev gave a speech before the Supreme Soviet in which he made two unprecedented public statements and announced one very significant policy change. The first statement was that the size of the army was no longer a factor in measuring military strength; nuclear firepower was the only determinant of victory in a future war, which would involve all-out strategic nuclear destruction in the opening minutes. In other words, combined forces no longer mattered very much. War would be won or lost in a short time frame. The second was that the Strategic Rocket Forces (SRF), a branch of the military created only a month earlier, had become the preeminent service within the Soviet military, replacing the Ground Forces in that role, and negating the long-range delivery significance of military aviation and surface naval ships. The policy announcement that accompanied these statements was that troop levels would be cut by one-third (1,200,000 men).[75] While the level of actual troop cuts waxed and waned throughout Khrushchev's tenure in office,[76] Khrushchev's doctrinal insistence on the superiority of Strategic Rocket Forces and the supplementary character of the Ground Forces was maintained.

By forcing his own strategic planning ideas on the military, Khrushchev succeeded in challenging the professionalized military order established after Stalin's death in 1953. His ideas, often referred to as the "one-variant war" hypothesis, do not seem to have been based on any discus-

sion of the issues within the military. As was noted above, after Stalin's <- sim. to
death in 1953, Soviet military officers carried on a lively discussion about Holloway's acct,
the impact of nuclear weapons on war planning. However, they tended
to view nuclear weapons as support forces for the ground troops, not as
independent strike forces that obviated the need for armies. There were
some writers, such as Marshal of the Armored Tank Forces P. Rotmistrov, who stated that the imperialists intended to use nuclear weapons in
a surprise strategic strike.[77] But most strategists concentrated on problems of tactical nuclear weapons use in conjunction with ground force
operations.[78] As late as 1959, the discussion in *Voennaia Mysl'* does not
seem to reflect any military interest in one-variant, massive nuclear strike
war. This finding is not unexpected; respected Western Sovietologist
Thomas Wolfe noted that before 1960, nuclear weapons were generally
viewed in the Soviet Union as being supplementary to the traditional
forces, not as an independent fighting force.[79]

It is unclear how and why Khrushchev developed his ideas about nuclear war. He told U.S. President Eisenhower during the Camp David
summit in 1959 about his plans for restructuring the Soviet services, and
said that he personally did not believe that aircraft and navy surface ships
retained any value in the modern era.[80] A representative of the Soviet
Foreign Ministry told an American official around that time that Khrushchev had also personally ordered the cessation of development of Soviet
tactical nuclear weapons.[81] It is therefore possible that the plan was
merely one in the stream of Khrushchev's idiosyncratic policy ideas. Perhaps Khrushchev was attempting to copy Eisenhower's New Look cost-
cutting example without Eisenhower's nuclear monopoly; if this is true,
then Khrushchev's doctrinal justification for force cuts was only a cover
for economic reasoning.

Edward L. Warner III suggests, on the other hand, that Khrushchev
was the political patron of retired Maj. Gen. N. A. Talenskii, a man who
deviated from the standard military viewpoint on future war and wrote
that nuclear weapons were unusable in the modern world. Warner believes that Khrushchev accepted Talenskii's arguments and used them to
create the justification for a minimum nuclear deterrent strategy.[82] John
Erickson also sees Khrushchev as a practitioner of minimum nuclear deterrence.[83] A third argument about the motives behind Khrushchev's policy has been made by some: that the troop cuts and budget cutbacks were
merely an excuse for a purge of the military officer corps and for punishing the individuals with whom Khrushchev was displeased.[84] If this latter
argument is correct, then the policy logic behind Khrushchev's decisions
is irrelevant.

There does appear to have been a major, official General Staff discussion of Khrushchev's ideas, but it *followed* Khrushchev's 1960 announce-

ment, rather than preceding it. *Voennaia Mysl'* published a "Special Collection" of articles in 1960 and 1961 which apparently focused on nuclear doctrine questions.[85] It may have been here that the Soviet military discussed Khrushchev's ideas.

Certainly powerful voices within the Soviet military did support the priority development of nuclear rocket weapons. According to one Soviet source, the decision to create a separate branch of the Strategic Rocket Forces, rather than to integrate intercontinental rockets into the Ground Forces or the Air Force (as was done in the U.S.) was made after a lengthy discussion in the General Staff, and was supported by a majority in the Central Committee, the Defense Ministry, and the High Command.[86] Another Soviet source states that a major military reconsideration of doctrine in the light of the development of strategic rocket weapons was undertaken in 1959.[87] In fact, long after Khrushchev's demise, the Soviet military continued to refer to intercontinental nuclear rockets as the foundation of Soviet military power.

However, it is vital to keep in mind that the priority development of strategic nuclear weapons would not in and of itself have necessitated the downgrading of the other forces and the rejection of the established doctrine that stated that nuclear war would involve a significant level of ground operations. There is no indication in any Soviet source that the Soviet military's reconsideration of doctrine included a reevaluation of the role of the Ground Forces in a nuclear war. Strategic nuclear rocket development and ground force development could have continued simultaneously, as they did when Leonid Brezhnev came to power.

Based on these findings, it seems likely that Khrushchev's 1960 speech was a declaration that he, not the military theoreticians, would control the direction of Soviet strategic planning, and that he would thereby control military budget allocations as a whole (by cutting troop levels and conventional weapons allocations) and among the services (by ensuring that the Strategic Rocket Forces would receive first priority).

The military reaction against Khrushchev's doctrinal statements arose immediately after his January 1960 speech, and continued for the remainder of his term in office. In his speech commenting on Khrushchev's 1960 announcement, for example, Defense Minister Malinovskii introduced a doctrinal modification of what Khrushchev had just said: "The rocket troops of our armed forces are indisputably the main type of armed forces, but we understand that it is impossible to decide all problems of war with one type of troops."[88] Malinovskii repeated this thought in his report to the 22d Party Congress of the CPSU in October of 1961,[89] and in his later doctrinal pamphlet, *Vigilantly Stand on Guard over Peace*, which was widely cited by military writers in the following years.[90] Malinovskii has been identified as a moderate in the doctrinal debate, who tried to reach a compromise that would unify Khrushchev's stress on strategic nuclear strikes at the start of the war and the military's belief in the need for large theater forces to fight a long, drawn-out nuclear war.[91] The fact that both Khrushchev's arbitrary Ground Forces policies and military press statements about the need for large troop numbers in a future nuclear war continued through 1964, however, seems to indicate that Malinovskii's efforts were not successful.

Examples of military writings about the need for large masses of troops in a future nuclear war abound.[92] Two particularly interesting lines of doctrinal argument were developed in the military journals during this time.

One line of argument, which appeared in the Soviet military historical journal, dealt with the strategic wisdom and error of great individuals in world military history. Maj. Gen. P. Zhilin contrasted the views of Napoleon and Kutuzov, the villain and the hero, respectively, of the first Patriotic War of the Russian people. He wrote:

> The fundamental component of [Napoleon's] strategy was the attempt to destroy the army of the opponent through one mighty strike in a decisive battle, and to [thereby] secure decisive victory in the campaign or war as a whole.
>
> Kutuzov correctly reckoned that various capabilities for struggle should find a place in war, and that one cannot turn the whole art of conducting war into only a decisive battle, as the sole possible means of attaining victory.[93]

Malinovskii repeated the parallel two months later in the same journal.[94]

In 1964, Col. of the Reserves V. Tsvetkov stated that the great Prussian military theorist, Carl von Clausewitz, also supported the idea that war could not be won with one great blow or battle. After describing the high Marxist-Leninist regard for Clausewitz's thinking (and after criticizing Stalin for disregarding Clausewitz), Tsvetkov wrote that Clausewitz, while believing that sometimes a single "general engagement" in a war was possible, predicted that it alone could not win a war if the popular masses became mobilized for defense and restored the forces of the army. "The effect [of the general engagement on the outcome of the war] especially declines in coalition wars." (A European war would, of course, have involved the NATO and Warsaw Pact coalitions.) Clausewitz's beliefs, Tsvetkov states, contrast specifically with those of Napoleon. Finally, according to Tsvetkov, Clausewitz believed that strategic offensives could not succeed in one fell swoop. They almost always faced difficulties in execution and demanded pauses as battle losses and supply problems mounted.[95] It seems clear that all three of these articles about the long drawn-out character of strategic offensive operations, and about the inability of single decisive strikes to achieve victory, are criticisms of Khrushchev's one-variant war doctrine.

The second interesting line of doctrinal argument appeared in the journal of the Main Political Administration, the voice of party propaganda within the military. This time, a conflict in thinking among the journal authors is clear. The fact that debate appeared in this journal is supporting evidence that the doctrinal conflict was not between the party and the military, but rather between Khrushchev and his political allies on the one side, and a variety of military officers on the other. The terms used in this argument were those of the Marxist-Leninist philosophical dialectic.

The first article in this series was a very wordy, complicated piece by Lt. Col. E. Rybkin, identified in the West as a "Red Hawk" who believed fervently in the 1960s that the Soviet Union could fight and win a nuclear war. While in this article Rybkin lauded the nuclear-rocket revolution in military affairs, he warned against ignoring the experience of World War II and against rejection of the old types of forces and weapons. The words he used to describe the coexistence of progress and continuity in military affairs were "the negation of the negation"; that is, while the new negated the old, the negation was itself negated by the need to retain what was useful from the old.[96]

In the next issue of the journal, the opposite viewpoint was aired by Col. I. Kuz'min, who, like Rybkin, was a Candidate in Philosophical Sciences. World War II experience was useful still for *political* preparation of forces, Kuz'min wrote, but on a military level, "thermonuclear war, if it is unleashed by the imperialists, will be qualitatively distinguished from the past." While the old weapons and forces will be used to support the new, nuclear rocket means of struggle, "As a result of the struggle of opposing tendencies, old military technology, military art, organization of forces and their separate aspects die off." Rather than a struggle between negations, Kuz'min stresses a struggle between old and new: "The old never gives up its position without resistance."[97] The following issue contained another volley in this debate, which seems to have been designed as a compromise between the two positions that somewhat favors the "modernist" outlook of Kuz'min.[98]

Although Khrushchev could not stop these debates in the military press from occurring, he apparently attempted to land some major blows against the organizational power of supporters of combined arms doctrine. In part, this was done through removal of key opposition personnel. Immediately following Khrushchev's January 1960 speech, Chief of the General Staff V. D. Sokolovskii and Commander-in-Chief of the Warsaw Pact Forces I. S. Konev were sent into retirement; it was probably not coincidental that the two of them stood out among others in the high command because they did not give public speeches praising Khrushchev's troop cut decision.[99] (Sokolovskii was obviously still greatly esteemed by those in the high command who were responsible for strategic planning, since he was chosen to edit the 1962, 1963, and 1967 editions of the Voenizdat book *Military Strategy*, which was described in the Soviet military press as the most important book written on the subject since 1929.)

A new piece of evidence has recently come to public light that Khrushchev went much further than this, and actually tried to destroy the General Staff Academy. According to commentary published in 1989 by Chief of the General Staff M. A. Moiseev, Khrushchev attempted to eliminate the General Staff Academy in March 1960, by cutting its faculty size in half, and turning what remained into the Operations Department of the Frunze Military Academy (a national academy which is prestigious, but which concentrates on tactics rather than strategy). According to Moiseev, "[Chief of the General Staff] M. V. Zakharov considered this a disaster for the Soviet Armed Forces. He became the initiator of the abolition of this act. In April 1961 a new resolution of the Council of Ministers was passed, 'On the retention of the General Staff Academy in the Armed Forces.' The Academy was resurrected."[100] In other words, Khrushchev must have seen the Academy as a threat to his usurpation of control over Soviet strategic planning. Zakharov challenged Khrushchev's attempts to overturn the existing power structures, and won. (Zakharov was known as a combined-arms traditionalist who opposed a one-sided concentration on missile development.) Perhaps as a result of this General Staff Academy struggle, Khrushchev fired Zakharov. Khrushchev claims that he was forced to relieve Zakharov of his command because he slept through important meetings.[101]

Zakharov was nonetheless sufficiently awake to regain his old post in 1964, within days of Khrushchev's ouster. He then presided over the shift in Soviet European war-planning that began shortly thereafter. He and his supporters got in their final lick against Khrushchev a few months after Khrushchev's departure from office. In an article seen in the West as a definitive military condemnation of Khrushchev's doctrinal meddling,[102] Zakharov, by then restored to the position of Chief of the General Staff, vented his frustration. He condemned any attempt to decide military questions without a deep understanding of military science; stressed that Lenin taught "that a serious, powerful army needs to be constructed 'not with phrases and exclamations . . . but with organizational work' [ellipses in the original]"; and stated that military generals, admirals, marshals, and other officers have the responsibility for giving recommendations on military construction, education, and preparation. Two quotations from the article stand out: "With the appearance of nuclear rocket weapons, cybernetics, electronics and computer technology, a subjective approach to military problems, hare-brained scheming [prozhekterstvo], and superficiality can have a very high cost and can lead to irreparable harm." And, to tie his arguments in to the tasks of the post-Khrushchev leadership: "It is important also to inculcate in the military leadership an attentive, respectful relationship toward military science and its recommendations, the correctness and vitality of which are not subject to doubt."[103] Zakharov's thoughts were echoed in a 1966 article in *Kommunist Vooruzhennykh Sil*, which contained an editorial note recommending it for use in officers' political classes.[104]

The importance of this debate about the role of combined forces in a nuclear war is confirmed by other Soviet military sources. For example, in the 1963 edition of Sokolovskii's edited volume, *Military Strategy*, a summary of the debate is provided: "These questions [of forms of strategic operations] are subject to polemics. Essentially, the argument is over the basic methods of conducting a future war, whether this is to be a ground war employing nuclear weapons in support of the ground forces, or a fundamentally new kind of war in which the chief means of carrying out strategic tasks will be nuclear-missile weapons."[105] The debate seemed to continue beyond the Khrushchev era; this is suggested in a 1970 book edited by Marshal of Tank Troops A. Kh. Babadzhanian.[106] Yet by that time the combined arms supporters were clearly in control of the General Staff.

There is thus no question that any Soviet military concern about strategy shifts occurring in the West in the 1960s had to contend with the pressing concern of domestic struggles over the content of military strategy and the role of the Ground Forces in fighting a nuclear war.

It would seem logical that to support their arguments against Khrushchev about the need for larger ground forces, military officers would argue that the Soviet Union should react to the Western adoption of Flexible Response with a corresponding development of its own conventional forces. Not only would this restore the military budget; it would also reassert military institutional control over military doctrine decisions. An innovative reaction to Flexible Response could have restored officers' autonomy on doctrinal issues.

However, these arguments do not appear to have been made by a significant number of military officers. There are some small indications that a variant of such an argument was tried. For example, Defense Minister Malinovskii (the voice of moderation) said in his May Day speech in 1961 that Kennedy's build-up of army forces over the Berlin Crisis demanded a Soviet response.[107] Yet Khrushchev did not appear to accept this argument, and at that point it seems to have been dropped by the military as well. The Soviet military thus seems to have neglected to take a position that would improve both its resource share and autonomy, and the Soviet international competitive military position.

This can be explained by the fact that Khrushchev's major opponents within the military tended to be those whose thinking developed in the doctrinal debates of the 1950s. As old-timers, well inculcated in tactical nuclear war–planning, these General Staff officers would undoubtedly resist not only Khrushchev's intrusions into their affairs, but also the innovative ideas about doctrine proposed by those who wanted to overturn the positions worked out in the previous decade. There were, altogether, three possible visions of future war in Europe to be considered: nuclear rocket-based war (with a small role for the Ground Forces); nuclear rocket-plus-ground-based war (with a large role for Ground Force troops and tanks); and limited, conventional war or war with a significant conventional pause (with a large role for the Ground Forces, but in a different mode from what thinkers in the 1950s envisioned). Both the first and the third challenge the precepts of the second. It was the second vision that had the support of the powerful General Staff officers who formed the heart of the anti-Khrushchev opposition in the military. In order to maintain a strong, unified coalition against Khrushchev, the issues of Ground Force resources and conventional war–planning probably had to be kept separate until Khrushchev was out of the way.

Innovation: Debate and Adoption

Articles in *Voennaia Mysl'* over the following years, through the early 1970s, said that a debate over strategy was occurring at that time in the General Staff, and argued that such debate should be considered a welcome prerequisite of innovative thinking.[108] The debate was echoed in the Polish General Staff, as well.[109]

Many articles during this period continued to deal with preparation for waging nuclear war at an operational and tactical level. This alone should not be surprising, since the Soviet military would need to be able to fight in a nuclear environment if the NATO side were to use nuclear weapons, even if this was not the preferred or expected scenario. Thus, articles appeared on using camouflage to force the enemy to expend his nuclear ammunition on false targets;[110] on resuming the offensive after troops have been subjected to enemy nuclear strikes;[111] on the need to improve training for dealing with nuclear conditions;[112] on the need to improve methods for predicting when and how the enemy will use nuclear weapons;[113] on the need to disperse artillery for survival under nuclear attack;[114] and on the need for tactical commanders to be aware of potential nuclear events in the operation as a whole.[115]

What would not be explicable if the Soviet military had in fact accepted the desirability of limiting conflict in Europe to the conventional level are the number of articles, appearing at least through 1973, which argued that war in Europe would be nuclear or that nuclear weapons would be the decisive determinants of ground operations in the theater.[116]

All through this era when conventional war came under reconsideration in the Soviet military, there were powerful, important voices among the group responsible for formulating and disseminating military plans who held to the idea that nuclear use was basic to operations against NATO.

Yet without doubt, conventional war was becoming a basic part of Soviet military planning. This is confirmed by an editorial stating that "military regulations and manuals" conformed with modern warfare requirements, and implied that these included "conducting military actions with ordinary weapons."[117] Army Gen. V. Penkovskii (not to be confused with Penkovskiy the spy), writing after the "Dnepr" exercise in the Soviet Union in the fall of 1967, which contained an extended conventional scenario, wrote that exercises should be conducted in simulation of both nuclear and conventional-only conditions.[118] Zakharov wrote in 1968 that "nonnuclear and nuclear" were distinguishable aspects of the theory of military art.[119]

But one cannot take this as proof that conventional war was generally accepted within the Soviet military as an alternative in Europe to nuclear war. Too many linking issues intrude. While some military officers did believe that a completely conventional war against NATO was possible, many others emphasized different reasons for paying attention to conventional weapons.

First of all, a recurring theme, at least through 1967, was that situations might arise in a basically nuclear war where the attacking troops lacked a sufficient number of nuclear weapons, and would be forced to accomplish their goals using conventional armaments despite the greater desirability of using nuclear arms.[120] Through 1972, occasional articles appeared which stated that conventional weapons might be used on secondary axes, while nuclear strikes were being carried out on the main axis.[121]

In addition, even among those Soviet military officers who accepted the possibility of a completely conventional pause before a nuclear attack in Europe, there were those whose reason for endorsing the pause concept was not, like many Western theorists' (including Chairman of the U.S. Joint Chiefs of Staff Gen. Maxwell Taylor's), to allow for the negotiated resolution of the conflict before nuclear holocaust broke out. Instead, a conventional pause was seen as a useful nuclear war–fighting technique. Col. Gen. M. Povalyi argued that the conventional pause would allow the preparation of the society and economy for war.[122] Maj. Gen. N. Vasendin and Col. N. Kuznetsov believed that the conventional beginning of war would allow the ideal positioning of nuclear weapons to take place for later use, and would be instrumental in achieving a surprise nuclear attack.[123]

Another point to consider when analyzing Soviet conventional operation intentions during this time period is that NATO was not the only possible target. Even within Europe, the invasion of Czechoslovakia in 1968
presents an example of conventional operations use that was not directed
against a nuclear enemy. But two other major geographic regions also
occupied Soviet military concerns during this time period.

First, there was China. Articles focusing on China as a military threat
to the Soviet Union began appearing in *Voennaia Mysl'* in 1967.[124] While
some of the articles stressed the Chinese nuclear threat, at least one from
1973 stated that China was preparing for both conventional and nuclear
war, justifying itself by reference to "the threat from the North."[125] Also,
in 1969, a historical article on "the defeat of the Japanese militarists on
the Kharka River," that is, in an earlier conventional ground conflict,
explicitly stated that this was a warning against those who had contemporary pretensions to the Soviet Far East.[126] The potential need to conduct conventional operations against a Chinese incursion into Soviet territory must have been a constant preoccupation during the late sixties and
early seventies.

Second, U.S. fighting in Vietnam, which was portrayed both in the U.S.
and in the USSR as an attempt to implement the Flexible Response policy,
apparently struck a resonant chord among those Soviet leaders who desired the expansion of Soviet military influence in the Third World. Soviet
military exercises of this time included simulated long-distance airlifts
applicable far beyond European borders.[127]

Yet once the caveats have been cleared away, it must be emphasized
that a significant number of writers from the mid-1960s onward did express interest in exploring the notion of conventional conflict in the European theater against a nuclear-armed enemy. These articles fall into four
categories.

The first group believed that a conventional pause was possible in a
war that would ultimately become nuclear. The eventual escalation scenario, whether the pause was viewed as being of short or long duration,
was explicitly described in each case.[128] This position would probably
be the most congenial of the innovative possibilities to the old-style thinkers, since it demanded a continuing focus on nuclear war–fighting in the
theater.

The second group of writers on European conventional options focused on extended conventional operations; they often mentioned that
these would occur under the threat of the use of nuclear weapons, and
that therefore dual capability was needed, but did not specify how the
conflict would end (i.e., whether or not eventual escalation would occur).
Examples of this group include articles by Marshal of the Soviet Union
and Commander-in-Chief of the Warsaw Pact I. Yakubovskii,[129] Col. G.

Ionin and Col. K. Kushch-Zharko,[130] and, perhaps the clearest example, Col. Gen. of Artillery G. Peredel'skii.[131]

The third group of conventional war–planning supporters use language implying that they are almost sure that war would escalate to the nuclear level, but that they are not completely sure. Col. Gen. N. Lomov wrote, "For everyone, including imperialist theoreticians of local war, it is obvious that the probability of the spread of limited war to world nuclear war, in the case of the inclusion in the local conflict of nuclear powers, is very high, and in certain conditions it may become inevitable."[132] Maj. Gen. V. Zemskov wrote that "it is hardly probable that military operations will succeed for any length of time in staying within a limited framework. Most likely they will grow into a general nuclear war."[133] Maj. Gen. M. Cherednichenko wrote, "[I]n case of initiation of a conventional or limited nuclear war in such an area as Europe, there would inevitably be a large probability of escalation into a nuclear world war."[134] This last statement seems to be an almost mind-bending attempt to avoid saying that nuclear war is inevitable, while still using old-style phraseology.

The final group of theorists who stressed the possibility of a conventional conflict in Europe honestly believed that a conventional European war could be fought through to victory. The two clearest statements of this are in articles by Army Gen. P. Kurochkin in 1968, Commandant of the Frunze Military Academy, and Col. P. Sidorov in 1969. In both cases, the use of the word "or" instead of "and" as a connector between conventional and nuclear weapons use sets the statements apart from others. Kurochkin wrote, "To the important achievements in the development of Soviet military science can be added the fact that, having correctly determined the main and decisive role of missiles and nuclear weapons, it did not consider and does not consider them as the only means for achieving victory. Such a conclusion permitted the harmonious development of all branches of the armed forces and a reliable defense of the interest of our homeland and the whole socialist camp, while taking into account the possibilities of a war being conducted with conventional weapons, or with the use of nuclear weapons, if such a war were to be unleashed against us by the imperialists."[135] Sidorov's statement used almost identical wording: "[Soviet military strategy] deserves great credit for its struggle against making a god out of any type of weapons, even the most powerful. Correctly assessing the decisive role of missiles and nuclear weapons, Soviet military strategy has not considered and does not consider this to be the only means of achieving victory. For this reason all branches of the armed forces are developing harmoniously in this country, thus guaranteeing a capability to wage war with conventional weapons or with nuclear weapons if such a war is unleashed by the imperialists."[136]

Those Soviet officers who believed that a conventional war could be fought through to victory came up with at least two different explanations for why this was so.

One group stressed that Soviet forces could destroy the imperialists' ability to launch nuclear strikes by using conventional weapons against their nuclear delivery vehicles. The primary threat was that the NATO powers would resort to nuclear weapons use at an unpredictable time, and the primary task in a war would thus be to strike those weapons early and wage continuous battle against them until they were incapacitated. Not all Soviet writers who advocated destruction of NATO nuclear weapons belonged to the conventional options school; some focused on the use of Soviet nuclear forces to accomplish this task, assuming that the conflict would be nuclear from the start.[137] But others clearly stated that nuclear escalation was dangerous, and believed that conventional destruction of NATO nuclear forces would keep the conflict conventional.[138] Despite the fact that these writers had different visions of how war would open, they shared the viewpoint that nuclear strikes against Soviet forces were to be avoided by using Soviet military action to deny NATO access to nuclear means. Otherwise, it was believed, NATO intended at some point to use those weapons.

Stephen M. Meyer interprets these two subsets of articles as evidence of contingency planning; the type of Soviet actions against NATO nuclear forces would depend on whether NATO appeared to be ready to use those forces, or not.[139] The differences in viewpoint which make the branches of such contingency planning are important. In contingency implementation during a crisis, someone must determine which branch of the contingency is relevant: namely, whether or not NATO was about to use its nuclear weapons. It seems reasonable that theorists who emphasize, during peacetime, that immediate escalation is the norm might have a different perspective on events during a crisis from those who in peacetime emphasize the likelihood of a conventional pause. Differences in viewpoint may be encompassed by a single official policy and operational plan, but may become crucial if that operational plan ever needs to be put into effect.

The second explanation given for how conventional war against NATO could be won was the argument that NATO would not dare to use its nuclear forces (or at least, in the view of some authors, would not dare to use them early on, thereby giving time for something else—such as the destruction of NATO nuclear weapons—to occur) because of the fear or stigma attached to nuclear weapons use. The argument is first made explicit in a 1969 article by the new Commandant of the General Staff Academy, Army Gen. S. Ivanov: "There is too great a risk of the destruction of one's own government, and the responsibility to humanity for the fatal consequences of the nuclear war is too heavy for an aggressor to make an easy decision on the immediate employment of nuclear weapons from the very beginning of the war without having used all other means for the attainment of its objectives."[140] The strongest statement of this type, highlighting the moral consequences of the use of nuclear weapons, was made by Naval Capt. 1st Rank B. Balev, who said, "[O]ne must be aware of the fact, as is asserted abroad, that under present-day conditions nuclear war is not inevitable, even if there occur military conflicts involving several nations possessing nuclear weapons. In World War II all belligerent nations possessed substantial quantities of chemical and even biological weapons. But in spite of the savage character of the war, and the most resolute aims of the belligerents, these weapons were not employed on a mass scale."[141] The implication is that nuclear weapons, like chemical and biological weapons, are morally unusable.

It is difficult to sum up these Soviet military debates over conventional and limited war–planning for the European theater. At an intellectual level, the debate over whether or not war in Europe could be kept limited and on whether it was even worth attempting a conventional force option first does not seem to have been completely resolved by the early 1970s. It probably has not been resolved to this day.[142] Nonetheless, by the late 1960s it seems clear that the beginnings of a consensus had been reached.

In 1965, official Soviet military doctrine apparently shifted to allow the possibility of limited war in Europe.[143] By the late 1960s, this shift was reflected in Soviet military exercises[144] and war games in the General Staff Academy,[145] which experimented with non-nuclear scenarios and phases in wars against nuclear-armed enemies, even though nuclear scenarios continued to receive a great deal of attention. The "Dnepr" exercise of 1967 began with an extended conventional pause; the "Dvina" exercise of 1970 apparently contained a conventional scenario, but focused much more on the connectedness of conventional and nuclear war–fighting in the European theater.[146] By the late 1960s, then, Soviet military planning seemed to take a conventional pause contingency into consideration, whether or not it was thought to be the most likely future war scenario.

Soviet military writings indicate that there was an important source for doubt about the sustainability of a conventional option. As Col. K. Spirov noted, "Inasmuch as bourgeois military science is not and cannot be a consistent scientific theory, there frequently occurs in the military affairs of imperialist states a break between theory and practice, between the views of military theoreticians and official views."[147] As critics in the West often admit, the Flexible Response decision was taken as a political compromise, and the Western ability to avoid nuclear escalation for any length of time was never fully ensured because of budget constraints and philosophical disagreements among the allies. The Soviet military seemed especially afraid of what the West Germans would do; many articles stressed that West German officers were trying to take over significant NATO personnel slots and were succeeding in these attempts, and that the Bundeswehr strategy was based on early or immediate nuclear use.[148]

Nonetheless, by the mid-1970s, official Soviet doctrine accepted the idea that a conventional pause in a European war could last for five to six days,[149] even though eventual nuclear escalation was thought to be the most likely outcome.[150] Soviet official doctrine appears to have been based on the assumption that NATO would resort to nuclear weapons when its conventional forces gave out. Nonetheless, the General Staff hinted that the Soviet Union would watch for evidence of preparation of such NATO escalation, and would preemptively use nuclear weapons first.[151]

Thus the General Staff seemed to believe that the end result of war in Europe would most likely be the same in the sixties and early seventies as it was in the fifties: mutual nuclear exchanges. However, the acceptance of the pause concept and of at least a slight possibility that conventional war in Europe would not escalate to the nuclear level was a major innovation in Soviet military doctrine.

This doctrinal innovation is reflected in the evolution of the Soviet force posture. By the early 1970s, the Soviet leadership had succeeded in creating a newly dual-capable (i.e., outfitted for both nuclear and conventional operations) military presence in Europe.[152] It may be significant that in 1968, a new ministry was created in the Soviet Union to oversee conventional munitions development and production.[153] While Western analysts doubted until the early 1980s the Soviet ability to keep a major conflict at a completely conventional level,[154] this build-up (which, according to standard Western estimates of time-lags between production decisions and deployments, must have been decided upon in 1966 or 1967) indicated serious Soviet military interest in matching the Western shift to planning for conventional scenarios in a future European war. Thus while the Soviet military's institutional reaction to Flexible Response seems to have been tempered by the realization that it could not yet hope to control the course of NATO decision-making, by the start of the 1970s the Soviet military as a whole was clearly interested in having a conventional option at hand, in case it could be used. Many Western observers believe that by the middle of the 1970s, the Soviet build-up in Europe was propelled by the hope that Soviet conventional forces could in fact control NATO's wartime decision-making; if conventional weapons destroyed NATO's theater nuclear forces, they could remove a step in the

NATO escalation ladder, and thereby possibly prevent nuclear use entirely.[155] The Soviet innovation in reaction to Flexible Response thus served dual purposes: it expanded Soviet military budget resources, and improved Soviet war-fighting capabilities in an environment that might look quite different from the one projected for the 1950s.

Makeup of the Policy Community

Turnover in the Soviet Military

Personnel turnover stagnancy might be a contributing factor in explaining the gradualism of the Soviet military's acceptance of this doctrinal innovation. Until the late 1960s, the Soviet High Command was dominated by the single cadre of officers who had held responsible command positions during World War II.[156] These officers had also borne the brunt of Stalin's heavy-handed postwar limitations on the discussion of nuclear doctrine. These men were "uniformly over the age of 60," and thereby "a collective infraction of the 1939 law (Article 57) which stipulated transfer to the reserve at that age."[157] Those responsible for forming Soviet military strategy were a well-entrenched and aging clique. Khrushchev had tried to create a new junior officer corps, with personnel turnover that rewarded the "new" technically trained thinkers who might share his approach to war, but this did not touch the top-level officers who were responsible for doctrine development.[158]

An October 1967 law on Universal Obligation for Military Service went a long way toward relieving this situation; it strengthened the mandatory retirement law at various age brackets, and it insisted that quality of performance, and not mere seniority, was a necessary condition for those who wished to remain on active duty.[159] The fact that respect for seniority had been such an important part of personnel policy up until that time indicates that it might have been difficult for innovative thinkers earlier in the decade to institutionalize their ideas; the tool of organizational control would not have been available to them, since old-fashioned thinkers with seniority could not be replaced.

After the "Dnepr" Soviet military exercise in 1967, which simulated an extended conventional phase in European war, a number of promotions in the Ground Forces and at the Military District command level did reward those who had performed well, and therefore presumably rewarded those who accepted a greater limited war and conventional emphasis in Soviet war planning.[160] Also, at the very end of the decade, a high number of senior officers died of natural causes in close succession.[161] While these changes affected some key positions, exceptions to the mandatory retirement law were apparently made to such a significant extent that by 1972—five years later—the top-level cadre was reportedly made up of almost the same members as it had been earlier, and was still dominated by World War II commanders.[162]

Thus it is not surprising that innovation toward the development of a conventional option moved foward only slowly within the General Staff. As long as 1950s thinkers and planners remained in positions of power, it would remain difficult for innovators to gain support for new ideas.

The Role of Civilian Analysts

While Khrushchev's ideas challenged professional military autonomy in the early 1960s, there is no evidence that his views were developed or supported by expert civilians. At this time, the military retained a monopoly over technical information on doctrinal issues. In the 1960s, there does not seem to have been a civilian institution capable of challenging the military and offering military-technical solutions to strategy problems.[163]

There was an academic institute in the Soviet Academy of Sciences, the Institute of World Economics and International Relations (IMEMO), which was given the responsibility of analyzing Western military issues.[164] The first article published in its journal, *MEiMO*, which summarized the Western strategy shift to Flexible Response appeared in 1966. While the analysis in this article was quite sophisticated, the five-year gap between the Western policy change and the institute's analysis is, in itself, evidence that the *institutchiki* were incapable of playing a military-technical policy advocacy role.[165]

This was the first in a long line of articles that did a very good job of summarizing military technical developments in the West. Summaries of these developments within the Academy of Sciences especially gained in quality with the establishment of the Institute on the United States (which would become the Institute on the United States and Canada, ISKAN), which was formed in 1968 to give advice to political leaders about parity, detente, and the Strategic Arms Limitation Treaty process.[166]

It is interesting that in almost every case, these technical articles were written or cowritten by either current or retired General Staff officers who had long-term associations with the institutes.[167] Articles on doctrine written by many of the civilian academics at the institutes tended to be clumsy and laden with party-line propaganda (for example, on the demise of NATO and the desirability of developing an all-European security community without U.S. participation), rather than with technical accuracy.[168]

It is not necessarily true that military officers writing for institute journals are bound to advocate the military viewpoint; these officers often held joint appointments in the military and at the institutes, which would probably dilute their military organizational interests. And in recent years, individual officers associated with the institutes, like V. V. Larionov and M. A. Mil'shtein, became advocates for the civilians urging defensive defense doctrinal reform under Gorbachev. Yet none of these articles advocated any kind of innovative Soviet responses to the technical developments happening in the West. There was no suggestion that an alternative solution was being developed by the institutes, or that something other than a Soviet conventional arms build-up should be considered in response to Western policies. These articles only provided information about the Western shifts, not policy recommendations for dealing with them.

Overall, there is no indication that any nonmilitary actors were involved in the policy community that was responsible for reacting to the Flexible Response decision. Had there been any Soviet recognition at that time that arms races and military doctrinal improvements were reciprocal, costly phenomena, creative analysis could have been presented to the top leadership which would have allowed them to experiment with conciliatory solutions to the competition. There is no evidence that any such solutions were proposed.

Moscow to the contrary officially condemned as empty gestures U.S. and NATO proposals for conventional arms reduction negotiations in Europe throughout the 1960s. These Western proposals included U.S. Secretary of Defense Robert McNamara's proposal for reciprocal force reductions, made before Congress in June 1966; U.S. President Johnson's "bridge-building" speech in October 1966, which made a similar proposal; the NATO announcement of the Harmel Plan in December 1967, which in conjunction with its own Flexible Response announcement became a de facto two-track decision calling for a conventional force build-up and expressing hope for a mutual troop reduction and the attainment of stability in Europe; and the communique from the NATO Ministerial Council meeting at Reykjavik, Iceland, in June 1968, which developed a set of principles for such negotiations.[169] While there were complex international political reasons for Moscow not to take up the Western powers on these offers (including the apparent need for a large Soviet troop presence in Eastern Europe to discourage instability there, the desire not to negotiate on European issues until the existence of two Germanies was recognized by the West, and the fact that the U.S. was unable to exert pressure on Europe for a military build-up while it was itself diverted by the Vietnam conflict), there would have been grounds for a sophisticated nonmilitary policy community to suggest that Soviet resources did not need to be so strongly concentrated on conventional defense efforts in the current international climate. Instead, in 1965 Brezhnev apparently achieved political consensus around the issue of an all-round defense build-up, and maintained this consensus through at least the mid-1970s.[170]

Conclusion

The period from 1960 to 1964 in Soviet military thinking was dominated by the desire of many officers to contain the threat to military autonomy and military resources that emanated from Khrushchev and his support-ers. Not all officers shared the view that Khrushchev was a misdirected meddler; in particular, Khrushchev had support within the Strategic Rocket Forces. Nonetheless, after Khrushchev was removed from office in late 1964, mainstream strategists within the Soviet military managed to ensure at the political level that the Ground Forces would be given a boost in their resource share and that a reaction to Flexible Response would be pursued by development of limited war options for Europe.

Doctrinal debate in the post-Khrushchev era did not seem to be con-ducted primarily between formally defined interest groups; instead, it was carried out among General Staff officers who had different visions of fu-ture war.

Not even the Khrushchevian debate about whether or not nuclear war involved a significant ground forces role was limited by service rivalry. Harry Gelman notes that in early 1965, before Brezhnev announced the expansion of the ground forces' budget, there were a number of hints in the Soviet military press about an intensified debate over the issue. He cites, as an example, a famous argument over the role of the tank, "the queen of the battlefield," which took place between Commander of Ar-mored Troops Marshal P. A. Rotmistrov and Deputy Chief of the Gen-eral Staff S. M. Shtemenko.[171] What is particularly interesting is that this debate was carried on by two army men. Rotmistrov was the Com-mander-in-Chief of the Soviet Armored Troops; it is logical that he would be in favor of extensive use of tanks in a future war. Shtemenko, who claimed that the queen was losing her crown to nuclear rockets, was the Chief of Staff of the Ground Forces. In September 1964, just before Khru-shchev was ousted from his position as First Secretary, the Ground Forces' independence as a separate command and branch of the Armed Forces was officially eliminated, and their activities were directly subordi-nated to the General Staff. Independent command was apparently not reestablished until 1967, when the name of a new Commander-in-Chief of the Ground Forces, I. G. Pavlovskii, was first mentioned in the Soviet press,[172] although some Western scholars believe that the decision to reactivate the Ground Forces was made in 1966, during a General Staff reassessment of SRF and Ground Forces policy.[173] It is possible that Shtemenko's views and the General Staff absorption of the Ground Forces are linked. While Western analysts have usually portrayed Ground Force independence as a victim of Khrushchevian wiles, it probably occurred too late for Khrushchev to have been able to influence events. Perhaps it was instead an attempt by the General Staff to bring pro-Khrushchevian elements in that branch under the control of the Zakharov coalition. (Shtemenko was promoted to Chief of Staff for Administration, however, and thus gained the title of Deputy Chief of the General Staff; this episode in Soviet military history remains somewhat of a mystery.)

Khrushchev's battle with combined arms supporters was probably not carried out in isolation, as a pure military technical issue. Instead it was one of many battles in the political war that characterized Khrushchev's later years in power.[174]

The Soviet military's reaction to Flexible Response also took place in a political atmosphere. In the early 1960s a number of maverick officers directed strategists' attention toward the NATO strategy shift. Yet the issue did not receive a wide amount of publicity in the Soviet military press. Perhaps it is significant that in Zakharov's famous condemnation of Khrushchev's military policy errors, lack of attention to Western military developments was not cited as one of Khrushchev's flaws. It therefore seems likely that it was difficult for the mavericks to win support for their views at that time, and that many of the most active strategy thinkers of that time were more immediately concerned about the Soviet domestic threat to military autonomy.

Interest in limited war grew by late 1963 and into 1964, and the possibility of limited war seems to have been recognized by official Soviet military doctrine within a year of Khrushchev's ouster; the battle with Khrushchev did not prevent the growth of military thinking about conventional operations and limited war. Instead, it merely delayed the achievement of initial consensus about the need to react to the Western strategy shift. This conclusion is supported by Col. I. Korotkov's 1964 article, cited above, which laments the lack of attention paid by debates over strategy to the problem of limited war as it was developing in Western strategy.

Once Khrushchev was gone, the innovators seemed to gain support rapidly for their viewpoint. Nonetheless, they continued to encounter resistance from those who saw conflict with the West only in nuclear war-fighting terms. The period from 1965 through the early 1970s in Soviet military thinking does not seem to have witnessed either a stubborn adherence to nuclear war–fighting plans in Europe, or a shift to general acceptance of a conventional option. Instead, the era was one of vitality in the analysis and building of theories and scenarios about war in Europe.

Policy communities theory seems to provide a good explanation for this gradualism in the acceptance of a reaction to the Western shift. The variety of viewpoints contained in military writings about strategy during this time, even among those that accepted the need for Soviet conventional war–planning, supports the notion that Soviet strategists were individual thinkers. Consensus was built slowly, and agreement was achieved because each individual strategic thinker had his own particular reason for falling into line, not because one common line was followed by them all.

The role of personnel turnover in the process of achieving consensus in the military is more difficult to determine, simply because it is impossible to trace the careers of all military writers. Nonetheless, a number of those who seem to have been conservatives in the debates of the late 1960s were indeed officers who participated in the working out of theater nuclear war plans in the late 1950s.[175] There is thus some anecdotal indication that personnel turnover and the influx of younger officers had an effect on the acceptance of the innovative shift in the Soviet military.

The Soviet military as a whole was interested in successfully competing against Western military planning for future war in Europe. It was cognizant of the Western shift to Flexible Response, and it eventually reacted in such an effective way that many Western planners from the mid-1970s onward feared a Soviet conventional victory in the event of a war in Europe. But this reaction was delayed by domestic bureaucratic battles over resources and military autonomy, and consensus was built in favor of the reaction only with much argument (and perhaps with a little organizational control over personnel, although less evidence is available here).

The case of the Soviet reaction to Flexible Response thus demonstrates that military organizations are attuned to both external threats to state security, and internal threats to military resources and autonomy. It also demonstrates that Soviet military strategists in general were neither hidebound bureaucrats who resist all innovation, nor unthinking followers of the Party line on questions of strategy and doctrine. They formed a community of individual policy experts, each with his own individual approach to strategy questions. Many of those individuals were creative thinkers, and a few were bold enough to risk damage to their careers in order to speak out about what they thought was necessary for Soviet security.

4

Soviet Reactions to the Schlesinger Doctrine

A Case Out of Focus

The U.S. adoption of the Schlesinger Doctrine and the Soviet reaction to that adoption present us with evidence of puzzles without clear solutions. One of the stated purposes of the 1974 United States military doctrinal shift was to create a variety of preplanned limited strategic nuclear strike options, usable by the President in the event of crises or wars, to signal U.S. intentions without unleashing a world nuclear holocaust.[1] Previous U.S. strategic nuclear targeting plans were seen to lack a sufficiently flexible selection of target sets; the President would be left with a choice between all-out nuclear war or no strategic nuclear weapons use. As a result, it was believed that a greater capability for limited and controlled strategic nuclear response to the Soviet threat was needed.

An attempt was made to give the U.S. President enough information about the progress of a strategic nuclear exchange and enough control over U.S. targeting to allow the use of a small number of intercontinental nuclear missiles for limited purposes. The aim of such use would not be the destruction of Soviet forces or Soviet society, but rather to warn the Soviet Union that further military action on its part would meet with heinous consequences. With this capability, the President could demonstrate that the U.S. was still coupled to Western Europe. Limited strategic targeting for political purposes was seen as a means of strengthening extended deterrence, the U.S nuclear guarantee of NATO's safety from the Soviet threat.

This stress on flexibility and control in strategic targeting options was obviously the next step, after Flexible Response, in official U.S. attempts to give political leaders a multitude of options for how to wage war in Europe against the Soviet Union. Its political intent was in line with U.S. declaratory doctrine of the past decade and a half. At the operational level, however, the doctrine was a clear departure from previous U.S. strategic targeting plans. Extremely limited use of strategic nuclear weapons had never before been seriously considered, and was certainly not included in the Single Integrated Operational Plan (SIOP) for nuclear weapons employment. In this sense, the Schlesinger Doctrine was a real innovation in U.S. doctrine, when doctrine is defined in terms of plans for future war.

From the Soviet perspective, too, such plans should have seemed novel. The Soviet military appears to have accepted by the early 1970s the idea that tactical nuclear war which did not touch Soviet territory could be kept limited, even if it hit Warsaw Pact territory in Eastern Europe.[2] There is no evidence that the General Staff at that point had accepted the idea that tactical nuclear war which touched Soviet territory could be limited. Therefore, the statement by the United States that now strategic nuclear weapons (whether Intercontinental Ballistic Missiles [ICBMs], or forward-based, medium-range U.S. systems in Europe[3]) would be targeted on Soviet soil for limited political warning purposes should logically have come as a shock to Soviet war planners. Never before had Soviet territory been explicitly targeted by the United States for purposes other than all-out destruction of forces or cities.

Yet it is far from clear in the open literature whether Secretary of Defense James Schlesinger's plans to include limited strategic options in the SIOP were ever realized. The actual contents of the SIOP are highly classified, and thus in the open literature one finds only informed speculation. Much of this speculation casts doubt on Schlesinger's success. Certainly at the time that the doctrine was adopted, many in the West believed that its attendant technological developments in command, control, communications, and intelligence (C^3I) were primarily intended to improve U.S. first-strike, massive counterforce capabilities, not really to create a limited strategic employment option.

Thus in trying to analyze Soviet reactions to the Schlesinger Doctrine, it must be recognized that the Soviet General Staff could have found itself in the proverbial situation of the blind men encountering the elephant. Officers might accept differing descriptions of the doctrine's intentions. Those who believed what Schlesinger said about the doctrine that bore his name, and who thought that the SIOP had been changed accordingly, would have been expected to react differently from those who saw Schlesinger's statements as either subterfuge or pipedream. Theoretically, it is possible that the Soviet General Staff knew more about the U.S. SIOP than can be learned from open Western sources; perhaps Soviet officers saw the elephant in its full glory. Given the extremely high classification level of information about the SIOP, however, this is unlikely.

Thus it should not come as a surprise that the evidence of Soviet officers' perceptions about and reactions to the Schlesinger Doctrine is comparatively scanty, enigmatic, and contradictory. Almost no one in the General Staff wrote anything that can be identified as a policy argument along the lines of the other cases studied in this book. Very few officers tried to describe the Schlesinger Doctrine; even fewer offered any clear suggestions for how to react to it. It is possible that this merely reflects the sensitive nature of strategic nuclear targeting issues in the Soviet press. However, from the bits and pieces available to us, it seems more likely that the General Staff was confused by the Schlesinger Doctrine than that it hid some clear-cut discussion occurring at a more highly classified level.

Nonetheless, the very turbidity of the Soviet response indicates that a simplistic model of the preferences of military officers is inadequate. If military officers always resist doctrinal innovation (especially when its effects are unclear), and if they always believe that decisive action which seizes the initiative is the best type of war plan, then we would expect a unified Soviet military effort to dismiss the Schlesinger Doctrine as foolhardy and to emphasize that it meant nothing to Soviet war planners. Many Western authors have in fact hypothesized that this is what the Soviet General Staff did. However, as the evidence presented below reveals, the Soviet military reaction to the Schlesinger Doctrine was much more ambiguous and complex than such an argument would predict. While it cannot be proven whether or not reactive innovation occurred in Soviet war planning (in great part because we have no evidence in the open literature concerning Soviet nuclear employment plans), it is clear that some in the General Staff thought that U.S. plans for limited strategic strikes were something new that had to be dealt with in new ways.

The U.S. Shift?

The Schlesinger Doctrine was primarily about giving the President control over the use of strategic nuclear weapons, so that they could be used for political purposes rather than for massive military destruction. U.S. Secretary of Defense Robert McNamara started talking about "controlled" use of strategic nuclear weapons as early as 1961 in his classified Draft Presidential Memoranda to the President. It was not until January 1968, however, that McNamara's use of the "control" concept began clearly to take on the connotations that have been used by those favoring limited strategic strike capabilities. Earlier, he had focused on two primary choices for the President: a massive counterforce option, designed to destroy Soviet military resources, and a massive countervalue option, designed to threaten the Soviet population with retaliation in the event of a Soviet first strike.[4] But in 1968 he stated, "What if deterrence fails and a nuclear war with the USSR occurs? If the war began with an all-out Soviet attack, including our cities, we would reply in kind. If the war started with less than an all-out attack, we would want to carry out plans for controlled and deliberate use of our nuclear power to get the best possible outcome. The lack of such nuclear war plans is one of the main weaknesses in our posture today."[5] This statement, admitting and lamenting the absence of a truly limited strategic strike option in U.S. nuclear planning, signals the germination of the official U.S. shift to the Schlesinger Doctrine. It is important to keep in mind that this germination occurred at a classified level; the beginning of a doctrinal shift was not revealed to the public.

Weeks before the Nixon Administration took office in January 1969, the new Secretary of Defense, Clark Clifford, listed "limited and controlled retaliation" as one of four potential U.S. strategic force missions. He added his assessment of current capabilities for meeting that mission:

> Although it is doubtful that a limited nuclear war would stay limited for very long, we have the weapons and reconnaissance systems needed for selective responses in such a war. Here we enjoy a marked technical advantage over the Soviets. However, the lack of complete plans and data processing centers for selective responses continues to be a major weakness in our strategic forces.
>
> To overcome this weakness, we are investigating improvements in two areas: (1) providing pre-planned options for the National Command Authority (NCA) for additional selected responses against military and industrial targets (for example, strategic strikes for support of NATO); and (2) providing the procedures, data processing equipment, and computer programs for planning new, selective responses on a timely basis during the crises.[6]

Ivan Selin of the Department of Defense Office of Systems Analysis had apparently been the first member of the Johnson Administration to become concerned about the absence of a limited strike option in the SIOP. During the late 1960s, his office, in cooperation with a number of Air Force officers, began a joint study with the RAND Corporation on possible solutions to this problem. The study was called Project NU-OPTS; James Schlesinger, Director of the RAND Strategic Studies Division, wrote a paper in support of the study.[7]

As this study progressed, a Nixon Administration review of U.S. targeting capabilities began in June 1969 under the direction of Selin, who was now Acting Assistant Secretary of Defense for Systems Analysis. Selin worked with Secretary of State Henry Kissinger on the development of National Security Study Memorandum (NSSM) 3, which argued for the need to create limited nuclear strike options in U.S. strategic planning. In 1970, this grew into a Department of Defense Office of Systems Analysis (OSA) Strategic Objectives Study.[8]

While President Nixon apparently had difficulty at first convincing military officers to take his proposals for more flexible targeting seriously,[9] this problem was overcome in January 1972 by involving the Joint Chiefs of Staff (JCS) and some Air Force officers in a parallel study chaired by Johnny Foster, DOD Director of Defense Resources and Engineering.[10] The chief liason between the Foster Group and the Strategic Air

Command (SAC) was Air Force Brig. Gen. Jasper Welch, who apparently gave the Pentagon civilian analysts credibility with the military.[11]

Schlesinger, whose name the doctrinal change would adopt, met regularly with one of the study panel members.[12] Nonetheless, at least some of the members apparently did not realize that the RAND analyst was involved in the study.[13] The Foster Group's study was called the National Nuclear Strategic Targeting and Attack Plan (N-STAP), and it was designed to develop instructions to be issued by the Secretary of Defense to the JCS on targeting issues.[14] It was the basis for NSSM-169, approved in late 1973, which in turn became National Security Decision Memo (NSDM) 242, "Planning the Employment of Nuclear Weapons," signed by President Nixon on January 14, 1974.[15]

NSDM 242, in combination with the Nuclear Weapons Employment Policy (NUWEP1) signed by now Secretary of Defense James Schlesinger on April 4, 1974, gave the JCS and the Joint Strategic Target Planning Staff (JSTPS) at SAC headquarters in Omaha, Nebraska, the necessary guidance for development of a new set of preplanned nuclear targeting options.[16] The result, SIOP-5, was approved in December 1975 and took effect on January 1, 1976.[17] While the doctrinal change therefore did not officially go into full effect until 1976, its contents were leaked to the press by Schlesinger in January 1974.

Nixon gave two public hints before 1974 that he wanted to change targeting policies, first in his Foreign Policy Message to Congress in February 1970,[18] and again in the same statement the next year. However, these hints were not very explicit, and did not reveal that the existing counterforce options of the SIOP allowed only relatively massive strikes. In this sense, Nixon's public statements could be perceived as merely following the *public* line set by Secretary of Defense Robert McNamara in 1962 and echoed by Defense Secretaries until 1974. While their private memoranda to the President revealed that they were dissatisfied with current SIOP target options, this was not revealed to the rest of the world. Publicly these leaders called for counterforce targeting flexibility, but did not state that current targeting policies were inadequate for limited counterforce strikes.[19]

In January 1974, U.S. Secretary of Defense Schlesinger made the first public statements indicating that a significant shift had occurred in American operational doctrine concerning the limited employment of strategic nuclear weapons.[20] It was because of these statements that Schlesinger's name appears on the doctrine. Apparently, the first of these statements was made because the President's National Security Council (NSC) had privately indicated some misgivings about NSDM-242; by going public, Schlesinger hoped to force the NSC's hand.[21]

Schlesinger's best public summaries and defenses of the doctrinal shift are found in his testimony before the U.S. Congress in 1974 and 1975. In testimony before a Senate Foreign Relations Committee subcommittee in March 1974, Schlesinger indicated that previous U.S. strategic nuclear weapons targeting practices had not allowed the President sufficient flexibility in decision-making. While the SIOP had included a number of options, allowing some choice about whether population centers or military installations would be the primary targets of American strategic nuclear missile strikes (i.e., whether the strikes would be countervalue or counterforce), Schlesinger said that even the counterforce plan would have involved massive destruction of population centers. Truly limited strike options, those that would target only one or a few key military targets, were not part of the standard operating procedures or mindsets of the Strategic Air Command officers responsible for implementing the SIOP. Although the President could, in theory, order a very limited strike, Schlesinger said that the absence of preplanned limited options in the SIOP meant that under crisis-situation pressure, it would be difficult to ensure the timely implementation of such a strike. His major fear was that the Soviet leadership would not be able to distinguish what was intended as a limited counterforce strike from a massive strike on Soviet cities, and that therefore the United States had no capability for preventing escalation to a nuclear holocaust once strategic nuclear weapons use began.[22]

Schlesinger wrote that in addition to improvements in targeting flexibility, better missile accuracy/yield combinations were needed in order "to destroy only the intended target and to avoid widespread collateral damage."[23] He added that such accuracy was important not only for destroying "hard" targets (such as hardened Soviet ICBM missile silos), but also for destroying "soft" military-related targets (such as oil production centers).[24]

In the hearings on Schlesinger's defense budget request to the Congress, Sen. Stuart Symington asked the Secretary why the Soviets would not interpret Schlesinger's call for improved accuracy as an indication that the U.S. was planning to create a first-strike capability against the Soviet Union.[25] Symington's question arose out of the deterrence theory which lay behind the American declaratory doctrine of the time, Mutual Assured Destruction (MAD). This theory argues that improved missile accuracy is destabilizing. According to this theory, deterrence exists when each side has the capability to launch a massive attack on the other side's population. Since the opponent would maintain such a capability even after an initial massive strike on his forces, neither side would gain by launching a first strike, and nuclear war would thus be deterred. This deterrent capability is thought to be threatened if very accurate missiles are developed: even small-yield, very accurate missiles can destroy hardened missile silos, while even relatively high-yield missiles below a certain accuracy level are only effective against soft targets.[26] According to Mutual Assured Destruction logic, the possession of a sufficient number of accurate missiles could seem to give one side the ability to destroy the other side's missiles in a first strike. This situation could prompt the opposing side to use its missiles first in the event of a crisis situation, since it might believe that if the missiles were not used, the country's forces could be completely destroyed by a disarming first strike. The acquisition of very accurate missiles in 1974 was therefore dangerous, in the eyes of Mutual Assured Destruction adherents, because Soviet leaders could decide that the United States intended to launch a first strike and disarm Soviet forces, and the USSR might therefore be tempted to launch a preemptive strike first in a crisis. This is sometimes referred to as the "use 'em or lose 'em" dilemma of nuclear crises.[27]

Schlesinger responded to Symington's question by saying that the operational accuracy of missile systems was never as high as their theoretical accuracy, and that therefore neither side would ever have sufficient confidence in its forces to attempt a first strike. He said that he did not believe that either side could develop an assured first-strike capability, and that he was sure that the Soviets realized this also.[28] In other words, Schlesinger denied that the Soviet leadership could in reality put a first-strike effort interpretation on the doctrinal shift enacted. In his prepared report to the Congress, Schlesinger explicitly wrote that the improved flexibility that he sought in strategic missile employment did not include the choice of a disarming first-strike option.[29]

Schlesinger instead saw two potential uses for accurate, limited strategic striking ability. First, it could be used to signal U.S. intentions to remain linked to its European NATO allies during a war with the Soviet bloc. If the Soviet Union were to threaten to overrun Western Europe during a major conventional or tactical nuclear conflict there, a single limited strategic counterforce strike, on either East European or Soviet territory, could be used as a demonstration that the U.S. had not been decoupled from Europe, and would not allow Western Europe to be defeated by the Warsaw Pact.[30] This use of strategic nuclear weapons would therefore be politically motivated, not militarily motivated. No particular military objectives would be achieved through such use. It would merely serve as a warning signal to Soviet policymakers.[31]

The issue of decoupling was a particularly acute one in the early 1970s because of a number of foreign policy issues that divided West European and American political leaders. These included the refusal of many West European countries to support the American position in the Vietnam conflict, the misgivings of some in the United States over West German Chancellor Willy Brandt's independent *Ostpolitik*, and the fears of some in Western Europe that the SALT negotiations were leading the U.S. to make too many decisions about NATO security without European input. President Nixon's declaration that 1973 was "The Year of Europe" only aggravated the situation, by creating the belief in Western Europe that the U.S. saw its Atlantic allies as pawns in the superpower détente process.[32] The coupling mission of the Schlesinger Doctrine thus had two purposes: reassurance of the European allies about U.S. intentions, and deterrence of a Soviet theater attack on Western Europe.

Schlesinger's second justification for the acquisition of limited strategic strike capability was that it was necessary to counter Soviet possession of that capability. He wrote that the Soviets had attained a selective target attack ability in recent years, and that for deterrence to be credible, the U.S. had to match the Soviet Union. Otherwise, the Soviets could hope to launch a limited nuclear attack which left the U.S. with only two options: doing nothing, or causing a nuclear holocaust.[33] Schlesinger wrote, "[W]e hope to prevent massive destruction even in the cataclysmic circumstances of nuclear war."[34] There do not seem to be any sources, at least in the open literature on U.S. threat assessment, that confirm Schlesinger's claims about Soviet selective targeting abilities or intentions at that time. It is therefore possible that this part of his justification for the doctrinal shift was designed primarily to achieve political approval at home.[35]

Schlesinger stated that the establishment of a preplanned limited nuclear strike option required four sets of specific technical improvements in the U.S. force posture. First, the Command Data Buffer, a system which allowed prompt remote-control retargeting of missiles (presumably to switch back and forth between limited and massive options), needed to be completed. It had been installed in one Minuteman III squadron (covering fifty missiles) in 1973, and was scheduled to be fully deployed by the end of Fiscal Year 1978.[36] Presumably, this improvement would be designed to allow the President more flexible control over targeting decisions in crisis. Missiles could be switched back and forth between different preplanned option sets. Second, missile accuracy and penetration abilities had to be improved. Schlesinger directly stated that new Minuteman III terminal guidance systems were to be developed,[37] and implied on the public record (part of his statement was deleted for security reasons) that the Poseidon warheads used in the SLBM force were also to be technically upgraded.[38] As was mentioned above, Schlesinger stated that these improvements in accuracy were needed so that limited numbers of strikes would clearly be seen by the Soviet side to be directed against limited targets. Third, Schlesinger called for increases in capabilities for detection and reporting of enemy missile activities, including both launches from the Soviet Union and nuclear bursts on U.S. territory.[39] Presumably, this would allow the President to decide whether or not an attack on the U.S.

was limited or total, and therefore what sort of response was appropriate. However, it would also serve to increase the efficiency and effectiveness of a massive counterforce strike from the U.S. side, by allowing the Strategic Air Command to worry about launching only those missiles that remained in their silos, aimed only at Soviet missiles that remained in *their* silos, without wasted damage-limitation effort. Finally, Schlesinger stated that the overall U.S. capacity for strategic data-handling and communications had to be raised.[40] In other words, all of the improvements in technical Presidential control over targeting had to be backed up by better and faster electronic operations.

Because missile accuracy and other counterforce technical capabilities (such as Multiple Independently-targetable Re-entry Vehicles (MIRVs) had been undergoing steady development and improvement for the better part of a decade in both the U.S. and the USSR, the key Schlesinger Doctrine-related innovation in the U.S. force posture was improvements in C^3I capabilities for Presidential control over targeting decisions. While the President could theoretically have ordered a very limited missile attack in the absence of these technical improvements, Schlesinger's fear was that such orders would become muddled or lost in the fog of crisis and war. Preplanning made the fulfillment of those orders more likely.

Western political reactions to the announcement of the Schlesinger Doctrine were mixed. Some American scholars raised objections to his call for targeting flexibility, but such criticism apparently did not take hold either within Congress,[41] or within the policy-making circles of the NATO allies.[42] Apparently, the European members of NATO seemed to believe that U.S. strategic nuclear targeting was U.S. business, and that their input was neither needed nor desirable.[43]

The sections of Schlesinger's proposals which did provoke sharp criticism and debate both in the U.S. and in unofficial European circles were those that dealt with improvements of missile accuracy and the counterforce option. Assured Destruction deterrence adherents raised objections similar to those made by Symington in Schlesinger's Senate testimony, and many feared that the true intent of the announced changes was to improve U.S. massive first-strike capabilities.[44] Many Europeans, especially West Germans, worried that the U.S. focus on limited counterforce nuclear war–fighting made nuclear use more likely; ironically, although Schlesinger intended the doctrinal change to enhance appearances of U.S. nuclear coupling with its allies,[45] some Europeans worried that it was a sign of increased U.S. willingness to fight a nuclear war limited to Europe without fear of retaliation on American territory.[46]

Despite such objections, throughout both the Carter and Reagan administrations the Defense Department's development of accurate counterforce targeting options continued and intensified.[47] The fact that calls for the establishment of truly limited strategic nuclear employment options continued during this time is itself evidence that the Schlesinger Doctrine might not have accomplished what Schlesinger claimed he wanted from it. Thus a caveat needs to be introduced concerning the effects of the doctrine. The contents of the SIOP change remain highly classified, and its effects over actual targeting practices therefore remain murky.

The caveat is raised strongly by Col. Richard Lee Walker of the U.S. Air Force, who served in the Strategic Air Command and has held a variety of defense research and planning posts. In a 1983 monograph dealing with the limited targeting options proposals of the Carter Administration, Walker notes that there can sometimes be a disjunction between targeting theory and practice. He cautions, "Although planning for increased flexibility appears straightforward in theory, in practice technical considerations limit the degree of implementation."[48] He adds that there is an urgent need to ensure that policy directives do not undermine the goals that they seek to accomplish: "The urgency stems from a concern that nuclear policy decisions may not reflect a complete understanding of the gap between theory and practice in strategic target planning."[49] Specifically on the issue of limited nuclear options, he cites at least three major technical problems that can complicate the achievement of truly limited strategic targeting: the prevalence of MIRVs can lead to a mindset that undermines the formulation of options best served by single warhead releases; insurmountable inadequacies in C^3I can limit the speed and accuracy of judgments about which option should be implemented; and shortfalls in intelligence can leave the specific characteristics of very limited targets unclear (presumably leading to a tendency to overestimate the amount of destructive power needed to destroy the target).[50] While Walker never directly indicates that the Schlesinger Doctrine lacked practical effect, the "urgency" of the problem he believes was facing those who wished to implement very limited strategic targeting options in 1983 indicates that U.S. strategic options might not have been as limited as Schlesinger would have desired.

A related argument is made by Janne Nolan, who writes that SIOP-5 merely gave the President targeting options utilizing hundreds, rather than thousands, of weapons, hardly the ability to avoid all-out nuclear destruction.[51] Nolan does not cite a source for this particular conclusion, and it is impossible to determine from the open literature exactly what the impact of the Schlesinger Doctrine shift on U.S. preplanned targeting options was. However, it is known that SIOP-5 contained, for the first time in SIOP history, Selected Attack Options (SAOs), Limited Nuclear Options (LNOs), and Regional Nuclear Options (RNOs) in addition to the more established Major Attack Options (MAOs).[52] Target numbers have never been publicly attached to the planned use of any of these options. How-ever, Kaplan has reported that Henry Kissinger once asked two JCS gener-als for a hypothetical RNO in case of a Soviet invasion of Iran. Kissinger believed that their example of an RNO containing two hundred nuclear weapons was not sufficiently limited, and they came back with an RNO which was limited to exploding an atomic demolition mine on one of two Soviet major roads into Iran, and launching two nuclear weapons at the other road. While Kissinger found this alternative too small to have the Soviets take U.S. intentions seriously, this example does illustrate how small an RNO planned by JCS generals could possibly have been.[53] It is therefore probable that at least some of the SIOP-5 options contain less than hundreds of targets, and that the U.S. capability for attempting to keep strategic nuclear war limited was improved by this doctrinal shift.

A different point of dispute about the doctrine's effects on SIOP plan-ning is raised by Terry Terriff. He notes that Henry Kissinger regarded the doctrinal change as a means to develop regional strategic strike op-tions targeted not only on Soviet territory, but on European and Middle Eastern areas peripheral to the Soviet Union.[54] Terriff believes that Kissinger's target preferences were reflected in the Foster Group's discus-sions of the shift, and included in the SIOP guidance that resulted from NSDM 242.[55] Terriff claims that Schlesinger pointedly ignored this portion of the guidance in his public testimony on the doctrinal shift; apparently, Schlesinger did not want to harm U.S.-NATO relations by mentioning the fact that non-Soviet European targets were included in the U.S. plans.[56] Furthermore, according to Terriff's interview data, this doctrinal shift led to the inclusion of U.S. tactical battlefield weapons systems in the SIOP, so that they would be usable for U.S. global strategic purposes, rather than for the battle purposes of the commanders in the field.[57] Thus the Schles-inger Doctrine seems to have included both Soviet and non-Soviet re-gional targets in its set of limited strategic strike options.

The confusion on the Western side about what the Schlesinger Doc-trine really meant must have affected Soviet discussions of the topic. If U.S. defense experts did not then and do not now agree about the doc-trine's effects, then it is likely that Soviet military officers would have reacted to the apparent shift with skepticism and confusion.

Soviet Perceptions of the Shift

It is not clear when the Soviet military first recognized that the U.S. was considering the addition of a preplanned limited strategic nuclear option to the SIOP. Throughout the 1960s there was a lively discussion of im-provements in U.S. technical strategic nuclear war–fighting capabilities. However, discussion of U.S. limited strategic nuclear war plans did not appear in even the semiclassified Soviet military literature until after Schlesinger's first public statement in January 1974. Several public Soviet news analyses of the doctrine far preceded the semiclassified Soviet discussion of the doctrine's importance.[58] This situation is in stark contrast to that observed at the time of the U.S. adoption of the Flexible Response doctrine in the early 1960s. A semiclassified military discussion of that impending Western doctrinal shift began in the mid-1950s.

It is impossible to tell in the case at hand whether the delay in discussion indicated a lack of access to information about the Western shift, or merely a delay in discussion of the problem at a less than highly classified level. It is possible, for example, that the General Staff was unwilling to disseminate even to a semiclassified audience (the journals in question state on their covers: "Only for generals, admirals and officers of the Soviet Army and Navy") the fact that it had access to information about the impending nuclear targeting shift before Schlesinger's January 1974 press leak. It is also possible that the U.S. announcement caught them by surprise.

It is clear that the Soviet military recognized that U.S. strategic nuclear warfare C^3I capabilities were being improved in the early 1970s. For example, a military publishing house (*Voenizdat*) book sent to the typesetter in October 1973 summarized SAC work on updating computers, on "defining methods for mathematical modeling of the values of different variants of plans for combat use of SAC forces," and on preparing "data for correction of plans of combat activity and re-planning of strikes" (i.e., retargeting).[59] However, there is no direct evidence that the Soviet military ever linked these U.S. C^3I improvements with the U.S. doctrine shift. No currently available Soviet analyses appear to discuss both topics together.

The first public Soviet acknowledgment of Schlesinger's announcement of a U.S. nuclear doctrine shift was apparently contained in a TASS report issued on January 25, 1974 and reprinted in the daily newspaper of the Soviet Ministry of Defense, *Krasnaia Zvezda*, on January 26 and in *Izvestiia* on the 27th. In a small news item about proposed increases in the U.S. defense budget, a few lines were included about the doctrine shift: "J. Schlesinger spoke about a change in the nuclear strategy of the US, the goal of which, in his words, is to secure 'greater flexibility' and 'the possibility of choice' in the utilization of current systems of armament."[60] No analysis of the new doctrine was given in this news note, except to say that it appeared to be inconsistent with the goals of detente.[61] From January through March, various East European newspapers and Soviet TASS press releases and radio programs commented on the doctrinal shift, but often made no analyses, or made inaccurate analyses of the policy (for example, portraying it as a shift from a countervalue to a counterforce targeting strategy. This mistake was made by a number of U.S. analysts as well; whether or not the Schlesinger Doctrine was intended to *improve* U.S. counterforce capabilities, it certainly did not initiate U.S counter-force targeting).[62]

The first public Soviet military analysis of the Schlesinger Doctrine was apparently the one published by Soviet General Staff Col. V. V. Larionov in *Pravda* on April 7, 1974.[63] Larionov stated that a shift in American strategic nuclear targeting practices was occurring, and said that this would have both a quantitative and qualitative impact on the arms race. However, he did not mention that the goal of the Schlesinger Doctrine was the improvement of limited strategic nuclear war–fighting capabilities.[64] It is therefore impossible to tell how Larionov interpreted the full impact of the Schlesinger Doctrine. It is clear, however, that the doctrinal change was linked in his mind with U.S. capabilities for fighting limited nuclear war of one sort or another. After briefly quoting Schlesinger on the doctrine change, Larionov immediately shifted to a discussion of U.S. plans for tactical nuclear war–fighting in Europe.[65]

One piece of evidence which further clouds the picture of how Larionov, one of the major commentators on the doctrine in the open Soviet press, interpreted the Schlesinger Doctrine is his article in *Krasnaia Zvezda* in July 1974. In this article, he never mentioned the Schlesinger Doctrine by name, despite the fact that the theme of his article was the foolishness of trying to control nuclear war. Instead, he appeared to make reference to the Schlesinger Doctrine in coded form. He wrote, "It was not so long ago, in the 60s of our century, that imperialist circles professed the formula of 'controlled' limited nuclear war. The essence of this formula was the same as before: the 'legitimation' of capabilities of war, the establishment of some kind of rules for waging it, although even then it was clear with what [consequences] for humanity nuclear war was pregnant."[66] The criticism of limited nuclear war strategies which his argument implies is certainly one that Westerners had applied to the Schlesinger Doctrine. It is not clear why he did not give the Schlesinger Doctrine as an example of U.S. attempts to control limited nuclear war.

A recognition that the Pentagon was newly concerned with selective nuclear targeting of a small number of Soviet military sites was nonetheless clearly in evidence in an article published in the journal of the Soviet Academy of Sciences Institute for the Study of the USA and Canada (ISKAN), *SShA*, later in 1974. It was written by two retired military officers attached to ISKAN, Gen. M. A. Mil'shtein (who had been a senior Soviet military intelligence analyst of U.S. strategic policy[67]) and Col. L. S. Semeiko. Mil'shtein and Semeiko said:

> [I]n military theories (which find reflection in a number of military construction programs) attempts are continuing to be made to find the means for widening the spectrum of "usableness" of nuclear weapons. This spectrum, in the views

of many Pentagon theorists, can stretch from limited nuclear strikes on selected military objects to a massed, essentially unlimited volume.

While earlier on they officially allowed for limitation in nuclear weapons use, it was only in certain remote theaters of military activity. That is, the "epicenter" of nuclear war with its devastating consequences for the United States was maximally removed from its territory. Now attempts are being undertaken to "legitimize" limited strikes on objects lying on the national territories of the two nuclear powers.[68]

Semeiko later stated, in a 1975 *Krasnaia Zvezda* article, that the Western doctrinal shift was toward limited strategic nuclear targeting of a minimum number of objects, to enable quick war termination.[69] The most complete statement indicating a Soviet perception that the Schlesinger Doctrine involved limited strategic nuclear targeting was made in 1980, by Mil'shtein and Semeiko along with a civilian researcher at ISKAN. In a book on the evolution of U.S. strategy, they noted that the Schlesinger Doctrine was distinguished by its plans for "infliction of strikes in a nuclear conflict only on an insignificant number of military objects utilizing an insignificant number of nuclear means," in order to terminate war quickly.[70]

It is curious that one of the retired military officers listed as authors of this work recently denied ever having written such a thing in an article, and denied having knowledge that this passage was included in the book.[71] Several retired military officers now say that they never thought of the Schlesinger Doctrine as involving the choice of only a small number of strategic targets; they claim that it was seen as a massive counterforce option. However, it is clear that senior Soviet military officers would have had the opportunity to learn from open sources at the time of the shift that the Schlesinger Doctrine may have signalled a change in U.S. plans toward selective, very limited strategic nuclear targeting, regardless of what these officers' memories now tell them.

This is especially important to keep in mind because many Soviet officers apparently interpreted differently the intention of the Schlesinger Doctrine. Schlesinger himself testified in September 1974 that Soviet civilians and military officers had expressed to "some of our people [deleted] . . . concern and surprise" over his own announcement of the doctrinal shift; "[they said] they always assumed that we would target this way, therefore, why do we now say so, what is the purpose of all this fanfare?"[72] Schlesinger's statement has been interpreted by some in the West as an indication that the Soviets might not have believed that the Schlesinger Doctrine was a real shift in strategic targeting policy.[73] It is possible that Schlesinger's source for his remarks on this subject in September 1974 was not particularly significant or reliable. That month there was a meeting in Moscow between an invited group of prominent

U.S. Sovietologists and Soviet scholars at ISKAN and IMEMO (the Soviet group did include at least one retired colonel). Apparently, at this meeting one unidentified Soviet scholar (not given a military label in an American summary report) "called the Schlesinger option the reemergence of the counterforce doctrine, which the United States had abandoned in 1963. He could not understand why this doctrine . . . was reaffirmed in 1974." As an American report of this meeting was at first classified "confidential" by the U.S. government, it is at least possible that this was the source of Schlesinger's statements. Both the context of the statement (a discussion with American Sovietologists who would undoubtedly brief the U.S. administration upon their return, thus giving the Soviets a Western audience ripe for propagandizing), and the fact that only one Soviet scholar was reported to have made this comment, would indicate that this Soviet perception of the Schlesinger Doctrine was not particularly significant.[74] No other independent open-literature source of that time appears to confirm Schlesinger's statement.

However, in the semiclassified and specialized military journals, there did seem to be a debate throughout the mid- to late 1970s on how to interpret the Schlesinger Doctrine. Many high-ranking officers described the Schlesinger Doctrine and/or U.S. selective nuclear targeting practices as being plans for massive, preventive counterforce strikes against the Soviet Union. (Given the fact that many of the technical improvements which Schlesinger proposed could have been used to improve U.S. launch-on-warning capabilities, this perception is understandable.) The doctrine was said to favor "limited" nuclear war only in the sense that it would be "limited" to destroying Soviet military capability, and would not destroy the United States.[75]

Nonetheless, other semiclassified articles described the Schlesinger Doctrine more in the sorts of terms that Schlesinger had used. For example, Col. N. A. Chaldymov said that the Schlesinger Doctrine foresaw "a limited exchange of strategic strikes on a small [nebol'shoe] number of military objects. Their results, supposedly, will compel both sides to believe in the decisiveness of actions, and will aid for this reason the active search for a way of averting the utilization of the whole might of strategic weapons, capable of 'guaranteed annihilation.' "[76] In the next sentence Chaldymov says that such strikes by the United States would be made "with surprise and decisiveness," and later he identifies the results of such strikes disparagingly as involving "only" five or six million deaths instead of ninety-five to one hundred million.[77] It is therefore not clear how Chaldymov interpreted the concept of limitation. However, it is clear that he did not believe that the Schlesinger Doctrine was synonymous with a massive counterforce strike aimed at achieving military victory through destruction of the USSR. He clearly saw it as having the goal of communicating political warning, not of achieving military victory.

There is one piece of evidence that at least some of those in the Soviet military who originally perceived the Schlesinger Doctrine in terms of counterforce preemption may have changed their interpretations of it with time. In 1975, Major General in the Reserves P. Sergeev and Colonel in the Reserves V. Trusenkov were among those who said that the Schlesinger Doctrine was primarily about surprise, massive counterforce strikes.[78] But by the end of 1977, those same two authors writing in the same military journal, *Zarubezhnoe Voennoe Obozrenie*, said that the U.S. concept of target selection, adopted in 1974, "foresees various versions of the use of nuclear weapons, from limited strikes on selected targets to a surprise massed strike carried out simultaneously on military objects and industrial centers of the Soviet Union."[79] While they did not specify how they interpreted the concept of limited strikes, this statement would seem to imply that they perceived a wider range of targeting possibilities than simply a choice between all-out counterforce and all-out massive retaliation.

Despite this one indication of change in perceptions over time, it is not clear that a consensus was ever reached in the General Staff community about how to interpret the significance of the Schlesinger Doctrine. Without such a consensus, no concerted effort at making a response to the doctrine could be expected to emerge. For innovation in doctrine to occur, policy entrepreneurs must gain organizational support for their innovative ideas. If there was no agreement in the General Staff that a significant change in the environment had occurred, then there is no reason to expect agreement on the need for reaction. Its very ambiguity probably made the Schlesinger Doctrine a nonstarter for Soviet innovators.

One technical issue needs to be mentioned before the Soviet reaction is discussed. Would it have been possible for Soviet radar to distinguish between a massive strategic attack and a truly limited one? Soviet antiballistic missile (ABM) capabilities at that time are now generally thought to have been weak. However, U.S. government estimates from 1985 indicate that as early as the mid-1960s, Soviet early-warning "Hen House" line-of-sight radar installations provided sufficient intelligence to allow the determination of the relative size of a U.S. strategic nuclear attack, at least in terms of whether it involved a handful versus hundreds of weapons.[80] Further supporting evidence is provided in a 1971 article in the Soviet military's journal on technical developments; the article claims that "contemporary classification of radar targets" for the air-defense forces of the country (which have responsibility for ABM defense as well as antiair defense) is divided into three major groups: point (individual), grouped (as in a formation of airplanes or a cluster of ballistic rockets and warheads) and spread (as in snow or ionospheric gases).[81] It is therefore likely that by the time the Schlesinger Doctrine was adopted, the Soviet military would have had the technical ability to distinguish a truly limited and controlled demonstration strike from an all-out counterforce strike or an Assured Destruction strike, even if the tracking radars and data-processing abilities were not adequate for a real defense mission.[82]

The Soviet Reaction

The Interests of the General Staff

The question of how the Soviet military should, logically, think about the possibility of limited strategic nuclear war is one that continues to divide Western scholars. The majority of Western scholars who have studied Soviet analyses of limited strategic nuclear options have concluded that the Soviet military would have had no reason to be interested in the possibility of limited strategic nuclear war. These analysts believe that from the 1960s onward, the Soviet General Staff held to the doctrinal position that any nuclear strike on Soviet territory would be answered by decisive, massive nuclear strikes on the United States. In particular, many note, Soviet targeting doctrine seems to have emphasized the importance of hitting nuclear command and control centers, thus negating the possibility of maintaining technical control over the magnitude of a nuclear conflict.[83] These analysts hold that while the Soviet military would have preferred to avoid any use of strategic nuclear weapons, recognizing their extreme destructiveness, Soviet officers believed that any attempt to place limits on strategic nuclear weapons use once nuclear conflict had involved Soviet soil would be futile.

These scholars have often made the argument that Soviet views have been conditioned by Soviet "strategic culture." According to this perspective, the historical experiences and philosophical leanings of militaries in various states are thought to be significantly different from each other, and to be determining explanations for the behavior of military officers. The concept of strategic culture has been used both to contrast American and Soviet approaches to general questions of military strategy[84] and to shed light specifically on the Soviet approach to the issue of limited nuclear war.[85] As Jack Snyder puts it, "Individuals are socialized into a distinctively Soviet mode of strategic thinking. As a result of this socialization process, a set of general beliefs, attitudes and behavior patterns with regard to nuclear strategy has achieved a state of semipermanence that places them on the level of "culture" rather than mere "policy." Of course, attitudes may change as a result of changes in technology and the international environment. However, new problems are not assessed objectively. Rather, they are seen through the perceptual lens provided by the strategic culture."[86]

The argument usually made in regard to Soviet views on limited strategic nuclear options is that because the Soviet military learned from experience (especially from World War II) that decisive offensive action is needed to win wars and prevent defeat, Soviet military officers believed that it was dangerous and foolhardy not to completely destroy the aggressor's means of waging war after the aggressor attacked Soviet territory. By responding to a limited strategic strike in a controlled and limited way, or by responding with a political offer to work out a cessation of hostilities, the Soviet Union would be leaving an aggressor with the means of continuing to launch nuclear strikes at his leisure. According to this line of argument, the Soviet military had a cultural preference for decisive, counterforce retaliation against any strategic strike on its own territory, no matter how limited or controlled the aggressor's strike may have been.

It is actually not necessary to make a strategic culture argument to find support for the idea that the Soviet military would want to focus its strategic planning on decisive offensive strategies. The political science literature on military organizations and the offense all indicates that military officers prefer to maintain control over the battlefield in the face of uncertainty, and to be proactive rather than reactive in war. This, too, would be a logical argument for a lack of Soviet military interest in limited strategic nuclear options. In fact, as was noted above, the U.S. Strategic Air Command seems to have resisted at first civilian calls for changes in the SIOP to allow controlled and limited nuclear targeting. Militaries have no business concerning themselves with political uses of military force; their business is to accomplish military objectives, which the limited use of strategic nuclear weapons cannot do alone.

However, it must be remembered that the contexts of the U.S. adoption of the Schlesinger Doctrine and the Soviet reaction to it were very different. The U.S. innovation was adopted in order to give the President political warning capabilities through the use of nuclear weapons; it does not seem to have been adopted in response to a new military threat. Military officers have no reason to support the use of military weapons for purely political purposes. On the other hand, by not matching the U.S. adoption once it was made, the Soviet military would have been allowing the U.S. to achieve a new type of superiority in military flexibility.

While few scholars have dissented from the view that the Soviet military would not be interested in limitation of strategic nuclear war, at least two respected analysts of Soviet military affairs have stated that Soviet strategic nuclear flexibility was possible. Raymond Garthoff bases his assessment of this problem on the desire for flexibility by the political leadership. He believes that limited U.S. nuclear strikes on Soviet territory might have provoked a limited Soviet response strike on U.S. territory, or might instead have led to a Soviet "offer to seek rapid war termination, above all in further nuclear attack employment."[87] Garthoff concludes that in the Soviet Union, "Conflict termination is . . . approached in terms of waging wars [if at all] in ways that minimize uncontrolled escalation and preserve options of termination," including limitations on nuclear usage at the strategic level.[88]

If this is a correct interpretation of the motives of political leaders, it leads to one possible incentive for the General Staff to implement a limited strategic nuclear employment planning option. According to arguments both about military organizations in general, and about Soviet military preferences in particular, passivity is the bête noire of military planners. Officers facing war want to take action; absorbing a nuclear strike on the homeland without reacting would be virtually intolerable. While logically officers might want to respond by punishing the aggressor to the full extent possible, the Soviet political leadership might not allow this to occur if it values the maintenance of options for the political settlement of war. Soviet and Western sources concur that it is the political leaders of the USSR that ultimately have responsibility for the decision of whether or not to use nuclear weapons.[89] If the only choice given to political leaders is between an all-out counterforce decisive strike (carrying the risk of countervalue retaliation from U.S. submarine forces) or nonaction, those leaders might very well choose not to act. In this case, it would be in the interests of military officers to be able to present the political leadership with another choice, such as a limited strategic nuclear option.

Thus, there may be a crucial difference in how military autonomy, a key interest of military organizations, would be affected by U.S. and Soviet decision-making on this limited strategic employment question. U.S. military autonomy might have been impaired if the political leadership decided to use nuclear weapons for political signalling purposes, rather than allowing the Joint Chiefs of Staff to retain those weapons for military destruction purposes. Soviet military autonomy, in contrast, might have been impaired if the political leadership tied the hands of the General Staff out of fear that massive counterforce retaliation against a limited strategic strike would lead to armageddon. (While it is theoretically possible that the Soviet political leadership would have wanted flexible nuclear options for the same political signalling reasons that the U.S. President wanted them, there is in fact no evidence that Brezhnev or any other political actor expressed such a desire.)

Notra Trulock III gives a different argument for why the Soviet General Staff would have preferred to have the capability of controlling strategic nuclear targeting. He argues that the General Staff had an incentive to maintain limits on nuclear use in order to prevent the disruption of command and control systems.[90] He states, "[I]t seems likely that initial Soviet use would be limited in both scope and scale."[91]

This, too, can be explained in terms of theories about the preferences of military organizations. If military officers want to keep control over the uncertainty of the battlefield, then they would not want to unleash a nuclear holocaust. Even if every single remaining accurate U.S. counter-force missile were destroyed by a massive Soviet counterforce retaliation (which is in itself highly unlikely), the remaining U.S. capability to wreak havoc on Soviet society and to disrupt military communication links through electromagnetic pulses emanating from relatively inaccurate sub-marine- or air-based weapons would undoubtedly weigh heavily on the minds of military planners.

It is not clear that those planners would necessarily want to adopt a matching doctrine to the U.S. shift. It is difficult to conceive of any real military use for a very limited nuclear launch. Nonetheless, the situation might lead Soviet military planners to forego their insistence on massive retaliation against any nuclear use on Soviet soil. In this sense, reaction to the Schlesinger Doctrine might entail a doctrinal shift away from immedi-ate counterforce retaliation plans, even if a matching limited employment doctrine did not result. The Soviet military might have chosen to absorb a very limited nuclear strike.

There is one logical reason why some type of a matching effort might be expected, however. When one side in a military competition has a new military force use capability that the other side lacks, such a situation is likely to provoke reactive doctrinal innovation. As was detailed above, the Schlesinger Doctrine was accompanied by improvements in U.S. com-puter technology for strategic C^3I. Whether or not the Soviet military ever intended to launch a limited strategic strike itself, it may have wanted to match that technological development. In this sense, an argument that the Schlesinger Doctrine needed to be matched might provide an excuse for the Soviet military to acquire this technology, and thereby maintain its place in the technological competition between East and West.

Various expert Western analysts have provided different justifications for why the General Staff either would or would not have wanted to match the Schlesinger Doctrine, or at least make changes in its own doc-trine in reaction to the U.S. announcement of a targeting change. There is no a priori reason to prefer one set of these arguments to another; justifi-cation for all of them can be found in the political science literature on the preferences of military organizations. This plethora of possible General Staff interests in one direction or another leaves us with no clear predic-tions about what the Soviet military should do. It does give us an idea, however, of how difficult it might be for General Staff entrepreneurs to create a pro-innovation consensus. The cloudiness of both the effects of the U.S. shift and the interests of the Soviet military if the U.S. shift were real leaves us with no reason to expect innovation to occur in this case. However, given the mix of military interests posited here, it would also be surprising if no debate took place on the question.

The Soviet Debate

In private conversations with the author, one Soviet general and four retired Soviet General Staff generals confirmed that there was a debate in the Soviet General Staff over whether or not nuclear war could be limited.[92] Two separate issues were involved here: the issue of limited *tactical* nuclear war, which could be conducted on the European battlefield but not touch the Soviet or American homelands; and the issue of limited *strategic* nuclear war, involving small numbers of intercontinental or intermediate-range strikes on the homelands of the superpowers.

Some of these Soviet generals have indicated that there was (and through at least 1990, continued to be) an ongoing debate among members of the Soviet General Staff about whether or not limited strategic nuclear war was possible. They claim that while the debate existed, it was not very important by the late 1980s; the issue had been decided. Nuclear strikes on the homelands of the U.S. and the USSR would not remain limited. A retired general who held top advisory positions in the Soviet General Staff during the 1970s and 1980s claims that a majority of officers never believed that the United States would actually attempt a Schlesinger Doctrine–type of limited strategic nuclear strike. Instead, he says, the Soviet military thought that the threat of the U.S. unleashing a limited tactical nuclear war in the European theater was much more real. Therefore, the debate over limited tactical nuclear war was much more important.[93] His statement that the General Staff never believed that a strategic limited nuclear strike would be tried by the United States was repeated, independently, by another retired General Staff general who worked on strategic air defense issues.[94]

As was noted above, the Soviet General Staff had already decided that *tactical* limited nuclear war in the European theater was possible by the late 1960s, as long as it did not touch Soviet territory. But in the mid- to late 1960s, Soviet military writings which dealt with future nuclear world war (i.e., war beyond limited nuclear war in the non-Soviet European theater) tended to repeat a series of four basic themes: that such war would involve tens of millions of deaths and massive property destruction;[95] that such war would be fought without mercy for the aggressors and without compromise;[96] that such war should involve the maximal destruction of the enemy's military potential in order to ensure his defeat;[97] and that decisiveness of action and of goals was one of the most important components of military activity in such a war.[98] Each of these attributes of potential future nuclear war had been identified as characteristics of the Soviet offensive in World War II, at a 1965 conference of Soviet military historians in Moscow.[99] Thus there does seem to be some validity to the argument that the strategic culture of the Soviet military determined its views on strategic nuclear weapons use.

It is clear that these views in the press were reflected in official doctrine of the time as well. A former student officer from Afghanistan smuggled to the West lecture materials from the Voroshilov General Staff Academy in Moscow, dating from his work at the academy between 1973 and 1975. According to Raymond Garthoff, these lectures, which were highly classified, undoubtedly represented accepted official Soviet military doctrine.[100] In these lectures, early, maximal, and decisive use of strategic nuclear forces in order to achieve military victory over the enemy in a strategic nuclear war is stressed, along with the importance of disruption of enemy nuclear control centers.[101] There are in fact indications in the lecture materials that the Soviet military would have interpreted an initial limited American strategic strike as merely a precursor for follow-up massive nuclear strikes.[102]

Yet suddenly, between 1974 and 1979, Soviet mention of the notion that limited nuclear attack on the USSR would be met by unlimited retaliatory strikes seemed to disappear. General Secretary Leonid Brezhnev did state, in a speech celebrating the thirtieth anniversary of victory in World War II in 1975, that "The unleashing of nuclear rocket war would turn inevitably to the destruction of the aggressor himself, not to mention the enormous losses for many other countries and peoples not even drawn formally into the war."[103] However, this is a far cry from his earlier speech at the 24th Communist Party Congress of 1971, where Brezhnev stated, "Any potential aggressor well knows that in the event of an attempt at nuclear rocket attack on our country, he will receive an annihilating retaliatory strike."[104] In the 1971 speech, he promised direct Soviet massive retaliation in the event that the U.S. used nuclear weapons on Soviet territory. In the 1975 speech, he gave a more philosophical statement about the general consequences of world nuclear war, and did not mention retaliation per se.

During the mid- to late 1970s, military writings on future nuclear world war echoed Brezhnev's circumspection. Articles on the subject would often dwell on the class essence of world nuclear war or on the decisiveness of the *political* goals to be achieved in such a war, while almost pointedly ignoring questions about weapons usage and the military-technical aspects of such a war. This was a departure from similar articles which appeared in the 1960s and early 1970s.[105]

Even in the semiclassified military literature of this time, the subject of Soviet retaliation after a U.S. strike on the Soviet homeland was discussed only in muted terms. Very few articles on nuclear war after 1973 and before 1979 state directly that such retaliation is inevitable; two which do say this quote Brezhnev's 1971 24th Party Congress statement as their authority on this doctrinal position.[106] No articles sent to the typesetter after 1974 (the 1975 article, published in January, was sent to the typesetter in late 1974) mention retaliation.

One retired Soviet general who wrote on strategic nuclear issues at the time recently said that he believes this circumspection was due to the progress of détente between the Soviet Union and the United States; as the SALT II negotiations progressed, the USSR did not want to jeopardize relations by seeming to threaten the U.S.[107] However, when the absence of such statements is put in the context of the broader discussion in the literature at this time on the question of limitation in strategic nuclear war, this retired general's interpretation becomes suspect.

Many statements made in open sources by Soviet military officers on the Schlesinger Doctrine in the mid- to late 1970s seemed to indicate that innovation in Soviet military doctrine was being considered. These officers did not argue that limited strategic nuclear war was impossible; they instead pointed out (and most American analysts, including those who are proponents of planning for limited strategic war, would probably agree) that the maintenance of control over strategic nuclear operations would be difficult and unlikely to succeed amid the fog of war. There is a significant difference between saying that controlled strategic nuclear war is impossible, and that it is improbable; this difference has been ignored by Western analysts of Soviet doctrinal development. If cultural variables predetermined an unfavorable Soviet reaction to the Schlesinger Doctrine, there would be no explanation for the changed character of the discussion on the course of strategic nuclear war.

This is especially true since it would have been to the Soviet advantage in terms of a deterrent posture to maintain that limited strategic nuclear war was impossible. If unity were maintained on that position, it could convince American leaders that any attempt to launch a controlled nuclear strike was dangerous folly. In other words, it was not to the Soviet advantage to reveal any cracks in the edifice of disbelief in the possibility of limiting strategic strikes.

The discussion of the Schlesinger Doctrine within the Soviet military was characterized by some of the same reticence as was used in talking about strategic nuclear issues in general at this time. One particular article which stands out for its lack of a definitive analysis of the Schlesinger Doctrine is the 1977 entry on "Military Doctrine" (not to be confused with the later entry on "Military Strategy" written by Ogarkov) in the *Soviet Military Encyclopedia*. While it mentions that the United States adopted in 1973 [*sic*] a doctrine of selective nuclear targeting, and says that the goal of such a doctrine was to prevent a retaliatory nuclear strike from the Soviet Union, it does not judge the feasibility of controlled strategic nuclear war. It also says nothing substantive about the content of

Soviet nuclear doctrine, merely claiming that such doctrine is governed by a system of laws.[108]

A variety of articles illustrate the semantic games played by those who criticized the U.S. shift without saying what Brezhnev had said earlier: that any strategic nuclear weapons use would be met by a full retaliatory blow. Mil'shtein and Semeiko, the Soviet officers attached to ISKAN, wrote in a 1974 article about strategic nuclear war: "Even if it began with the infliction of strikes on several selected military objects, such a conflict . . . would *most probably* [skoree vsego] quickly grow into a general war. . . ."[109] They added that it was difficult to imagine (but thus, not impossible) that significant collateral damage to civilians could be avoided. Semeiko wrote in a solo article in *Krasnaia Zvezda* the next year: "Having begun with a limited exchange of strikes, nuclear war *can* reach an unlimited scale significantly more quickly than a war with use of conventional means."[110] The 1980 book by Bogdanov, Mil'shtein, and Semeiko, mentioned above, similarly places the consequences of limited strategic nuclear weapons use in the conditional: "[The Schlesinger Doctrine was adopted] in spite of the growing recognition of the fact that attempts by the U.S. to utilize all or even part of its nuclear potential *can* have suicidal consequences."[111]

Maj. Gen. R. Simonian, a doctor of military science and a professor at the prestigious Frunze Military Academy, wrote in 1976 that "To every healthy-minded person it is clear, that any war unleashed by the aggressor, in the course of which strategic nuclear weapons are used, even in limited quantity and on 'selected targets,' conceals in itself a real *threat* of widening and turning into a strategic (general) nuclear war with all its fatal consequences."[112] Simonian repeated this conditional phrase in a late 1978 article he wrote in the IMEMO journal, and in a 1979 article in the semiclassified General Staff journal, *Voennaia Mysl'*.[113]

Simonian's position on this issue is made somewhat unclear by the fact that he was one of the Soviet General Staff officers who interpreted the Schlesinger Doctrine in terms of massive counterforce strikes. It seems as though he may be straddling a fence in the strategic limited nuclear war debate, by claiming that on the one hand the Schlesinger Doctrine is nothing new, and on the other that limited strategic nuclear war may not escalate to general strategic nuclear war.

This puzzle may be clarified by Simonian's 1976 article in the Soviet journal which analyzes foreign military developments. Simonian's words are set in the context of his discussion of U.S. limited nuclear war plans. He states, "It is believed that such a [limited nuclear war] should not leave the bounds of a single theater of war, for example the European, and the exchange of nuclear strikes should not touch U.S. territory. In inflicting nuclear strikes, a small part of strategic nuclear forces can be utilized."[114]

It is not clear what Simonian meant by the "European" theater of war. It is possible that he interpreted the Schlesinger Doctrine as planning strategic strikes on what the Soviets may have thought of as expendable territory: Eastern Europe, but not the Soviet Union. When added to Simonian's earlier repeated statements that nuclear exchanges carried the "threat" of escalation to all-out war, it would seem that he may have believed that a very limited strategic nuclear exchange not touching the U.S. and Soviet homelands was a possibility. Put in the context of Schlesinger's concerns about a Warsaw Pact overrun of Western Europe (and given the evidence recently uncovered by Terriff, noted above), it might have made sense for Simonian to believe that not all Schlesinger Doctrine targets were on Soviet territory. U.S. intercontinental or intermediate-range weapons targeted for political warning purposes could be launched on non-Soviet Eastern Europe. Simonian may have been trying to fit the Schlesinger Doctrine into the established framework of the Soviet doctrinal mindset. If this interpretation held, then no innovation in Soviet military doctrine would have been necessary, since no new threats presented themselves from the U.S. side.

There clearly was a discussion in the Soviet military over what the Schlesinger Doctrine meant. There may have been a very limited discussion about whether the Soviet approach to nuclear war should be changed as a result. It is unusual that most of the analyses of what the Schlesinger Doctrine meant were done either by retired officers at the academic institutes, or by serving officers (such as Larionov) who were attached to the institutes (Larionov was a consultant to ISKAN before his retirement; he became an ISKAN employee). While these analyses often appeared in the military press, and while Larionov provided a link to the General Staff, it seems that "regular" General Staff officers did not usually express themselves on this issue.

It may be telling that at least two of the individuals identified here as associates of ISKAN—Larionov and Mil'shtein—made explicit arguments in their public pieces linking the U.S. doctrinal shift to an unfortunate continuation of the arms race. Larionov praised the serious pursuit of détente and arms control, and condemned the efforts of "reactionary circles" (and, significantly, he did not modify this term with the adjectives "American" or "imperialist") to continually improve the quality of nuclear rocket weapons. He then juxtaposed against the new American doctrine the existence of international opposition to the use of nuclear weapons, and he emphasized the necessity of "reduction of the most dangerous means for unleashing and waging" nuclear war.[115] While it was commonplace for Soviet officers to call the Schlesinger Doctrine an infringement of détente, Larionov's article stands out for its strong support of qualitative arms control. Mil'shtein wrote an article in a second academic institute journal, *Mirovaia Ekonomika i Mezhdunarodnye Otnosheniia* (*MEiMO*), which made a very sophisticated argument about how Schlesinger Doctrine–type concepts can hurt détente and fuel the arms race. He said, "It is necessary to renounce once and for all efforts to use nuclear weapons as 'flexible' and 'acceptable' foreign policy means. In contemporary conditions it is senseless to try to achieve strategic superiority, for such attempts in the end will not bring any kind of political dividends, but will lead only to an additional waste of means on the arms race."[116] He repeated these thoughts in an article in *SShA* two years later.[117] Essentially he argued that any attempt by one side to get an advantage over the other through a new strategic concept is useless, because it will be matched.

In both Larionov's and Mil'shtein's writings, it is qualitative improvements in missile accuracy, not improvements in C³I, that are singled out for criticism as contributors to the arms race. Such missile improvements were not at the heart of the Schlesinger Doctrine; C³I improvements were. In fact it would be illogical for Soviet military officers to conclude that the Schlesinger Doctrine was responsible for some new direction in U.S. planning for accurate, MIRVed missiles usable in a first strike. Mutual superpower fears of the other side's development of a first-strike capability had flared up already in 1969, when the Soviets first tested MRVs (multiple re-entry vehicles for missiles, which sprayed several warheads out of one missile) and when the United States intensified its own research on MIRVs (which gave each warhead independent navigation toward separate targets once the warheads left the missile "bus"). In 1969, members of the U.S. Congress publicized their realization that Secretary of Defense Melvin Laird had shifted his arguments for why MIRVs should be developed; while earlier he had said they would be used on inaccurate missiles in order to improve American abilities to avoid Soviet antiballistic missile (ABM) defenses during an Assured Destruction strike, he switched to arguing that accurate MIRVed missiles were needed for use against Soviet hardened targets.[118] The first U.S. MIRVed missiles, the Minuteman III, were deployed in 1970; and the Soviets had already deployed their first MIRVed missile by 1974. By the mid-1970s the Soviets had deployed a variety of highly accurate, large throw-weight, MIRVed missiles.[119] Given the lead-times involved in Soviet missile deployments, these missiles must have been in development by the late 1960s. In fact, many Western observers believe that the Soviet push toward accurate counterforce missiles began in the mid-1960s with the entrance into service of the SS-9, and that early models of this missile were only stopgaps on the way to this goal.[120] Further evidence for continuity in Soviet perceptions about the U.S. development of a first-strike potential is provided by the record of Soviet work on missile silo hardening. Technical improvements in silo protection were implemented under a silo conversion program that began in 1970.[121] From the Soviet perspective, the Schlesinger Doctrine's *innovative* contribution to the military competition between the two sides could not primarily have concerned missile accuracy or MIRVing improvements.

Therefore, it is likely that Larionov and Mil'shtein were arguing not about the effects of the specific provisions of the new U.S. policy, but rather against a battle of strategic concepts that would justify further expenditure of resources on potentially destabilizing qualitative missile improvements.

In more recent years, both Larionov and Mil'shtein spoke out in favor of radical doctrine reform under Gorbachev.[122] It is possible that by bringing the U.S. shift to the attention of the attentive Soviet public and linking it to an unwanted increase in the level of military competition between the two sides, these officers were making an early attempt at opposition to those in the Soviet military who preferred weapons buildups. Presumably, those in the Soviet military who stated that the Schlesinger Doctrine was evidence of U.S. massive first-strike intentions could use such an analysis for certain ends: to argue for the further development of both accurate Soviet missiles to match the U.S. developments, and improved early-warning systems to secure the Soviet state against the U.S. threat. By arguing that arms control was a good outcome and that any attempts to achieve strategic superiority would fail, Larionov and Mil'shtein could have been making an argument for a different, negotiated solution to the U.S. nuclear threat.

Soviet Civil-Military Relations and Doctrine

In the mid- to late 1970s the threat level emanating from the political leadership to military autonomy on doctrinal issues was very low. It is therefore not surprising that discussion of the Schlesinger Doctrine began in the Soviet military immediately in 1974. Unlike the situation during the initial period of the Soviet reaction to Flexible Response, there is no evidence of strong political-military friction in the Soviet Union from the late 1960s through the late 1970s. Most Western analysts consider Brezhnev's relationship with the military to have been very cordial during this time period.[123] While one American analyst has posited that the Soviet military was greatly distressed by the Soviet signing of the SALT I accords in 1972,[124] this does not seem very likely. The Soviet military does seem to have been initially unhappy about the Soviet political leadership's decision to enter arms control negotiations in the mid- to late 1960s.[125] The military may also have been upset by the fact that the negotiations forced them to reveal information about the Soviet force posture that they would have otherwise preferred to keep secret.[126] However, those Americans who participated in the SALT negotiations and later analyzed Soviet behavior at them and after them seem to agree that the Soviet military acquiesced in the agreements without argument.[127] While the agreements did affect the Soviet military's doctrinal freedom by limiting the development of ABM systems (which may in fact have been agreeable to the General Staff, since both U.S. ABM and MIRV technology seemed to be improving frighteningly fast at that time), they did not limit qualitative improvement of strategic missile systems, and thus did not greatly restrict either the military's resources or doctrinal autonomy. The Soviet military would have had no logical reason to resent the Brezhnev leadership at this point, especially since Soviet military budgets and societal prestige were at very high levels.

A sore point in Soviet civil-military relations may have appeared in the mid-1970s because in 1977, for the first time in the Brezhnev era, there appears to have been a slowing of the yearly increase in the defense budget.[128] Articles in the Soviet press written by officers at this time seem to indicate some displeasure over the possibility of defense spending cuts.[129] Particularly noteworthy is an article on the need to maintain sufficiently strong strategic nuclear forces, written by Chief of the General Staff Viktor Kulikov in 1976.[130] Within a few months of writing the article, Kulikov was replaced as Chief of the General Staff by Nikolai Ogarkov, and sent instead to the less politically powerful post of Commander-in-Chief of the Warsaw Pact forces. Some Western analysts have postulated that this personnel change occurred because of the political leaders' desire to control military displeasure over the defense budget trimming.[131]

Because the defense budget increase cuts fell particularly on the Strategic Rocket Forces, some Western analysts have linked the cuts to doctrinal pronouncements made by General Secretary Leonid Brezhnev and the Soviet High Command officers in the early 1980s about no first use of nuclear weapons and about the impossibility of victory in a nuclear war.[132] Jeremy Azrael in particular has argued that Brezhnev made "ex cathedra" pronouncements on doctrine beginning with his famous speech in Tula in 1977, and that these alienated military officers as much as Khrushchev's had in the early 1960s.[133]

However, the Tula speech is only recognizable in hindsight as the beginning of Brezhnev's penchant for making nuclear doctrine pronouncements, which really began to be observed in the Soviet Union in the early 1980s. In the 1977 speech, Brezhnev merely stated that the Soviet Union was interested in defense sufficiency, not nuclear missile superiority, and offered his support for a mutual superpower declaration of no first use of nuclear weapons.[134] He did not make any doctrinal pronouncements on nuclear war, but instead seems to be justifying decreased defense expenditures. This interpretation of Brezhnev's speech is confirmed by a Soviet military source of the time, which explicitly links the Tula speech to arms control for economic reasons, and does not mention the possibility of doctrinal change.[135]

Beginning in 1981, Brezhnev did make several statements about the "madness" of starting a nuclear war and about the impossibility of victory in such a war.[136] Brezhnev's statements contradicted Soviet Chief of the General Staff Nikolai Ogarkov's rather optimistic view about the end result of nuclear war–fighting, presented in his 1979 article in the *Soviet Military Encyclopedia* on "Military Strategy." Ogarkov had implied that general nuclear warfare was winnable.[137] As we will see below, Brezhnev's 1981 statements appeared to influence the Soviet military's later declaratory doctrine.

David Holloway, and Thomas Bjorkman and Thomas Zamostny note that some civilian journalists and academics who were close to Brezhnev, notably Aleksandr Bovin and Georgii Arbatov, made a concerted effort, beginning in 1973, to argue that victory in nuclear war was impossible. These Soviet liberals concluded that Clausewitz's famous dictum that "War is the continuation of politics by other means" no longer applied in the nuclear era, since no policy could be furthered by nuclear war.[138] These civilian scholars were repeating an argument that had been made by a dissident retired military officer, N. Talenskii, in the early and mid-1960s.[139] Many powerful military officers argued against these civilian analysts in 1973 and 1974, as they had argued against Talenskii earlier.

In spite of this debate between military officers and civilians at the institutes over Clausewitz's dictum, in the late 1970s the military seemed to accept Brezhnev's Tula line about the need for balance in strategic weapons systems.[140] Bjorkman and Zamostny interpret this acceptance, along with the earlier and later military/civilian debates about the winnability of nuclear war, as evidence of see-sawing in military officers' attitudes on a particular issue; they believe that the prospect of agreement on SALT II led the military to abide by the "no win" dictum, and that the dashing of SALT II by the U.S. in 1979 led to a reemergence of hardline military views. A more logical explanation is that it was the issues, and not the military opinions, which differed. Two separate issues were involved. Belief in the desirability of nuclear arms control and of the maintenance of a strategic balance does not necessarily lead one to believe that a nuclear war would be suicide. Scholars and liberals in the Soviet Union may have been arguing for linkage of the two issues, but there is no evidence that they had a great deal of influence in defense issue debates in the early 1970s.[141] Therefore, there is no evidence that military officers had to deal with a real civilian political threat on this issue in the 1970s.

It may be significant that Brezhnev's statements on nuclear war as suicide *followed* by two years the 1979 establishment of a Scientific Research Council on Problems of Peace and Disarmament in Moscow; this
group was designed to coordinate the efforts of civilian scholars on arms
control issues,[142] and probably also to act as a lobbying organization for
the scholarly liberal viewpoint on nuclear peace issues (this would fit arguments made now by academics about the growth of their influence on
these issues in the early 1980s). In other words, civilian scholars were
given increased access to the political agenda in the early 1980s, at the
time of the Brezhnev/Ogarkov split on the consequences of nuclear war.
Before that, the civilian scholars lacked a power base. The apparent doctrinal conflict between the political leadership and Ogarkov seemed to
break out in the early 1980s, rather than at the time of the budget con-
straint. It does not seem to be a case of civil-military doctrinal conflict
resulting from a change in economic priorities. It should not have affected
the Soviet General Staff's discussion of the Schlesinger Doctrine.

In fact, there is no evidence that civilian scholars tried to influence the
Soviet military debate about how to respond to the Schlesinger Doctrine.
The policy community on doctrinal issues in the 1970s did not seem to
have expanded to include experts not in the military. However, the fact
that retired Soviet military officers at the institutes were the major participants in the Schlesinger Doctrine discussion may indicate the beginnings
of the defense policy community shift under Gorbachev that is detailed in
the next chapter.

A few times, civilian analysts mentioned the Schlesinger Doctrine in
passing as evidence of the U.S. Defense Department's hypocrisy on
détente and arms control issues.[143] One civilian analyst seems to have
inaccurately reported both the intention of the Schlesinger Doctrine shift,
and the Soviet reaction to that shift. Genrikh Trofimenko argued in a
1974 article that the Schlesinger Doctrine shift could not possibly have
been real, since the Pentagon would never reveal its true strategic targeting plans. He therefore interpreted the announcement of the doctrine
change as nothing more than political propaganda, designed to frighten
the Soviet Union.[144] There is no apparent evidence that Soviet military
officers shared his interpretation; while many of them cited the Schlesinger Doctrine as merely an evolutionary step in the development of U.S.
flexible counterforce strategic planning, all of the officers who mentioned
the new doctrine seemed to believe that some sort of real policy move had
been made. Trofimenko did not stop there. In a 1976 book, he claimed,
"[P]entagon theorists cannot but take account of the fact that if it were to
come to 'a trial of main forces,' then the Soviet Union would not act in
accord with American 'rules,' which are called upon to maximize the
marginal advantages of the U.S., but in accordance with its own military

doctrine, 'with the goal of full defeat of any aggressor, who tries to en-
croach on the socialist homeland.'"[145] Trofimenko incorrectly cites Soviet
Defense Minister Grechko on this point.[146] Since there is no reason to
believe that Trofimenko was influential in military policy circles in the
Soviet Union, there is also no reason to believe that his assessment of
Soviet military doctrine at that time was correct. His statements were not
repeated in even the semiclassified Soviet military press.

Overall, there is no evidence that in the mid- to late 1970s Soviet civilian academics played any significant role in the Soviet military's consideration of the problems of strategic nuclear doctrine and targeting.

Nonetheless, by the early 1980s a striking congruence appeared between statements by General Staff officers and statements by civilians,
including Brezhnev, on the character of future nuclear war.

Soviet Nuclear Doctrine in the 1980s: Innovation?

Soviet military statements about nuclear war in the early 1980s, when
détente had reached a low point, did not return to their predétente feroc-
ity. The Soviet general who claimed that the circumspection of General
Staff statements about nuclear war in the 1970s was due to the progress
of détente could not have gotten the whole story right.

It is true that in the early 1980s, public statements by the General Staff
began once again to declare that it was not possible to limit nuclear war.
This was a departure from the mid-1970s statements which called nuclear
war limitation improbable, not impossible. The new "no limitation" line
remained constant through the 1980s, probably indicating that some sort
of doctrinal decision had been made. It is not clear, however, whether it
was an operational decision made by the General Staff, or a declaratory
decision made by the General Secretary. Two alternate explanations are
possible.

First, Soviet military sources in the mid-1970s had always been ambiguous in their analyses of how nuclear war would end. While some implied
that an exchange of limited strikes might be possible, none ever directly
stated that such an exchange could end a war. It is thus possible that the
General Staff by the early 1980s reached an operational decision not to
consider the possibility that strategic strikes could remain limited for
long. The decision could have come from the General Staff, and been a
reflection of officers' war planning preferences.

However, it is also possible that the unity of statements reflected the
growing influence of civilians on Soviet declaratory doctrine in the early
1980s. If civilians at the institutes had long believed that nuclear war was
suicide, and now were given access to the top political agenda, then the
"political" half of Soviet military doctrine could now belong to them.

This view is particularly plausible since the first official statements about the impossibility of winning nuclear war came from Soviet General Secretary Leonid Brezhnev in 1981; military statements about the impossibility of limiting nuclear war seemed to begin appearing again in about 1983. Brezhnev's statements appeared to be directed against Chief of the General Staff Nikolai Ogarkov, who argued that massive counterforce strikes could achieve nuclear victory. Limitation of controlled nuclear strikes and victory through a controlled massive nuclear strike are obviously related issues.

Regardless of the source of this new doctrinal unity, the Soviet military as a whole nonetheless did not return to the type of statements made in the early 1970s. The majority of officers never again argued that any strike on Soviet territory should receive immediate massive retaliation. Instead, they tended to state that nuclear war would not remain within any preset bounds.[147] This could imply that a temporary exchange of limited strikes was possible.

In a major statement (in a civilian Academy of Sciences journal, which may be telling) on Soviet nuclear doctrine in 1983, Chief of the General Staff Marshal Sergei F. Akhromeev, Ogarkov's replacement, said that limited nuclear war was impossible: "If nuclear war is touched off, it inevitably will become general, with all the resulting consequences. . . . The theory of 'limited' nuclear war arises from an erroneous understanding of the essence of the matter, and from an attempt to make the idea of nuclear war acceptable to societal opinion, to suggest to people that nuclear conflict could be waged by 'rules' worked out in advance."[148] However, his only statement about the consequences of an American strike on Soviet territory referred specifically to the impossibility of a disarming U.S. first strike. He did not say, as other officers had in the early 1970s, that immediate massive retaliation was inevitable following a limited strike.

In 1979, a few Soviet military writings did harken back to the old view of strategic nuclear warfare, emphasizing early and maximal Soviet retaliation for any nuclear strike. Prominent among these was the article in the *Soviet Military Encyclopedia* on "Military Strategy," written by then-Chief of the General Staff Ogarkov.[149] One would think that an article in the *Soviet Military Encyclopedia*, a basic reference work for Soviet officers to consult, would seem to be a statement of official Soviet doctrine, and not merely an argument being made personally by Ogarkov. The fact that the article is signed by the Chief of the General Staff should give the positions stated in the article extra weight (not all articles in the encyclopedia are signed).

Yet, subsequent statements made by Ogarkov himself in the 1980s failed to repeat this threat of immediate and decisive retaliation. They reaffirmed that strategic nuclear warfare could not remain limited, but did not specify that the escalatory step would come because of Soviet massive retaliation. Even when Ogarkov talked about immediate escalation to massed use of nuclear weapons, he said that this step would be taken "by the [warring] sides," not by the USSR alone.[150] When Ogarkov's later writings and the statements of other Soviet military sources in the 1980s are combined, Ogarkov's 1979 encyclopedia article begins to look like a trial balloon that did not float. There is no indication that it set the tone of future Soviet statements on doctrine. Instead, the article seems to be the last volley in the Soviet military's debate on how to react to the Schlesinger Doctrine.

There are at least two possible interpretations of the evolution of doctrinal statements at this time. First, operational doctrine may have changed to admit the possibility that limited strategic strikes could be exchanged, even if no one believed that this exchange would end the war. (Both military and political leaders could have *hoped* that it would end the war, rather than destroying the world, even if they did not have much confidence that it would.) Second, it is possible that in the early 1980s the USSR did not want to say anything that might seem aggressive or unreasonable, since it was trying to build bridges with the anti-INF peace movements in Western Europe. By not directly threatening massive retaliation in its declaratory doctrine, the Soviet Union might seem more reasonable and flexible, even if its operational doctrine for war followed the line set by Ogarkov's encyclopedia article.

The problem in deciding whether or not innovation took place in reaction to the Schlesinger Doctrine is a lack of hard evidence one way or the other. For both of the other cases considered in this book, changes in declaratory statements can be checked against changes in deployment patterns, in exercises, in arms control behavior, or in weapons acquisitions. For this case, no such unclassified evidence exists.

Reliable Western sources do tell us that the Soviet Union probably did not have the C^3I capability for fighting strategic nuclear war in a flexible manner in the mid-1970s, but did have it by the mid-1980s. According to an estimate made by the U.S. Air Force, as of 1976 Soviet military C^3I capabilities still lagged far behind what American technology provided, especially in regard to computer and satellite developments that would be required for "an efficient flexible deterrent posture." Instead, according to Edgar Ulsamer, "[T]he makeup of the Soviet C^3 system . . . seems to be oriented toward a preemptive all-out strategic posture that requires only relatively simple communications functions."[151] Notra Trulock III estimated in 1987 that a flexible strategic posture had become possible for the USSR, and that Soviet ICBMs were capable of fulfilling limited and controlled strike options.[152] It is impossible to tell for sure whether this capability grew in reaction to a doctrinal decision related to the Schlesinger Doctrine, or whether instead it was a natural technological progression that was designed to improve Soviet command and control capabilities for fighting an all-out counterforce war.

From the mid-1960s on there was a constant discussion and debate in Soviet military circles about whether improvements in Soviet cybernetic military technology were needed, and about the whole question of command and control of military troops and weapons.[153] From 1966 on, the development and use of computer technology in all aspects of the Soviet economy and industry became a major concern of the Brezhnev regime; in the early 1970s this concern resulted in the development of new training programs and scientific institutes for programmers and systems analysts, especially in relation to problems of operations research and management (a civilian parallel to the military field of C^3I).[154] The most recent history of the Soviet General Staff Academy notes that from 1972 through 1987, a major new concern of the academy was work on command and control for both nuclear and conventional war scenarios, using computer electronics and complex automated control systems.[155]

While it is possible that a perceived need to match the Schlesinger Doctrine might either have provoked these improvements or been an excuse for making them, it is important not to overstate the relationship between a Soviet military interest in limited nuclear war options and a Soviet military interest in C^3I improvements. Many of the articles that appeared in the Soviet military press in the mid-1970s on the question of "command and control" [upravlenie] in nuclear war were obviously not geared to the question of fighting limited strategic nuclear wars. Instead, they dealt with command and control of troops and weapons in fighting a nuclear ground battle in the European theater.[156] As Notra Trulock notes, the mid-1970s development of a Soviet conventional option in Europe meant that nuclear command and control also had to be improved to prevent a premature launch of nuclear weapons, so that a clear transition point from conventional to nuclear operations could be maintained.[157] Furthermore, inadequacies in Soviet ballistic missile defense capabilities in the late 1960s could have led to a concern over C^3I improvements for the sake of all-out, massive nuclear war–fighting, apart from any interest in limited nuclear war–fighting.[158] An article published in *Voennaia Mysl'* in 1970 confirms that fear of a massive counterforce first strike was indeed an issue, and implies that automated launch-on-warning plans may have been a result of this fear. Lieutenant General of the Engineering Technical Services A. Vasil'ev and Colonel of Engineering N. Pimenov wrote, "Real-time warning of the opponent's rocket launches, automatic analysis of the information received from various systems of the [early warning] complex, with confirmation of the high reliability of the discovery of some guaranteed set number of rockets in flight, and automatic issuing of the command for a prompt launch [*vstrechnyi udar*] excludes the possibility of the destruction of strategic rockets on the ground in practically all conceivable combinations of military-strategic situations."[159]

One of the most eloquent supporters of improvements in Soviet command and control capabilities for nuclear war–fighting was Col. V. M. Bondarenko. He repeatedly wrote, from the late 1960s on, that a "third stage" in the nuclear revolution of military affairs was underway. The revolution itself was "the transition from conventional weapons to nuclear-rocket weapons as the chief means of achieving the fundamental goals of war." The first stage had been the development of the atomic and thermonuclear bombs; the second stage had been the development of strategic rocket delivery systems. The third stage was the utilization of complex automated control systems for directing troops and weapons in waging such a war.[160] Beginning in 1971, Bondarenko began to identify this third stage as an element of a scientific research and development competition between socialism and capitalism.[161] In a 1973 article which repeated each of these themes, he specifically tied the command and control improvements question to the forces responsible for strategic nuclear war–fighting: the Strategic Rocket Forces (which would launch ICBMs) and the Anti-Air Defense Troops of the Country (the PVO Strany, which manned the early-warning radars and would be responsible for tracking and shooting down incoming missiles).[162] He particularly emphasized the desirability of real-time data processing, as well as the danger that signals might be distorted or lost in the fog of war.

Several other Soviet military writings also deal with the problem of strategic C³I and competition with the West in technology development. In 1974, two Soviet military officers published a book which described Western automated command and control systems, and which gave a fairly detailed summary of current U.S. Strategic Air Command (SAC) development work.[163] While never mentioning the Schlesinger Doctrine by name, the two authors seem to have hit upon exactly the C³I improvements that Schlesinger mentioned in his testimony before the Senate. In their conclusion, these officers highlight the deficiencies of the U.S. system and caution against "the danger of overestimating the potentials of the operational automized systems of control in the armed forces of foreign countries."[164] Perhaps this is an indication that they did not believe that the Schlesinger Doctrine shift demanded a response.

Yet five years later, another *Voenizdat* book claimed that the future plans of the U.S. military were based on continuing improvements in electronic control and ballistic missile accuracy. The author cited in particular the growing role, from 1973 on, of electronics experts in the highest echelon of the American Defense Department.[165] He focused on U.S. efforts to correct some of the deficiencies that the previous authors had noted.[166]

Without access to data about Soviet strategic nuclear exercises and war games, it is simply impossible to tell whether or not this focus on technical improvements was matched by any operational innovation in planning for future nuclear war. There is one indication in open Soviet sources that the official codification of strategic nuclear doctrine could have been changing during the mid-1970s. In the 1976 edition of the official history of the Soviet General Staff Academy, it is noted that in 1975 a textbook with a "new" view on nuclear war was published by the Strategy Department.[167] However, the "new" quality of the view is not specified, and the 1987 edition of the book on the Academy does not appear to mention any changes occurring in the views of the Strategy Department during the 1970s.[168] It is therefore not clear whether this textbook change has any relationship to the changed tone of military and official civilian words on limited strategic nuclear warfare.

Conclusion

We are left with several enigmas:

- Was the U.S. announcement of the Schlesinger Doctrine a real doctrinal innovation? Did it in fact change U.S. targeting options and operational planning for strategic nuclear warfare?
- Did the Soviet General Staff ever agree to treat the Schlesinger Doctrine as an innovation, whether or not it was a "real" innovation?
- How should the General Staff have defined its own interests if it perceived the Schlesinger Doctrine as a genuine innovation? Would it make the most sense for the General Staff to do nothing in response, to eliminate its doctrine of immediate and massive retaliation against any strike on the Soviet homeland, or to develop a matching limited strategic strike capability for political or resource acquisition reasons?
- How were the discussions in the General Staff in the 1970s on limited strategic nuclear warfare resolved? Did the declaratory doctrinal unity on nuclear war issues observed in the early 1980s indicate that the General Staff had reached an operational decision, or instead that political leaders had declared the subject of strategic limited warfare taboo?
- Did the improvement of Soviet strategic nuclear C³I capabilities between the mid-1970s and late 1980s have anything to do with the Schlesinger Doctrine?

The two other cases studied in this book do not present us with such enigmas. In them it is much easier to demonstrate both the achievement of consensus in Soviet press debates, and the operational effects of Soviet reaction to foreign threats. Part of the problem here is undoubtedly that strategic nuclear targeting doctrine is an extremely sensitive issue. None-theless, given the ambiguity of the U.S. doctrinal shift, the ambiguity of the Soviet response is not surprising.

Given the composition of the Soviet senior officer corps at that time, it would have been surprising if the possibility of innovation in nuclear war–fighting doctrine had not been considered in the Soviet General Staff. The officer corps was relatively young and filled with those interested in technological improvements, particularly in regard to computers and C^3I. According to Kulikov's history of the Soviet General Staff Academy, for example, the Strategy Department (whose responsibilities included strat-egy research and formulation, not just teaching) underwent a personnel turnover that changed almost the complete cadre between the mid-1960s and the mid-1970s.[169] American analyst Richard Woff noted in 1985 that Soviet military concerns about C^3I in the late 1970s were reflected in a massive promotion of technical signals experts within the officer corps.[170] And according to John Erickson's 1976 table of data on the Soviet High Command, three-fourths of the members of the command had received promotion to their current position in 1967 or later (the old-timers were concentrated in the Main Political Administration (MPA) and the Navy, not in the two services expected to be most directly concerned with the Schlesinger Doctrine—the SRF and the PVO Strany).[171] It would seem that adding new options to Soviet strategic planning might have been attrac-tive to this group of young technocrats.

It is curious that one particular young advocate of Soviet C^3I improve-ments was Marshal Nikolai Ogarkov,[172] the man who wrote the 1979 encyclopedia article denying the existence of a Soviet controlled strike option. One would have thought that Ogarkov in particular would have valued the creation of flexibility in strategic targeting. His encyclopedia article seems even more puzzling given his penchant for technological mil-itary competition with the West.

It is not clear whether or not a doctrinal innovation occurred in this case. However, it is clear that there was a military debate about how to react to the Schlesinger Doctrine, and about the probable character of strategic nuclear warfare in the future. It is also clear that the tenor of open Soviet comments on strategic limited nuclear warfare changed after the early 1970s. The evidence presented here suggests that a number of Soviet military officers responsible for doctrine formulation did react with some sort of interest to the Schlesinger Doctrine. Some of them may have accepted the possibility of an exchange of limited strategic nuclear strikes before the outbreak of general nuclear war. Those Western theorists who have argued that the Soviet military would never demon-strate any interest in anything other than massive, decisive options in war have not captured the complex reality of General Staff debates on that issue.

What is perhaps most valuable about this case from a theoretical perspective is its very ambiguity. It serves as a caution against assuming that organizational perceptions of the environment are always discernable, and that organizational interests are always clearcut. Even in an organization such as the Soviet General Staff in the 1970s and early 1980s, where the basic goal of the organization was set (the defense of the state against external threat) and the basic character of the environment was decided (it was hostile, with the primary threat emanating from the United States), ambiguity seems to have existed both in the organization's understanding of the causal world (i.e., whether a change in U.S. declaratory doctrine for limited nuclear war–fighting meant anything) and in organizational objectives (i.e., if it did mean something, what the organization's interests were in reacting to it).[173] While organizations do react to threats from the environment, it is not always clear when a threat exists, or how it should be overcome.

5

Soviet Reactions to Western
Deep-Strike Doctrines

SOVIET PRESIDENT Mikhail Gorbachev said in a speech at Stanford University on June 4, 1990:

> Science has played a major role in the arms race. Yet science was the first to speak out authoritatively against this folly and to look for a way out. Here we have to give credit to the joint efforts of Soviet and American [scholars]. . . . I am referring to the development of the basic principles of such concepts as international security and strategic stability. Without a serious and objective approach to defining stability and mutual security, without a scientific analysis taking into account all factors—political, scientific, military, technical and political-military—it is impossible to make the right decisions on cardinal issues, nuclear and conventional force reductions.[1]

This chapter argues that the Soviet reaction to the Western doctrinal shifts of Follow-on Forces Attack (FOFA) and AirLand Battle (ALB) was qualitatively different from Soviet reactions to previous doctrinal shifts in the West, and that this difference is attributable to the efforts of Soviet civilian academic scientists and scholars to decelerate the arms race, to lessen the defense budget burden on the Soviet economy, and to create a more stable military situation in Central Europe. For the first time since the era of Trotskii in the early 1920s, civilian theorists joined military debates in the Soviet Union about the direction of doctrinal developments, and they seem to have had significant influence.

Military officers on their own, in the absence of discussion within a broader policy community, tend to make reactive doctrinal innovations that lead to increases in their own resources and autonomy. The result is often a new cycle in the ongoing military competition between two potential adversaries. In this case, as is demonstrated below, Soviet military officers added a new defensive component to their basically offensively oriented doctrine, a component which would better prepare them to protect their own forces in case of an attack by the West. This did lead to an innovation in doctrine, in the sense that the old, purely offensive approach to future war was modified. However, the military retained the view that its basic mission was still victory in war, and that victory was achievable only through decisive offensive activities on the territory of the opponent. A component of strategic defense was merely added to a basically offensive plan.

In the mid-1980s, a group of civilian academics joined forces with reformist politicians to propose an alternative reaction to the Western doctrine shift. They thought that a better reactive innovation would be a conciliatory one. Specifically, they argued for a reaction which would encourage the achievement of "nonprovocative defense" or "defensive defense" formations by both sides in Central Europe. These defensive defense plans differed from the strategic defensive planning component originally favored by the Soviet military, in that defensive planning was to pervade all war preparations; the strategic defense would be the sole plan for the initial stage of future war, and the sole plan for the entire conduct of war. These proposals envisioned defensive operations which would be undertaken for the sole purpose of repelling an invading enemy. They criticized the pursuit of "victory" in war as dangerous and illusive, and instead aimed only for the restoration of the *status quo ante bellum*, that is, the state borders that existed before the start of war.

There were at least two variations in thinking about how the status quo ante bellum could be restored. Some saw the issue the way that the designers of NATO's Follow-On Forces Attack doctrine did (detailed below), where counteroffensives would be launched over state borders to stop attackers, but without any political intention to carry an offensive attack on to another state's territory. Other Soviet civilians went so far as to argue that in the event of an attack, the counteroffensives launched by the defending side should not cross state borders. In other words, deep strikes on enemy forces over the border would not be acceptable.

The impact of the Soviet military's "defensive defense" doctrine on operational planning became moot as other, more pressing issues overtook the Soviet Union in 1991. It is clear, nonetheless, that these civilian visions of future security in Europe influenced the direction of doctrinal debates among Soviet military officers to an unprecedented extent. Despite civil-military conflict under Gorbachev, the ideas of some civilian scholars seem to have penetrated the barrier of professional expertise that had earlier limited civilian access to military officers. Through his support of a novel, cooperative, community-building strategy of civilian intervention into technical military issues, Gorbachev succeeded in shaping the military's doctrinal planning process to a degree that Khrushchev never approached. It is my prediction that a defensive orientation will pervade Russian military planning as it develops in the coming years.

Before turning to the Western doctrinal shifts and the variety of Soviet reactions to those shifts, this chapter will begin by discussing the expansion of the Soviet defense policy community in the mid- to late 1980s.

The Changed Soviet Defense Policy Community

Many Western scholars noted the surge of Soviet civilian academic participation in discussions about conventional force doctrine and structure in the late 1980s. Some have argued that Soviet President Gorbachev attempted to set up an alternate source of policy advice on doctrinal issues.[2] Many respected Western analysts, including Edward Warner III, Jack Snyder, and Stephen M. Meyer, argue that the civilian scholars (or *institutchiki*), while perhaps competent to talk about strategic nuclear force issues, lacked the background that would allow them to be taken seriously in discussions about the technical characteristics of the ground forces. As a result, these Western scholars claim, the Soviet military was bound to dismiss them as incompetent interlopers.[3] And in fact, one senior scholar at Moscow's Institute for World Economy and International Affairs (IMEMO) admitted that most Soviet academics initially lacked one key advantage in dealing with the military on conventional force questions that they possessed on nuclear questions: experience in international arms control negotiation sessions.[4]

Nonetheless, a few Western scholars do recognize that a certain degree of cooperation and tolerance grew up between certain military officers and certain civilian scholars at the institutes. For example, Jacob W. Kipp et al. have written that in the Gorbachev era, the Soviet military apparatus "displays new vitality in reaching out to its civilian academic counterparts," and that networking between the military and civilian institutions "enables the Soviet political and military leadership to draw upon a mixture of traditional and newer views."[5] Similar comments about the development of means for military and civilian academic cooperation are found in the discussion of John Hines's arguments at a 1989 RAND workshop on Soviet military politics.[6]

The argument I make in this chapter is that there was an expansion in the Soviet defense policy community as civilian scholars became participants in policy debates on military doctrine issues. In this section, I will demonstrate the extent to which these scholars entered the policy community in the Gorbachev era. (Their continuing influence in post-Soviet Russian defense policy formulation is now evident.)

Those who question the military's acceptance of civilian defense views under Gorbachev often stress the high level of conflict that existed between members of the two groups under Gorbachev. There certainly are a number of examples of direct confrontations in the Soviet press between individual civilian scholars and military officers. Sometimes this seemed to have occurred because the civilian scholar intentionally provoked the confrontation by engaging in name-calling directed against the military.[7]

Other times it was because civilian scholars proposed structural reforms akin to those of Khrushchev—for example, the elimination of the Strategic Defense Forces as a separate military branch (the PVO Strany).[8] At least once, it was because a reform proposal made by civilian scholars seemed unreasonable even from the standpoint of a disinterested observer.[9] Still other times, however, some military officers objected to civilian involvement in defense debates at any level, even in the absence of name-calling, institutional threats, or obvious civilian naivete.[10]

There were thus plenty of cases of civilian scholars being criticized by military officers for incompetent meddling. However, it would be wrong to see the entire relationship between Soviet military officers and civilian defense-expert scholars as having been one of conflict and name-calling. Some Soviet scholars actively cooperated with some military officers in various defense reform issue-areas, including doctrinal reform, and many officers seem to have more or less accepted the civilians' role in this process. The community of defense policy experts in the Soviet Union expanded as these civilian scholars joined the ranks of those whose views were respected, and whose contributions were valued, by both political and military leaders. As a result, opinions in the military gradually shifted away from supporting traditional, confrontational reactions to external threats, toward looking for more creative solutions that changed the parameters of the East-West military competition.

Civilian scholars were introduced into the policy community by efforts both from above—that is, through efforts of the Soviet political leadership to place them in positions where the military was forced to listen to them—and from below, as the scholars themselves tried to make themselves respectable in the eyes of military officers.

The push from above seems to have taken three different forms. First, Soviet President Gorbachev, Foreign Minister Eduard Shevardnadze, and Politburo member and presidential adviser (with responsibility for foreign affairs) Aleksandr Yakovlev apparently all insisted, from the beginnings of their terms in office, that representatives from the institutes play a large role in the international negotiations on the elimination of intermediate-range nuclear missiles (the INF negotiations). This is not surprising; Yakovlev himself was director of IMEMO for a few years before being appointed to a policy-making role. Up until this time, the only civilian scholars who were allowed to actively participate in arms control negotiations were physicists and engineers, who could give advice about the technical properties of various weapons systems. There was no real voice in negotiations for academic experts on international security. In the INF negotiations, however, many Moscow scholars believe that the Soviet positions taken reflected their own views, and that the military was forced to cooperate with this new perspective.[11] The eventual Soviet positions on the INF negotiations were unprecedented; the USSR allowed the elimination of an entire class of weapons that it had substantially modernized only a few years before, and agreed to an asymmetrical reduction of forces (the Soviet side had the greater number of weapons), rather than staying with the traditional "bean-counting" equivalence approach of previous Soviet negotiating behavior. These differences in negotiating behavior seem to be evidence of the entrance of a new set of players into the policy process.

As a second means for increasing the role of civilian scholars in military policy, Shevardnadze tried to create within the Ministry of Foreign Affairs a group of analysts who would be capable of competing with the military in giving advice to the top leadership about arms control and other security issues. He set up a new section within the Foreign Ministry on Arms Reduction and Disarmament, headed by Viktor Karpov, chief Soviet negotiator at the SALT II talks and in the earlier part of the INF negotiations.[12] Military officers apparently participated both in this section, and in a similar new section that was set up in the Communist Party Central Committee International Department.[13] Shevardnadze also set up a Center for Scientific Coordination in order to encourage contacts between the Foreign Ministry and both the military and the Academy of Sciences institutes (including ISKAN and IMEMO). This allowed the scholars who remained at the institutes an additional channel of influence.[14] Aleksei Arbatov, an IMEMO department head, became a special arms control adviser to the Ministry.[15]

In addition, the ministry set up conferences which featured joint participation by military officers and civilian scholars. In November 1988, for example, a roundtable conference at the Foreign Ministry's Diplomatic Academy was held on "Strategic Stability in a World Without Nuclear Weapons." Participants included representatives from the Ministry of Defense Directorates on Estimation and Planning and on Arms Limitation and Disarmament, as well as Foreign Ministry representatives and scholars from ISKAN, IMEMO, and the Institute of Europe.[16] While those attending such conferences did not necessarily take away with them a new outlook on security issues, such meetings nonetheless provided an opportunity for cross-fertilization of ideas between military and scholarly civilian communities. A senior official in the Center for Scientific Coordination stated that meetings between civilian scholars and officers from the General Staff Academy were particularly meaningful, since General Staff Academy officers, as academics, were already favorably disposed toward the idea of discussing military reforms, and could thus find a common language with the civilians.[17]

Shevardnadze personally was a vocal advocate for ending the military's monopoly on defense information in the Soviet Union.[18] Shevardnadze's uncompromising positions on the issues of *glasnost'* in the military budget and in arms control, on the necessity of giving up Soviet control over Eastern Europe, and on assisting United Nations efforts to oust Saddam Hussein's forces from Kuwait, certainly brought him into conflict with hardline, high-ranking Soviet military officers.[19] Undoubtedly, his conflict with officers such as Defense Minister Marshal Dmitrii Yazov contributed to his decision to resign as Foreign Minister in December 1990.[20] However, it should not be concluded from this that the Foreign Ministry's role as a whole in doctrinal debates was circumscribed by military hostility. At conferences and meetings in the West, several reformist civilians said that Shevardnadze was widely viewed as being overly idealistic, and that his departure actually made things easier for reform-minded professionals at the Foreign Ministry staff, since they were then able to deal with other Soviet institutions at a more practical level. Furthermore, despite his senior position, Yazov was probably not typical of the military officer corps. He was one of the participants in the August 1991 coup attempt against Gorbachev; most high-ranking military officers did not participate, and many worked actively to put down the putsch.[21]

A final means that the top leadership used to encourage the development of ties between the institutes and the military was through structural changes at the institutes themselves. Pat Litherland provides a useful summary of how this occurred at IMEMO, starting under the leadership of General Secretary Yurii Andropov in 1983.[22] Through top-level intervention, institute scholars who dealt with military issues were granted more autonomy and power. Top political leaders also apparently exerted pressure on top military leaders to meet with representatives from the institute departments dealing with security issues. According to one ISKAN scholar, both Generals Mikhail Moiseev and Sergei Akhromeev, when each served as Chief of the General Staff, met with ISKAN Deputy Director Andrei Kokoshin because they were told to do so by someone (unnamed) at the top.[23] In other words, top political leaders can create opportunities for initiating contacts between institutions, leaving the scholars with the responsibility for using those contacts well.

As chapter 2 noted, the Soviet military traditionally maintained a virtual monopoly of power on technical doctrine questions. The military was often led by hardline officers, whose doctrinal policies were perceived as threatening by Western policymakers. It is therefore not surprising that political leaders concerned about international stability and the possibility for Soviet integration into the Western world economy would focus their efforts on taking doctrinal power away from the military. Gorbachev obviously fits this description. Some scholars, both Western and Soviet, believe that Yurii Andropov also fit this profile.[24] This might explain why many of the attempts to alter the defense policy community in the Soviet Union had their roots in the period from 1982 through 1984; many of Gorbachev's policies were based on the ideas of those scholars whom Andropov cultivated.

But in this case, the *institutchiki* did not rely only on pressure from the top to make their way into military circles. They actively worked to gain technical expertise, which they saw as a prerequisite if they were to be taken seriously by the military. They then used the sources of expertise available to them to build alliances with military officers. There are a number of illustrations of this.

First there is the example of Andrei A. Kokoshin, Deputy Director of ISKAN and a major voice in Soviet doctrinal reform efforts. (In April 1992, Russian President Boris Yeltsin appointed Kokoshin First Deputy Defense Minister, indicating the augmentation of Kokoshin's military reform role.[25]) Kokoshin received a degree from the N. E. Bauman Higher Technical University in Moscow before he went on to study history and to join ISKAN.[26] Bauman in general gives its students a broad technical and engineering education; its specialization is in radio electronics and communications, and many of its students and graduates worked in the Soviet defense industry. Kokoshin gathered around him at ISKAN a number of senior and junior scholars who also had a technical education, either from Bauman or from other Moscow institutes with ties to the defense industry (for example, the Engineering-Physics Institute, which apparently specializes in warhead design, and the Aviation Institute).[27] Similar patterns were repeated in some sections at IMEMO.[28]

There were other means through which institute scholars could obtain an education in military and technical matters. Aleksei Arbatov of IMEMO is widely respected among his fellow civilian scholars because he became very highly self-educated in these areas, using Western publications as his textbooks.[29] Aleksei Arbatov has argued strongly in the press that civilian scholars who wish to analyze arms control and security issues need to do so from a sufficient scientific-technical background to allow them "to give concrete recommendations."[30] Beyond self-education, some members of the institutes (those who worked in departments at the institutes which were "classified") have also apparently had the opportunity to attend three-week short courses at the General Staff on military-technical topics.[31]

Andrei Kokoshin has an additional background benefit that he has used to his advantage in gaining respect among the military; he comes from a military family. In an interview he gave to *Krasnaia Zvezda*, the daily newspaper of the Defense Ministry (which was titled "Our Man in Congress," perhaps indicating the military's respect for him), Kokoshin said:

I know the military life, [and] not from hearsay. I was born into an officer's family. Almost all of our men were military [people], not merely in one genera-tion, either. My father participated in the Victory Parade; he served more than 40 years [in the armed forces]. My uncle still serves in the Armed Forces. My paternal grandfather fought in both the Civil War and the Great Patriotic War as a common soldier. But my uncle has the biggest combat past in my family—Vadim Vladimirovich Chudov, who fought on the Baltic. I myself in childhood wanted to join the navy; military history attracted me. My father believed that if I wanted to be a military man, then from the beginning I should receive a basic engineering education.[32]

One measure of the degree of respect that Kokoshin engendered among military men may be that Sergei Kirshin, the son of Maj. Gen. Yurii Kir-shin (then Deputy Director of the Institute of Military History in Mos-cow), became a graduate student working in Kokoshin's ISKAN group.

An additional means for the civilian scholars to use in building bridges (both of expertise, and of personal networks) with the military were the many retired Soviet military officers, most of them generals of one rank or another, who have been associated with ISKAN and IMEMO, and also with institute scholars through other organizations (such as the Center for Scientific Research of the Committee of Soviet Scientists for Peace). While it is not clear that all of these retired officers were sympathetic or useful to the civilian scholars, some of them have written or cowritten promi-nent articles indicating their support for the academics' ideas. These men were very powerful in their active service days, and are therefore un-doubtedly very well informed about military technical issues and General Staff decision-making. Maj. Gen. Valentin V. Larionov (who spent the Gorbachev years at ISKAN, in Kokoshin's group) was responsible for all three editions of the major Soviet military book, *Military Strategy*, which created a stir in the 1960s; he was also the personal adviser to a former Defense Minister;[33] and he was a professor in the Strategy Department of the General Staff Academy through 1989, even after his retirement from active military duty. Maj. Gen. Vadim Makarevskii (at IMEMO during the Gorbachev years, in Aleksei Arbatov's department) was a General Staff officer and Deputy Commandant of the Kuibyshev Military Engineering Academy. Lt. Gen. Mikhail Mil'shtein (at ISKAN during those years) was apparently a top Soviet military intelligence officer specializing in analysis of U.S. developments,[34] and was formerly a department head at the Gen-eral Staff Academy.

The exact role played by these retired generals in institute and schol-arly life is not clear. No published Soviet sources appear to discuss their role. Several ISKAN senior scholars and retired officers based at that insti-tute have said that the military men acted as consultants, commenting on papers that civilians wrote to make sure that there were no military-technical errors in them.[35] Many institute articles were cowritten by civilian scholars and retired military men; presumably the coauthors shared perspectives and expertise with each other in the process of preparing these articles. Some of the retired officers led classes for institute scholars.[36] Many of them apparently retained friendships and business contacts with active officers on the General Staff;[37] since opportunity in the Soviet Union depended so heavily on whom one knew, this presumably would have assisted civilian scholars at the institutes in their efforts to build networks with the military. In addition, many of the retired officers were members of a group called "Soviet Generals and Admirals for Peace and Disarmament," which met with its Western counterpart, Generals for Peace and Disarmament, to exchange ideas on such topics as nonprovocative defense.[38] These officers likely provided the institutes with an additional conduit for information about Western military thinking, and for testing the reactions of Western audiences to institute proposals.

These various means for academics to achieve respect among the military seem to have worked. There is a certain amount of evidence that respect for civilian scholars grew over time within the Soviet military. In 1990, several articles appeared in the military press which indicated that the civilian experts were being taken seriously.

First, a colonel wrote in to *Kommunist Vooruzhennykh Sil* to say that he supported Aleksei Arbatov's efforts to become involved in the discussion over military construction questions. He accused one of Arbatov's critics within the military, General Lieutenant Liubimov, of being "tendentious," and said, "The experience of the military reform of 1924/25 in our country, [and] the reconstruction and improvement of the armed forces in the developed capitalist countries affirms the necessity of an open confrontation of views, with the drawing in of a wide circle of military and civilian specialists."[39]

Second, Maj. Gen. N. A. Chaldymov and Lt. Col. B. V. Molostov, in a report on a November 1989 international conference in Moscow on "New Thinking in Military Policy," gave prominent place to a quote from Kokoshin about the dangerous lag in military technology faced by the Soviet Union. This article appeared in *Voennaia Mysl'*, the General Staff journal.[40] Since the threat of a Soviet loss in this arms competition was an obvious concern of military officers for many years, the fact that this quotation was selected from a civilian scholar might have been meant to indicate that Kokoshin appreciates the military viewpoint. It is probably also significant that several articles written by civilians on military reform were published in *Voennaia Mysl'* during the Gorbachev years; this indicates a certain level of tolerance for the civilian viewpoint.

Finally, Major General Kirshin wrote on the topic of military reform in the journal *New Times* in March 1990, and said, "It pays to enlist social scientists concerned with problems of war and peace, as well as military theoreticians, in working out the general provisions of military doctrine."[41] This statement is not surprising, given that his son was working with Kokoshin at the time.

One other inroad that the civilians seemed to have made into the military officer corps is their alignment with the disaffected group of midlevel, younger officers that Soviet civilians referred to as "the young turks." Some of these younger officers banded together with the more left-wing members of the Congress of People's Deputies, complaining of conflict with their superiors in the military, and demanding the appointment of a civilian defense minister in the Soviet Union and the establishment of a "professional" (volunteer) military.[42] Others of them resolved their conflicts by leaving the armed forces, or at least trying to leave.[43] The fact that the military bloc in the Congress of People's Deputies (the body which fed candidates into the Gorbachev-era Supreme Soviet) was not unified in its views was reported in a set of interviews in *Kommunist Vooruzhennykh Sil*, the MPA journal.[44] According to a number of ISKAN scholars, the institute reached out directly to this "young turk" group by appointing Sergei Rogov, head of the Political-Military Department at ISKAN, as a liaison to them. While these officers were not necessarily primarily interested in doctrinal reform issues, the fact that they were antiestablishment is said to have made them automatically opposed to the old military way of thinking about doctrine and armaments.[45]

Many of the civilian scholars believe that their expertise and influence in military-technical affairs was best demonstrated in practice a few years ago on the issue of the Soviet reaction to the American Strategic Defense Initiative (SDI). U.S. President Ronald Reagan announced in 1983 that a new priority of his administration would be the research and development of advanced technology for defense against strategic nuclear ballistic missile strikes. According to several Soviet civilian scholars, the Soviet military as a whole wanted to match these efforts with a Soviet version of SDI. A group of civilians, including Andrei Kokoshin and defense-industry physicist Academician Velikhov (Vice Chairman of the Soviet Academy of Sciences, Chairman of the Supreme Soviet Committee on Defense and State Security, and reportedly "Gorbachev's science adviser"[46]), worked together to present a counterposition to this argument. They believed that SDI would never work as a complete defensive system, and that therefore a smaller, asymmetrical Soviet program would answer Soviet needs sufficiently.[47] This counterposition was presented in a number of works by the Committee of Soviet Scientists for Peace, Against the Nuclear Threat; the committee was headed by Kokoshin and by Academician Roald Z. Sagdeev, Director of the Institute of Space Research.[48] Also, according to Kokoshin, "There were . . . maybe for the first time, open debates in the Soviet Union. There was a substantial participation of civilian scientists. A committee of Soviet scientists where I am the vice chairman, headed by Academician Velikhov, have conducted a series of studies for the first time maybe in our history, published in an unclassified version. There were a lot of technical details in it."[49] According to a number of civilian scholars at ISKAN, Velikhov's participation in this group was key, because he knew more technical details about the construction of the weapons systems than the military men did, and they were therefore forced to respect the expertise of the civilian group.[50] The scholars claim that they emerged victorious from this discussion with the military, and that as a result, they had a direct impact on limiting the SDI arms race. They claim that the Soviet military finally accepted the idea of an asymmetrical reaction to a new technological development in the West.

Apparently one consequence of this discussion was that the civilian group began a project on the modelling of stability under radical disarmament. Their 1987 study on stability under radical nuclear cuts reportedly was the foundation for many of Gorbachev's disarmament proposals.[51] In 1989, one subgroup of that committee came out with an additional report on stability under radical conventional force cuts in Europe.[52] Thus the initial cooperative work on SDI soon grew into work on nuclear armaments in general, and then on conventional armaments and doctrine in Europe.

As will be discussed below, the decision made by these civilian policy entrepreneurs to put their expertise to use on conventional doctrine issues meant that the Soviet-NATO doctrinal competition changed course. Supported by the political power of the Soviet civilian leadership, these academics tried to convince the Soviet officer corps that reacting to a threatening doctrinal shift in kind would be dangerous and disadvantageous to Soviet state interests.

The Western Shifts

In the late 1970s and early 1980s, developments in weapons technology and the evolution of Western thought about future war in Europe led to separate but similar innovations in U.S. and in NATO military doctrine. Both the new U.S. Army operational doctrine of AirLand Battle (ALB) and the NATO conventional war–fighting strategy of Follow-on Forces Attack (FOFA) changed the focus of military planning. Whereas previously defensive operations were to be waged at the zone of immediate contact with the enemy offense (in military terminology, the forward edge of the battle area, or FEBA), now the defense would be fought through deep strikes into the enemy's second echelon, or follow-on, formations. The desire to strike deep behind Soviet lines stemmed from the Western recognition that traditional Soviet military planning was based on an offensive which consisted of two interconnected parts: the first echelon, which would strive to break through the enemy's prepared defense; and the follow-on forces (a Western, not Soviet, term), whose mission was to build on that breakthrough, to wreak havoc behind the enemy frontline so that a coherent defense became impossible and defeat of the enemy resulted. These follow-on forces could be of basically two types: traditional second-echelon tank-heavy forces, which would roll through the breakthrough point into the enemy's depth;[53] or the apparently new Operational Maneuver Group (OMG) (a reworking of the Soviet World War II Mobile Group concept), which would use stealth and mobility, rather than the shock and firepower of large tank formations, to slip deep behind enemy lines and create command and control chaos from within.[54] For a variety of reasons discussed below, Western defense planners began to focus on the Soviet follow-on, rather than first-echelon, threat.

Simultaneously, the "emerging technologies" (or ETs) for warfare, especially for conventional land and air warfare, began to come to fruition in the West. ETs involve "incorporation into weapons and reconnaissance systems of advanced data-processing systems and a variety of optical, radar, infra-red and laser sensors that offer extraordinarily accurate target acquisition in all types of climatic conditions and at great distances."[55] In other words, highly advanced technological achievements are used to create a lethal combination of conventional weapons accuracy and range. The eventual importance of these ETs for Western military planning was already becoming visible to Western specialists in the early 1970s.[56] However, in the early years their accuracy and range combination was primarily viewed as a means for fulfilling "stand-off" attack missions, where the troops which controlled the weapons could be based far behind their own lines of defense and still hit targets on the enemy's side of the FEBA. It was not until the late 1970s that these technological capabilities combined with Western doctrinal planning to create a new wartime mission: deep strikes against enemy offensive follow-on forces. Such planning appears to have reached fruition in Operation Desert Storm against Saddam Hussein in 1991.

The U.S. Adoption of AirLand Battle Doctrine

In July 1976, the U.S. Army Training and Doctrinal Command (TRADOC) published a new version of FM 100–5, "Operations," the basic "how to fight" field manual of the U.S. Army. It spoke of the increasingly high lethality of precision-guided projectiles and of the importance of electronic (communications) warfare in disrupting the command and control of forces on the ground, taking into account the experience of the 1973 Arab-Israeli War.[57] The manual had thus been updated to account for technological change. It had also been updated to account for the Army's disastrous experience, both militarily and politically, during the protracted U.S. war in Vietnam. It therefore emphasized the importance of winning the first battle in a war that was expected to be short and intense.[58] It also emphasized preparation and organization of a defense that was as close to the FEBA as possible,[59] and as risk-free as possible.[60] While the manual contained a chapter entitled "AirLand Battle," the theme of the chapter was on the need for land army and air force cooperation in combat; the term had not yet taken on its current meaning.[61] Also, while the chapter on "Offense" mentioned in passing the ideal of attacking the enemy in his depth, this was not a theme of the manual.[62]

This new manual was immediately criticized both within the Army and among a wider circle of American defense analysts for its perceived emphasis on combat passivity. A debate was aired in the pages of U.S. military journals; TRADOC paid special attention to the "Lind Critique," published in *Military Review* in early 1977.[63] Critics believed that the manual placed too much emphasis on firepower, and not enough on maneuver; in their view, this limited U.S. options and forced the use of an attrition defense, where efforts would be made to wear down the enemy offense from certain fortified positions, but where the enemy retained all of the initiative. Furthermore, some said, the emphasis on winning the first battle, along with planning for a single Soviet breakthrough, ignored the realities of Soviet planning for a multipronged, echeloned offensive.

These criticisms spawned an effort to review and rewrite the manual, which began in 1978. This process was supervised by the new TRADOC Commander, Gen. Donn A. Starry, who had been appointed in 1977 and who was an advocate of neutralizing Soviet second echelon forces.[64] Starry believed that such neutralization was important because of the temporal breathing space it would give U.S. troops. Deployed conventional forces could continue to battle the advancing Soviet first echelon, and meanwhile, before the second echelon had time to regroup after its initial deep-strike destruction, release authority for battlefield nuclear weapons could be obtained from U.S. political leaders. In other words, deep strikes against the second echelon were to be used as a delaying tactic for domestic political purposes; nuclear weapons use was still seen to be a major element of combat. Starry used this argument explicitly when he made internal briefings to other Army officers on the new concept in early 1980.[65]

In March 1980, work on a new FM 100–5 began.[66] In October of that year, the preliminary work on the document was presented at an Army

Commanders Conference, and was approved by the Army Chief of Staff, Gen. E. C. Meyer.[67] In January 1981, Starry put the "AirLand Doctrine" label on the new concept.[68] Starry then made the first public argument in favor of the new concept in March, in an article in *Military Review*.[69] Also in March, the first official document concerning the new concept was circulated Army-wide. Apparently one of the justifications given for the change was that "the enemy had to be led to perceive from United States military doctrine and action that the situation he [the enemy] had created would not be one which would eventuate in a status quo ante bellum, but one that 'will be resolved on new terms.' "[70] Also in 1981 the concept was put into practice in U.S. Army field training.[71] Throughout 1981 and 1982, the concept was "sold" to the Pentagon and the Congressional Defense Reform Caucus in well-received briefings that stressed the danger of attrition warfare planning. It was stated in these briefings that the purpose of using military force was not "to avert defeat," but "to win."[72]

In August 1982, the new FM 100–5 was published. It did not emphasize early nuclear use in the way that the Army briefings apparently had; it merely stated, "The manual emphasizes the application of conventional weapons; however, the United States Army must be capable of operating in any environment, including the nuclear and chemical battlefield."[73] It also said that "the AirLand Battle may mean using every element of combat power from psychological operations to nuclear weapons."[74] There is no hint here about the political delay purpose for deep-strike attack.

Nonetheless, it did clearly identify the deep-strike offensive as the Army's primary mission. A series of excerpts illustrate its tenor:

We must retain the initiative and disrupt our opponent's fighting capability in depth with deep attack, effective firepower, and decisive maneuver.[75]

The object of all operations is to destroy the opposing force. . . . [AirLand Battle] doctrine is based on securing or retaining the initiative and exercising it aggressively to defeat the enemy. . . . Our operations must be rapid, unpredictable, violent, and disorienting to the enemy. The pace must be fast enough to prevent him from taking effective counteractions.[76]

The offense is the decisive form of war, the commander's only means of attaining a positive goal or of completely destroying an enemy force. . . . Once the attack is underway, the attacker must move fast, press every advantage aggressively, and capitalize on each opportunity to destroy either the enemy's forces or the overall coherence of his defense.[77]

While reactive measures halt the enemy, early counterattacks improve the chances for total victory. The reactive phase of the battle should end with a decisive counteroffensive.[78]

And on the war's intended outcome: "Exploitation is the bold continuation of an attack to maximize success. Pursuit is the relentless destruction of retreating enemy forces who have lost the capability to resist."[79] Finally, "Successful pursuit requires unrelenting pressure against the enemy to prevent reorganization and preparation of defenses. Pursuit completes the destruction of the enemy force that has lost the ability to defend and is attempting to disengage."[80]

It must be noted here that the shift to AirLand Battle was not dependent upon new achievements in the development of emerging technologies. While ETs would contribute to the success of ALB's deep-strike mission, they were not necessary for it; its strikes were planned at a distance of only 150 km behind the FEBA, within the range of existing technology.[81] FOFA plans were for much deeper strikes, initially up to 300 km, and were thus much more dependent on the latest technological achievements, although some of the necessary systems were already available by the time of its approval in 1984–1985.[82]

The NATO Shift to FOFA

Gen. Bernard W. Rogers, the Supreme Allied Commander for Europe (SACEUR) who was most responsible for the institutionalization of the FOFA concept in NATO planning, claims that FOFA and ALB developed independently of each other, and that deep-strike planning also developed independently in each of the concepts.[83] He is careful to point out the differences between the concepts, which are basically twofold. First, FOFA was explicitly designed to involve conventional forces only, and in fact to raise the nuclear threshold; its objective was to avoid nuclear weapons use as long as possible.[84] This contrasts with Starry's plans, noted above, to use ALB for expediting nuclear release authority. Second, FOFA was oriented only toward the defense; despite its deep-strike planning, the NATO Command was committed to not firing the first shot, and to not crossing the border to develop a major counteroffensive. Instead, counterattack was seen as a means only toward restoration of the status quo ante bellum.[85] This is directly opposed to the stated purpose of AirLand Battle as it was presented to the U.S. Army.

Furthermore, Rogers is careful to point out, once NATO forces had been committed to a conflict, as they would have been in the event of a Soviet attack on Western Europe, it would have been the Allied Command of Europe (ACE) that headed the chain of command for operations, and not the U.S. Army. Therefore, the NATO concept would have superceded the U.S. Army concept in the event of war.[86] The 1982 FM 100–5 explicitly agrees with this: "National commands relinquish operational command of these forces to NATO," on alert of impending hostilities in Europe.[87] Nonetheless, it is not clear how well this operational command shift would work in practice, in the fog of war, with American troops trained and equipped for decisive offensive penetration into the enemy's depths.

The stimuli for FOFA are found in the 1960s. As soon as the Flexible Response Doctrine was adopted by NATO in 1967, it became clear that NATO lacked the conventional force strength necessary to fulfill the doctrine's intent of establishing an alternative to quick nuclear escalation. The situation was aggravated by a number of factors which seemed to point toward Soviet conventional force superiority in the European Central Region. The Soviet invasion of Czechoslovakia in 1968 left five additional Soviet divisions permanently stationed in Central Europe. The Mansfield Resolution, introduced into the U.S. Senate in April 1970, called for a unilateral redeployment of U.S. forces out of Europe in order to conserve resources during the Vietnam War; while the resolution was not adopted as U.S. policy, it introduced doubt about U.S. intentions in regard to support forces for Europe. Simultaneously, Belgium, Canada, and the Federal Republic of Germany hoped to cut their NATO force deployments for domestic reasons.[88]

Throughout the 1970s, a series of efforts were undertaken to improve NATO's conventional defense capabilities. In 1974, the NATO Flexibility Studies were carried out with SACEUR participation; 865 potential ways of improving NATO force flexibility were found, but the results of the study were never approved by the Defense Ministers group.[89] In 1976, SACEUR Alexander Haig tried again, with his "3 R's" program for Readiness, Rationalization, and Reinforcement. He drew heavily on the results of the Flexibility Studies, and achieved some success; 80 percent of his initiatives were implemented by the time the program ended in 1982. However, they tended to be low-cost or no-cost items at the military level, without any political commitment components.[90]

Yet another attempt at conventional force improvement was made with the Long-Term Defense Program (LTDP), introduced by U.S. President Jimmy Carter at the May 1977 NATO Summit Meeting, and approved at the May 1978 NATO Summit. The allies committed themselves to a 3 percent annual growth in NATO defense budget outlays, and the LTDP identified problems to which special attention was to be given, including Haig's "3 R's" and alliance standardization and interoperability. However, most of the conventional improvement programs were never implemented, and the 3 percent growth goal was, for the most part, not met by the European members of the alliance.[91]

This history of the European NATO countries' unwillingness to commit to large financial outlays made a deep-strike technological solution to

NATO's conventional defense problem seem attractive to many alliance representatives. As Soviet conventional power and mobility improved, it seemed unlikely that NATO would increase the size of its forces, add reserves to counter Soviet breakthrough operations, or even deploy a sufficient quantity of the new technology to allow a spread-out, across-the-board improvement of close-in fighting capabilities.[92] The FOFA alternative meant fewer troops would need to be committed to NATO, and that weapons improvements were needed only in certain select areas, not everywhere along the frontline.

SACEUR Gen. Bernard W. Rogers states that he and his staff at the Supreme Headquarters for Allied Planning in Europe (SHAPE) began work on the FOFA concept in late 1979.[93] SHAPE's purpose in pursuing this work was "reducing to a manageable ratio with conventional weapons the number of enemy forces arriving at our General Defensive Position."[94] When SHAPE began its work, it was thought that the primary threat in the event of war would be the arrival of Soviet second-echelon tank forces. According to Rogers, it was the Zapad-81 Warsaw Pact exercise, which used the Operational Maneuver Group, that convinced him to focus not only on attacking the second echelon, but attacking all "follow-on" forces, including echelons, reserve forces, and OMGs.[95]

In October 1981, ACE submitted a document to the NATO Military Committee which contained the force proposals resulting from the study. SACEUR Rogers then defended these proposals before the Defense Planning Committee at the NATO Ministerial Session of December 8, 1981, and the proposals were approved by the Ministers in the spring of 1982.[96] The approval came only after a great deal of controversy. Many of the European states in particular argued that FOFA was based on too many unproven and expensive technologies; that the Soviet OMG might be deployed in the first echelon, and that if OMG penetration occurred as a result the FOFA forces would be destroyed before they could be used; that the plans were too offensively oriented for a defensive alliance, and too destabilizing in a crisis, since they encouraged preemptive strikes on the enemy's depth; that the prospect of a longer conventional war was evidence of the erosion of the U.S. nuclear guarantee of NATO; and that the plans hurt arms control efforts in Europe by encouraging a new round of the arms race.[97] Nonetheless, the approval went forward.

In June 1982, U.S. Secretary of Defense Caspar Weinberger outlined for the Defense Ministers' group yet another conventional force improvement plan, this one called the "Emerging Technologies Initiative." This initiative called for the establishment of joint NATO projects for development of technologies for target acquisition, command, control, communications and intelligence (C^3I), accuracy, and lethality. Weinberger explicitly tied this to improving the alliance's conventional posture in the Central European region. This initiative was met by a "frosty reception" from several of the European members of the alliance, mainly because they feared it was an American means for forcing U.S. technological dominance onto European markets.[98] Nonetheless, by 1984 the National Armaments Directors Representatives managed to submit to the Ministers a list of thirty-three potential projects, and obtained agreement on sixteen of these.[99]

In September 1984, SHAPE recommended that FOFA be included in a revision of NATO's "Land Force Tactical Doctrine," ATP-35(A). The proposal was accepted by the Land Force Tactics Working Party meeting, and the new ATP-35(A) was circulated for national ratification in 1985.[100] In November 1984, in the Defense Planning Committee, the NATO Defense Ministers accepted FOFA as the basis for the Long-Term Planning Guideline.[101]

Meanwhile, the ET and FOFA development strands were brought together by NATO's Military Committee in MC 299, referred to as the "Conceptual Military Framework," which related the two initiatives to long-term alliance defense planning. The intention of the document was to bring some sense of unified purpose into the variety of recent conventional force planning initiatives. The NATO Defense Ministers endorsed this document in the Defense Planning Committee meeting of December 3, 1985.[102]

Apparently this final agreement on the adoption of FOFA and ET planning in NATO was reached without the level of rancor and indecision that has characterized some other NATO decisions, such as the double-track decision on Intermediate-range Nuclear Forces.[103] However, as in the case of many past NATO efforts at force posture improvements, it is not clear that the decision was ever implemented to any significant extent in the policies of the individual alliance members. U.S. pressure for implementation slackened in following years, as the Strategic Defense Initiative became the major U.S. defense planning issue and as the Gramm-Rudman Act impeded the extension of U.S. defense budget commitments.[104] As a result, in April 1989 the new SACEUR, Gen. John R. Galvin, complained that NATO's Defense Review Committee had found the implementation efforts to be "less than adequate," especially in regard to the near-term lynchpin of the policy: aircraft.[105] He cited as problems the failure to provide adequate electronic warfare and NBC (nuclear, biological, and chemical) warfare protection; to provide sufficient night and all-weather equipment; to arm the planes with "the latest generation of munitions"; to provide an adequate number of pilots to the Central Region; and to eliminate regional disparities in flank air defense.[106]

Soviet Recognition of the Shift

Despite the fact that FOFA may never have been fully implemented and that many ETs remain either on the drawing board or in prototype stage (and in some cases, with doubtful potential for success), the seriousness with which this project was pursued and the effects that it had on NATO field manuals must have given the Soviet military cause for concern. The effect of the FOFA decision on the Soviets must have been amplified by the U.S. AirLand Battle doctrine decision; on the American side there was no sign of wavering or of failure to meet the demands of a changed doctrine. Even though the U.S. doctrine would be legally subordinated to the NATO doctrine in wartime, it is in itself clear evidence of American military thinking about deep strikes and offensive attacks using high technology weapons, where U.S. research and development was generally agreed to be significantly more advanced than its Soviet counterpart. Furthermore, it was quite clear that FOFA was being pushed on the Europeans from the American side (albeit with a different set of American players than were involved in the ALB decision); the American view of future war in Europe remained key for the direction of NATO doctrinal development.

By 1978, the Soviet military had definitely noticed Western development of emerging technologies for conventional theater warfare. The unclassified Soviet military journal which comments on Western developments, *Zarubezhnoe Voennoe Obozrenie*, described from that year onward how the U.S. and NATO were developing complex automated tactical command and control equipment,[107] radioelectronic intelligence and target location systems,[108] precision air strike systems,[109] lasers,[110] and sophisticated antitank weapons.[111] Often these articles recognized the fact that these emerging technologies combined precision location and striking abilities with increased striking distance capabilities.

However, until 1983, this journal treated such a combination in the way that it had been treated in the West in the mid-1970s: as allowing a stand-off striking capability, so that enemy forces could be hit by defensive forces located far behind the zone of contact. There was no hint at this time that the weapons were being considered in deep-strike counterattack or offensive terms.[112] Western work on stand-off weaponry during this time period certainly was continuing; however, the important point is that this was the only mission for long-range weapons that the Soviet open literature noted. In fact, in the early 1980s ZVO wrote summary articles on U.S. army doctrine which implied that nothing had changed since the appearance of the 1976 version of FM 100–5.[113]

The first article in this journal which recognized a significant change in Western war-planning for the European theater appeared in August

1983.[114] The next few months saw an explosion of summaries and analyses of the U.S. and NATO concepts.[115]

Three facets of these analyses are particularly important for understanding the Soviet viewpoint. First, while it was recognized that ALB and FOFA were not equivalent, the assumption was made that for all practical purposes their combat outcome would be the same. No one seemed to accept the NATO claim that their planning was only for defensive purposes, and thereby distinct from AirLand Battle. Maj. Gen. V. Kozhin and Col. V. Trusin wrote:

> Although the concept of "AirLand Battle" is still officially not accepted in NATO, its separate positions, judging from the reports of the Western press, are already being assimilated into the troops of the bloc. In particular, in the course of numerous exercises of the joint armed forces [OVS], special attention is given to working out means for waging highly maneuvering offensive actions of the ground forces in cooperation with tactical aviation, [and to] disorganization of the movement and disruption of the entrance of the second echelons into the engagement of the opponent.[116]

Second, writers in the journal cited NATO exercises as evidence of the success of deep-strike planning in destroying the opposing second echelon forces, and in delaying use of nuclear weapons in the battlefield. Maj. Gen. N. Ivlev and Lt. Col. V. Viktorov summarized the results of one such exercise:

> The "Blues," while conducting a number of measures of political and diplomatic nature and assuring themselves that war was inescapable, began to move the first units out toward the border, in order to implement under their cover a transfer at high tempo of the armed forces from a peaceful to a wartime position. In short order they were moving out into the region of operational designation, and actively striving not to allow a frontline breakthrough by the opponent; and they were inflicting destruction on the second echelon and reserves of the "oranges" through counterstrikes, and were restoring the situation on the "state border."[117]

The authors then conclude that while the "oranges" succeeded in breaking through the depth of the opponent's first echelon, "they had insufficient reserves for the development of the offense."[118] In other words, the FOFA mission succeeded. About a year later, Col. V. Levadov and Lt. Col. V. Viktorov summarized another NATO exercise:

> In the "Autumn-Forge 83" maneuvers, the results of the qualitative improvement of conventional armaments, as foreign specialists hold, have been made manifest in the increase of the nonnuclear period of "limited" war and, correspondingly, in the volume of tasks resolved by troops utilizing only conven-

tional means of destruction. In the majority of exercises . . . a situation was created which allowed the NATO armed forces formations to inflict destruction with first echelon troops on the operational formations of the probable opponent for 15 days, waging conventional war. At the end of the 1970s . . . it was thought that the joint armed forces [OVS] of the bloc could fulfill military tasks for only 5 days without use of nuclear weapons. In this period their first groupings had been given the task of defeating only first echelon troops.[119]

The conventional-only period was thus perceived to shift from a few days to two or so weeks, and this shift was tied to the development of second-echelon striking capabilities.[120]

The final key point of the Soviet analyses in this journal at this time is that many authors stressed that Western planning was becoming more offensively oriented. While admitting that the superiority of the defense was growing under the new technology, Soviet military authors stressed that its superiority came from an ability to launch more active and decisive counteroffensives.[121]

There is thus ample evidence that by 1983 the Soviet military believed that the changes in Western doctrine (and technology) for fighting a future war in Europe were real, that they left the West better able to meet and defeat a Soviet offensive, and that they were potentially threatening to Soviet defenses because of their capability of being used offensively as well as defensively.

It is not clear why the journal did not speak about these changes before 1983. One possibility is that because this journal was an open source, available for subscription in the West, it was not allowed to report changes in Western doctrine until they had been officially announced in late 1982. Earlier analyses of Western doctrinal change could have been perceived by the Soviet military as breaches of Soviet state security. (This would leave the journal in a role that contrasts with its semiclassified predecessor, *Voennyi Zarubezhnik*, which, as was shown in chapter 3, accurately reported trends in Western doctrinal thinking before they entered the policy realm in the late 1950s and early 1960s.) Support for this explanation is found in an article out of the semiclassified General Staff journal, *Voennaia Mysl'*, from 1980. Maj. Gen. I. N. Vorob'ev, a professor of military science, mentioned that weapons were currently becoming more accurate, mobile, fast-acting, and long-range. As a result, he wrote:

One of the peculiarities of modern fire confrontation of the offense and defense is the strengthening of struggle at far distances. If the offenders will be striving to achieve simultaneous influence on the whole depth of the combat construction of the defending troops, then the defending side also will be taking measures to transfer the center of gravity of their fire efforts on the distant approaches to the defensive borders, to inflict destruction on the offender not in the course of struggle for the tactical or operational zone of defense through "pulverization" of the enemy forces in combat (as it was in the last war), but during the opponent's preparation for the offensive, or during the movement of his troops toward the borders of the transition to attack.[122]

While Vorob'ev does not directly mention Western doctrine in this article, it is clear that he foresaw a change in the defensive practices that Soviet offensive forces might be encountering in the future. Thus, the Western doctrinal shift was a potential stimulus for change in the Soviet view of the relationship between offense and defense before its impact was publicly admitted.

Soviet Reactions to the Shifts

This section will be broken into five parts: a discussion of the original reaction by Soviet military officers to the Western shifts in the early 1980s; a discussion of the civilian expert community's reactions to the Western shifts, from 1985 onward; a discussion of the civilian entrepreneurs' movement into a coalition with political leaders; a review of the resulting policy actions taken by the top civilian leadership to implement "defensive defense"; and finally, a discussion of the debate within the military segment of the policy community following the civilians' entrance into the community. I hope to demonstrate that the military's own reactions to the shift were somewhat innovative, but constrained by organizational interests; that the civilian academics favored an innovative reaction that would lead to international conciliation, rather than an aggravation of the military competition; and that the civilian academics, by combining their own political support with bridge-building efforts toward military officers, had a real impact on military debates on doctrinal issues.

The Military Reaction to FOFA and ALB

In chapter 1 it was hypothesized that military organizations often innovate in response to threatening changes in the international environment. In the case at hand it is clear that many Soviet officers adopted a preference for innovative *weaponry* as a result of the Western shift. It is also clear that attention to the strategic defense as a necessary component of military activity at the beginning of war was heightened, in a way that it had not been in the Soviet Union since the early 1930s. This qualifies as somewhat of a "doctrinal innovation" under the definition provided in the Introduction: planning for future war was changed so that initial preparations included the possibility of either offensive or defensive actions; previously, only a strategic offensive had been considered. However, there is no indication that in the absence of civilian ideas, the military would have replaced the offensive with the defensive as the only plan for the initial period of war, much less as the basic direction of Soviet military thinking about and planning for war after the initial period. In fact, some military officers stressed that the Western shift should actually be met by more intensive offensive, deep-strike planning on the Soviet side.

This is fully consistent with the theories about military officers' preferences that are laid out in chapter 1. Military officers prefer to react to foreign threats with solutions that augment military resources and autonomy. Posen has argued convincingly that to exchange an offensive doctrine for a defensive one would compromise military budgets and prestige.[123]

A definitional digression is needed here so that the reader is not confused about Soviet expectations concerning Western war plans. While NATO planners insisted that their intentions were purely "defensive," their defensive plans by the mid-1980s included the possibility of launching a "counteroffensive" on attacking (i.e., "offensive") Soviet troops. It will be remembered from the earlier section on the Western doctrinal shift that NATO claimed that this counteroffensive would be geared toward restoring the status quo ante bellum, while U.S. Army plans seemed more geared toward "victory." In any case, the West would not have passively defended its territory, but would have launched weapons across its borders. The Soviet side, meanwhile, would have found it necessary in this scenario to defend its "offensive" (attacking) troops against the Western "counteroffensive." The Soviet side might therefore move to the "defensive" in the midst of its own "offensive."

In addition, it must be remembered that while it may be easy for Westerners to speak of the use of counteroffensive plans and weaponry as fulfilling defensive goals, and while NATO ground forces have never been large enough or strong enough to launch a surprise offensive attack, it is impossible to distinguish in advance between a "defensive counteroffensive" use of weapons, and an eventual out-and-out "offensive" use of those weapons after an initial defensive period. In other words, in the event that a hypothetical military crisis had occurred in the 1980s which led to skirmishing in Europe (an example might have been a new Berlin crisis following a failed attempt at German reunification), the NATO forces which had been designated for a "counteroffensive defensive" mission could just as well have been used for a major offensive on to Soviet territory, especially after American reinforcements arrived.

Thus, when Soviet military planners spoke of the growing utilization of counteroffensive planning in NATO defense, and when they spoke of the growing offensive character of NATO plans, they were really speaking about the same phenomenon. Usually, in open sources NATO is presented as the "offensive" side; sometimes in semiclassified sources, a hypothetical "defender" (i.e., NATO) is presented as having developed a counteroffensive component. What is at issue in these discussions is not Soviet perceptions of the political intentions of either side, but rather their perceptions about how military force would be utilized, regardless of whose fault it was that the war started.

What occurred within the Soviet military officer corps at this early stage was not a true innovation, but instead a shift in views about proper development priorities within existing war plans. Recognizing that they might not be able to keep control over events at the start of war, the Soviet General Staff began to plan for the possibility of a surprise offensive attack from abroad. According to Stephen D. Shenfield, data from the mid-1980s on Soviet military exercise behavior confirm that a "mixed strategy" had been adopted, where strategic defensive and offensive activities were carried out simultaneously along the front.[124]

Soviet military discussion of how to react to the Western shift began as early as 1979, when Western plans were being developed but were not yet officially approved. There were two basic types of reaction among military officers to the Western shift (and to the development by Western militaries of emerging technology weapons systems).[125] The first type of reaction was a direct one which called for matching the Western technology shift. The second type of reaction was a more indirect, philosophical one which concerned the proper relationship between defensive and offensive preparation and planning in current combat.

A major component of the first type of reaction, calling for direct matching of the new Western threat, was an accusation that the West was trying to achieve military-technical superiority over the Soviet Union, and a call for Soviet matching of Western (and particularly, American) conventional weapons improvement plans. Sometimes the policy prescription—Soviet matching of Western technical developments—was stated only vaguely, couched in terms of increasing Soviet military preparedness or readiness, or in terms of Communist Party concern about the issue.[126] Other times, more direct advice was given to the leadership.

Major General of Engineering in the Reserves N. Maksimov wrote in 1979, "American specialists think that the equipping of forces with precision guided weapons [and] with new means and systems of reconnaissance and control is an objective process, which proceeds, in their estimation, in the armed forces of both the NATO countries and their potential enemies. Therefore the consequences and advantages [of these developments] relate in an equal degree to both sides. The question is only who will realize this concept faster, whose weaponry and technology will be of higher quality and combat potential."[127] Col. V. V. Afinov chimed in, "It is fully understood that the side against which new types of [reconnaissance-strike complex] weapons are being readied will not only not remain indifferent, but will do everything to have at its disposal no less effective weapons."[128] Nikolai V. Ogarkov, former Chief of the General Staff and afterward still an active military exponent of conventional weapons technical development and competition with the West, brought out the old argument from the early 1960s about the "negation of the negation." It will be remembered from chapter 3 that the argument in this vein during the 1960s was over whether nuclear rocket weapons had made large conventional ground forces obsolete. In 1985, Ogarkov said, "New technology and weapons, generation after generation, with inevitability, push out [and] negate the old technology and weapons."[129] He continued, "The process of dialectical negation in military affairs is continuing. At present various, including airborne, means of struggle against tanks, airplanes and to a significant degree also against ships are stormily developing. They have already achieved a quantitative and qualitative state that . . . demands an attentive investigation of these new tendencies and possible consequences of their development. To ignore these tendencies is dangerous."[130]

Thus many Soviet officers, including some in the General Staff and the High Command, believed that Soviet participation in this new round of technological arms development was imperative. In the entire period before "new thinking" in security affairs took hold, there seems to be only one military officer arguing for a different approach. Col. N. Volkov wrote an article in 1978 about technological developments; while it did not only focus on conventional weapons, it did mention two of the components of the ALB and FOFA threat often cited by Soviet officers: lasers and cruise missiles. Volkov stated:

> The economy [and] science and technology in our country are now at a sufficiently high level that we are in a position to create in a very short time any kind of weapon on which the enemies of peace wish to stake their bet.
>
> The Soviet Union has more than once declared that we do not want to take such a path. It is precisely therefore that [the USSR] has more than once proposed to the United States [that we] mutually refrain from working on new types and systems of weapons.[131]

There is no evidence that any military officers who preferred such a negotiated resolution of the arms race engaged in discussion with the technological progress advocates of the early 1980s. However, this article does seem to provide evidence of the existence of at least a latent anti-arms competition group of Soviet military thinkers.

Another manifestation of this call for a direct, matching reaction to the new Western doctrines was one which said that growing Western deep-strike defense capabilities required an even further development of Soviet deep-strike offensive capabilities. In other words, one group of Soviet military officers reacted to the Western shift by arguing for an intensification of the Soviet doctrine that the Western shift had hoped to nullify. If defensive deep-strike weapons were a threat to Soviet plans, then they had to be destroyed through a deep-strike offensive before they could be used.

Maj. Gen. I. N. Vorob'ev, for example, wrote that the concept of deep strikes was no longer merely an operational principle, governing the use of the second echelon for follow-on development of the offensive, but a tactical battle principle influencing the actions of the Soviet offensive first echelon at the beginning of combat.[132] He wrote, "The necessity of realizing a deep strike is called forth by the fact that [the opponent's] most powerful, fast-acting means of destruction are deployed most often at a significant distance from the frontline. . . . It is clear that without continual, practically unbroken influence on these most important objects using fire and troops, the offensive side cannot achieve a decisive defeat of the defenders."[133] He added, "Now the necessary material conditions are there for the realization of deep strike on a tactical scale. All of this, in our view, allows [us] to make the conclusion that simultaneous infliction of strikes on the opponent in his whole depth has in contemporary conditions the significance of an independent principle of general forces battle."[134]

Major General Manzhurin wrote a few years later, "As is noted in the Western military press, the primary task of the defender now is not so much to retain territory as to defeat the offensive forces." Therefore, "as the experience of local wars and exercises shows, the greatest result . . . can be achieved by inflicting on the reserve groupings of the enemy, upon the initiation of their activity, such destruction as would maximally hamper or make impossible the realization of the projected counterstrikes."[135]

Other theorists showed special concern about protection, both passive and active, of Soviet forces in the offensive. The Soviet military history journal, *Voenno-Istoricheskii Zhurnal*, published a series of articles in 1982 on "Studying the Experience of Protecting Troops in Offensive Operations." An editorial note said that contemporary defensive weapons development had made this problem more complex than it had been earlier.[136] Topics in the series included the use of reconnaissance and anti-reconnaissance means,[137] operational concealment,[138] and technological improvement of the offensive forces themselves.[139]

Colonel Yu. Molostov wrote a summary article of these points, arguing that against NATO precision antitank systems, such as the Assault Breaker system, the offensive side should use masking features of the locale for camouflage, create false targets with heat and radar, use smoke cover for movement and keep the second echelon so spread out that it did not present a good target, and hide the tanks' visual and radar profile using new technology. He also posited that the offensive side should use electronic warfare to disorganize the troop control, intelligence, and targeting functions of the Western precision strike complexes, which depend on exact, near-real-time electronic information in order to be effective.[140]

On these technical questions concerning which weapons were needed in the Soviet arsenal and how the new weapons changed the old operational plans for waging offensive operations, there seemed to be no disagreement at all. Consensus seemed to be reached immediately on the need for direct, reactive development of new Soviet weapons technology for both the offense and defense. It was in another type of reaction, a philosophical reconsideration of the balance between the offense and defense, that evidence of some debate exists.

There have always been occasional articles in the Soviet military press which focus on conducting the defense and on the meaning of defense in warfare.[141] However, before 1979 these articles were few and far between, and did not seem to be part of a coherent discussion of various ideas. Apparently, the Soviet military up until this point had not made very many serious efforts at planning for the possibility of a strategic defensive. All efforts were concentrated on launching and developing offensive activities in Europe; the assumption seemed to be that any attempt at offensive incursion by the West could be overcome if the Warsaw Pact merely seized the initiative.[142]

This sole emphasis on the strategic offensive in theater warfare began to be challenged within the Soviet military in 1979. The key semiclassified article which seems to have set off the Soviet military's discussion throughout the 1980s about the relationship between offense and defense was written by Maj. Gen. V. V. Turchenko, a *dotsent* (assistant professor) of strategy at the General Staff Academy. Turchenko stated that the strategic offense and defense exist in dialectical unity.[143] He then observed, "The principally new means of waging armed activities, the growing spatial scale of contemporary wars, the coalition makeup of the opposing sides—all of this predetermines the impossibility of achieving full superiority over the opponents [necessary for] waging only the strategic offensive from the beginning of war."[144] He stated that the Soviet military needed to devote more study to the problem of strategic defense, and cautioned that "the rejection of the defense, the neglect of the necessity of its theoretical analysis, unpreparedness for it in general or an inability to carry it out when the situation demands it—[this] led to serious strategic losses and severe consequences" in World War II and in several large local wars.[145] He wrote specifically about the circumstances of Hitler's invasion of the Soviet Union in 1941, saying, "There was no clearcut plan of strategic defense, the creation of the defensive groupings of the Armed Forces was not thought out in advance, strategic defensive borders in the rear were not built. The basing of aviation, the system of material mainte-nance also did not answer the conditions that were present. In connection with this, the strategic defense had to be created in the midst of repelling the offensive of the enemy, in extremely difficult conditions; that was one of the reasons for the lack of success of our forces in 1941–1942."[146]

This rediscovery of the strategic defense launched a discussion on de-fensive doctrine in the Soviet military, which eventually segued into the later discussion about defensive defense and the "new thinking" in mili-tary affairs.

Turchenko's basic theme[147] was repeated by Maj. Gen. I. N. Vorob'ev, one of the first Soviet officers to write about the combat implications of change in the West (see the discussion in the previous section), in 1980. Vorob'ev added, "The border which divides combat means into offensive and defensive [types] is being erased more and more. In the final result, both the offense and defense use in essence one and the same means of struggle (with few exceptions) in the achievement of their goals."[148] Since the defensive was now using "offensive" capabilities, the development of defense and offense was occurring in parallel; the result was a "leveling" (*nivelirovka*) of offensive and defensive actions.[149]

In 1981 and 1983 there were conferences at the General Staff Acad-emy, with participation by representatives of the Ministry of Defense and Main Political Administration, on the fortieth anniversaries, respectively, of the outbreak of the Great Patriotic War and of the "radical turning point" in that war, where Soviet forces finally seized the initiative from the invading German forces and went over to the counteroffensive. At these conferences M. M. Kozlov, Commandant of the General Staff Acad-emy, presented two major papers on the strategic defense/strategic of-fense interaction theme.[150] Kozlov's statements in those lectures probably were elaborations of his 1980 article on a similar theme, where he argued, "The principally new means of struggle [and] the growing scale and deci-siveness of contemporary operations predetermines the utilization of var-ious forms of military activity, including the strategic defensive. It will be distinguished by high activeness, dynamism and decisiveness of goals."[151] Col. Gen. Makhmut A. Gareev, Deputy Chief of the General Staff and head of the General Staff's Military Science Directorate, and therefore probably the key person in the General Staff's consideration of doctrinal developments at the time, wrote on a similar theme in 1983: "[W]ar has begun completely differently from the strategic and operational situation in which the majority of exercises and maneuvers have taken place. Troops prepared themselves chiefly to be on the offensive, but were forced to defend and retreat. This once more speaks to the fact that war is a two-sided phenomenon, and therefore it is impossible to proceed only from what is profitable or preferred by us. It is necessary to consider without fail that the opponent will be trying to undertake those actions which we least of all expect."[152]

The argument that the Soviet military had to be prepared for the unexpected was extended in an article by Maj. Gen. A. P. Maryshev, a *dotsent* at the General Staff Academy and coauthor of a 1985 textbook on military art in the postwar period. Maryshev noted that there were two types of possible defensive operations: those which were prepared in advance, in order to attain operational advantage over the enemy; and those which were forced on troops by an unexpected offensive.[153] He argued that while it was preferable to have a prepared defense at the ready, so that combat could quickly move over to the counteroffensive (as it did at the Battle of Kursk in 1943), training with prepared defense alone was not sufficient. "It follows that one should try to create precisely such a defense [as at Kursk]. However, it is necessary to keep in mind that there might not be such favorable conditions. Therefore, more intent attention should be given to the experience of defense in the first period of the Great Patriotic War."[154]

There did not seem to be any open debate in the Soviet military about whether or not to consider and prepare for the strategic defensive as a response to Western doctrinal and technological developments. No one appeared to claim that this was not needed. However, the fact that articles which decry the lack of attention being paid to the strategic defense appeared many times over a space of at least seven years may be an indication that there was some sort of passive resistance to this change.

There is definite evidence of debate and discussion about certain aspects of the changing offense/defense relationship. One of these debates was another "great figures in history" discussion, in some ways parallel to the discussion on that topic which appeared in the Soviet military press back in the early 1960s (see chapter 3). In 1980 and 1981, articles appeared in *VIZh* which analyzed the offensively oriented military thinking of three great European generals: Clausewitz, the great Prussian strategic theorist;[155] Suvorov, the hallowed Russian commander who achieved stunning victories in a series of wars for the tsarist empire in the late 1700s;[156] and Tsar Peter the Great, whose military victory against Sweden in 1709 established Russia as a great power in Europe.[157] While each of these three articles said that the general in question believed that the defense was an integral part of offensive planning, all of them emphasized the necessity for decisive offensive action in order to achieve victory. Clausewitz knew that "only great, decisive victories lead to great, decisive results."[158] Suvorov believed that attack was "the soul of contemporary war."[159] And, "Peter understood that the ruling 'classical strategy' in the West, in which commanders in fear of losing their army tried to avoid decisive engagements, was not profitable for the Russian state. Such a strategy led to paltry results in war. For him a full victory over Sweden was needed."[160]

While not directly countering those who demanded consideration of the strategic defense, these articles certainly gave an indication of where their authors' priorities lay.

In contrast to this set of articles which uniformly emphasize the offense are another set of articles and books, again on great figures in history, but this time about great figures from Soviet military history of the 1920s and 1930s. The primary pieces in this set were a number of publications which appeared on the one hundredth anniversary of the birth of M. V. Frunze, who was officially considered by the Soviet military to be the greatest theoretician (after Lenin and Engels) of Soviet military doctrine and strategy. Some of these pieces emphasized the traditional Soviet military view of Frunze, identifying him with the offensive. General of the Army G. Obaturov, Commandant of the Frunze Military Academy, wrote, "If in the leading, political part of Soviet military doctrine M. V. Frunze emphasized its defensive directedness, then [he believed] the military-technical part, that is, the capabilities for waging war in defense of the USSR, should be active [and] offensive."[161]

Others, however, took a different approach and instead emphasized Frunze's contributions to building a theory of the strategic defense. The leader of this school was M. A. Gareev, the Deputy Chief of the General Staff who had written in 1983 about the need to devote more attention to the defense. In 1985 Gareev published a biography of Frunze which highlighted his work on the strategic defense. He wrote, "M. V. Frunze in many of his works emphasized that the operations of the Red Army should be imbued with an active offensive impulse, should carry a decisive character, and should not limit themselves to deflecting the strikes of the opponent. [But] together with this he explained that in a given case the question is about the general goal of military doctrine and military strategy, and not about recognizing the offensive as the only possible form of strategic action."[162] In other words, even if the ultimate direction of Soviet military doctrine was still toward achieving a decisive offense, Frunze did not limit himself to thinking only about offensive activity. In fact, according to Gareev, Frunze thought that "the more widely defense is used, the more favorable conditions are created for successful waging of offensive operations."[163]

According to Gareev, Frunze did not even limit himself to thinking about an active, maneuvering defense. Positional defense, or defense that was designed to hold and defend particular objects or pieces of territory, was also a major component of Frunze's theoretical work. "[S]uccessful operational-strategic maneuver is unthinkable without wide utilization of positional forms of struggle on certain particularly important borders."[164] Gareev here engaged in a direct debate with Ogarkov, the former Chief of the General Staff. Ogarkov wrote, also in 1985, that as a result of the experiences of World War I, where attempts at offensive maneuver were mowed down by machine-gun fire from trenches, many countries fell into the "positional dead-end," and were unprepared for the superiority of offensive maneuver in World War II. Only the Soviet Union, he said, correctly predicted in the 1920s and 1930s that offensive maneuver would be the hallmark of future war.[165] Gareev wrote instead that Frunze's recognition of the interconnectedness of position and maneuver allowed "an exit from the positional dead-end."[166] He went on, later in the book, to criticize the lack of sufficient Soviet preparation for World War II.[167]

In other words, the theme of Gareev's book seems to be that all kinds of combat—offense, defense, positional, and maneuver warfare—have their place in modern operations, and that the key to success is combining them wisely, not in holding fast to a dogma of offensive maneuver. A review of Gareev's book in *Voenno-Istoricheskii Zhurnal* explicitly stated that this balanced approach to "military-scientific problems" was the necessary answer to imperialism's current attempts to achieve military technical superiority over the Soviet Union.[168]

A notable addition to this discussion is provided by a 1985 Soviet military biography of Marshal M. N. Tukhachevskii, who is generally seen as the strongest Soviet proponent from that era of offensive maneuver, and particularly of deep offensive operations. While Tukhachevskii by the late 1930s, under pressure from Stalin, did turn to some consideration of the defense and of positional warfare, he had earlier strongly criticized A. A. Svechin's advocacy of positional attrition-defense combat.[169] Yet it was Tukhachevskii's later contribution to defensive theory that was mentioned in the book. According to V. M. Ivanov, "At that time [in the pre-war years] far from everyone was in agreement with Tukhachevskii's opinion. The positional form of defense, especially in the strategic plan, in the pre-war years did not receive the attention it should have; questions of organizing it were not worked out seriously."[170] In other words, by 1985 the strategic positional defense had become fashionable enough within the Soviet military that even Tukhachevskii's contribution to it needed to be lauded.

One of the most complex and comprehensive discussions of the military theorists of the 1920s and 1930s and their understanding of the offense/defense relationship was provided by Col. Gen. V. N. Lobov in 1989. His conclusion indicated his support for the continuation of debates in the 1990s on these issues. He wrote, "The catalyst of creative activity was the atmosphere [in the 1920s and early 1930s] of discussion, of a critical approach to any, to even the most authoritative opinion. The achievements of the theory of strategy at that time are a clear reflection of the progressive character of Soviet military science, of its rich potential."[171]

There was one additional Soviet military discussion at this time which seemed to reflect the debate over the relative position of the offense and defense in light of Western doctrinal developments. This was a discussion of the reasons for Soviet failure at the beginning of the Great Patriotic War in 1941. As was shown above, the fact of this failure was used as an example in the original statements of 1979 and 1980 about the need to turn more toward study of the strategic defense. The argument which grew out of this was between those who said the failure was due precisely to this lack of study and implementation of the principles of strategic defense,[172] and those who said that the Soviet military correctly anticipated the offensive maneuver character of the war, but that the troops were nonetheless insufficiently prepared to wage a strong counteroffensive from the start.[173] With only a little extrapolation, this becomes an argument about whether or not to discard the traditional purely offensive approach of Soviet military thought.

Overall, then, there is clear evidence of a discussion and debate within the Soviet military over the proper response to shifts in Western doctrine and technological developments. Some officers saw the problem in simple terms of technological matching of Western weapons characteristics; others saw the need to alter Soviet planning concepts. Within the latter group, some believed that an even stronger deep-strike offensive orientation was needed; others favored (and apparently got) a movement toward recognition of the importance of strategic defense in the initial period of war. None of the positions taken were radical, but each contributed to the overall picture of a reactive policy community.

Soviet Academic Reactions to FOFA and ALB

This early discussion, which seems to have been limited to the Soviet officer corps, was about the military necessity of having a strategic defensive prepared in the event of war in Europe. Sometime in the mid-1980s, however, a new type of "defensive doctrine" began to be discussed in the Soviet Union. The new discussion was not about the military necessity of preparing for the strategic defense, but about the political, economic, and international stability benefits of radically changing the offensive orientation of Soviet war-fighting plans. In other words, the issue was no longer the addition of a strategic defensive contingency plan to a basically offensive military doctrine. Instead, the issue became replacing the offensive orientation of the doctrine with a defensive orientation.

This change in focus was not a result of efforts by the officer corps. Instead, it was created by reformist political leaders and civilian academics, working hand in hand to effect a *perestroika*, or reconstruction, of Soviet relations with the Western world. It was recognized that the Soviet offensive doctrine threatened the West, and thereby contributed both to a conventional weapons arms race and to the lack of Soviet international economic integration with the West. As such, the doctrinal discussion was part and parcel of the broader reform efforts of the Gorbachev era.

The probable starting point of this new discussion about defensive doctrine was an article on FOFA written by Andrei Kokoshin in September 1985. As a publication of the pre-*glasnost'* era, this article is striking for its originality and its policy advocacy.[174] In 1985, it was extremely uncommon for any article in the Soviet press to make a new policy recommendation. While Kokoshin's article did not directly state which policy should be taken, it is clear that he is proposing an alternative to the standard military reaction to FOFA. Kokoshin seems to have been one of the major policy entrepreneurs responsible for the innovative policy shift toward defensive defense in the USSR.[175]

In the article Kokoshin begins by summarizing what FOFA entails, calling it "the first significant change in NATO strategy for waging military actions in 15 years." He emphasizes that he believes it will increase the danger of war's outbreak in Central Europe.[176] He mentions that NATO is attempting to gain military-technical superiority over the Warsaw Pact in conventional weaponry, and also mentions that ALB, as opposed to FOFA, foresees the deep-strike use of nuclear and chemical weaponry as well as conventional weapons.[177] He mentions that emerging technologies are very expensive, and that in practice they have feasibility problems.[178] Then he lists the reasons why he believes that the strategy changes are destabilizing and detrimental to overall security in Europe.

First, he writes, although FOFA may prevent the outbreak of nuclear war in Europe, it may make a small conventional war more likely. He does not go into detail about why he believes this is so, but instead concentrates on the possible consequences. Even a small conventional war in Europe, he says, could lead to the destruction of life in the sectors it covers, because "on the territory of the European countries, especially in Central Europe, enormous stores of highly flammable hydrocarbons are kept, highly toxic chemical industry wastes are stored, and it has a large number of atomic power stations and so forth."[179] Second, Kokoshin argues, it will be impossible for commanders in the field to tell if the rockets which are aimed at the second echelon are carrying conventional or nuclear warheads. Since military commanders are likely to accept worst-case scenarios, they may assume that the warheads are nuclear, and as a result, the nuclear threshold may actually be lowered.[180] Third, the fact that the systems are based on automated command and control may mean that in the fog of war, political control over military activities may be lost, making a peaceful resolution of military hostilities impossible.[181] Finally, these developments are likely to lead to a new round of the arms race, and therefore will call forth a less stable strategic situation in Europe. They definitely will not lead to a lowering of the military competition.[182]

In other words, Kokoshin predicts that the Soviet military will react by developing its own version of FOFA and its own ETs, and the resulting competition will be both costly and destabilizing. Already this article is a departure from most analyses appearing in the Soviet press. What comes next makes it the first of its kind. Kokoshin writes:

> An important peculiarity of the debate in Western Europe and the U.S. over the "Rogers Plan" and the "AirLand Battle" concept is (in parallel with the criticism of their positions stated above) the advancement of alternative variants of guaranteeing security of Europe as a whole and of several countries of the continent. . . . The advancement of such alternatives of military concepts is included in the general volume of antiwar, antinuclear movements, and the politicization of many questions connected with this, not only of military-political doctrine [and] strategy, but also of operational art and tactics.[183]

In other words, there are military alternatives which do not involve a direct reaction to these Western doctrinal shifts, but which can preserve state security in the face of these doctrinal changes; and it is up to those outside the military to "politicize" the issues by becoming involved in military-technical issues.[184] According to Kokoshin, the goals of these alternatives are "the lessening of the danger of the outbreak of war in Europe, lowering the level of military confrontation, [and moving] toward a significant lowering of military expenditures."[185]

The specific proposals he notes are focused on reducing the confrontation on the (then) inter-German border, replacing heavy divisions on both sides with light infantry "not capable of waging any significant offensive operations, and only appropriate for effective defensive actions"; and also withdrawing long-range systems from the zone of confrontation to make deep, echeloned strikes on the opponent impossible. The proposals include withdrawing all offensive conventional force structure capabilities and nuclear weapons to a distance of seventy-five kilometers behind the inter-German border, so that surprise attack is impossible.[186] The direction he is suggesting is toward nonprovocative defense, where neither side feels threatened by the other, because neither side has the capability

to launch any large offensive action, even as part of a "defensive" counteroffensive.

He concludes with the standard comment about the Warsaw Pact
needing to take measures to ensure its defense and to maintain the military balance, while preferring to engage in constructive arms negotiations. He also mentions Warsaw Pact unilateral measures already taken
to further European stability, but at this time this included only the nuclear testing moratorium and some small pre-Gorbachev Soviet troop
withdrawals from Eastern Europe.[187]

Kokoshin's article quite clearly sets the stage for public academic discussions about conventional doctrine in Europe from that time on. Proposals for Soviet policy became more direct with time, but many of them
(both those of Kokoshin and of others) reflect the same themes of this
article: mutual force reductions within mutual doctrinal concepts of nonprovocative defense, where the threat of surprise attack is eliminated, and
where both sides are limited in their abilities to wage a large-scale offensive.[188] With time, many of the arguments made by Kokoshin in this article would be given a deeper and more sophisticated treatment by civilian
scholars.

For example, Kokoshin did make one small mention in this article of
the high expenditure and feasibility problems associated with Western
emerging technology weapons. ISKAN scholars A. Vasil'ev and M. Gerasev went further than this a few years later, arguing that Western plans
for using those weapons were in fact not yet realistic. They wrote, "Despite the noisy publicity campaign worked out in the [U.S.] ground forces
concerning the concept of second echelon strikes, which is tied to the
Airland Battle doctrine, it has been recognized after a detailed discussion
that [this concept] is not [being] provided with the corresponding technical and military-economic means."[189] The authors then added that as
technological improvements appear in the future, progress in realization
of the concept may be made. Given the fact that these two scholars were
involved in the SDI project summarized above, where civilian scholars
attempted to convince the Soviet military that a direct, matching reaction
to SDI was not necessary because of SDI weapons feasibility problems, it
is likely that they were trying to make a parallel argument here about the
Soviet reaction to FOFA and ALB.

A puzzling addition to this argument is made by Kokoshin in his 1989
book. He once again mentions the difficulties of introducing high technology weapons into the U.S. ground forces, but then states that the problem
seems to be the lack of knowledge held by the U.S. volunteer forces. "In
the opinion of knowledgeable specialists," he concludes, "an army
manned on the basis of general military obligation has greater possibilities for mastering the new technology."[190] This is a strange argument to

make, since many of the "young turks" in the Soviet military had been making the opposite argument, namely, that in a "professional" volunteer army time can be taken to educate each soldier on the proper use of the relevant pieces of equipment. This is one of the arguments used by the "young turks" for Soviet abolition of the draft. It is also a strange thing for Kokoshin to say because in all of his other works he seems to be arguing against a direct Soviet matching reaction to the Western threat. The implication here is that the Soviets, with their almost-universal military service obligation system, would do better at high-tech integration than the Americans. The logical conclusion is therefore that the Soviets should push ahead with ET development. Kokoshin's argument here almost seems to be one against the Soviet adoption of a volunteer army. It is possible that Kokoshin's statements are an indication of ambivalence in his own attitude toward reform issues, especially if he really was someone whom the military then saw as "our man in Congress."

The second issue raised by Kokoshin in his 1985 article which received an increasingly sophisticated treatment with time is the question of Soviet responsibility for the continuation of a destabilizing European military competition. Oleg Amirov et al. wrote in the 1987 IMEMO Yearbook that it was Soviet doctrinal positions that were at least partly responsible for the Western adoption of deep-strike strategies. The West, according to their analysis, recognized that the Soviet military saw offensive action as the basic means of warfare, and "these provisions of the Soviet military doctrine and strategy caused the West to form a distorted idea of the Soviet Union's military and political course and to make a broad use of that interpretation."[191]

Aleksei Arbatov states the problem more directly in 1989: "[T]he development of the military potential of our likely opponent is not only an objective reality for our planning, but also a process on which our measures exert the most direct influence. Our actions are capable of attracting an intensification and broadening of their programs, or, on the other hand, their slowing down and curtailment."[192] In other words, not only did Soviet actions contribute to the causes of FOFA and ALB; they could also contribute to those doctrines' continuation or disappearance.

Kokoshin also expanded on this theme in his 1989 book. He notes that American analysts believe that counteroffensive capabilities can create the perception of an offensive threat in the eyes of the opponent.[193] Kokoshin particularly notes the importance of the West's belief that the Soviet Union had the ability to launch a surprise attack in Central Europe,[194] and then points out that the U.S. and NATO were at that time reevaluating their strategic concepts. He posits, "The results of these actions will in large part depend on the policy of the USSR and its allies, which have already put in their two-cents' worth [*vnesli svoiu leptu*] in the process going on in the NATO countries of reexamination of the military-political aspects of East-West mutual relations."[195] Kokoshin's implication seems to be that since the USSR and its allies have already made their contribution concerning the *military-political* aspects of the confrontation, it is now time for them to go further, perhaps into the *military-technical* arena of doctrine.

It may be significant that Kokoshin's book was sent to the typesetter (and therefore, presumably, was finished) in August 1988, several months before Gorbachev's announcement at the United Nations of Soviet unilateral force reductions connected with defense sufficiency. A variety of Western defense analysts, including those in the U.S. Defense Department, said at the time that if the announced cuts were implemented as promised, then within three years Soviet short-term surprise attack ability would be significantly cut as warning time for the West would be increased to several weeks.[196] Obviously, these projections were later overtaken by even more radical Soviet troop withdrawals from Eastern Europe. While there is no evidence that Kokoshin participated directly in the force cut decision-making process, it is nonetheless possible that his ideas motivated those who were responsible for writing the United Nations policy announcement.

Kokoshin's work on fleshing out the defensive, or nonprovocative, defense concept with historical examples evolved with time. The first published attempt he made in this direction was a 1987 article he cowrote with Valentin Larionov, one of the retired generals at ISKAN. The subject of the article was the 1943 Battle of Kursk, where the Soviet troops successfully carried out a preplanned defensive operation against the Germans, and then turned their success into a large-scale counteroffensive that eventually drove the Germans off of Soviet soil and moved the Soviet forces toward Berlin. (The Soviet military's original discussion of the strategic defense, summarized above, had also mentioned the Kursk battle example.) Kokoshin and Larionov said in the article that they picked this example as a counter to those in the Soviet military who claim that "only a decisive offense leads to victory." Here, they said, was an example of how a reliable defensive plan could be more profitable than the offensive.[197] Kursk, they wrote, was an example of the "classical positional defense."[198] (A positional defense is one which is designed to protect territory, rather than to launch counteroffensives against an invading force.)

This article contains an anomaly that many Western analysts have noted: the "positional defense" at Kursk was followed by a huge counteroffensive operation. The capabilities for waging such operations certainly do not jibe with the requirements of nonprovocative defense. Some Western analysts have implied that they suspect some duplicity on the part of "the Soviets" here, and that this model was somehow supposed to fool the West into believing that Soviet doctrine had changed, when in fact it had not.[199] However, such analysis is unfair to Kokoshin and Larionov. They explicitly admit in the conclusion to this article that this model does not fit the requirements of nonprovocative defense, but that it does serve a purpose in getting the Soviet military interested in the concept of positional defense. They write:

> No direct analogies between the Kursk Battle and nonprovocative defense on both sides of the line dividing the Warsaw Treaty Organization and NATO today are possible. The defense then was created in the course of the war, and had completely different motives from a nonoffensive strategy and structure of armed forces, [which would be] based on mutual agreement in peacetime and supported by various control measures, including local inspections. However, the Kursk Battle disproves doubts about whether capabilities for fundamentally preparing a positional defense would [be able to] resist the powerful onslaught of offensive means which [would be] effective in other conditions.[200]

In other words, Kokoshin and Larionov were not proposing the Kursk Battle as a model for future defense planning. They were instead trying to point out to the Soviet military that a positional defense (which would be a major component of a real nonprovocative defense concept) was capable of stopping the German attack in the first half of the Kursk Battle, before the counteroffensive began.

Within a few months, Kokoshin explicitly wrote in favor of replacing the current conventional arms race by establishing on both sides in Europe "purely defensive groupings and concepts, strategic and operational forms. . . ."[201] In this later article he first broached the name of A. A. Svechin, the former Tsarist officer who led the Soviet school in the 1920s that praised the superiority of the defense over the offense, and that emphasized the utility of the positional defense. Kokoshin wrote in this article that the Soviet military had for years overestimated the importance of the offensive, and that this error was due to the discarding of Svechin's ideas in the late 1920s.[202]

A few months after this, Kokoshin and Larionov presented a new system for modeling defensive defense concepts. In this system, four types of thinking about defense are possible. In each case, Kokoshin and Larionov assume that both sides have the same concept; none of their variants recognize the possibility that only one side is oriented toward defensive activity.

First, it is possible for both sides to believe that only decisive offensive activities from the beginning of the outbreak of hostilities are sufficient for defense. This concept orients both sides toward meeting engagements, where each side will be attempting to attack the other with strikes on the opponent's second echelon.[203]

Second, the Kursk Battle planning variant is possible. Here both sides are oriented toward the defense at the beginning, including deep echeloning of the defense and a basically positional set-up. However, the final intention is to pursue a decisive, preplanned counteroffensive on to enemy territory.[204] (Obviously, in the actual Kursk Battle both sides were not oriented toward the defense at the beginning; the battle occurred because the Germans attacked.)

Third is the Khalkhin-Gol Battle (1939) model (sometimes called the Korean War model, since the combat situations were similar). Both sides here are oriented toward defense only, with counteroffensive capabilities that are aimed only at restoring the status quo ante bellum. (Again, the real-life Khalkhin-Gol Battle occurred because of one side's invasion of the other; the model name refers to the Soviet decision not to pursue the offensive in that battle.) The authors note the difficulties inherent in this situation: the victims of aggression want to be compensated for the crime committed against their territory. How will this be accomplished? (The unspoken but implied caveat is "How will attempts at compensation be stopped?" if each side has the capability for counteroffensive activities.)[205] The Khalkhin-Gol border battle, fought between the Japanese and the Soviet-supported Mongolians, was over an artificial line in a desert, not over valuable property. This model contains an important ambiguity: it is not clear how political intentions to limit the extent of the battle would be reflected in military realities, if both sides, as in this historical case, have the theoretical combat capability of launching a counteroffensive.

Fourth and finally is a real "nonoffensive defense" model, where neither side has the material capability to wage either an offensive or a significant counteroffensive operation. This, according to the authors, is the preferrable model, and this is the one, they say, toward which the 1986 Budapest Appeal of the Warsaw Pact (discussed below) was heading.[206]

Kokoshin repeatedly used these models to describe his proposals for doctrinal change.[207] With time he seemed to retreat from his espousal of the fourth model; while he still talked about the importance of eventually establishing nonprovocative defense, in his later works he tended to emphasize more the value of the Khalkhin-Gol model over the Kursk model, and to leave open the question of the threatening character of the counteroffensive capabilities that this model allows.[208] At Khalkhin-Gol, the Soviet forces stopped their counteroffensive at the border because of a political decision to do so, and not because they lacked the ability to take the counteroffensive on to the other side's territory. In Kokoshin's testimony before the House Armed Services Committee, Chairman Les Aspin called him on this point.[209]

Rather than portraying this as further evidence of Soviet skulduggery, as some in the West have done, it is perhaps more accurate to see this situation as a case of Kokoshin walking the middle line between reformist ideals and military interests. He himself said in his testimony in the U.S.:

> [A]rmed forces need to have some definition of victory. They need some purpose until we get rid of them completely in some distant future, as we hope. The objective of the armed forces of each side . . . would be simply to restore the situation which existed before the outbreak of hostilities—status quo ante bellum—without crossing the border of the other side and without trying to retaliate by responding to a strike with a "double strike."
>
> Ideally, the ability of the two sides to take energetic actions aimed at restoring the situation by delivering counterattacks against enemy incursion should not, in my opinion, extend on a reciprocal basis, beyond the operational and operational-tactical scale.[210]

We know from other of Kokoshin's writings that this is probably not really his ideal; his ideal is most likely the fourth model of truly nonprovocative defense, which goes beyond the Khalkhin-Gol model. However, what Kokoshin is probably pointing out here is that in the transition period, the fourth model was unacceptable to the military (and, given the success of the U.S.-led counteroffensive against Iraq in 1991, it probably will remain unacceptable to the militaries of both countries into the future). Aleksandr Savel'ev, a senior scientific fellow at IMEMO, implied that even the Khalkhin-Gol model was difficult for the military to accept. He writes, "[T]he overwhelming majority of the military leadership of the USSR believes that armed forces cannot fully reject the waging of offensive operations. They think that the activity of the USSR in repulsing a possible aggression should be based on defense with a subsequent counteroffensive with the goal of destruction of the opponent. This has been emphasized in the works of [Defense Minister] D. T. Yazov, [former Commander-in-Chief of the Warsaw Pact forces] V. G. Kulikov, Commander-in-Chief of the PVO troops I. M. Tret'iak, and others."[211] The Khalkin-Gol analysis alone would lead to fairly radical changes in the Soviet force structure, and would thus be opposed by military conservatives.

Savel'ev joined Aleksei Arbatov in detailing how a status quo ante bellum counteroffensive capability could be separated from a threatening, deep-strike counteroffensive capability. They suggested that divisions can act either offensively or defensively at any given time, and that what separates a defensive from an offensive strategic-operational posture is one which is either spread out thinly along the frontier (positional defense) or concentrated into "fists" for mobile strikes (maneuvering offensive or counteroffensive). The solution, in their view, is to keep offensive reserve divisions in the second echelon, far behind the positional defensive line, and to keep the reserves at a level which is smaller than an offensive, deep-strike reserve would be.[212] While the article gives no clues about how both sides can reach agreement about these relative sizes and intentions, it at least indicates that some thought was being given to how nonprovocative defense concepts could be put into practice.

More suggestions were put forth by Kokoshin and Army Gen. Vladimir N. Lobov, the Chief of Staff of the Warsaw Treaty Organization Supreme Command, who cowrote an article in *Znamia*, the journal of the Soviet Writers' Union. (Again, Kokoshin's standing among military officers was demonstrated by the fact that one so high in the High Command deigned to put his name on an article with the civilian analyst.) The theme of the article is Svechin's contributions to Soviet military theory, and especially Svechin's thinking about defense. The article identifies reasonable defense sufficiency with "a nonoffensive structure," and describes such a structure as involving "limitation in strike systems; changes of deployment in consideration of fulfilling strictly defensive tasks; a lowering of the mobilized deployment parameters, and also of the volume of military production."[213] While again not providing much detail as to how these structural changes would be implemented in practice, this article provides further evidence that academic discussions of nonprovocative defense were leading to practical considerations of one sort or another by military officers.

Probably the best description of the problems which faced those who were trying to argue for nonprovocative defense and reasonable defense sufficiency is provided by G. Kunadze, then a sector head at IMEMO. Kunadze points out there can be no agreed-upon definition of such concepts in advance, because too many particulars remain to be worked out. For example, does nonoffensive defense entail only defense of one's own territory, or instead, of all of one's "national interests"? And how can the latter be defined? Is nonoffensive defense unilateral or not, and if not, who constitutes the other set of players—the United States, Europe as a whole, or some combination of those two? Who should be responsible for defining defensive sufficiency in terms of military potential; and at an abstract level, what is sufficiency? Does it matter whether other countries recognize one's own definition of sufficiency as legitimate? And finally, a question that had special significance as the Union of Soviet Socialist Republics was wearing thin: Is sufficiency something that is defined for the country as a whole, or instead for particular regions?[214]

In other words, it would be unrealistic to expect any quick or neat resolution of this problem. All that should be expected is further discussion and experimentation, until all of the many reform issues now facing the former Soviet Union are eventually resolved. While it would be ideal if it were possible to obtain evidence confirming or denying the operational status of defensive defense doctrine by 1991, such evidence is not likely to be meaningful for the future until the reform process is finished.

The Academic/Policymaker Link

According to a well-informed source at ISKAN, Andrei Kokoshin participated in the drawing up of the 1986 Warsaw Treaty Organization Budapest Appeal on conventional arms reductions in Europe.[215] According to this source, Kokoshin's participation helped to ensure that the appeal focused not merely on arms reductions, but arms reductions based on defensive military concepts for future war in Europe. This appeal came out a year before the 1987 Warsaw Treaty Organization declaration (discussed in the following section) on the defensive character of WTO military doctrine.

Kokoshin is said to have made two significant contributions to the 1986 appeal. First, he is said to have made sure to emphasize the importance of zonal reduction of troops and armaments along the line of contact between NATO and the Warsaw Pact. This would assist in eliminating the danger and fear of a surprise offensive, and would be a movement toward a defensive defense concept. Second, he is said to have inserted into the appeal the phrase that "the military concepts and doctrines of the military alliances should be based on defensive foundations."[216] According to the source, this was significant because the Soviet military was fond of saying that its doctrine had always been defensive; what was meant by this was that the *political* side of the doctrine, the part that determines aims in war, is defensive. In other words, the Soviet Union would only enter war when its security was threatened from without, and did not have aggressive aims. This does not prevent the waging of surprise attacks or large-scale offensives. By inserting the words "military concepts," Kokoshin was apparently breaking new ground; he was now indicating that the *military-technical* side of doctrine, the part that governs combat planning, should also be based on defensive (i.e., nonoffensive) thinking.

While there is no published confirmation of Kokoshin's participation in this meeting, there is one indication that not everything that was discussed in the meeting appeared in the official appeal. According to ISKAN scholar A. A. Konovalov, "at the Budapest meeting of the PKK (the Political Consultative Committee) of the WTO states in June 1986, it was proposed to restructure the army and armaments so as to 'exclude not only the possibility of surprise attack, but also the waging of large offensive operations.' "[217] This proposal does not appear in the official *Pravda* report of the conference. It does, however, correspond to much of Kokoshin's writings about European security. Therefore, this might be indirect evidence of Kokoshin's participation in the meeting. According to Eberhard Schneider, Kokoshin and Larionov were also involved in drawing up the 1987 Warsaw Pact document in Berlin about the defensive character of Soviet military doctrine.[218]

What is clear from Soviet sources is that the formulation of the new concept behind Soviet military doctrine began in 1985,[219] and received its first political presentation in the draft of the new edition of the CPSU program before the 27th Party Conference, publicized in January 1986.[220] It was also in late 1985 and early 1986 that Gorbachev first used the term "reasonable sufficiency" to describe his vision for a reduction of the balance of conventional weapons in Europe; previously, the term had only been applied to strategic nuclear weapons.[221] (Gorbachev's use of the term to describe Soviet unilateral budget-cutting goals did not begin until February 1987.[222]) Presumably, Gorbachev did not invent the reasonable sufficiency concept on his own, nor did he decide on his own that military doctrine needed to be restructured toward the defense. He did not have a history of expertise on military affairs, and would presumably have relied for these policies on advisers who did have such expertise. The timing would suggest that Kokoshin could have been involved in this discussion, since his first public article on the defensive defense concept appeared in September 1985. Especially in the pre-*glasnost'* era, it was commonly the case that any new and controversial article in the open Soviet press was a signal of some significant behind-the-scenes policy debate activity by its author. Whether or not Kokoshin helped to initiate the policy debate on this issue, he certainly acted as a conduit between civilian reformers and General Staff officers as the reforms progressed.

Defensive Defense and Official Soviet Policy

The first unambiguous policy evidence of a strong Soviet political priority on defensive military doctrine was the May 1987 Warsaw Pact [WTO] declaration on that subject.[223] The declaration stated that war prevention, and not war fighting, was the ultimate goal of the Warsaw Pact military doctrine. The WTO pledged not to begin military activities unless one of its member states was already the object of an attack; that it would not use nuclear weapons first; that it had no territorial pretensions against any state; and that it did not consider any state an enemy. The declaration further stated that the armament goals of the WTO states were tied to the concept of "sufficiency for defense." Finally, the declaration proposed that the WTO and NATO engage in consultations about the military doctrines of both sides, "having in mind the removal of accumulated years worth of mutual suspicion and distrust." In particular, the declaration stated that the eventual goals of such consultations would be "The reduction in Europe of armed forces and conventional weapons to a level at which neither side, while preserving its own defense, would have the means for surprise attack on the other side, [or] for the unfolding of offensive operations in general."[224]

In other words, the eventual declared political aim of the WTO states was the establishment of mutual defensive defense deployments and doctrine in Europe, so that mutual distrust could be eliminated and the outbreak of war could be permanently prevented. This declaration was signed not by the WTO generals, but by the General Secretaries of the Communist Parties of each of the WTO states. While undoubtedly military leaders were used as consultants on this declaration, it seems clear that this was not written on the initiative of military officers.

Instead, it is the first clear evidence that reformist political leaders and their civilian advisers had decided to snatch the reins of doctrinal initiative away from the Soviet military. While it is unclear that this declaration alone would have had any immediate or lasting effect on Soviet military doctrine, it became a rallying point for debates between and among Soviet military officers and civilian defense experts. While the declaration alone may not be responsible for changes in Soviet military planning, without it the new civilian members of the Soviet defense policy community would not have had public evidence that the reformist political leadership backed their actions. In other words, this doctrinal declaration should not be seen as the final word on Soviet defensive military doctrine, but instead as the turning point, giving official sanction to the civilian experts to participate in conventional doctrine debates. It was primarily intended to be a message to Soviet military officers that the technical specifics of military doctrine had become a political issue in the eyes of the leadership.

This declaration also became the foundation for the security policy changes that Gorbachev instituted in the years to come. A prime example of this was his December 7, 1988 announcement at the United Nations that Soviet forces would be cut unilaterally by five hundred thousand men and ten thousand tanks, with a reconfiguration of the remaining European Soviet divisions and units in a clearly defensive posture.[225] According to Western defense experts as diverse as François Heisbourg, Director of the International Institute for Strategic Studies in London, and Phillip A. Karber, a senior vice president of the BDM Corporation in Washington, D.C., the implementation of these Soviet plans (which have since been overtaken by the radical Soviet withdrawal from Eastern Europe) would have left the Soviet Union unable to launch a surprise attack on

NATO forces in Europe without significantly improved warning time for NATO.[226] While Gorbachev probably instituted these cutbacks for economic and East European relations reasons as much as for doctrinal reform reasons, he nonetheless referred to the 1987 declaration when announcing the policy. In this sense, the 1987 declaration has become a justification for civilian attempts to implement military reforms.

Changing Views within the Soviet Military

It is probably too early to expect to find evidence of academic scholars having a lasting policy impact on Soviet and post-Soviet military affairs. Too many unresolved specific doctrinal questions remain, especially given the military control conflicts between Russia and Ukraine and Russia and some of its own autonomous republics (flaring up as this book went to press). What we should expect to find, if academics were indeed drawn into the policy community, is evidence of their impact on discussions among military officers. What remains to be reviewed are the debates about reasonable sufficiency and defensive defense that have occurred between military officers since the 1987 defensive doctrine declaration. Does the military discussion of these changes reflect the impact of civilian scholars who were concerned about the effects of FOFA and ALB on European security?

The ideas of the academics have certainly been reflected in the independent writings of the "bridge group" members, the retired generals who became associated with the institutes. The late Mikhail Mil'shtein, a retired military intelligence officer and General Staff Academy department head, focused on the dangers of further development of conventional emerging technologies weapons. He wrote, "The escalation of the race in the latest conventional arms is extremely dangerous. . . . Unless we bar the development of new types of weapons today, tomorrow it may prove far more difficult to do so."[227] He tied this directly into the Rogers Plan. He also decried "the worship of military technologies [and] improvement of arms," and states that "many people still find the present situation to their liking" and that there is "direct or indirect opposition of certain groups, which are eager to continue the arms race and are thwarting new thinking."[228] While he did not consider here the issue of military doctrines in any depth, this article clearly stands in contrast to mainstream military articles from the early 1980s on the need to match Western technology developments.

An even clearer example of the bridge group's acceptance of the academic approach is provided by Vadim Makarevskii. He first brings up the military argument from the early 1980s about the leveling of offense and defense under current technological developments, and repeats Mil'shtein's argument that the only solution to the instability this creates is negotiated agreements on stopping weapons development.[229] Then he goes on to detail the importance of nonprovocative defensive doctrines in eliminating the arms race, and explains his view of what a mutual solution would look like: "[T]he concept essentially boils down to creating purely defensive structures of conventional armed forces and armaments of lesser strength, without offensive-oriented major tank and air-force units, and without clearly offensive armaments (while defensive ones may be improved). It is also essential to station troops in a way which would rule out not only a sudden attack but also, other limitations taken into account, in-depth offensive operations."[230]

It must be noted that it cannot be assumed that the only impact on the thinking of this "bridge group" was from Soviet sources. (Nor can it be assumed that these officers themselves wrote the articles that bear their names. They could instead merely be "lending" their names to civilian reformist writers.) Makarevskii, like Kokoshin before him, cites a variety of views coming from the European peace movement as the sources of his own proposals. Mil'shtein served as a scientific adviser to the Independent Commission on Disarmament and Security Issues, also known as the Palme Commission, which met between 1980 and 1982; and Kokoshin has cited the Palme Commission as one of the major influences on *his* thinking about nonprovocative defense.[231] Furthermore, it is not clear that the academic and "bridge" groups have had the only impact on the liberalization of Soviet military officers' views. Kokoshin wrote in 1988 that "interest in concepts of nonoffensive defense has intensified among the professional militaries in the USSR and other socialist countries, even though 5–6 years ago they considered such ideas very skeptically."[232] Rather than attributing this to his own skills, Kokoshin cites as the key event in this evolution a March 1988 meeting in Hamburg between Soviet and West German civilians and military officials to discuss defense concepts.

Regardless of the precise source of the ideas of each individual, it is clear that the ultimate source of all these ideas was in the European peace movements, and it is also a good guess that none of these ideas would have been discussed by military officers if the Soviet civilian scholars had not gotten actively involved in the discussion.

Discussion about defensive defense in the Soviet military since the 1987 Berlin Declaration on the defensive goals of Warsaw Pact military doctrines (and thus, after civilians had been officially ushered into the community) proceeded along a variety of axes. The first axis was the question of whether the declared doctrine was something new, or whether it was merely a new statement of the way that things had been all along. An implication that the statement was nothing new was made by at least one high military officer in 1987; in an interview, then-Chief of the General Staff of the Warsaw Treaty Organization Supreme Command, Army Gen. A. I. Gribkov, was asked, "Anatolii Ivanovich, if I understand you correctly, it may be confirmed that all of the most important positions of the military-technical side of the military doctrine of the Warsaw Pact are already incarnate in the construction and preparation of the unified armed forces, of each allied army. . . ." Gribkov apparently interrupted and said, "Yes, this is so."[233] However, early in 1989 newly retired Chief of the General Staff Sergei Akhromeev confirmed, also in an interview, that a "new defensive doctrine" had been adopted.[234] The fact that at least most of the High Command in the military believed that a new doctrine had been adopted is demonstrated by the number of statements that have come out since the end of 1988 indicating that the doctrine is leading to military-technical reassessments inside the General Staff. Col. O. Nikonov reported on a General Staff Communist Party conference which revealed that "With regard to defensive military doctrine, plans are being reworked, documents and positions are being made more precise and improved, [and] other work is also being conducted."[235] Col. Gen. M. A. Moiseev, Chief of the General Staff, stated two months later that discussion was running so high in the General Staff on this issue that many positions that had "lost touch with life" were being put forward, including the notion of unilaterally cutting the size of the army by 50 percent and instating a territorial militia.[236] Maj. Gen. Yu. Liubimov, a critic of civilian reformer Aleksei Arbatov, stated that military policies "are undergoing changes in the form of utilization of troops in operations. In conformity with defensive doctrine, new tactical methods for waging battle are being worked out."[237] Chief of the Directorate for combat preparedness in the Ground Forces Col. Gen. A. Demidov talked about the fact that "the structure, technical equipping [and] combat potential of the army are being brought to reasonable and reliable sufficiency for defense; the branches of the Armed Forces, the types of troops, the [operational] groupings and [tactical] formations are being reconstructed. The operational and combat preparation of personnel is being organized in strict correspondence with the tenets of our defensive doctrine."[238] And in April 1990, the High Command held a "regular session of the commission to elaborate a concept of Armed Forces development in 1991–1995," which concentrated on the question of finalizing defensive military reform at a practical level.[239]

While there is no way for outsiders to know exactly what such work involves, or whether it has any correspondence with what academic scholars have been talking about, it is at least clear that most military officers thought of the defensive doctrine as something new.

The second discussion issue that arose in the Soviet military as a result of the doctrinal statement is related to the first; that is the question of whether the doctrinal statement was primarily of *military-political* signif- icance, or *military-technical* significance. In other words, the question was of whether the doctrine would affect actual technical military plan- ning. Doubts about this were expressed early on; some said the doctrine applied primarily to military-political goals.[240] It had seemed that the issue was resolved with Chief of the General Staff Akhromeev's Decem- ber 1987 statement that "the defensive character of the Warsaw Pact doc- trine extends in equal measure not only to the political, but also to the military-technical aspect [of the doctrine]."[241] This statement was re- peated by the new Chief of the General Staff Moiseev in March 1989, shortly after he took office.[242] However, a new and ambiguous state- ment appeared in *Voennaia Mysl'* in February 1990. Maj. Gen. N. V. Meshcheriakov, a professor, wrote, "In the most capacious and concen- trated aspect, new thinking has found its manifestation in change in the character of military doctrines, a review of the contents of this important *military-political* category. The socialist states in distinction from the cap- italists have adopted military doctrines of an especially defensive direct- edness, that will introduce much [that is] new into the theory and practice of military affairs, military science, preparation and education of the per- sonnel of the socialist armies."[243] This hard-line article also defended pre- perestroika Soviet military policy: "[A]ttempts by several publicists to portray the history of Soviet military construction before the appearance of this new level of thinking as a chain of mistakes is groundless, unnatu- ral, amoral in its moral-ethical regard to those people who honorably served in the army, strengthened its military preparedness, and in the harsh years of military experience defended the Fatherland."[244] It would therefore seem that the acceptance of new doctrinal thinking in the Soviet military was not universal, despite what appear to be efforts by the High Command to achieve consensus on this point.

The final set of conventional doctrinal issues around which the military discussion revolved is the set that is parallel to academic discussions of defensive doctrine. The questions discussed include whether defensive doctrine is to be implemented bilaterally and mutually, or unilaterally; exactly what "defensive" means; whether or not defensive doctrine has a decisive counteroffensive component; and where the problem of mutual threat perceptions enters the equation. While certainly not reflecting the liberalism or creativity of the academic and "bridge group" positions, there is good evidence of evolution in these discussions.

Originally, all Soviet military articles on the question of defensive doc- trine stressed that movement toward such doctrines had to be made mu- tually and on the basis of bilateral force reductions.[245] These authors held to such arguments even if they were made illogical by the rest of their analysis. For example, two of these authors stressed that the West was trying to use the conventional arms race to undermine the Soviet economy, to force the Soviets to divert resources from more useful sectors of the economy into weapons procurement.[246] If the conventional arms and doctrine race was an intentional Western ploy to break the Soviet economy, then it would have been unlikely for the West to agree to mutual limits on such policies.

Once it was agreed that any doctrinal shift should be mutual, the question then became how to define a "defensive" directedness in doctrine. Many writers emphasized that defensive doctrines would rule out the possibility of a surprise attack; that is, they would do what Gorbachev's unilateral cuts announcement of December 1988 is thought to have accomplished.[247] One naval writer, however, remained convinced as late as August 1988 that surprise attack was the essence of victory in war, and therefore a basic principle of military art.[248]

Those who believed that the doctrine ruled out surprise attack emphasized that it did not rule out offensive operations. On the contrary, passivity in the defense was to be avoided, and the final goal of any defensive operation was still to smash the enemy through a decisive counteroffensive.[249]

Some argued that defensive defense implies the inability to wage large-scale offensives. However, they stressed that this could only be achieved through mutual negotiated measures, and that in the presence of a NATO offensive capability, the Soviets needed to maintain their own.[250] One of the more interesting writers in this group is Makhmut Gareev, whose views seemed to turn completely around in the space of a year. In his 1988 book he wrote, "It is impossible to achieve a full defeat of the opponent with defense alone. Therefore, in the course of war (after repulsing the aggression of the opponent) the basic means of combat action will be, during the transfer to the counteroffensive, decisive counteroffensive action in combination with defensive [action], in consideration of the situation."[251] But by the end of that year his position changed: "Is it possible to have a reliable defense without an offensive potential? We believe the answer is yes, but only if current stocks of weapons are considerably reduced and if all states fully adhere to the principle of sufficiency for defense, without the forces and means for offensive operations."[252] It thus seems that the academic viewpoints on doctrinal reform were beginning to have an impact on the military.

Some in the military went even further, and said that what defines "defensive" doctrine is the perception of other parties. Defensiveness is identified with the absence of threat. For example, Army Gen. P. Lushev, Commander-in-Chief of the Warsaw Pact, said in March 1989, "Its essence consists of lowering expenditures on defense to have armed forces at a level that would allow them to repel any attack from without on any member-state of the Warsaw Pact. This level should not call forth from even one country any kind of danger, even imagined, to their security."[253] This definition of "defensiveness" was also part of the Soviet delegation's presentation to the first seminar on military doctrines sponsored by the Conference on Security and Cooperation in Europe (CSCE), held in Vienna in January and February 1990. Moiseev stressed in his closing speech that a mutual understanding should be worked out such that neither side's military doctrine or activity would be considered threatening by the other side.[254]

By 1989, even the unity of military views on the need for mutual doctrinal revision was gone. Undoubtedly, Gorbachev's announcement that unilateral force cuts had been made in part in order to implement the defensive doctrine was the major cause of this change. Yet some statements went beyond what Gorbachev said. Even Chief of the General Staff Moiseev seemed to imply that Gorbachev's statement was not the only unilateral policy which would be made. He wrote:

> In the practical plane the principle of defensive sufficiency, in our view, signifies: attachment to the Armed Forces of an unoffensive structure; a maximal limitation in them of the volume of strike systems; changes in their deployment on account of the fulfilling of strictly defensive tasks; lowering of the parameters of the mobilized deployment of the Armed Forces, and also of the volume of military production.
>
> . . . . These are not simply plans for the future. The share of the measures which can be adopted without damage to defenses in a unilateral fashion are already being realized. Not in one stroke, of course, since restructuring requires time, and careful analysis of the external situation.[255]

Lieutenant General Starodubov, head of a Soviet General Staff Academy delegation that visited the West German Bundeswehr Staff Academy in Hamburg in December 1989, is reported to have said that the Soviet unilateral policy moves extended to refusing the initiative at the beginning of a war. According to a Western report, he stated:

> [B]oth the theory and the practical part of military art are determined by the concept of a defensive strategy. In practice this means that the Soviets, at the outset of an aggression, deliberately assume the more difficult role of the defender, i.e., of reacting, while leaving military initiative to the aggressor. This effort to harmonize the political and the military/technical side has been carried out consistently through all levels of strategic and operative planning. The combination of offensive and defensive operations, which was admitted in the past for countering an aggression, has now been discarded.[256]

A March 1990 article in *Voennaia Mysl'* suggests that the unilateral reform initiative may have gone even further, beyond the idea of a defensive posture at the beginning of war, to the Khalkhin-Gol model of non-offensive restoration of the status quo ante bellum. Maj. Gen. A. S. Kulikov and Maj. Gen. A. D. Nefedov, writing on the effects of the Soviet adoption of the defensive doctrine, say, "The appendage to military doctrine of a . . . defensive directedness defined the status of the defense as the basic type of combat action, especially during the waging of the first defensive operations. Its goal is to repulse the invading aggressor, to inflict defeat on him, and to reconstruct the lost position."[257] While not specifically denying that this could continue on to include a major counteroffensive, the article does not mention such a possibility, nor does it make this planning conditional on mutual agreement. It thus seems to be breaking new ground in the General Staff debate. This argument follows from public statements made by Soviet military representatives at the CSCE Conference on Military Doctrines in Vienna in February 1990. According to a Western report of the meetings, "Lt. Gen. Burutin in his presentation renounced preventive or preemptive strikes on a probable enemy and established WTO boundaries as the limit of any offensive action. In addition, 'the entire system of operational and combat training of the leadership and the organs of control and forces in our Armed Forces has been corrected.' This resulted from a complete reanalysis of Soviet military science and led to a revision of Soviet military art."[258]

It is important to realize that no matter how defensive the Soviet and post-Soviet doctrines become, there are no apparent plans to forego force modernization with emerging technologies. In fact, many sources equate the new defensive doctrine with an emphasis on quality over quantity in weaponry, identifying improved quality with complexity of defensive systems.[259] It is not clear how these force modernization plans relate to plans for nonoffensive defense.

The overall level of confusion over just what defensive defense meant to the Soviet military is illustrated by an anecdote from the January-February CSCE meeting in Vienna on military doctrines. According to the report issued by Stephen R. Covington and James F. Holcomb, Soviet Chief of the General Staff Moiseev said at the meeting (this is not a direct quotation of Moiseev) that "The USSR will only 'respond' to aggression and conduct operations to restore the ante bellum status quo. Soviet forces will acquire a 'nonoffensive structure' which is not capable of conducting large-scale offensive operations. This non-offensive structure will demand limitations of strike systems, changes in the force groupings and their deployments, and a lowering of military activity in general.

Strategic plans are being reworked."[260] Later, Soviet Lieutenant General Markovskii expressed concern about FOFA, since it did not meet this criterion of supporting a nonoffensive structure. According to Holcomb and Covington:

> The U.S. delegation defined FOFA in strictly defensive terminology, that is, it would be used only after a violation of alliance boundaries. The Soviets and some [non-Soviet WTO representatives] expressed concern that the deep strike nature of the systems allows them to fire across state boundaries. The U.S. then quoted the Soviet definition of "counterpreparation" which includes preemption and deep strikes as elements and asked if the Soviets were prepared to change or renounce the counterpreparation [sic] under their defensive doctrine and asked how that was different from FOFA. The Soviets provided a rambling answer. . . . The FOFA issue appeared to evaporate as a result of this challenge.[261]

Soviet Foreign Minister Eduard Shevardnadze may have given an accurate summary of the situation when he asked rhetorically, "We have declared that our military doctrine was defensive, but have we implemented this doctrine?"[262]

Yet at the end of 1990, after German reunification and the de facto end of the Warsaw Pact, a hopeful sign appeared in the military press. A special issue of *Voennaia Mysl'* contained a draft Defense Ministry document entitled "On the Military Doctrine of the USSR."[263] In the section of the draft which discusses "the military-technical aspect of doctrine," that is, the part for which the General Staff professionals have had the greatest responsibility, two statements stand out. First, the draft says that in the event of aggression against the USSR, the chief tasks will be "its repulsion, the defense of sovereignty and the territorial integrity of the state, the creation of conditions for the speedy end of war and the reestablishment of a just and lasting peace."[264] There is nothing mentioned about the need for counterattacks, much less for victory over the aggressor. The final goal is restoration of the status quo ante bellum.

Second, the draft defines conventional military sufficiency as "that minimum quantity [of armaments and armed forces] which is necessary for the guaranteeing of a reliable defense, but not sufficient for the waging of large-scale offensive actions."[265] While not defining what the terms "reliable defense" or "large-scale offensive actions" mean, this statement at least confirms the direction which the General Staff officially promulgated at the 1990 Vienna meeting. A source who is very knowledgeable about work at *Voennaia Mysl'* told me in December 1990 that civilians did not participate in drawing up this draft, and that it was wholly a Defense Ministry document.

Some Western observers are bound to treat this draft document as a ruse intended for Western audiences. David M. Glantz warns of the possibility that the General Staff will use supposedly defensive structures as a cloak to hide true offensive preparations, as the Soviets did in their 1945 Manchurian operation.[266] And Mikhail Tsypkin has recently written convincingly about the Soviet military institution's ingrained habit of lying—to Westerners, to Soviet political leaders, and to its own employees.[267] Certainly it is impossible to prove that the Soviet military's thinking really changed.

But perhaps the best evidence that this draft document in particular is not mere camouflage for more sinister General Staff planning is the fact that it attracted criticism from so senior a source as Marshal of the Armored Forces O. Losik, in a review article in *Krasnaia Zvezda*, the daily newspaper of the Defense Ministry. Losik attacked the draft's alleged "passivity," and championed both counteroffensives based on the Kursk model and the retention of parity with an untrustworthy Western adversary.[268]

If the draft document were really a ruse, one would think that Western analysts would be made to feel more certain about Soviet intentions if Defense Ministry unanimity about its value had been maintained. Theoretically, of course, the critique could be part of an overarching campaign, designed to make the draft look more real by criticizing it. However, this would demand a degree of cohesion and planning from the General Staff which did not seem to be evident anywhere else in Soviet society during 1991.

Furthermore, a mid-1991 analysis in the General Staff journal reaffirmed that counteroffensives "are thought of as a means for reestablishing the position occupied before the beginning of the aggressor's attack; a transition to ground forces activity on his territory is not foreseen."[269] A significant group of General Staff officers saw the counteroffensive in defensive defense terms.

Thus the proper conclusion to draw seems to be that powerful representatives of the General Staff and Defense Ministry, those who determined official policy stances, were taking into account the arguments of civilian scholars about the value of truly defensive planning with restoration of the status quo ante bellum as the ultimate military goal. This was not inevitable, even with the demise of the Warsaw Pact. Operational planning within Soviet borders could still have been based on quick seizure of the counteroffensive, with defeat of the aggressor as the ultimate goal. Thus, such planning does not seem to have been forced on the General Staff by events. A significant debate continued among General Staff officers about whether or not such innovation was a good idea, even as the Soviet Union drew to a close.[270] (Especially around the time of the

August 1991 coup attempt, offense proponents sent articles to the *Voennaia Mysl'* typesetter.) Yet civilian influence in setting the General Staff's agenda seems to have reached an unprecedented level in the post-Stalin era, and it has done so by stressing cooperation and the building of community rather than confrontation or terror.

Civil-Military Relations under Gorbachev

While it is clear that military statements about the meaning of defensive doctrine have changed over time, and while it is clear that one of the original engines for this change was the Western adoption of FOFA and ALB, it might still be argued that this demonstrates nothing except Gorbachev's control over the military. Perhaps Gorbachev faced a hostile military organization, and used the power of personnel appointments to gain the upper hand.

There is no question that Gorbachev did in fact made a plethora of personnel changes in the military. According to Jacob Kipp, a large turnover in General Staff and Ministry of Defense personnel began in the summer of 1986, and the new generation "owes its rise to Gorbachev's patronage."[271] Gorbachev did not undertake this task all alone; Minister of Defense Yazov was his pointman. According to Alexander Rahr, Gorbachev praised Yazov during the 1989 Supreme Soviet Committee on Defense and State Security hearings about Yazov's reappointment to his post: "Gorbachev said that Yazov had performed very well 'in cleaning up the defense ministry, the general staff, and other organizations connected with the ministry.' Gorbachev identified the system of patronage by which generals gave posts and favors to their friends and protégés as one of the armed forces' major problems, saying that he had received many letters from junior officers who complained about the practice."[272] According to Dale Herspring, there was almost a complete turnover in top-level Soviet officers by the end of 1988.[273] Eighty percent of the officer corps is now under the age of forty,[274] and Soviet military pension expenditures increased by almost 5 percent between 1989 and 1990 in order to pay off the early retirees who were cut from the personnel roster as a result of Gorbachev's unilateral force reductions.[275]

However, while it is clear that the newer personnel are reformists, it is not clear that their reformism originally extended to doctrinal or arms control issues. Most of the new appointees were technocrats who desired qualitative improvements in Soviet weapons and troop skills; they may have been indifferent (or even hostile) to doctrinal reform efforts.[276] While such an influx of young officers to top positions and a high level of personnel turnover is bound to bring in people who are receptive to innovative thinking, it did not necessarily bring in people who already accepted the need for doctrinal change.

Thus personnel turnover was probably a contributing factor to doctrinal innovation in the Soviet military under Gorbachev, but not the major explanation for it.

One more question remains to be answered: has doctrinal change in the Soviet Union been accompanied by a high level of civil-military animosity, as was the case under Khrushchev? There is no question that the moderate political reform coalition's views on doctrine and strategy greatly threatened traditional military interests. The defense budget and deployments were drastically cut; military autonomy in the military-technical aspects of doctrinal decision-making was taken away; and the old offensive doctrine was replaced by a defensive one. However, Gorbachev tried to soften that threat as much as possible by including the military in policy decisions. The best example of this is that the General Staff seems to have been included in the process of working out the unilateral force reductions announced by Gorbachev in December 1988. Statements that the military played a large role in analyzing the options that Gorbachev considered and put into effect appear in numerous military publications.[277] According to Peter Schweizer, Gen. G. A. Stefanovskiy stated that the troop cuts were "a General Staff initiative," and that the military rationale of quality over quantity was primary in the decision.[278] Certain high-ranking military officers later privately denied that such participation actually took place;[279] they claimed that those military officers who stated that the policy was designed cooperatively were merely trying to calm public opinion. However, given the impact of those unilateral cuts on the Soviet officer corps, high-ranking military officers would have good reason now to deny that they were involved in the decision; there is no housing or employment for many of the laid-off officers.

As Stephen M. Meyer has noted, Gorbachev also tried to give military officers perquisites, including such things as restoration of the title of Marshal of the Soviet Union (given to Yazov in late April 1990), which contribute to the appearance of military prestige.[280] There can be no question that the Soviet military nonetheless by 1990 felt less integrated into Soviet society than it ever had before. The biggest challenge at that point was no longer doctrinal change, but rather the collapse of the Soviet military economy and the breakdown of general societal respect for the military profession. The Soviet officer corps as a whole must have seen the military as an institution under seige.

Nonetheless, the fact that the Soviet military entered a state of flux may have made it easier for the new concepts of defensive defense to be institutionalized. As the coherence of the officer corps was weakened by social conflict, and as the military's whole basis for offensive planning crumbled, the old doctrinal concepts became obviously unworkable. According to a report by the U.S. House Armed Services Committee Defense Policy Panel, all of the experts in Soviet military analysis who were called to testify in hearings in April 1990 agreed that "using Soviet forces outside of Soviet borders would be very difficult, if not impossible in some instances."[281] Stephen Meyer in particular testified that "he could not 'imagine how any Soviet military planner could plan' to attack Western Europe or retake Eastern Europe"; John Hines stated that "It would be a relatively ineffective force and essentially one I think any serious commander would not want to take into an offensive operation."[282]

The breakdown in Soviet military order meant that the old doctrine lost its meaning. An alternative doctrine was (and still is) clearly needed. The fact that some civilians, such as Kokoshin, are respected by military officers, both for their expertise and for their military sympathies, may mean that their alternative scenarios for nonoffensive defense in Europe become the only attractive choice in the midst of chaos. Even if the military as a whole feels itself to be under attack by the civilian reformers as a group, the attempt to build civil-military bridges on the particular issue of doctrine may pay off in the long run.

Gorbachev and his advisers were repeatedly verbally attacked by military officers on virtually every political decision made in his later years in office, from the loss of Eastern Europe to attempts to reform the economy. Yet one political decision does not seem to have been subjected to such unified political attack by military officers, and that was the decision to pursue defensive defense doctrine. Gorbachev's doctrinal innovation effort thus had a very different conclusion from the one faced by Khrushchev in the early 1960s.

Conclusion

The hypotheses from chapter 1 that are relevant to this case explain the Soviet reaction to FOFA and ALB very well. There was a discussion which occurred solely within the military at first, and which showed some signs of debate and disagreement. This discussion nonetheless flowed generally in the direction of reacting to the new Western threat with a slight change in Soviet doctrine and weapons development, a change that the West would probably find even more threatening than the policy it was consciously reacting against with its own doctrinal innovations. If the military had been left to itself, the competition in offensive doctrines could have continued ad infinitum.

Instead, Gorbachev and his reform coalition (perhaps continuing the efforts of Andropov) helped to empower a new set of actors to make contributions to the discussion on doctrinal change. These new actors and their political benefactors were probably moved to act by a combination of motives: a real desire to see the military competition in Europe reach a level of greater stability, because of their own fear of the consequences of war; a desire to find a way to cut the military budget without harming state security, in order to put more resources into social and consumer welfare programs and high technology development; and a desire to break the military's monopoly on technical information in the Soviet Union. These actors brought in new ideas from the Western peace movements, and argued in favor of these ideas in many cases with their own hard-earned technical expertise.

The fact that these ideas, shared by scholars from a variety of nations, seemed to have an impact on Soviet military planning means that this might be one area where "epistemic communities" can have a policy impact, where interacting groups of experts or scientists who share policy-relevant ideas can see those ideas implemented.[283]

Arguments about the role of ideas in fostering change in the international system are strongest when it can be shown that the natural interests of states would not lead them in the same direction as these ideas pointed. In the case at hand, a deceleration of the international military cooperation does seem to have been in obvious Soviet state economic interests. Change in state policy might have occurred even in the absence of the academics.

However, such innovation does not seem to have been in the interests of the Soviet military as an institution; and therefore ideas, combined with the new political empowerment of experts with differing opinions, may be the critical variable explaining change in Soviet military doctrine. A Khrushchev-type leader, who suddenly announced (without prior consultation or warning, and without arguments that might appeal to a military mindset) that Soviet forces were being withdrawn to within state borders and that offensive planning must stop immediately, would likely have been ignored at best or hounded out of office at worst. Most military officers did not support the August 1991 coup attempt against Gorbachev. (Defense Minister Marshal Yazov's participation in the putsch, and the seeming support given by Chief of the General Staff Moiseev and former Chief of the General Staff Akhromeev, mistakenly led many Americans and Russians to believe that it was a military coup attempt. However, the individuals at the top of this effort did not receive support from most high-ranking officers.)

Not all of the newly empowered expert actors have been accepted into the defense policy community, and even those who were have not necessarily seen their ideas ensconced in military-technical policy yet. However, the new actors definitely contributed to making the discussion of how to react to the Western shift more innovative, and both the actors and the ideas clearly gained respect with time.

Partly this is due to personnel turnover in the original policy community. A more innovative body of military officers has achieved a higher level of power than has been true in decades in the Soviet Union; presumably, these younger, more innovative officers are more open to change than are their older and more organizationally established colleagues. Partly, the increased respect is due to the fact that the civilian scholars have sacrificed some of their ideals in the short run, in order to gain military support in the long run.

Policy community expansion involves mutual compromise. Konstantin Pleshakov identified in the Soviet reform process something he calls the "Zhukovskii dilemma." In 1826, the poet Vasilii Andreevich Zhukovskii was offered a choice: he could continue absolute allegiance to his friends martyred in 1825 in the revolutionary Decembrist movement, and go on with the war against tsarist repression; or he could "abandon the cause of his life" and accept a position as tutor to the heir of the Russian throne. He chose the latter, in the hopes that he could "harmonize" the future Tsar Aleksandr II to the notion of reform, and accomplish change through evolution.[284] (Zhukovskii's measure of success may be that Aleksandr II has gone down in history as the reformer-tsar who abolished serfdom, although many Western scholars believe reform was forced on Aleksandr against his will by historical circumstances.) According to Pleshakov, "Extremism . . . will have only one result—chaos. . . . We do not need new Decembrists, we need Zhukovskiis."[285]

It is too soon to say for sure whether or not the civilian Zhukovskiis will ultimately be successful. We know that Khrushchev's extremism was not. Statements by some senior Soviet military officers on doctrinal issues now seem to be moving closer to the civilian scholars' positions with time. So far, the expanded policy community seems to be taking root; and on this issue at least, an evolutionary "harmonizing" approach appears to be working. We will only know for sure once Russia finds its answer to the many current dilemmas of military reform.

6

Doctrine, Innovation, and Competition

Summary of Results

As the three case studies demonstrate, each of the hypotheses outlined in chapter 1 contributes to a correct understanding of the process of military doctrinal competition and innovation in the Soviet Union. Each of them highlights particular aspects of the historical problem that have often received insufficient attention in Western analyses.

Foreign Threats and Innovations

Hypothesis #1 states: "Military organizations are likely to develop innovative doctrines on their own, in the absence of civilian intervention, when they interpret a foreign doctrinal shift as a threat to the success of their current war plans." The Soviet reaction to the Western adoption of the Flexible Response doctrine in the 1960s is probably the best example of a case where this was so. Innovators within the Soviet military recognized that the United States was moving away from a strategy for future war in Europe that relied solely on nuclear weapons use, and they believed that the new Western doctrine had operational effects for future battle. Specifically, they believed that the first hours or days of war would see only conventional weapons use by the Western side. As a result, these Soviet military innovators pushed for the development of a Soviet conventional option, more useful than a purely nuclear doctrine would be for at least the opening stage of a future European war. The new doctrine was thought at a minimum to give the Soviet military new battlefield opportunities, for less risky destruction of enemy theater nuclear weapons, with less cost to Soviet troops and command and control capabilities. At a maximum, some officers apparently thought that the ravages of nuclear warfare could be avoided entirely. The effects of the innovation became noticeable for the first time in the late 1960s, when Soviet military exercises and war games in the European theater began to experiment with conventional scenarios, and when the Soviet military industry began to develop significantly new conventional and dual-use weapons. The innovation probably reached its fulfillment in the mid- to late 1970s, when Western analysts came to agree that the Soviet military intended to use its conventional option to prevent a Western resort to tactical or theater nuclear weapons in the event of a military conflict in Europe.

In the case of the Soviet reaction to the Schlesinger Doctrine, there is insufficient evidence to know for sure whether any change in Soviet military operational doctrine resulted from the U.S. shift to limited strategic nuclear war–planning. We simply don't have access to open-source data about Soviet strategic targeting plans, and about any changes that might have been instituted in them. It does seem that the Soviet military may have decided at some point in the mid- to late 1970s that a strike on the Soviet homeland would not necessarily result in a massive counterattack on the United States, and this may have been tied to the Western doctrinal shift. But the discussion in semiclassified military sources indicates that no one seemed to believe that there was much chance of limiting strategic nuclear warfare permanently, once it had begun.

The Soviet military's reaction in this case is notable because it was so muted. This Western shift was not discussed as often or in such great detail as were the other two cases studied here. There are a variety of possible explanations for both the low level of discussion and for the ambiguity of the Soviet response to the shift; perhaps the most convincing is that the General Staff was unable to reach agreement about how to interpret the Western shift, and thus was incapable of formulating a coherent response. In the semiclassified Soviet military press, disagreement continued through the late 1970s about whether the Schlesinger Doctrine really meant that the U.S. planned limited, warning strategic strikes on Soviet territory, or whether instead the new doctrine was merely a cover for U.S. massive counterforce strike plans. The greatest problem for the researcher in this case is the Soviet military's obsession with secrecy; the policy process is cloudy, and we must rely on scant data.

In the case of the Soviet military's reaction to AirLand Battle (ALB) and Follow-on Forces Attack (FOFA), officers succeeded in altering their doctrine to take account of new Western counteroffensive capabilities and intentions, both by improving their offensive and counteroffensive abilities and planning, and by further developing plans for the possible use of a strategic defensive. Yet no officers seemed to believe on their own, before civilians entered the policy community, that a complete revision of the Soviet conventional offensive doctrine for war in Europe was necessary. Given that such revision would damage their institutional interests in preserving resources and offensive planning, the absence of radical innovation among the Soviet officer corps in this case is not surprising.

The overall conclusion to draw about this hypothesis is that reactive innovations are not implemented frequently or easily by the military; however, when military officers do make doctrinal innovations on their own, they can have significant impact on international military competitions. Therefore, Barry R. Posen's discussion of doctrinal innovation is incomplete. It is probably true that innovation within military organizations is rare. However, militaries do not only innovate when civilians intervene in the doctrinal process, or when the state or one of its client states loses in war.[1] Militaries sometimes innovate in response to threatening innovations in the future war plans of their potential enemies. Even when true reactive innovations do not occur, military officers are basically reactive to foreign threats; when foreign military doctrines change, military officers often change their own doctrines in response.

Organizational Interests

Hypothesis #2 states: "Military officers will prefer innovations which augment military resources and autonomy." Both the Soviet military's reactions to Flexible Response and to AirLand Battle/FOFA provide solid evidence in support of this hypothesis. In both cases, Soviet military officers chose policies that demanded further development of new weapons and technologies, and which preserved the offensive élan of the Soviet army. In the Flexible Response case, the offensive spirit was furthered by plans to use the Western doctrine against Western forces; Soviet troops would use the conventional pause to destroy Western nuclear weapons in the theater, and thereby would force the West to choose between fighting a completely conventional war or escalation to strategic nuclear weapons use. Soviet forces would seize the initiative that the Western pause allowed them. In the FOFA and ALB case, even as the Soviet military developed its plans for a strategic defense in case of surprise attack, officers emphasized that the counteroffensive was necessary for victory, and that victory was the eventual aim.

The Schlesinger Doctrine reaction, however, provides us with another anomaly. By reacting to the Western shift with a development of Soviet limited war–fighting capabilities, the Soviet military could have lobbied for improvement of strategic C^3I capabilities, an area where the USSR lagged behind the United States. Because the Soviet military had, at that time, a virtual monopoly of information in the Soviet Union on weapons and their usage, adding another option to Soviet war plans would not have significantly decreased the military's autonomy relative to the political leadership. (The Soviet case was thus not parallel to the American case, where Defense Department civilians had to force a change in SIOP plans on the military.) In fact, the addition of a new option to the Soviet version of the SIOP would have given the Soviet military more freedom for maneuver and initiative in war. Without such an option, future war could force the Soviet Union to choose between surrender and holocaust after a very limited strategic nuclear strike by the United States. Given the existence of American nuclear submarines and bombers, the Soviet military could not have been sure of destroying American military potential in a retaliatory counterforce strike. The absence of a more limited option thus left the Soviet Union vulnerable, as retired Col. L. S. Semeiko seemed to recognize.[2] Here, as in the discussion of the previous hypothesis, there is insufficient information to reach a conclusion about why a Soviet military lobbying effort seems not to have been made.

In the absence of information, it is not possible to describe the limits which the Schlesinger Doctrine reaction case suggests should be placed on Hypothesis #2. Perhaps strategic nuclear weapons are "different"; maybe the Soviet military believes that civilian decision-making is more allowable on strategic doctrinal questions. Or perhaps it is merely that the General Staff could not achieve the consensus necessary for a lobbying effort.

What is clear is that Hypothesis #2 held for two out of the three cases.

Domestic Threats

Hypothesis #3 states: "Military officers will react to domestic threats to their organizational health and autonomy first, before reacting to foreign threats to state security." Only one of the case studies examined here unfolded in a context where this hypothesis is relevant; Khrushchev threatened military interests, but Brezhnev, for the most part, did not. While Gorbachev's policies certainly unleashed a social situation that threatened military interests, he tried to prevent the alienation of the military as much as possible. At any rate, there were not any cases of threatening Western doctrinal innovations during the Gorbachev era which could be used to test this hypothesis.

Instead, we are left with only one case where a Western doctrinal shift occurred simultaneously with a domestic threat to Soviet military autonomy and resources, and that is the case of the reaction to Flexible Response. It is quite clear that in this one case the hypothesis held. Some Soviet officers explicitly said that the Soviet consideration of limited and conventional war was sidetracked by debates over the use of nuclear weapons in war, debates that were launched by Khrushchev's declaration that the outcome of all future wars would be determined primarily by nuclear rocket weapons.

However, from an objective perspective, it would be premature to decide that this strong hypothesis is necessarily correct for all cases. This hypothesis declares that a political threat to military autonomy is not only *related* to delays in reaction to foreign threats, but that domestic threats are a *sufficient condition* for such a delay (in other words, given a domestic threat to the military, a delay in reaction *will* occur). While nothing in this study disproves this hypothesis, the hypothesis should be considered a subject for future research; the support of one case study does not make the hypothesis definitive.

Debate in the Policy Community

Hypothesis #4 states: "Policy innovations will be institutionalized slowly within the expert policy community; discussion and debate will permeate the community." All three case studies follow this pattern (although the reaction to the Schlesinger Doctrine is again an anomaly, because the public discussion of the reaction to the Western shift was carried on almost solely by those officers and retired officers who were associated with the academic institutes in Moscow). In all three cases, debating positions can be traced.

In the first case, the Soviet reaction to Flexible Response, the major question was whether, and for how long, conflict in Europe could be limited to conventional weapons use. At least four positions in this debate were visible: those who said it could not be limited; those who said it might start in a limited fashion but would inevitably escalate to nuclear use relatively quickly; those who said merely that conventional conflict between nuclear powers *might* escalate (implying that it might not); and those who expressed confidence that the West would not use nuclear weapons. This debate continued even after policy shifts began to be implemented in the Soviet Union. Thus, perhaps Gen. Makhmut Gareev's analysis (outlined in chapter 2) is correct: bold decisions about doctrine may sometimes be made before a consensus has been reached in the General Staff about their benefits.[3]

In the second case, the Soviet reaction to the Schlesinger Doctrine, there seems to have been debate about two issues. First was the question of how to interpret the Schlesinger Doctrine: as a new doctrine of limited strategic strikes made for political warning purposes, or as merely a new attempt to justify U.S. massive counterforce strikes on Soviet territory. Second, two positions seemed to be held on the question of strategic warfare in general. One stated that it was impossible to keep strategic nuclear war limited, and therefore the Soviet Union should respond to a limited strategic nuclear attack with a crushing blow; the other, in contrast, implied that while it would be *difficult* to keep strategic nuclear war limited, immediate escalation to massive strikes might not be necessary. It is not clear whether either debate ever had any policy impact, although by the early 1980s the old declaratory formula, about strikes on Soviet territory leading to immediate crushing blows on the enemy, disappeared.

In the third case, the Soviet reaction to ALB and FOFA, the positions held within the policy community shifted as the community membership itself shifted. Originally, before civilian scholars became involved, two basic positions were taken, with most officers falling somewhere in the middle. One held that much more attention had to be paid to the possible necessity of waging an unexpected strategic defensive operation; the other held that the best reaction to the Western shift was an augmentation of Soviet offensive capabilities and planning. Once civilian scholars entered the community, a number of new issues arose. Some issues were procedural; for example, positions varied on whether civilians belonged in the defense policy community, and if so, in what capacity. Other issues were substantive, and revolved around the problem of defensive defense in doctrine. A variety of positions arose on this issue. Some said that it was a new concept, affecting military-technical developments; others said it was an old concept that reflected only political goals. Some said that it necessitated only the removal of plans for surprise attack offensives at the beginning of war; others said that it meant that counteroffensives had to be limited to expelling the enemy from inside one's own borders. Some said that it involved only mutual doctrine shifts between East and West; others said that it should be implemented unilaterally. Many of these positions criss-crossed each other, and increased the variety of possible policy preferences expressed.

In each of these cases discussion and debate were real and prolonged; in no case did the primary issue seem to be a division along service interest lines. While in the latter case there is evidence of a civilian/military split on the issues, especially early on, the split does not seem to have been either complete or eternal.

Community Building vs. Interest Acrimony

Hypothesis #5 states: "An expansion of the policy community, to include different types of actors, can result in a new type of reactive innovation to a foreign doctrinal shift." The first case, the Soviet reaction to Flexible Response, demonstrates that even a significant change within the existing policy community (in this case, a significant number of promotions and retirements of officers) seemed to be associated with a willingness to innovate, and to accept a reactive shift in doctrine. The third case, the Soviet reaction to FOFA and ALB, demonstrates the impact that new entrants into the community can have.

The strongest lesson of the third case in this regard is that new entrants into the community, if they are to be accepted into the existing community and respected by it, must attempt to build bridges with that community. It is such bridge-building efforts that primarily distinguish the doctrinal innovation efforts of the Gorbachev era from those of the Khrushchev era. Those civilians who seem to have had the most policy impact on conventional force planning in the Gorbachev era were those who accepted military officers' demand that policy be made by technical experts; they tried to make themselves experts, and they tried to use the military scientists available to them (namely, the retired officers working at the Moscow institutes) to add legitimacy to their work.

It is probable that these efforts could not have succeeded as much as they did without high-level political support; bridge-building alone might not have convinced the General Staff to take civilian scholars seriously. Civilians had to be institutionally empowered, as well. They were granted policy responsibility, and this forced military officers to deal with them.

However, this did not force military officers to accept them or to work with them, rather than against them. A repeat of Khrushchev-era doctrinal acrimony was possible. Only with a combination of expertise and respect for the existing community could civilians be accepted by the community. Because the instincts of institutional preservation are strong, new entrants into the community will have greater success in the long run if they threaten existing institutions as little as possible.

From these five hypotheses a new theoretical approach to the question of doctrinal innovation and international competition has been built. This approach can be generalized and applied to other foreign policy problems. It can be summed up in three postulates:

1. Institutional and organizational interests constrain beliefs and behavior, but do not determine beliefs or behavior. Individuals and their ideas matter.[4]

2. External competition motives and internal political and organizational motives coexist within individuals and organizations, and these motives influence each other. Institutional perspectives color reactions to foreign threats; foreign influences change institutional perspectives. A key example of this is that Soviet academic scholars used the arguments of West European peace movements to counter the Soviet military's viewpoint on reactions to FOFA and ALB. Foreign policy-making is a "two-level game."[5]

3. Policy outcomes are determined not only by interest groups, but also by policy communities that extend through and beyond interest groups. Communities can create constellations of interest and support around innovative policies, whereas simple interest group competition tends to leave the policy losers alienated and determined to undo what has been done. Therefore, foreign policy reform efforts will have the greatest chance of successful implementation if they are developed within communities that encompass the most powerful interest groups.

Beyond the Soviet Example

It might be argued that the case study results concerning military doctrine innovation and competition apply only to the Soviet example. Obviously, the approach used here could be tested by in-depth case studies which focus on other states. This is a task for other area specialists. However, the process can be started here with one "mini-case study" which has already been used by a Soviet reformist author as a comparison to the Gorbachev-era Soviet situation.[6] Andrei Kortunov wrote that Soviet reform efforts should draw on the lessons provided by Jack Snyder's analysis of French preparations for World War I in 1914.[7]

France before World War I

In his case study of the development of French military doctrine before World War I, Snyder makes it clear that French officers did not innovate in reaction to what was happening in the doctrine of their potential enemy, Germany. If that sort of reactive relationship had existed, Snyder argues, the French doctrine would have been a lot more attuned to the reality of German planning. Instead, the French command planned for a type of attack that was unlikely to occur. Snyder argues that the French army almost consciously misperceived German doctrine, in order to justify a doctrine that the military institution preferred.[8]

Nonetheless, Snyder demonstrates that the French military as an institution did formulate innovative doctrinal policies on its own. These innovations changed the tenor of the doctrine from basically defensive (with a strong counteroffensive element) to basically offensive (where seizing the initiative from the start was the key). Snyder argues that although the loss of territory to Germany in 1870 was an impetus for minor reforms in this direction, the major reforms occurred because of an institutional interest in fighting off a civilian threat.[9] Thus, doctrinal innovation came about not because of losses in battle, and not because civilians forced it on the military, but in reaction to civilian attempts at control. While this type of innovation does not match the types that occurred in the Soviet case, it does indicate that militaries sometimes innovate from within in order to stave off a threat (this time, a domestic threat rather than a foreign one).

Snyder demonstrates that one of the major reasons for the French officer corps' support of an offensive doctrine was that it necessitated a large, active, and continuously trained army. The French staff wanted to avoid civilian attempts to civilianize the army and to make it an army of reservists, who would be called up only when an invasion seemed imminent. As Snyder states, the proponents of a reservist army recognized that "French reservists were best suited for defensive operations. Consequently, if people could be convinced that offensive operations were the sine qua non of success on the battlefield, the professional army would be saved."[10] Thus the French staff reacted to the increasing possibility of a German attack by building up army numbers and autonomy. The French military demonstrated its concern for standard military institutional interests.

In regard to whether civilian threats to military autonomy delay military reactions to foreign innovations, Snyder makes an even stronger argument than the present study does: he claims that domestic threats to the organizational health and autonomy of the French army did not merely become the first priority for the command staff, they became the *only* priority. Reaction to the foreign threat (in this case, German plans for using reservists to extend the line of their offensive into France) was lost because the military concentrated so heavily on the domestic threat. The domestic threat blinded the French staff to foreign innovation.

Snyder does illustrate that support for a purely offensive doctrine was not held by the entire French command, and that in fact the military community was suffused by debate over the issue. In some cases, the defensive orientation was preferred by officers who supported the efforts of republican politicians to civilianize the army.[11] In other cases, the old defensive/counteroffensive doctrine was preferred by officers who were themselves older; they were steeped in the old way of thinking, and believed (as it turns out, correctly) that the new ideas were foolhardy denials of tried and true doctrinal precepts.[12] The debate over the doctrinal shift began in the 1880s, but did not begin to affect war planning until 1911, at which time a personnel change in the General Staff leadership changed the balance of internal power in favor of the offensively oriented "young turks."[13] In other words, innovation in policy did not come suddenly, and when it did come, individuals and their ideas mattered.

Snyder presents no evidence that the civilian leadership in France attempted to create an expanded policy community, using cooperative methods, in the early part of the twentieth century. Instead, those civilians who were opposed to the military's way of operating attacked the military from without. As Snyder describes it:

> The new government concluded that the old formula for civil-military entente had been proved a failure. It set out to "republicanize" the French officer corps by direct interference in appointments, promotions, and war college admissions. The network of Masonic lodges was used to check on the political opinions of candidates for promotion. At the same time, the length of service was reduced to two years, officers were told to educate their recruits in nonmilitary

subjects, and traditional disciplinary powers were curtailed. . . . Under such onerous conditions, the French army needed its organizational ideology to defend itself against further encroachments and, if possible, to regain lost ground.[14]

In other words, the French government approached the military in a way that was similar to the way that Khrushchev approached the Soviet military in the early 1960s. Decisions were taken suddenly and without apparent discussion, and no attempt was made to empower a set of expert civilians who could build bridges toward those in the military command hierarchy. If such attempts had been made, the intelligence failures Snyder notes concerning German developments might have been avoided. The result could have been a doctrinal innovation in a different direction; rather than favoring a new, purely offensive style of planning, using a standing army that was as large as possible, the doctrine could have changed within the old defensive/counteroffensive framework, using the new reservist planning style that civilians preferred.

Andrei Kortunov has used Snyder's study to argue in favor of the development of independent civilian doctrinal expertise in the Soviet Union. However, Kortunov does not draw the lesson from the French case which the present study suggests is most crucial for the Soviet experience. To expand the policy community, not only must independent experts be educated and empowered; they also must use their ideas in a way that does not cut military interests to the quick. Civilians alone, without military acquiescence, cannot force a new strategy on the army. If commanding officers do not approve of the new strategy, they can undercut it from within. Therefore, bridges between the army and civilians must be built.

The French case does not demonstrate that militaries innovate in reaction to foreign threats. My hypothesis on reactivity is not relevant here. However, the hypotheses concerning military institutional interests, policy debates, and policy communities do shed light on the French case. Military institutional interests can overwhelm reasoned debate within the military about doctrinal shifts, especially if civilians attack those interests, instead of trying to build an expanded policy community. If bridges had been built with the older traditionalists in the French army, perhaps the French would not have fared so badly in 1914.

Postscript

After the Cold War

THE PRESENT STUDY demonstrates that the competitive bipolar international atmosphere of the 1950s through the 1980s had a significant impact on Soviet doctrinal innovation attempts. As the United States innovated, the Soviet military was concerned to keep up its end of the competition, not only in weapons development, but also in the doctrines that explained how those weapons would be used.

Now a new international atmosphere has emerged. Leaders of both sides in the competition have declared that the Cold War is over, and that each side no longer considers the other an enemy. Through various forums, NATO has actively drawn Russia into what has been called a "partnership" on defense policy management.[1] What impact will this changed international atmosphere have on the process of doctrinal competition? Will Russia and the United States leave such competition permanently in the past? Will a new doctrinal opponent emerge for the United States?

The hypotheses of chapter 1 lead to the prediction that the military organizations involved in the Cold War competition will want to retain their resources and institutional prestige in the new environment. In the new international political situation, military budgets and the importance of the military as an institution are under challenge by the public and by politicians in both the NATO countries and the former Soviet Union. Military organizations define their professional missions in terms of defending the state from foreign threats. Therefore, it is predicted that most officers will continue to see the external environment as threatening.

Innovators in all states are likely to view the changed international situation as a "policy window," an opportunity for them to jump into the fray with their ideas, and to change the dominant community's paradigm. These innovators are likely to be of two types: civilians who want to redirect budget priorities away from military expenditures, and maverick strategists (either civilians or officers) who believe that their doctrinal ideas will improve state security. In order to alter the dominant paradigm, these innovators will either have to change the power structure standing behind the old way of thinking, or convince the existing community that the new ideas are better. Barring a sudden replacement of personnel, any shift to a new paradigm is likely to be a protracted process, as the old policy community will resist change. A paradigm shift will not result when only scholars, or even elected officials, declare that the Cold

War is over and that new international relations alternatives must be found. It will only succeed when it has penetrated the thinking of those who are responsible for formulating doctrine, and who are capable of creating and implementing specific new policies which further the new paradigm.

The demise of the old Soviet governmental and military structures, and the advancement of new (presumably pro-reform) military personnel in Russia, may mean that the Russian military institution will be in a better position to adapt to a changed environment than the U.S. defense policy community will be. President Boris Yeltsin's April 1992 elevation of policy entrepreneur Andrei Kokoshin to a senior position in the Russian Defense Ministry may especially aid this transition. Kokoshin is likely to continue to work to build bridges between political leaders and military officers. Military officers' feelings of alienation are thus likely to be kept in check as much as is possible, given the radical nature of Russian reforms. The simple fact that practically no facet of military officers' lives in Russia remains unchanged may mean that change in the international environment is accepted, too. Since top-level changeover and radical reform in the defense policy community in the United States has remained limited thus far, the Pentagon may be more likely to retain its enemy images for a longer period than the Russian defense policy community does.[2]

The theoretical model presented here would further predict that if the old paradigm becomes discredited within the group responsible for doctrinal policy, military organizations will adopt a new threat-paradigm in its place. As members of the institution responsible for maintaining state security from foreign threats, military officers see their professional mission in terms of external threats. Most likely, since military organizations prefer to maintain a sense of predictability and control over events, the new threat will be seen to be of a specific type and scope. The old specific menace will be replaced by a new one. As soon as a threat is specified, a military opponent is created; and as soon as military opponents face each other, competitions in doctrinal concepts are once again likely. Many writers of American editorial columns have postulated that the end of the Cold War mission is one of the reasons why the U.S. military and the American defense industry have latched on to future Third World missions so quickly as a source of future threat to the United States. While the U.S. military leadership did not appear eager to begin fighting in the Gulf War, it does seem keen now to convince politicians that a hypothetical Third World dictatorship enemy demands continuing high outlays in the U.S. defense budget. The Russian military, too, seems newly concerned with potential threats from its non-European neighbors, particularly in Central Asia and the Middle East.

Two alternatives not covered by this scenario are possible. First, a state controlled by innovators could choose to force a shift of its defense policy paradigm without including the military institution in the process. The results in such a case would parallel those in pre–World War I France or Khrushchev's Soviet Union: the military would become centered on containing the domestic threat to its corporate identity, and might neglect its external competition role. Such results seem unlikely in any NATO member state. Military officers in most Western democracies are well integrated into broad policy communities, and accustomed enough to political intervention into military policy, that there is very little military turf to protect against outsiders. These results also seem unlikely under present conditions in Russia, where significant actors among those currently empowered in the civilian defense policy community are arguing for moderation and bridge-building in relation to military policy, and are trying to avoid alienation of the officer corps. However, if radical Russian reformers were to become powerful enough to unseat the more moderate bridge-builders, and were to decide that the military institution per se was an enemy, then senior officers could wage a pitched bureaucratic battle that included doctrinal issues.

One factor which would mitigate this civil-military split in the Russian case is the fact that the officer corps has become politicized, and thus divided.[3] The end result of a concerted civilian attack on the military would therefore depend on two things: the quality of relations between the civilians and the reformist officers, and the relative power of the reformist officers within the military organization. Sufficient evidence is not yet available for confident predictions on this point.

The second possible alternate scenario would be one where policy community innovators are marginalized by a conservative political backlash. Such a split is again unlikely in any NATO member state, where defense policy communities are fairly broad and well established, and change in one direction or another comes slowly. It would be possible in Russia, if hardline ideologues became powerful enough to unseat the reform coalition now arguing for international economic integration. The events of the past several years make such an effort seem unlikely to succeed. Despite concerted conservative and reactionary pushes against Soviet and Russian reforms in fall 1990, summer 1991, and spring 1992, Gorbachev and Yeltsin both consistently managed to emerge with at least moderate reform packages relatively intact. Even if a conservative overthrow of the leadership did succeed, it is not clear that it would result in the rebirth of the Cold War in Europe. It is unlikely now that Russia could marshall sufficient resources—economic, political, or geographical—to pose a threat to Central or East European feelings of security. (Most likely, the U.S.-Russia strategic nuclear competition would flourish under this scenario, however, since the Russian strategic nuclear arsenal would regain its menacing aspect in Western eyes.) However, it is possible under this scenario that the Russian military institution would continue to find the West militarily threatening, and would therefore maintain its reactive mission. If this occurred, Russia would be marginalized in the international economic system, since outsiders would view it as a distrustful (and therefore, untrustworthy) militaristic state. Given the current economic hardships of Russian life, and given the relatively high level of education and sophistication of much of Russia's urban population, it is unlikely that the state could maintain such a Stalinist regression for long.

The current Russian political situation is volatile enough that trying to predict which if any of these three scenarios will win out is somewhat foolish. Yet the conclusions of this study, about both the reactivity and the slow pace of change in military institutions, suggest that the West's approach to doctrinal questions in the future can have a significant impact on Russian security developments.[4]

The military doctrines and operational planning which were products of the East-West confrontation in Europe in the 1980s may have lingering, detrimental effects in the post–Cold War world. These effects could potentially hinder the full realization of rapprochement between East and West, and could remain a destabilizing element in efforts to achieve lasting peace and security in the region. Doctrines are based not merely on capabilities, but on intentions; and defense planners can have future intentions that are not necessarily reflected in present capabilities. It is a well-established tenet in the Western theoretical literature on military doctrine that military officers prefer offensive doctrines, and resist civilian attempts to interfere with those offensive doctrines. Offensive planning gives military officers more resources, more control over the battlefield, and more organizational autonomy. It would therefore not be surprising if conservative military officers tried to undercut official state attempts to alter doctrine, in the belief that in the future, their offensive way of war would again come into its own.

As chapter 5 demonstrates, the military planning of both sides in Europe contained a significant offensive component in the 1980s. Soviet planning focused on using strategic and operational offensives, surprise, and the maintenance of the initiative to achieve victory in the event of the outbreak of war. U.S. and NATO planning contained a precision deep-strike counterattack component, and the U.S. Army doctrine of AirLand Battle in particular intended to carry a hypothetical future war on to Soviet territory, to aim for victory in war, and to integrate nuclear weapons into deep-strike planning if necessary.

In the post–Cold War world, where neither side believes that a war with the other is likely, and where both sides profess to no longer consider each other threats to peace, movement away from these offensive doctrinal components will be crucial. Offensive conventional war doctrines are more costly financially than defensive doctrines, because they require higher troop levels and more weapons (the classic "3:1" rule of thumb states that the offender must have a threefold point superiority in order to achieve a successful offensive breakthrough of a prepared defense); in certain cases, such as deep-strike doctrines, counteroffensive doctrines also require a greater variety of high-technology weapons systems.

Offensive doctrines are also more destabilizing than defensive doctrines. When faced by an enemy with a significant offensive potential, it is to each side's military advantage to move first during a crisis, to avoid losing its own military forces to the other's surprise attack. In the case of the East-West European confrontation in the 1980s, the U.S. and NATO doctrines officially targeted Soviet offensive staging grounds and troop movement choke points. In order to retain the ability to implement its own plans successfully, it would have been to the USSR's advantage to move out quickly into attack formations, and to get beyond those staging grounds and choke-points if it seemed that crisis was moving toward war, even if the Soviet Union had no immediate intention of launching an attack. Simultaneously, NATO and the U.S. might have felt that it was necessary to assume that significant troop movements indicated preparations for an attack; for their plans to be implemented successfully, Western leaders might have been tempted to launch at least some conventional deep strikes preemptively, as a warning signal. A scenario can be imagined where offensive planning on one side, and counteroffensive planning on the other, could lead to a war which neither side wanted.

A better alternative, for both financial and stability reasons, is a doctrine of nonoffensive defense (NOD) (also called nonprovocative defense or defensive defense). NOD doctrines fulfill three basic criteria:

1. They are purely defensive, designed to repel an invading enemy but not to pursue a counteroffensive significantly beyond state borders. They are thus backed by forces with restricted ranges and destructive power.

2. They are nonprovocative; that is, they do not provide the opponent with an incentive to attack first or to escalate. For our purposes, this means that the opponent recognizes that the state does not have a counteroffensive potential which must be decommissioned for the attack to succeed.

3. They provide an effective defense against aggression or the threat of aggression; they are designed to deny the aggressor victory. In other words, deterrence is ensured not by the threat of punishment (as it is with a counteroffensive doctrine), but rather through a solid defense.[5]

It is understandable that when one side believes that the other is likely to attack, it is unlikely to favor moving unilaterally to NOD. If an attack seems likely, one side is not likely to be willing to cede the initiative completely to the other side. In a world where mutual threats are perceived, NOD doctrines may be perceived as too risky.

But in the post–Cold War world, where neither side believes that a war with the other is likely, and where both sides profess no longer to consider each other threats to peace, movement away from offensive doctrinal components is beneficial to each side's state interests.

Several Soviet General Staff officers complained about the continuation of U.S. and NATO deep-strike doctrines into 1990.[6] Undoubtedly, this complaint about NATO doctrine fed into the refrain which then echoed among the conservative members of the Soviet High Command and General Staff: that NATO still constituted a military threat, particularly with a reunited Germany, and that Gorbachev and Shevardnadze gave away the store. Certainly, all powerful General Staff and High Command officers did not believe that the Soviet adoption of an official state doctrine of defensive defense was a satisfactory situation.

NATO leaders have now adopted a "New Strategic Concept," one that emphasizes cooperation with the former Warsaw Pact states, and flexible forces not devoted primarily to repelling a major invasion from Russia. There is no doubt that this strategy is a radical departure from the Follow-on Forces Attack doctrine.

Yet NATO has not publicly declared whether or not this concept constitutes a nonoffensive defense strategy. The official NATO statement remains ambiguous. Its goals are focused on convincing a potential aggressor that the risks of invasion outweigh the gains, and on restoring the status quo ante bellum if such deterrence fails. It thus definitely meets two of the three NOD criteria. Yet it also mentions "stop[ping] an aggressor's advance as far forward as possible," as well as the *maintenance*, not merely the restoration, of territorial borders in the event of war.[7] This implies that deep-strike weapons and counteroffensive strikes may remain part of NATO's new European defense vision. William H. Taft IV, the U.S. Permanent Representative on the North Atlantic Council, confirmed this impression with a statement emphasizing the relevance of the coalition victory against Saddam Hussein in 1991 for future NATO planning: "We were right to focus on buying the most modern high-tech weapons for our forces, and we should continue to do this. These weapons proved their effectiveness against the enemy and saved our soldiers' lives."[8] Many of the most effective weapons used against Iraqi forces were designed for deep-strike counteroffensives, and were in fact among those that Soviet military officers found threatening in the early 1980s.

The continuation of deep-strike NATO planning would be destabilizing. The Russian military, whose forces lag behind the West in technological developments, might continue to believe that armaments competition with NATO was necessary. The General Staff might also retain at some level an ingrained belief that these NATO weapons are designed for offensive purposes. The realization of a true defensive defense doctrine in Russia might be hampered as a result.

This issue is especially thorny since Russia has traditionally lacked a civilian Defense Ministry, as well as established independent sources of classified information about its own defenses. Despite concerted efforts to get access to accurate military-technical information, Russian civilian state officials have undoubtedly not yet succeeded in completely penetrating the General Staff fortress. Russian civilians may demand that the military adopt a defensive doctrine, and may cut force levels to the extent that only defensive plans can be implemented; military leaders may publicly affirm that exercises, textbooks, and General Staff planning are now being changed to conform to defensive defense guidelines. Yet it is not clear that anyone outside the General Staff really knows what these new exercises, textbooks, and plans contain, even if a civilian sits at the top of the Defense Ministry hierarchy. Russia may not be currently capable of launching a large-scale offensive, but this does not mean that such a situation will remain in force in a decade, when today's General Staff Academy students are moving up the planning hierarchy. If those students are today being taught in the Academy that NATO and the U.S. are the primary future probable enemies, that NATO and U.S. planning is geared toward counteroffensives, and that today's situation for the Russian military is only a temporary setback, then official defensive defense doctrine may be meaningless in the long run.

Political intentions and military capabilities have changed, and the level of mutual trust has grown between Russia and the West. Nonetheless, the adversarial relationship has not been completely disavowed by military planners. Military officers, as the professionals whose mission it is to preserve state security, are likely to plan for worst-case scenarios. On the Russian side, this may mean planning for the possibility of a future NATO deep-strike attack, perhaps with the collusion of former Soviet republics or allies. (The General Staff must be uncomfortable about the civil wars now raging both within and just outside Russian borders.) What is needed therefore is an effort to change military leaders' perceptions about the level of threat emanating from the other side. Military officers have the responsibility to view foreign threats conservatively, and to doubt the removal of threats to state security.

Certain U. S. and NATO policy initiatives could help to further the establishment of trust in the Russian officer corps about Western intentions. As the present study has shown, military organizations are not homogeneous. Different officers have different perceptions about which policies are best for the state to follow. In the current situation, there are undoubtedly both senior Russian military officers who believe that nonoffensive defense doctrines in Europe are foolish, because such doctrine would leave them vulnerable to attack from a still-aggressive opponent, and others who believe that the old offensive and counteroffensive doctrines have lost their meaning in the new order, and who recognize the toll taken on the rest of society by the financial and destabilizing costs of such doctrines.

Military-to-military conferences and exchanges between Russia, the U.S., and European states have already begun to cement trust. This process would be greatly assisted if NATO were to declare its doctrine to be one of nonoffensive defense. Such a declaration, followed by withdrawal of deep-strike weapons from Europe, could help tip the balance of support in the Russian military organization in favor of the defense-oriented thinkers. The initiatives would serve to substantiate the idea that the old offensive threats are gone, and that there is no remaining reason not to move to a defensive doctrine. As evidence of a threat disappears, it becomes increasingly difficult for old thinkers to hold on to their traditional notions; there are fewer and fewer pieces of evidence to support their conservative perspectives. A good example of this is the flow of foreign policy politics in the United States. In early 1989, there were still quite a few foreign policy experts who doubted Gorbachev's intentions and the final extent of foreign policy reforms. The crash of the Communist regimes in Eastern Europe and the emergence of a unified Germany has removed all reasonable doubts on this score.

It is now clear that domestic political and budgetary pressures in both the United States and Russia will force each side to restructure its armed forces. It would be very dangerous to allow domestic budgetary pressures alone to determine future force structures. Knowing that cuts will be made, defense policymakers should go to their domestic audiences with well-thought-out plans for maintaining security and stability in the face of cuts, rather than allowing cuts to fall haphazardly. The adoption of nonoffensive defense doctrines could contribute greatly to stability in Europe by changing the threat perceptions of military officers.

The costs of such a NATO doctrine in the current climate are low enough that a reciprocal move from Russia would not be necessary. Given the long lead-times now present before a Russian offensive capability could be reestablished, and given that precision weapon research and development is likely to continue anyway in order to deal with Third

World threats (and thus reconstitution would not be impossible), it is unimaginable that NATO security could be hurt by the dismantling of European deep precision strike planning. Such strikes are unlikely to be useful in any peacekeeping missions NATO forces might take on.

The future of the Russian political system is now unclear. Rather than seeing continuing American military technological superiority only in terms of its possible positive consequences, the flip side of the coin should also be considered. The pressure of such superiority could be used by the Russian military and its conservative supporters as an argument for an antireformist backslide. The West has been granted an opportunity by Soviet and Russian reforms; now powerful, innovative American policy entrepreneurs must grab that opportunity to move the post–Cold War world forward into a new era.

Despite its current economic difficulties, Russia is so rich in natural resources and scientific talent that, in the event of a reactionary, praetorian coup, especially one supported by terror, it would not be unthinkable for the defense industry to once again hold up its end of the East-West arms competition. In fact, the November 1990 draft "Military Reform Concept" of the Soviet Defense Ministry calls for "decreasing the military-technical lag behind the NATO country armies, especially in such weapons as conventionally armed, long-range precision rockets and automatic command and control systems for troops and weapons."[9] The United States should not expect that its current edge in high technology weaponry will permanently erase any Russian competitive drive.

Some semiofficial NATO sources seem to have recognized these problems. Eckhard Lubkemeier of the Friedrich Ebert Foundation wrote in NATO Review in 1991 that "emphasis should be placed on the defensive orientation of the conventional potential," and that "what is needed . . . is a reduced military presence in the forward area, with defensive constraints imposed on the mobile elements (e.g., by static logistics and command structures), and suitably tailored engagement doctrines."[10] He concludes, "Material resources are being liberated and a political breathing space created in which the structural causes of antagonistic conflicts can be addressed. Countries take arms against each other because of such conflicts but weapons can lead to their intensification. This is a further reason why the political primacy of strategic planning must always be upheld."[11]

Doctrinal competitions can only be overcome if there are powerful innovators on both sides of the international game, who challenge the old confrontation with new cooperative approaches. Even major changes in declaratory strategy, military budgets, and deployment patterns are unlikely to erase the competition permanently unless training styles and operational combat missions change as well. Now that both Russian and Western leaders have declared that the Cold War is over, truly innovative thinkers must take control of the policy agenda. The enemy will only be truly defeated when all perceptions of threat have vanished. Work remains on both sides to ensure that this is realized.

Notes

Introduction

1. See Jack Snyder, *The Ideology of the Offensive* (Ithaca: Cornell University Press, 1984); Snyder, "Civil-Military Relations and the Cult of the Offensive, 1914 and 1984," *International Security* 9 (Summer 1984): 108–46; Scott D. Sagan, "1914 Revisited," *International Security* 11 (Fall 1986): 151–75; and Stephen M. Walt, "The Search for a Science of Strategy," *International Security* 12 (Summer 1987): 140–65.

2. Barry R. Posen, *The Sources of Military Doctrine* (Ithaca: Cornell University Press, 1984). Stephen Peter Rosen has challenged Posen, arguing that innovation happens within military organizations without civilian intervention when a pro-innovation coalition of officers emerges and gains power. Rosen, "New Ways of War," *International Security* 13 (Summer 1988): 134–68, and *Winning the Next War: Innovation and the Modern Military* (Ithaca: Cornell University Press, 1991).

3. A recent work which uses a different set of organization theories to criticize the arguments of Posen and Snyder is David R. Mares and Walter W. Powell, "Cooperative Security Regimes: Preventing International Conflicts," in *Organizations and Nation-States: New Perspectives on Conflict and Cooperation*, ed. Robert L. Kahn and Mayer N. Zald (San Francisco: Jossey-Bass, 1990).

4. This latter statement is borrowed from the definition of innovation offered by James Q. Wilson, *Bureaucracy: What Government Agencies Do and Why They Do It* (New York: Basic Books, 1989), p. 222.

5. My definition differs from the service mission definitions of doctrinal innovation proposed by Rosen, "New Ways of War," p. 134, and by Paul N. Stockton, "Services and Civilians," Doctoral Dissertation, Harvard University, 1986, p. 17. The definitional difference is only due to a difference in the choice of subject matter ("doctrine" defined as service missions versus "doctrine" defined as grand strategy), and should not be taken to indicate a theoretical disagreement over what innovation is. While Posen does not explicitly define doctrinal innovation, I believe that our definitions are similar.

6. For parallel definitions, which separate "innovation" from "invention," see Lawrence B. Mohr, "Determinants of Innovation in Organizations," *American Political Science Review* 63 (1969): 112; Jack L. Walker, "The Diffusion of Innovation among the American States," *American Political Science Review* 63 (September 1969): 881; and Everett M. Rogers, *Diffusion of Innovations*, 3d ed. (New York: Free Press, 1983), p. 11.

7. Those who study innovation in the American states are also turning to interactive explanations in their work; they are studying the interplay between political situations in the states and the influence of neighbor-state policy innovations. See Frances Stokes Berry and William D. Berry, "State Lottery Adoptions as

Policy Innovations," *American Political Science Review* 84 (June 1990): 395–415.

8. This is the approach taken by Posen, *The Sources of Military Doctrine*. Kenneth N. Waltz, *Theory of International Politics* (New York: Random House, 1979); Graham T. Allison, *Essence of Decision* (Boston: Little, Brown and Co., 1971).

9. In fact, Waltz did not present his theory as a competitor with Allison's for explaining the motives behind individual examples of foreign policy decision-making. He states that the structure of the international system acts as a selector, not an agent; it rewards or punishes the choices of policymakers, without necessarily guiding them. While wise policymakers who wish to preserve their states' health will conform to balance-of-power expectations, there is no a priori reason to expect that any particular policymaker at any one time is wise in that way. Furthermore, policies chosen for the "wrong" reasons in balance-of-power terms may still lead to favorable balance-of-power outcomes for the state, if their outlines conform to what balancing demands. Waltz, *Theory of International Politics*, pp. 73–74.

10. This approach is successfully used by Matthew Evangelista, *Innovation and the Arms Race* (Ithaca: Cornell University Press, 1988); and by Jack Snyder, "The Gorbachev Revolution," *International Security* 12 (Winter 1987/88): 93–131.

11. Alexander L. George, "Case Studies and Theory Development," in *Diplomacy*, ed. Paul Gordon Lauren (New York: Free Press, 1979), pp. 43–68. Obviously, George's requirements can never be perfectly met by any study of history; one can never demonstrate that a particular policy decision is independent of earlier policy decisions, nor can one ever control for all variables (in this case, for example, technology changes with time).

12. The author has chosen not to study the Stalin era because information about genuine Soviet military preferences in the immediate postwar era is difficult to obtain; Stalinist press restrictions prevented the military from publicly reacting to the advent of nuclear weapons, and delayed the Soviet reaction to the American deployment of theater nuclear forces, as well as to the American adoption of the Massive Retaliation strategy. See Raymond L. Garthoff, *Soviet Strategy in the Nuclear Age* (New York: Praeger, 1958); Herbert S. Dinerstein, *War and the Soviet Union*, rev. ed. (New York: Praeger, 1962); and Matthew Evangelista, *Innovation and the Arms Race*, pp. 156–63 especially.

13. Interesting perspectives on this question have been presented by Jack Snyder, "Averting Anarchy in the New Europe," *International Security* 14 (Spring 1990): 5–41; and John J. Mearsheimer, "Back to the Future: Instability in Europe after the Cold War," *International Security* 15 (Summer 1990): 5–56.

14. For discussions of this phenomenon, see C. N. Donnelly, "Future Soviet Military Policy, Part I: Doctrine and Economics," *International Defense Review* 22 (Jan. 1989): 20; Raymond Garthoff, *Soviet Military Policy* (New York: Praeger, 1966), p. 50; and Condoleezza Rice, "The Impact of Institutional Norms and Development on the Evolution of the Central Staff Systems of the United States and the Soviet Union," unpublished paper prepared for delivery at the 1987 Annual Meeting of the American Political Science Association. For a solid argu-

ment about the sources and effects of U.S. decentralized military service struc-tures, see Daniel J. Kaufman, "National Security: Organizing the Armed Forces," *Armed Forces and Society* 14 (Fall 1987): 85–112.

15. The recent Goldwater-Nichols Act reforms in the JCS system may have had some impact in reducing the effects of this competition on policy outcomes, because they have strengthened the centralized power of the JCS Chairman. See Vincent Davis, "Defense Reorganization and National Security," *Annals of the American Academy of Political and Social Science* 517 (September 1991): 157–73.

16. See Colin S. Gray, *The Soviet-American Arms Race* (Lexington, Mass: Lexington Books, 1976); Arthur J. Alexander, *Decision-Making in Soviet Weapons Procurement*, Adelphi Paper 147/8 (London: International Institute of Strate-gic Studies, 1978); David Holloway, *The Soviet Union and the Arms Race*, 2d ed. (New Haven: Yale University Press, 1984); Stephen M. Meyer, "Soviet National Security Decisionmaking: What Do We Know and What Do We Understand?" in *Soviet Decisionmaking for National Security*, ed. William Potter and Jiri Valenta (London: Allen and Unwin, 1984), pp. 255–97; and Matthew Evangelista, *Inno-vation and the Arms Race*.

Chapter 1
Military Organizations and Innovation

1. This point is most strongly made by Barry Posen, *The Sources of Military Doctrine* (Ithaca: Cornell University Press, 1984). One scholar who has criticized this trend is Stephen Peter Rosen, *Winning the Next War: Innovation and the Modern Military* (Ithaca: Cornell University Press, 1991).

2. Jack Snyder makes this argument in both *The Ideology of the Offensive* (Ithaca: Cornell University Press, 1984), and "Civil-Military Relations and the Cult of the Offensive, 1914 and 1984," *International Security* 9 (Summer 1984): 108–46.

3. Variations on this theme appear in works by Morris Janowitz, who coins the term "routine innovation," in *The Professional Soldier* (New York: Free Press, 1960), pp. 27–28; by Posen, *The Sources of Military Doctrine*, who argues that new technology is often grafted on to old doctrine, p. 55; by Matthew Evangelista, *Innovation and the Arms Race* (Ithaca: Cornell University Press, 1988), who posits that the Soviet military in particular incorporates new technol-ogies into its old strategies, pp. 7–8; and by James Q. Wilson, *Bureaucracy: What Government Agencies Do and Why They Do It* (New York: Basic Books, 1989), who argues that most military changes called "innovations" are really just revers-ible alterations in what he calls the "peripheral tasks" of the organization, pp. 225–26.

4. This theme is developed concerning national security policy-making in gen-eral by Laura Reed, "The Rise and Fall of a Divided Europe: What Do Organiza-tional Models Tell Us About Changes in the Security Agenda After World War II and at the End of the Cold War?" Unpublished paper prepared for delivery at the Annual Meeting of the American Political Science Association, August 1990.

5. The strongest theoretical statement along this line is found in Morton H.

Halperin's classic, *Bureaucratic Politics and Foreign Policy* (Washington, D.C.: Brookings, 1974).

6. See, for example, Graham T. Allison, "Questions about the Arms Race," in *Contrasting Approaches to Strategic Arms Control* (Lexington, Mass.: Lexington Books, 1974), pp. 37–38; and Dieter Senghaas, "Arms Race Dynamics and Arms Control in Europe," *Bulletin of Peace Proposals* 10, no. 1 (1979): 10.

7. Evangelista makes a point similar to this one in his *Innovation and the Arms Race*, p. 12.

8. As the term "professional military officers" is used here, it refers to the standard definitions of professionalism used by Samuel Huntington, *The Soldier and the State* (Cambridge, Mass.: Harvard University Press, 1957), and by Timothy P. Colton, *Commissars, Commanders and Civilian Authority* (Cambridge: Harvard University Press, 1979). I thus refer only to professional militaries in stable states where military intervention into general political decisions and activities is not considered normal. I do not mean to include Alfred Stepan's broadened definition of the term, where political intervention is considered to be a new professional role for military officers. See Stepan, "The New Professionalism of Internal Warfare and Military Role Expansion," in his *Authoritarian Brazil* (New Haven: Yale University Press, 1973), pp. 47–65.

9. Janowitz, *The Professional Soldier*, pp. 6–7.

10. Huntington, *The Soldier and the State*, pp. 64–67.

11. Some of these Soviet discussions are summarized by Serge Schmemann, "Soviets Say Their Weapons Were Not Iraqis' Weak Spot," *New York Times*, March 1, 1991.

12. General theoretical support for the proposition that militaries are concerned with the preservation of their autonomy is found in Amos Perlmutter, *The Military and Politics in Modern Times* (New Haven: Yale University Press, 1977); Posen, *Sources of Military Doctrine*; and Snyder, *Ideology of the Offensive*. In the Soviet case this situation was amplified, since for many years there was no civilian representation in the Ministry of Defense, and there were no civilian think tanks parallel to those in the West which could provide alternate sources of military advice to national political leaders. For discussions of the Soviet military's desire for autonomy on certain issue areas, see Roman Kolkowicz, *The Soviet Military and the Communist Party* (Princeton: Princeton University Press, 1967); and Timothy P. Colton, *Commissars, Commanders*, p. 288. Specifically on the question of the Soviet military's desire to maintain its monopoly on military expertise, see Condoleezza Rice, "The Party, the Military and Decision Authority in the Soviet Union," *World Politics* 40 (October 1987): 55–81; and Stephen M. Meyer, "The Sources and Prospects of Gorbachev's New Political Thinking on Security," *International Security* 13 (Fall 1988): 130–31.

13. Two examples of this are U.S. President Eisenhower's "New Look" strategy of 1954, and Soviet First Secretary Khrushchev's similar strategy of 1960. Both leaders apparently sought to emphasize less expensive nuclear weapons in their nations' military strategies and to constrict the resources devoted to higher-cost conventional forces, in order to free budget resources for other areas of the economy; both leaders spent the next several years in struggle with senior officers of their respective armies.

14. The two classic examples of such work are Jeffrey Pfeffer and Gerald R. Salancik, *The External Control of Organizations: A Resource Dependence Perspective* (New York: Harper and Row, 1978); and Howard E. Aldrich, *Organizations and Environments* (Englewood Cliffs, N.J.: Prentice-Hall, 1979). A useful discussion of the variety of arguments made within this school is provided by Richard W. Scott, *Organizations: Rational, Natural, and Open Systems*, 2d ed. (Englewood Cliffs, N.J.: Prentice-Hall, 1987), pp. 110–11.

15. The term "domain" is used by Scott, *Organizations*, p. 120.

16. Kenneth E. Boulding refers to this as a competition of "milorgs," when military and military-industrial organizations compete in a fashion resembling ordinary firms, but with different sets of consumers. See his "The World War Industry As an Economic Problem," in *Disarmament and the Economy*, ed. Emile Benoit and Kenneth E. Boulding (New York: Harper and Row, 1963), pp. 7–10.

17. James G. March and Herbert A. Simon, *Organizations* (New York: John Wiley and Sons, 1958), p. 176.

18. Ibid., p. 183.

19. James G. March, "Footnotes to Organizational Change," *Administrative Science Quarterly* 26 (1981): 563–77.

20. Charles E. Lindblom, "The Science of 'Muddling Through,' " *Public Administration Review* 19 (Spring 1959): 79–88. Similar arguments about the American political system have been made by Aaron Wildavsky, *The Politics of the Budgetary Process*, 4th ed. (Boston: Little, Brown and Co., 1984). Valerie Bunce and John M. Echols III have applied the same incrementalist framework to Soviet administrative policy-making in the 1970s. See their "Power and Policy in Communist Systems: The Problem of 'Incrementalism,' " *The Journal of Politics* 40 (August 1978): 911–32.

21. March, "Footnotes to Organizational Change," p. 564.

22. March and Simon, *Organizations*, pp. 188–89.

23. James G. March and Johan P. Olsen, *Rediscovering Institutions: The Organizational Basis of Politics* (New York: The Free Press, 1989), p. 34.

24. March et al. have been careful to note that negative environmental pressure is not the only factor associated with organizational innovation. Sometimes when organizations face almost no pressure, and organizational slack is high, their members are given sufficient resources to allow them to be creative, and to experiment on company time. This can also lead to innovation. See March, *Decisions and Organizations* (Cambridge, Mass.: Basil Blackwell, 1988), pp. 4–5; and March and Olsen, *Rediscovering Institutions*, p. 60. Nonetheless, innovation under environmental pressure is a continuing theme of their work on organizational change.

25. James N. Rosenau, "Before Cooperation: Hegemons, Regimes, and Habit-Driven Actors in World Politics," *International Organization* 40 (Autumn 1986): 849–94.

26. John D. Steinbruner, *The Cybernetic Theory of Decision* (Princeton: Princeton University Press, 1974).

27. Ibid., pp. 54, 80.

28. This has been a continuing theme in modern organization theory. See Pfeffer and Salancik, *The External Control of Organizations*, p. 13; Karl E. Weick,

The Social Psychology of Organizing, 2d ed. (Reading, Mass.: Addison-Wesley, 1979); Anna Grandori, *Perspectives on Organization Theory* (Cambridge, Mass.: Ballinger, 1987), pp. 14–15; March and Olsen, *Rediscovering Institutions*, pp. 41–45; and Scott, *Organizations*, pp. 134–36. It is also a theme of work on the sociology of knowledge and science, where it is often referred to as "the social construction of reality." Basic discussions are found in Peter L. Berger and Thomas Luckmann, *The Social Construction of Reality: A Treatise in the Sociology of Knowledge* (New York: Irvington, 1966); and David Bloor, *Knowledge and Social Imagery* (Boston: Routledge and Kegan Paul, 1976). The theme has been brought into the field of security studies by Donald Mackenzie's work on the social construction of data on nuclear weapons characteristics; see his *Inventing Accuracy: A Historical Sociology of Nuclear Missile Guidance* (Cambridge, Mass.: MIT Press, 1990). It is also found in the international relations literature on the organizational psychology of decision-making; see Alexander L. George, *Presidential Decisionmaking in Foreign Policy: The Effective Use of Information and Advice* (Boulder, Colo.: Westview, 1980), especially pp. 56–62.

29. Weick, *The Social Psychology of Organizing*, pp. 172–73.

30. Ibid. See also Erving Goffman, *Strategic Interaction* (Philadelphia: University of Pennsylvania Press, 1969), especially pp. 3–81.

31. Lawrence Freedman, *US Intelligence and the Soviet Strategic Threat*, 2d ed. (London: Macmillan, 1986), p. 184.

32. This argument is made strongly by Charles Perrow, *Complex Organizations: A Critical Essay*, 2d ed. (Glenview, Ill.: Scott, Foresman and Company, 1979), p. 156.

33. See Herbert A. Simon, *Administrative Behavior*, 2d ed. (New York: Macmillan, 1961), pp. 76–77.

34. James G. March, "The Business Firm as a Political Coalition," *Journal of Politics* 24 (1962): 662–78.

35. See Pfeffer and Salancik, *External Control of Organizations*, p. 24; and David J. Hickson et al., *Top Decisions: Strategic Decision-Making in Organizations* (San Francisco: Jossey-Bass, 1986), passim.

36. Robert B. Albritton, "Measuring Public Policy: Impacts of the Supplemental Security Income Program," *American Journal of Political Science* 23 (August 1979): 563.

37. Policy communities theory is being developed by a school of scholars influenced by the work of the late Jack L. Walker. See Walker, "The Diffusion of Innovation among the American States," *American Political Science Review* 63 (September 1969): 880–99; and also Walker, "The Diffusion of Knowledge, Policy Communities and Agenda Setting," in *New Strategic Perspectives on Social Policy*, ed. John E. Tropman, Milan J. Dluhy, and Roger M. Lind (New York: Pergamon, 1981), pp. 75–96.

38. Nina P. Halpern, "Policy Communities in a Leninist State," *Governance* 2 (Jan. 1989): 23–41.

39. Matthew Evangelista, "Sources of Moderation in Soviet Security Policy," in *Behavior, Society, and Nuclear War*, vol. 2, ed. Philip Tetlock et al. (New York: Oxford University Press, 1991).

40. See Jack Walker, "The Diffusion of Knowledge," p. 79; and John W.

Kingdon, *Agendas, Alternatives, and Public Policies* (Boston: Little, Brown and Co., 1984), p. 123.

41. See Ernst B. Haas, *When Knowledge Is Power: Three Models of Change in International Organizations* (Berkeley: University of California Press, 1990); Peter M. Haas, "Do Regimes Matter? Epistemic Communities and Mediterranean Pollution Control," *International Organization* 43 (Summer 1989): 378–403; Peter M. Haas, *Saving the Mediterranean: The Politics of International Environmental Cooperation* (New York: Columbia University Press, 1990); and the *International Organization* special issue, "Knowledge, Power, and International Policy Coordination," ed. Peter M. Haas, vol. 46 (Winter 1992).

42. Peter Haas, "Do Regimes Matter?" p. 304.

43. Ibid., p. 402.

44. For a discussion of this process on the issue of global interdependence, see Stephen Shenfield, *The Nuclear Predicament: Explorations in Soviet Ideology*, Chatham House Papers no. 37 (New York: Routledge and Kegan Paul, 1987), especially p. 83.

45. See Eberhard Schneider, "Soviet Foreign-Policy Think Tanks," *Washington Quarterly* 11 (Spring 1988): 145–55.

46. Walker, "The Diffusion of Knowledge," p. 86.

47. Kingdon, *Agendas, Alternatives, and Public Policies*, especially pp. 85–87. John S. Odell, in his work on policy development, seems on the surface to disagree with this analysis, claiming that new ideas gain popularity in jumps, not steadily. See *U. S. International Monetary Policy* (Princeton: Princeton University Press, 1982), p. 368. Nonetheless, a closer look indicates that Odell's argument is really about state agendas changing quickly, not about sudden changes in the thinking of policy communities. For example, he cites the Kennedy administration's adoption of Flexible Response as an example of the establishment of a new idea in policy at a sudden, particular moment (p. 71); but the development of Flexible Response as an alternative to Massive Retaliation was a long, drawn-out process within both the U.S. and West European strategic policy communities (see my discussion of this in chapter 3). Kingdon in fact modifies his own statement about fast-changing agendas in relation to issues that fall within what he calls the "visible arena," issues (such as defense) which are always of concern to the government, p. 100.

48. See Walker, "The Diffusion of Knowledge," pp. 79–80.

49. Kingdon, *Agendas, Alternatives, and Public Policies*, pp. 129–30.

50. Ibid., pp. 131–32.

51. Ibid., p. 135.

52. Ibid., p. 133.

53. The term "salience" is used by Odell, *U. S. International Monetary Policy*, p. 65.

54. Wilson, *Bureaucracy*, p. 227.

55. Freedman, *US Intelligence and the Soviet Strategic Threat*, p. 5.

56. Deborah Welch Larson, *The Origins of Containment* (Princeton: Princeton University Press, 1985).

57. Examples of Larson's demands which cannot be met are the need to definitely determine authorship of speeches and articles and distinguish between real

perceptions of the speaker or "author" and those of the writer; and the need to determine exactly which information the policymaker read or was told about the subject at hand, how such information was interpreted by the policymaker, and then how this interpretation affected the policymaker's beliefs about the subject. Ibid., pp. 60–63.

58. Walker, "Diffusion of Innovation," notes that an influx of new personnel can be a catalyst of innovation, p. 80.

59. Ibid., pp. 79, 83–84.

60. Vincent Davis, *The Politics of Innovation: Patterns in Navy Cases*, vol. 4, monograph 3 of the Social Science Foundation and Graduate School of International Studies University of Denver Monograph Series in World Affairs, Denver, Colo., 1966–67, pp. 33–34.

61. Stephen Peter Rosen, "New Ways of War," *International Security* 13 (Summer 1988), pp. 134–68. This argument is seconded by Wilson, *Bureaucracy*, p. 227.

62. Davis, *Politics of Innovation*, pp. 36–37.

63. Franklyn Griffiths, "A Tendency Analysis of Soviet Policy-Making," in *Interest Groups in Soviet Politics*, ed. H. Gordon Skilling and Franklyn Griffiths (Princeton: Princeton University Press, 1971), pp. 335–77.

64. Certainly, I do not mean to imply that all civilians are by nature more inclined than military officers to favor cooperation over confrontation in resolving international problems. I mean instead that civilian participants in the doctrine process can be selectively chosen for their opposition to the standard policy opinions of the military.

65. Posen, *The Sources of Military Doctrine*, p. 56.

Chapter 2
Doctrinal Debate and Decision in the USSR

1. Burkart Holzner and John H. Marx, *Knowledge Application: The Knowledge System in Society* (Boston: Allyn and Bacon, 1979), pp. 333–38.

2. "Polozhenie o sluzhbe General'nogo shtaba Raboche-Krest'ianskoi Krasnoi Armii," signed by V. Molotov, Commissar for Defense; accompanied by Colonel in the Reserves Professor V. D. Danilov, "Kommentarii voennogo istorika"; both in *Voennaia Mysl'*, no. 11 (1990): 49–56. According to the commentary accompanying this draft, it failed to be approved in April 1937 only because its authors suffered under Stalinist repression. It is portrayed as a useful summary of what General Staff service entails.

3. Ibid., p. 56.

4. V. G. Kulikov, "General'nyi Shtab," in *Sovetskaia Voennaia Entsiklopediia*, vol. 2 (Moscow: Voenizdat, 1976), p. 513. For similar descriptions, see the Soviet military dictionary's definition, "General'nyi Shtab," *Voennyi Entsiklopedicheskii Slovar'* (Moscow: Voenizdat, 1984), p. 186; and Colonel in Retirement Ya. M. Gorelik, "Trud neprekhodiashchei tsennosti," (an article commemorating the sixtieth anniversary of the publication of B. M. Shaposhnikov's seminal work on General Staff systems, *Mozg Armii*), *Voennaia Mysl'*, no. 7 (1989): 77–78.

5. "Voennaia Nauka," in *Voennyi Entsiklopedicheskii Slovar'*, p. 136.

6. *Voennyi Entsiklopedicheskii Slovar'*, p. 240. While Soviet definitions of military doctrine have undergone slight permutations at various times in history, the basic thrust of the definition given above has remained intact.

7. "Voennaia Politika," ibid., p. 137.

8. These interpretations, both of political leaders' supremacy in doctrinal policy, and of fuzziness in the boundaries of political and military leadership responsibility for specific doctrinal questions, are well established among Sovietologists. See, for example, David Holloway, *The Soviet Union and the Arms Race*, p. 30; and Tsuyoshi Hasegawa, "Soviets on Nuclear-War-Fighting," *Problems of Communism* 35 (July/August 1986): 69.

9. Stephen M. Meyer, "Civilian and Military Influence in Managing the Arms Race in the USSR," in *Reorganizing America's Defense*, ed. Robert J. Art, Vincent Davis, and Samuel P. Huntington (Washington, D.C.: Pergamon-Brassey's, 1985), especially p. 40; and Condoleezza Rice, "The Party, the Military, and Decision Authority in the Soviet Union," *World Politics* 40 (October 1987): 55–81. Rice makes clear that the further one moves out from purely military questions, the less influence the General Staff had, simply because on those broader questions there were more alternative sources of information for the political leadership to use. For example, international relations analysts and economists wielded information influence in such areas as arms control and state budgeting decisions; the General Staff then became only one source of information in those more diffuse policy areas.

10. Some works with slightly different guesses about who has been on the Defense Council include David Holloway, *The Soviet Union and the Arms Race*, 2d ed. (New Haven: Yale University Press, 1984), pp. 109–10; Ellen Jones, *Red Army and Society* (Boston: Allen and Unwin, 1985), pp. 6–10; and Rice, "The Party, the Military, and Decision Authority in the Soviet Union," pp. 66–67.

11. See Ellen Jones, *Red Army and Society*, ibid.

12. Condoleezza Rice, "The Party, the Military, and Decision Authority in the Soviet Union," pp. 66–67.

13. Uri Ra'anan and Igor Lukes, eds., *Inside the Apparat: Perspectives on the Soviet System from Former Functionaries* (Lexington, Mass.: Lexington Books, 1990), pp. 85–88.

14. Ibid., p. 88.

15. From the report by Alexander Rahr, "Gorbachev Discloses Details of Defense Council," *Radio Liberty Report on the USSR* 1, no. 36 (September 8, 1989): 11–12.

16. The description of the debating positions is found in Danilov, "Kommentarii voennogo istorika," pp. 53–54; the character assessments of the officers involved are made by Timothy J. Colton, "Perspectives on Civil-Military Relations in the Soviet Union," in *Soldiers and the Soviet State: Civil-Military Relations from Brezhnev to Gorbachev* (Princeton: Princeton University Press, 1990), pp. 18–20.

17. M. V. Frunze, *Izbrannye Proizvedeniia*, reissued (Moscow: Voenizdat, 1984), p. 156. The original document was titled "On the Reorganization of the

Military Apparatus," and was delivered by Frunze as a speech at the Military Academy of the Red Army on April 18, 1924.

18. B. M. Shaposhnikov, *Vospominaniia/Voenno-nauchnye Trudy*, reissued (Moscow: Voenizdat, 1974), p. 429. This is a fragment from Shaposhnikov's famed three-volume work, *Mozg Armii* [*Brain of the Army*], written over a period of years from the mid-1920s through the 1930s.

19. Ibid., p. 445.

20. Ibid., pp. 456–57.

21. Ibid., p. 538.

22. This debate is discussed well by J. M. Mackintosh, "The Red Army, 1920–1936," in *The Red Army*, ed. B. M. Lidell Hart (New York: Harcourt, Brace and Co., 1956), pp. 52–64; John Erickson, *The Soviet High Command: A Military-Political History, 1918–1941* (New York: Macmillan and Co., 1962); and Condoleezza Rice, "The Making of Soviet Strategy," in *Makers of Modern Strategy, from Machiavelli to the Nuclear Age*, ed. Peter Paret (Princeton: Princeton University Press, 1986), pp. 648–76.

23. The clearest exposition of this history is Vitaly Rapoport and Yuri Alexeev, *High Treason: Essays on the History of the Red Army, 1918–1938*, ed. Vladimir G. Treml; Bruce Adams, co-ed. and trans. (Durham, N.C.: Duke University Press, 1985), especially pp. 127–37. See also Rice, "Making of Soviet Strategy," and Erickson, *Soviet High Command*.

24. V. N. Lobov, "Aktual'nye voprosy razvitiia teorii sovetskoi voennoi strategii 20-x-serediny 30-x godov," *Voenno-Istoricheskii Zhurnal*, no. 2 (1989): 50.

25. Albert Seaton, *Stalin as Warlord* (London: B. T. Batsford, 1976), p. 82.

26. Ibid., p. 270.

27. Both of these points are made by Rice, "The Party, the Military, and Decision Authority in the Soviet Union," p. 57.

28. Colton emphasizes the degree of professionalization of the Soviet military despite Stalin's repression; "Perspectives on Civil-Military Relations in the Soviet Union," p. 21.

29. This is discussed by J. M. Mackintosh, "The Red Army," p. 63; and by Leonard Schapiro, "The Great Purge," in *The Red Army*, ed. B. M. Lidell Hart, pp. 65–66.

30. Schapiro, "The Great Purge," p. 68. See also Timothy R. Colton, *Commissars, Commanders and Civilian Authority: The Structure of Soviet Military Politics* (Cambridge, Mass.: Harvard University Press, 1979).

31. Ibid., pp. 68–69; Erickson, *The Soviet High Command*, p. 463.

32. Erickson, ibid., p. 470.

33. This is summarized by Condoleezza Rice, "Soviet Staff Structure and Planning in World War II," in *Contemporary Soviet Military Affairs: The Legacy of World War II*, ed. Jonathan R. Adelman and Cristann Lea Gibson (Boston: Unwin Hyman, 1989), pp. 41–42. In the 1980s, analysis of the reasons why Operation Barbarossa succeeded so fully became a major theme in writings by Soviet military officers.

34. Colton, "Perspectives on Civil-Military Relations in the Soviet Union," p. 20.

35. Rice, "Soviet Strategy," pp. 668–69.

36. Danilov, "Kommentarii voennogo istorika," p. 55.

37. Holloway, *Soviet Union and the Arms Race*, p. 36.

38. This is discussed in detail by Garthoff, *Soviet Strategy in the Nuclear Age*; and Dinerstein, *War and the Soviet Union*.

39. Holloway, *Soviet Union and the Arms Race*, p. 36; and Rice, "Party and Military in the Soviet Union," p. 60.

40. This is summarized in Raymond L. Garthoff, *Soviet Military Policy*, pp. 48–49.

41. Ibid., p. 51. Even when Khrushchev felt threatened by the growing domestic political power and popularity of Defense Minister and war hero Marshal Zhukov, the terror weapon was not invoked. Zhukov was stripped of his rank in both the military and the Communist Party, yet lived out his life in peace, was allowed to publish his memoirs during the Brezhnev era, and has in the past few years been rehabilitated posthumously. The Zhukov incident is discussed in depth by Timothy J. Colton, *Commissars, Commanders, and Civilian Authority*.

42. David Holloway, *Technology, Management and the Soviet Military Establishment*, Adelphi Paper 76 (London: International Institute for Strategic Studies, 1971).

43. For discussions of this control and how it was both manifested and partially overcome during the SALT negotiations of the early 1970s, see Raymond L. Garthoff, "The Soviet Military and SALT," in *Soviet Decisionmaking for National Security*, ed. William Potter and Jiri Valenta (London: George Allen and Unwin, 1984), pp. 145, 154; and Thomas W. Wolfe, *The SALT Experience* (Cambridge, Mass.: Ballinger, 1979), p. 61.

44. Amy Knight believes that the GRU concentrated on "hard" data collection, while the KGB provided "soft" human intelligence indicators on strategic warning issues. Knight, "The KGB and Civil-Military Relations," in *Soldiers and the Soviet State: Civil-Military Relations from Brezhnev to Gorbachev*, ed. Timothy J. Colton and Thane Gustafson (Princeton: Princeton University Press, 1990), p. 97.

45. See M. M. Kozlov, ed., *Akademiia General'nogo Shtaba* (Moscow: Voenizdat, 1987), passim; and Army General I. E. Shavrov, Commandant of the General Staff Academy, "Sorok let voennoi akademii General'nogo Shtaba," *Voennaia Mysl*, no. 11 (1976): 3–14.

46. This is suggested by Maj. Gen. A. G. Khor'kov, "Istoricheskii opyt v razvitii voennoi nauki," *Voennaia Mysl'*, no. 6 (1990): 28–36.

47. Col. A. Tonkikh, "Voenno-nauchnye konferentsii—vazhnaia forma voenno-nauchnoi raboty," *Voennaia Mysl'*, no. 12 (1971): 36.

48. A shortened version of the article is reproduced in M. V. Frunze, *Izbrannye Proizvedeniia*, pp. 30–51.

49. Makhmut Akhmetovich Gareev, *M. V. Frunze, Military Theorist*, trans. from Russian by an unnamed source (Washington, D.C.: Pergamon-Brassey's, 1988), p. 64.

50. Ibid.

51. David Alan Rosenberg, "Reality and Responsibility: Power and Process in the Making of United States Nuclear Strategy, 1945–1968," *Journal of Strategic Studies* 9 (March 1986): 35–52.

52. The journal which chronicles OPFOR activities and provides new informa-

tion to the OPFOR about Soviet and other potential opponent tactics is *Red Thrust Star*, published for the U.S. Forces Command OPFOR Training Program by the S-2, 177th Armored Brigade, Fort Irwin, California.

Chapter 3
Soviet Reactions to Flexible Response

1. See, for example, Jane E. Stromseth, *The Origins of Flexible Response* (New York: St. Martin's Press, 1988).

2. The speech is reprinted in the *Department of State Bulletin* 30 (Jan. 25, 1954): 107–10. It is summarized and analyzed by Fred Kaplan in *The Wizards of Armageddon* (New York: Touchstone, 1983), pp. 174–75.

3. Jane E. Stromseth quotes JCS 2101/113 to this effect in *The Origins of Flexible Response*, p. 13.

4. David Alan Rosenberg, "The Origins of Overkill," *International Security* 7 (Spring 1983): 28–29.

5. Stromseth, *Origins of Flexible Response*, p. 14.

6. Stromseth, *Origins of Flexible Reponse*, summarizes U.S. troop commitment levels in Europe, p. 89.

7. Lawrence Freedman, *The Evolution of Nuclear Strategy* (New York: St. Martin's Press, 1981), p. 86.

8. The development of this thinking and the debates that surrounded the issue are traced by a variety of excellent Western historical studies, including Freedman, *Evolution of Nuclear Strategy*; Stromseth, *Origins of Flexible Response*; and Kaplan, *Wizards of Armageddon*.

9. This is noted by Robert Osgood, *NATO: The Entangling Alliance* (Chicago: University of Chicago Press, 1962), p. 125.

10. A. J. Bacevich presents a summary of these events in *The Pentomic Era* (Washington, D.C.: National Defense University Press, 1986), pp. 43–46.

11. Osgood, *NATO*, pp. 161–62.

12. This is reported by David N. Schwartz, *NATO's Nuclear Dilemmas* (Washington, D.C.: Brookings, 1983), pp. 140–41.

13. This shift is documented in detail by Robert A. Wampler, *NATO Strategic Planning and Nuclear Weapons, 1950–1957*, Nuclear History Program Occasional Paper 6 (College Park, Md.: Center for International Security Studies at Maryland, 1990).

14. See Stromseth, *Origins of Flexible Response*, p. 19.

15. Kaplan, *Wizards of Armageddon*, provides a fascinating summary of developments at RAND.

16. The text of the note is found in U.S. Senate Foreign Relations Committee, *Documents on Germany, 1944–1961*, 87th Congress, 1st Session (Washington, D.C.: GPO, 1961), pp. 348–63. A detailed history of the second Berlin crisis is provided by Jack M. Schick, *The Berlin Crisis, 1958–1962* (Philadelphia: University of Pennsylvania Press, 1971).

17. Gregory M. Pedlow, "Multinational Contingency Planning During the Second Berlin Crisis: The Live Oak Organization, 1959–1963," paper prepared for delivery at the Third Study and Review Conference of the Nuclear History Program, Ebenhausen, Germany, June 1991.

18. Schick, *The Berlin Crisis*, p. 140.

19. The speech is reprinted in the *New York Times*, March 29, 1961.

20. The specifics of this build-up are detailed by William P. Mako, *U.S. Ground Forces and the Defense of Central Europe* (Washington, D.C.: Brookings, 1983), p. 17.

21. Schick, *The Berlin Crisis*, pp. 151–52.

22. This is noted by John P. Rose, *The Evolution of U.S. Army Nuclear Doctrine* (Boulder, Colo.: Westview, 1980), p. 76.

23. See Michael A. Molino, "Division Defensive Operations for Nuclear and Nonnuclear Environments," *Military Review* 53, no. 12 (Dec. 1973): 13.

24. U.S. Army, FM 100–5, "Operations," February 19, 1962; examples of the new recognition of limited war as a possibility in Europe appear on pp. 4 and 8.

25. Ibid., p. 12.

26. See the table in Stromseth, *Origins of Flexible Response*, p. 89.

27. Three excellent books trace the course of Flexible Response in these three countries: Catherine McArdle Kelleher, *Germany and the Politics of Nuclear Weapons* (New York: Columbia University Press, 1975); Wilfrid L. Kohl, *French Nuclear Diplomacy* (Princeton: Princeton University Press, 1971); and Andrew J. Pierre's study of British defense debates, *Nuclear Politics* (London: Oxford University Press, 1972).

28. Freedman, *Evolution of Nuclear Strategy*, p. 285.

29. The title page of each issue of the journal bears the inscription, "Only for generals, admirals and officers of the Soviet Army and Navy."

30. It was replaced by the unclassified journal *Zarubezhnoe Voennoe Obozrenie* in 1973.

31. These included Maj. Gen. in the Reserves of the Belgian Army Emile Wanty, "Vliianie atomnogo oruzhiia na organizatsiiu i taktiki voisk," *Voennyi Zarubezhnik*, no. 2 (1956): 3–4; H. A. DeWeerd, "Meniaiushchaiasia voennaia politika Velikobritanii," ibid., pp. 50–51; and Lt. Col. F. Miksche, "Soobrazheniia po organizatsii budushchikh sukhoputnykh voisk," *Voennyi Zarubezhnik*, no. 6 (1956): 4.

32. For example, Gen. Willard G. Wyman's article which originally appeared in *Armor*, "Osnovnye printsipy doktriny Armii," *Voennyi Zarubezhnik*, no. 7 (1958): 4–6 especially, and Maj. R. Allen's article which originally appeared in *Military Review*, "Polevaia armiia pri razvitii uspekha," ibid., p. 13.

33. Col. M. Mikhailov, "Sukhoputnye voiska v ogranichennoi voine," *Voennyi Zarubezhnik*, no. 10 (1958): 82.

34. Maj. D. Vladimirov, book review, *Voennyi Zarubezhnik*, no. 12 (1959): 73–76.

35. Col. of the Reserves G. Iofin, book review, *Voennyi Zarubezhnik*, no. 10 (1960): 81–88.

36. This information is found in annotations made by Herbert S. Dinerstein, Leon Gouré, and Thomas W. Wolfe in their translated edition of *Soviet Military Strategy*, original editor V. D. Sokolovskii (Santa Monica: RAND, 1963), pp. 530–33.

37. Pedlow, "Multinational Contingency Planning," p. 34.

38. *Pravda*, January 15, 1960.

39. For examples, see Col. A. Khrisanfov, "Nachalnyi period sovremennoi

voiny po vzgliadam burzhuazhnykh voennykh ideologov," *Voennyi Zarubezhnik*, no. 10 (1960): 61–71; Col. P. Vasil'ev, "O roli vnezapnosti v sovremennoi voine i sposobakh ee dostizheniia," *Voennyi Zarubezhnik*, no. 3 (1961): 50–59; and again by Khrisanfov, "Vzgliady komandovanniia armii SShA na primenenie raketno-iadernogo oruzhiia," *Voennyi Zarubezhnik*, no. 5 (1961): 66–75, which argued that the U.S. planned to use nuclear-rocket weapons in all wars, including limited ones.

40. An unsigned editorial, "Novyi voennyi biudzhet SShA—usilenie gonki vooruzhenii," *Voennyi Zarubezhnik*, no. 8 (1961): 16–17, mentioned that conventional weapons development was receiving a larger share of the U.S. defense budget than it had previously; while the article connected this with the new emphasis on local war doctrine, it implied that such doctrine was intended for conflict on the periphery (i.e., not in Europe). But two issues later, a summary article stated that the U.S. was now preparing for both nuclear and conventional war, and did not add any limiting phrases about where such conventional war might take place. Col. N. Andreev and Col. I. Aleksandrov, "Izmeneniia v organizatsii soedinenii sukhoputnykh voisk SShA," *Voennyi Zarubezhnik*, no. 10 (1961): 69–75.

41. Col. V. Machalov, "Voennaia programma SShA," *Voennaia Mysl'*, no. 1 (1962): 49–58; Col. K. Ivanov, "Izmeniia v voennoi politike i strategii SShA," *Voennaia Mysl'*, no. 7 (1962): 46–56; Maj. Ye. Fedulaev, "Strategiia bezrassudnogo avantiurizma," *Kommunist Vooruzhennykh Sil* (*KVS*), no. 16 (1962): 83–87; and Col. S. Konstantinov, "Voennaia doktrina amerikanskogo imperializma," *KVS*, no. 23 (1962): 79–85.

42. While Western policymakers took a "wait and see" approach to recent Soviet claims of military doctrine change toward defensive defense and reasonable sufficiency, it must be remembered that these Soviet changes were in the direction of a decrease in the level of competition, not an increase. Flexible Response did not represent a decrease in the level of military competition; it represented the expansion of that competition to an additional arena beyond nuclear weapons and nuclear planning.

43. See, for example, Benjamin S. Lambeth, "On Thresholds in Soviet Military Thought," *Washington Quarterly* 7 (Spring 1984): 69–76; Joseph D. Douglass, Jr. and Amoretta M. Hoeber, *Conventional War and Escalation: The Soviet View* (New York: Crane, Russak and Co., 1981); and Thomas W. Wolfe, "The Convergence Issue and Soviet Strategic Policy," in *The RAND 25th Anniversary Volume* (Santa Monica: RAND, 1973), pp. 137–50.

44. Michael MccGwire, *Military Objectives in Soviet Foreign Policy* (Washington, D.C.: Brookings, 1987); and Andrew C. Goldberg, *New Developments in Soviet Military Strategy*, CSIS Significant Issues Series, vol. 9, no. 7, Washington, D.C., 1987.

45. See James M. McConnell, *The Soviet Shift in Emphasis from Nuclear to Conventional*, vols. 1 and 2, Center for Naval Analyses Research Contribution 490, Alexandria, Va., June 1983.

46. "Deistvie atomnogo oruzhiia," *Voennaia Mysl'*, no. 3 (1954): 69–78.

47. Col. R. Murav'ev, "O sisteme boevoi podgotovki amerikanskoi armii," *Voennia Mysl'*, no. 5 (1954): 64–65.

48. Col. S. Volkov and Lt. Col. A. Zaletnyi, "Vozrozhdeniie fashistskoi voen-noi ideologii v Zapadnoi Germanii," *Voennaia Mysl'*, no. 5 (1954): 70–73; and Col. V. Mochalov, "Osobennosti nastupatel'nykh deistvii polevoi armii v sovre-mennykh usloviiakh," *Voennaia Mysl'*, no. 7 (1954): 74–84.

49. See Maj. Gen. V. Yemelin, "Zametki o literature po protivoatomnoi zashchite," *Voennaia Mysl'*, no. 6 (1959): 83, which emphasizes protection of troops in the battlefield.

50. Col. B. Khabarov, "Nekotorye voprosy upravleniia voiskami v nastu-patel'noi operatsii," *Voennaia Mysl'*, no. 7 (1959): 80–87.

51. The most in-depth criticism of Soviet operational plans is provided by Richard Ned Lebow, "The Soviet Offensive in Europe: The Schlieffen Plan Revis-ited?" *International Security* 9 (Spring 1985): 44–78. See also Jack Snyder, "The Gorbachev Revolution: A Waning of Soviet Expansionism?" *International Secu-rity* 12 (Winter 1987/88): 123–24.

52. See, for example, "Leninizm—nashe vsepobezhdaiushchee znamia," *Voennaia Mysl'*, no. 1 (1954): 15.

53. See Maj. Gen. V. Kuvshinnikov, "Nekotorye voprosy sovremennogo vstrechnogo boia," *Voennaia Mysl'*, no. 5 (1959): 17–27; Maj. Gen. B. Golov-chiner, "Counterattack and Repulse of Counterattacks," *Voennaia Mysl'*, no. 6 (1959): 13–24 (an English title for *Voennaia Mysl'* articles in my citations will indicate that the version being used is a U.S. Central Intelligence Agency or De-fense Intelligence Agency translation); and Maj. Gen. M. Smirnov, Col. I. Baz', Col. S. Kozlov, and Col. P. Sidorov, "K voprosu o kharaktere sovetskoi voennoi nauke, ee predmete i soderzhannii," *Voennaia Mysl'*, no. 7 (1959): 5, who discuss the use of tanks in atomic conditions.

54. Col. I. Korotkov, "O razvitii sovetskoi voennoi teorii v poslevoennye gody," *Voenno-Istoricheskii Zhurnal* (*VIZh*), no. 4 (1964): 39–50; quotation is from p. 48.

55. V. D. Sokolovskii, ed. *Voennaia Strategiia* (Moscow: Voenizdat, 1962), p. 325.

56. Col. A. Zhelnov, "O deistvii zakona otritsaniia otritsaniia v voennom dele," *Voennaia Mysl'*, no. 3 (1962): 18–32; and Col. V. Larionov, "Za tvor-cheskoe razvitie sovetskoi voennoi nauki," *Voennaia Mysl'*, no. 10 (1962): 17–24.

57. Maj. D. Kazakov, "Teoreticheskaia i metodologicheskaia osnova so-vetskoi voennoi nauki," *KVS*, no. 10 (1963): 11–12.

58. See Col. Ye. Sulimov and Maj. A. Timorin, "Osnovye cherty sovremen-nogo etapa v razvitii vooruzhennykh sil SSSR," *KVS*, no. 24 (1962): 38–44; Col. V. Sergeev, "Partiinost' voennoi nauki," *KVS*, no. 1 (1963): 20–27; Lt. Col. V. Petrov, "Gotovit' podchinennykh k aktivnym boevym destviiam v usloviiakh pri-meneniia raketno-iadernogo oruzhiia," an article highlighted for use in political classes in the military, *KVS*, no. 12 (1963): 70–77; and Col. A. Iolev, "Trebova-niia XXII s'ezda partii i programmy KPSS k voennym kadram," *KVS*, no. 15 (1963): 42–50.

59. Summarized in Col. L. Belousov, "Konferentsiia o sovetskoi voennoi doktrine," *VIZh*, no. 10 (1963): 122–23.

60. Ibid., p. 123.

61. R. Ya. Malinovskii, "Revoliutsiia v voennom dele i zadachi voennoi

pechati," answers to questions posed by reporters, *KVS*, no. 21 (1963): 8–10; Col. P. Derevianko, "Nekotorye osobennosti sovremennoi revoliutsii v voennom dele," *KVS*, no. 1 (1964): 15–25; Col. V. Glazov, "O nekotorykh osobennostiakh vedeniia boevykh deistvii v iadernoi voine," *KVS*, no. 3 (1964): 41–46; Maj. Gen. S. Bronevskii, "The Factors of Space and Time in Military Operations," *Voennaia Mysl'*, no. 7 (1963): 36; A. Iovlev, "On Mass Armies in Modern War," *Voennaia Mysl'*, no. 10, pt. 2 (1963): 1 and 9; and Maj. Gen. of Tank Troops A. Zhilin, "Some Questions of Meeting Engagements of Large Tank Groupings," *Voennaia Mysl'*, no. 2 (1964): 2.

62. See Col. K. Lapshin, "Surmounting Obstacles and Zones of Destruction and Radioactive Contamination of the Offense," *Voennaia Mysl'*, no. 10, pt. 1 (1963): 15; and Capt. 1st Rank V. Kulakov, "Problems of Military-Technical Superiority," *Voennaia Mysl'*, no. 1 (1964): 14.

63. Maj. Gen. K. Bochkarev, "An Evaluation of the Results of the June Plenum of the Central Committee of the Communist Party USSR [*sic*]," *Voennaia Mysl'*, no. 7 (1963): 9.

64. Maj. Gen. I. Anureev, corps of engineers, et al., "The Aims and Content of the Theory of Operations Research," *Voennaia Mysl'*, no. 7 (1963): 27.

65. Col. L. Balansov and Col. L. Sapozhnikov, "Troop Combat Operations under Conditions of Radioactive Contamination of Terrain," *Voennaia Mysl'*, no. 7 (1963): 48–61.

66. Col. I. Vorob'ev, "Maneuver in Operations and in Combat," *Voennaia Mysl'*, no. 9 (1963): 19–30.

67. Roman Kolkowicz, *The Soviet Military and the Communist Party*, pp. 161–62.

68. S. Kozlov, "The Development of Soviet Military Science after World War II," *Voennaia Mysl'*, no. 2 (1964): 47.

69. S. Kozlov, "Voennaia doktrina i voennaia nauka," *KVS*, no. 5 (1964): 9–16.

70. S. Kozlov, "Voennaia nauka i voennye doktriny v pervoi mirovoi voine," *VIZh*, no. 11 (1964): 31–41.

71. Ibid., p. 41.

72. S. Kozlov, "The Formulation and Development of Soviet Military Doctrine," *Voennaia Mysl'*, no. 7 (1966): 57.

73. N. Liutov, comment, *Voennaia Mysl'*, no. 10 (1964): 41.

74. A report of a similar doctrinal debate in the Polish General Staff journal, *Mysl Wojskowa*, indicates that 1964 was the starting point for the flexible response discussion in the Warsaw Pact as a whole. See Col. Ernest Vishnevskii and Col. Zdzislav Golomb, editors of *Mysl Wojskowa*, "Voennye deistviia bez primeneniia iadernogo oruzhiia," *Voennaia Mysl'*, no. 2 (1970): 62–70.

75. *Pravda*, January 15, 1960.

76. Earlier, beginning in 1955, Khrushchev had made several troop cuts, totalling around two million men, without provoking any apparent protest from the military; see Wolfe, *Soviet Power and Europe*, p. 162. In July 1961, Khrushchev announced that the troop cut would be suspended in response to U.S. President Kennedy's force expansion during the Berlin Crisis; *Pravda*, July 9, 1961. Some Western observers have expressed doubt about whether the Berlin Crisis was the

reason for the troop level reinstatement, or merely the excuse given for a policy that Khrushchev was forced to take because of pressure from Party hardliners. See Michel Tatu, *Power in the Kremlin* (London: Collins, 1969), p. 171. In December 1963, Khrushchev proposed yet another troop cut, but it is unclear whether or not any serious attempt was made to implement it. See Wolfe, *Soviet Power and Europe*, p. 165.

77. P. Rotmistrov, "O roli vnezapostni v sovremennoi voine," *Voennaia Mysl'*, no. 2 (1955): 19.

78. Col. R. Murav'ev, "Osobennosti vedeniia boevykh deistvii v pustyne," *Voennaia Mysl'*, no. 2 (1955): 77–84, may have been expecting the U.S. to use tactical nuclear weapons even in a war outside of Europe; Col. M. Novokhatko, "Voennye voprosy v proizbedeniiakh V.I. Lenin," *Voennaia Mysl'*, no. 4 (1955): 12, reminded his readers that Lenin thought that the army needed to master the techniques of its enemies, and that "new military technique calls forth the necessity of new tactics."

79. Wolfe, *Soviet Power and Europe*, p. 161.

80. See George B. Kistiakowsky, *A Scientist at the White House* (Cambridge, Mass.: Harvard University Press, 1976), pp. 227, 160.

81. Ibid., p. 106.

82. Warner, *The Military in Contemporary Soviet Politics* (Westport, Conn.: Praeger, 1977), p. 128.

83. John Erickson, *Soviet Military Power* (London: Royal United Services Institute, 1971), p. 43.

84. See Oleg Penkovskiy, *The Penkovskiy Papers* (New York: Doubleday and Co., 1965), p. 230. Oleg Penkovskiy was a spy for the West, executed by the Soviets in 1963. The authenticity of this book has been questioned.

85. Penkovskiy mentions this, *Penkovskiy Papers*, pp. 248–49. At the time that this book went to press, this collection had not been declassified either by the Soviet or Russian General Staff, or by the U.S. Central Intelligence Agency, and is not yet available in the United States to those without security clearances.

86. V. I. Tolubko, *Nedelin* (a biography of the first Commander-in-Chief of the Strategic Rocket Forces by his deputy and successor) (Moscow: Molodaia Gvardiia, 1979), p. 181.

87. Penkovskiy, *Penkovskiy Papers*, p. 249.

88. *Pravda*, January 15, 1960.

89. Ibid., October 25, 1961.

90. R. Ya. Malinovskii, *Bditel'no Stoiat' na Strazhe Mira* (Moscow: Voenizdat, 1962), pp. 25–26.

91. See Wolfe, *A First Reaction to the New Soviet Book "Military Strategy,"* RM-3495 (Santa Monica: RAND, 1963), pp. 11–12.

92. See, for example, articles by Col. A. M. Iovlev, *Krasnaia Zvezda*, April 5, 1961, as reported in *Current Digest of the Soviet Press* (*CDSP*) 13, no. 13: 8–9; Col. I. Sidelnikov, *Krasnaia Zvezda*, May 11, 1962, as reported in *CDSP* 14, no. 22: 13–15; and Chief Marshal of Tank Troops P. Rotmistrov, *Izvestiia*, October 20, 1962, as reported in *CDSP* 14, no. 43: 20–21.

93. Maj. Gen. P. Zhilin, "Polkovodcheskaia deiatel'nost' M.I. Kutuzova v Otechestvennoi voine 1812 goda," *VIZh*, no. 7 (1962): 29–41.

94. Marshal of the Soviet Union R. Malinovskii, "Znachenie pobedy Rossii v Otechestvennoi voine 1812 goda," *VIZh*, no. 9 (1962): 9.

95. Col. of Reserves V. Tsvetkov, "Vydaiushchiisia voennyi myslitel' XIX veka," *VIZh*, no. 1 (1964): 47–59.

96. Lt. Col. Ye. Rybkin, "Zakony materialisticheskoi dialektiki i ikh proiavlenie v voennom dele," *KVS*, no. 7 (1964): 45–51.

97. Col. I. Kuz'min, "Bor'ba novogo so starym v razvitii voennogo dela," *KVS*, no. 8 (1964): 40–45.

98. Capt. 1st Rank B. Demidov, "Zakony dialektiki i voennaia nauka," *KVS*, no. 9 (1964): 92.

99. This is argued by Michel Tatu, *Power in the Kremlin* (London: Collins, 1969), p. 70.

100. M. A. Moiseev, "Ob avtore i ego knige," addendum to M. V. Zakharov, *General'nyi Shtab v Predvoennye Gody* (Moscow: Voenizdat, 1989), p. 305.

101. *Khrushchev Remembers: The Last Testament*, trans. and ed. Strobe Talbott (Boston: Little, Brown and Co., 1974), p. 17.

102. John Erickson, *Soviet Military Power*, p. 8.

103. Marshal of the Soviet Union M. V. Zakharov, *Krasnaia Zvezda*, February 4, 1965. While Zakharov's last quotation, about the need to inculcate respect for military science in the "military leadership," might seem confusing, it is comprehensible when it is remembered that the state, by definition, has ultimate leadership responsibilities over military doctrine. I am assuming that Zakharov was not accusing the General Staff of failing to listen to the advice of military professionals; such an accusation would not make sense.

104. Col. I. Prusanov, "Deiatel'nost' partii po ukrepleniiu vooruzhennykh sil v usloviiakh revoliutsii v voennom dele," *KVS*, no. 3 (1966): 8–16, especially p. 12.

105. The quotation and translation are made by Leon Gouré, *Notes on the Second Edition of Marshal V. D. Sokolovskii's "Military Strategy,"* RM-3972 (Santa Monica: RAND, 1964), p. 49.

106. A. Kh. Babadzhanian, ed. *Tanki i Tankovye Voiska* (Moscow: Voenizdat, 1970), p. 199.

107. *Pravda*, May 2, 1961.

108. M. V. Zakharov, "New Horizons of the Military Press," *Voennaia Mysl'*, no. 9 (1966): 5; I. Korotkov, "Some Questions on the History of Soviet Military Science," *Voennaia Mysl'*, no. 11 (1973): 107; Kh. Dzhelaukhov, "The Evolution of U.S. Military Doctrine," *Voennaia Mysl'*, no. 9 (1967): 94.

109. Vishnevskii and Golomb, "Voennye deistviia bez primeneniia iadernogo oruzhiia."

110. Col. V. Shchedrov, "Camouflaging Troops during Regrouping and Maneuver," *Voennaia Mysl'*, no. 6 (1966): 61.

111. Lt. Col. Ye. Galitskii, "Restoration of Combat Effectiveness of Troops and Elimination of the Effects of Enemy Nuclear Strikes during an Offensive," *Voennaia Mysl'*, no. 8 (1967): 42–48.

112. Army Gen. A. Yepishev, "The Question of Moral-Political and Psychological Training of Troops," *Voennaia Mysl'*, no. 12 (1968): 16.

113. Col. D. Samurokov, "On the Question of Foresight," *Voennaia Mysl'*, no. 9 (1971): 27–40.

114. Col. Gen. of the Artillery G. Peredel'skii, "Evolution of Forms and Methods of Artillery Control," *Voennaia Mysl'*, no. 3 (1972): 90–102.

115. Col. Gen. I. Shkadov, "Contemporary Art of Warfare and Some Questions on the Training of Military Personnel," *Voennaia Mysl'*, no. 11 (1973): 19.

116. R. Malinovskii, "Historical Exploits of the Soviet People and their Armed Forces in the Great Patriotic War," *Voennaia Mysl'*, no. 5 (1965): 27; M. Kalashnik, "Actual Questions of Ideological Work in the Armed Forces," *Voennaia Mysl'*, no. 8 (1966): 2; M. Skovorodkin, "Some Questions on Coordination of Branches of Armed Forces in Major Operations," *Voennaia Mysl'*, no. 2 (1967): 36–37; Col. Gen. V. Margelov, "Airborne Troops of the Soviet Army," *Voennaia Mysl'*, no. 8 (1967): 18; P. Poluboiarov, "The Armored Troops of the Soviet Army," *Voennaia Mysl'*, no. 9 (1967): 26–27; G. Semenov, "The Content of the Concept of an Operation," *Voennaia Mysl'*, no. 1 (1968): 92; Maj. Gen. S. Begunov, "The Maneuver of Forces and Materiel in an Offensive," *Voennaia Mysl'*, no. 5 (1968): 42; Lt. Gen. I. Zav'ialov, "Evolution in the Correlation of Strategy, Operational Art and Tactics," *Voennaia Mysl'*, no. 11 (1971): 36; Maj. Gen. R. Simonian, "The Development of Military Intelligence," *Voennaia Mysl'*, no. 8 (1972): 74; and Gen. I. Shavrov, "Soviet Operational Art," *Voennaia Mysl'*, no. 10 (1973): 11–12. Shavrov's statement here is somewhat odd, since lectures which he gave at the General Staff Academy sometime between 1973 and 1975 clearly stated that a conventional pause in European war was a contingency which demanded consideration. See *The Voroshilov Lectures*, vol. 1, comp. Ghulam Dastagir Wardak, ed. Graham Hall Turbiville, Jr. (Washington, D.C.: National Defense University Press, 1989), pp. 68–69, 237–39, 249, 253. While most of the lectures in the volume are not identified by author, Shavrov is identified as the deliverer of two specific ones.

117. "Let's Raise Military-Scientific Work to the Level of Party Demands," *Voennaia Mysl'*, no. 3 (1966): 2.

118. V. Penkovskii, "Combat Training of Troops at the Present Stage," *Voennaia Mysl'*, no. 11 (1967): 60.

119. M. Zakharov, "Soviet Military Science over Fifty Years," *Voennaia Mysl'*, no. 2 (1968): 51.

120. See Maj. Gen. B. Golovchiner, "Encirclements and Annihilation of Groupings of Defending Troops," *Voennaia Mysl'*, no. 8 (1964): 42–52; Col. M. Shmelev and Col. A. Sinaev, "Comment," *Voennaia Mysl'*, no. 10 (1964): 32; Maj. Gen. Kh. Dzhelaukhov, "The Infliction of Deep Strikes," *Voennaia Mysl'*, no. 2 (1966): 47; Col. P. Shkarubskii, "Artillery Before and Now," *Voennaia Mysl'*, no. 2 (1966): 51; Maj. Gen. V. Reznichenko and Col. Ye. Bob, "Consolidating a Gain in an Offensive Operation," *Voennaia Mysl'*, no. 3 (1966): 47; and Col. N. Smirnov, "A Meeting Engagement in Nuclear Warfare," *Voennaia Mysl'*, no. 9 (1967): 48–49.

121. See Col. M. Fedulov, "Problems of Modern Combined-Arms Combat," *Voennaia Mysl'*, no. 10 (1964): 28–29; and Col. A. Rodin, "Increasing Antitank Stability—A Trend of Modern Defense," *Voennaia Mysl'*, no. 8 (1972): 59, as

excerpted by Joseph D. Douglass, Jr., and Amoretta M. Hoeber, in *Index to and Extracts from Voyennaya Mysl', 1971–1973* (Alexandria, Va.: Systems Planning Corporation, 1980), p. 124.

122. M. Povalyi, "Development of Soviet Military Strategy," *Voennaia Mysl'*, no. 2 (1967): 71.

123. N. Vasendin and N. Kuznetsov, "Modern Warfare and Surprise Attack," *Voennaia Mysl'*, no. 6 (1968): 45.

124. See, for example, "Triumphal Step of Leninism," *Voennaia Mysl'*, no. 4 (1967): 8.

125. V. Akimov and A. Damor, "The Foreign Press on Military-Economic Preparations of the Chinese People's Republic," *Voennaia Mysl'*, no. 9 (1973): 104.

126. Col. M. Vilinov, "An Object Lesson of History," *Voennaia Mysl'*, no. 5 (1969): 79–85.

127. The idea that the build-up of Soviet conventional capabilities during this era was due at least to some extent to a new Third World power projection mission is presented by Thomas W. Wolfe, *Soviet Power and Europe, 1945–1970* (Baltimore: Johns Hopkins University Press, 1970), pp. 428–50, and by a Yugoslavian analyst of Soviet military affairs, Andro Gabelic, "New Accent in Strategy," *Military Review* 48, no. 8 (August 1968): 83–87. McConnell has argued that the entire Soviet discussion of "local war" in this era dealt only with the Third World, and thus had no relevance for planning in Europe. However, at least since the 1962 edition of Sokolovskii's *Military Strategy*, Soviet officers clearly saw that local war in Europe was a possibility. See McConnell, *Soviet Shift in Emphasis*, pp. 10–11; and Sokolovskii, *Voennaia Strategiia*, pp. 311–12.

128. Col. B. Samurokov, "Combat Operations Involving Conventional Means of Destruction," *Voennaia Mysl'*, no. 8 (1967): 29; Lt. Gen. N. Sliunin, "Nuclear Resistance of Ground Troops," *Voennaia Mysl'*, no. 12 (1967): 44; Maj. Gen. S. Shtrik, "The Encirclement and Destruction of the Enemy during Combat Operations Not Involving the Use of Nuclear Weapons," *Voennaia Mysl'*, no. 1 (1968): 53; and Maj. Gen. M. Kir'ian, "Weapons of Mass Destruction in the Aggressive Plans of NATO," *Voennaia Mysl'*, no. 12 (1971): 108.

129. I. Yakubovskii, "50 Years of the USSR Armed Forces," *Voennaia Mysl'*, no. 2 (1968): 31–32.

130. G. Ionin and K. Kushch-Zharko, "Defense in the Past and the Present," *Voennaia Mysl'* no. 7 (1971): 62–75.

131. G. Peredel'skii, "Artillery in the Struggle to Attain Fire Superiority," *Voennaia Mysl'*, no. 10 (1973): 57–67.

132. N. Lomov, "Vliianie sovetskoi voennoi doktriny na razvitie voennogo iskusstva," *KVS*, no. 21 (1965): 16.

133. V. Zemskov, "Wars of the Modern Era," *Voennaia Mysl'*, no. 5 (1969): 61.

134. M. Cherednichenko, "Military Strategy and Military Technology," *Voennaia Mysl'*, no. 4 (1973): 53.

135. P. Kurochkin, "A Chronicle of Heroism and Victories," *Voennaia Mysl'*, no. 5 (1968): 91.

136. P. Sidorov, "The Leninist Methodology of Soviet Military Science," *Voennaia Mysl'*, no. 4 (1969): 26.

137. See Lt. Gen. of the Reserves B. Arushanian, "Combat Operations by Tank Units against Operational Defense Reserves," *Voennaia Mysl'*, no. 1, pt. 2 (1966): 29–35; Col. A. Shliapkin, "Air Support of Ground Troops," *Voennaia Mysl'*, no. 8 (1968): 35; and the unsigned editorial, "The Tasks of Soviet Military Science in Light of the Decisions of the 24th CPSU Congress," *Voennaia Mysl'*, no. 8 (1971): 6.

138. Col. I. Liutov, "Some Problems of Defense without the Use of Nuclear Weapons," *Voennaia Mysl'*, no. 7 (1966): 36–46; and Col. P. Shakarubskii, "The Artillery in Modern Combat Operations," *Voennaia Mysl'*, no. 6 (1968): 61–66.

139. Stephen M. Meyer, *Soviet Theatre Nuclear Forces, Part 1: Development of Doctrine and Objectives*, Adelphi Paper 187 (London: International Institute of Strategic Studies, 1984), pp. 25–27, 33.

140. S. Ivanov, "Soviet Military Doctrine and Strategy," *Voennaia Mysl'*, no. 5 (1969): 49.

141. B. Balev, "Sea and Ocean Communications and Warfare on Them," *Voennaia Mysl'*, no. 10 (1971): 50.

142. John F. Burns in a *New York Times* article on the replacement of Gen. Viktor G. Kulikov as Commander-in-Chief of the Warsaw Pact ("Moscow Replaces Military Chief of Warsaw Pact," February 3, 1989) quoted "Western military experts" to the effect that Kulikov held the "view that any military confrontation with Western forces in Europe would rapidly grow into a nuclear exchange."

143. I was told that 1965 was the key year, by a retired Soviet General Staff officer in Moscow who was in a position to influence doctrinal discussions in the 1960s. This seems logical, since it is in 1966 that the General Staff journal began to mention changes in military planning. Michael MccGwire, *Military Objectives*, states, based on his analysis of the Soviet military press, that 1966 was the year that marked a sea-change in Soviet military thinking about future war. The case study presented here does not support his view, since debate over the issue began in the early 1960s and continued throughout at least the early 1970s.

144. See William F. Scott, "Changes in Tactical Concepts within the Soviet Forces," in *The Future of Soviet Military Power*, ed. Lawrence L. Whetten (New York: Crane, Russak and Co., 1976), p. 77; Malcolm Mackintosh, *The Evolution of the Warsaw Pact*, Adelphi Paper 58 (London: International Institute of Strategic Studies, 1969), pp. 7–8; and Jeffrey Simon, "Evaluation and Integration of Non-Soviet Warsaw Pact Forces into the Combined Armed Forces," *Signal* 40, no. 4 (December 1985): 52.

145. As summarized by V. G. Kulikov, Chief of the General Staff, in *Akademiia General'nogo Shtaba* (Moscow: Voenizdat, 1976), p. 207.

146. See John Erickson, *Soviet Military Power*, p. 68. While the Soviet military published many articles and one book (*Dvina*, ed. Maj. Gen. V. S. Riabov [Moscow: Voenizdat, 1970]) about the exercise, almost no mention was made of its nuclear or conventional character. One exception is an article by Engineering Lt. Col. A. Volkov and Lt. Col. of the Reserves N. Zapara, "Nauchno-tekhni-

cheskaia revoliutsiia i voennoe delo," *KVS*, no. 2 (1971), which states on p. 12 that the Dvina exercise demonstrated the role of landing forces in utilizing the results of strategic nuclear strikes.

147. K. Spirov, "Criticism of the Philosophical Foundations of the Imperialist Military Ideology," *Voennaia Mysl'*, no. 3 (1966): 43.

148. See Maj. Gen. of Aviation V. Kruglov and Col. M. Yegorov, "The Military Doctrines of the NATO Countries," *Voennaia Mysl'*, no. 8 (1966), especially pp. 94 and 96 on allied disagreements; Col. D. Ivanov, "The Hotbed of Militarism and Tension in Europe," *Voennaia Mysl'*, no. 7 (1967): 73–83; Maj. Gen. A. Marionov, "On a Dangerous Path," *Voennaia Mysl'*, no. 1 (1968): 90; Col. N. Glazunov, "The Bundeswehr—Weapon of Aggression and Revenge," *Voennaia Mysl'*, no. 1 (1969): 75–81; Col. O. Rubtsov, "West Germany: Politics and the Bundeswehr," *Voennaia Mysl'*, no. 3 (1971), especially pp. 106–7 and 112; and Col. V. Tumas and Col. N. Sergeev, "The West German Army Corps in Basic Types of Combat," *Voennaia Mysl'*, no. 1 (1972): 97–108.

149. Statements to this effect were made in lectures on official Soviet doctrine and strategy given at the Voroshilov General Staff Academy to future General Staff officers. See *The Voroshilov Lectures*, volume 1, pp. 74, 249.

150. Ibid., pp. 74, 262.

151. Ibid., pp. 271, 312–13.

152. See Stephen Meyer, *Soviet Theatre Nuclear Forces, Part 2: Capabilities and Intentions*, Adelphi Paper 188 (London: International Institute for Strategic Studies, 1984), pp. 22, 54; and Wolfe, *Soviet Power and Europe*, p. 471.

153. Arthur J. Alexander, *Decision-Making in Soviet Weapons Procurement*, Adelphi Papers 147 and 148 (London: International Institute for Strategic Studies, 1978/1979), p. 22.

154. Meyer, *Soviet Theatre Nuclear Forces, Part 2*, p. 24.

155. The most authoritative account of this development is provided by Meyer, *Soviet Theatre Nuclear Forces*.

156. Thomas W. Wolfe, *The Soviet Military Scene: Institutional and Defense Policy Considerations*, RM-4913 (Santa Monica: RAND, 1966).

157. John Erickson, "Rejuvenating the Soviet High Command," *Military Review* 50, no. 7 (July 1970): 83–84.

158. Erickson, *Soviet Military Power*, p. 13. Khrushchev's "rejuvenation" effort did cause intense upheaval within the military, nonetheless. Friction erupted between those in the military who valued engineering expertise and technical education of military cadres, and those who felt threatened by the young technocrats. See David Holloway, *Technology, Management and the Soviet Military Establishment*, Adelphi Paper 76 (London: International Institute of Strategic Studies, 1971).

159. Erickson, *Soviet Military Power*, p. 17.

160. Ibid., pp. 19–20.

161. Ibid., p. 22.

162. This is according to Matthew P. Gallagher and Karl F. Spielmann, Jr., *Soviet Decision-Making for Defense* (New York: Praeger, 1972), p. 42.

163. Many Western scholars and policymakers noted this lack of Soviet civilian military-technical expertise at the beginning of the SALT I negotiations in

1969, and credited Soviet civilian participation in SALT with overcoming the military's information monopoly. See Raymond L. Garthoff, "The Soviet Military and SALT," in *Soviet Decisionmaking for National Security*, ed. William Potter and Jiri Valenta (London: Allen and Unwin, 1984), pp. 154–55; Marshall D. Shulman, "SALT and the Soviet Union," in *SALT: The Moscow Agreements and Beyond*, ed. Mason Willrich and John B. Rhinelander (New York: Free Press, 1974), pp. 115–16; and Thomas W. Wolfe, *The SALT Experience* (Cambridge, Mass.: Ballinger, 1979), p. 61.

164. Eran Oded claims that this responsibility was given to the institute only under Brezhnev, and that before 1965 IMEMO did not deal with military strategy issues; see Oded's book, *Mezhdunarodniki* (Ranat Gan, Israel: Turtledove Publishers, 1979), p. 242. This is not correct; as early as 1963 the IMEMO journal had an article on NATO nuclear weapons policy (N. L'vov, "Iadernaia politika NATO— protivorechiia i razdory," *Mirovaia Ekonomika i Mezhdunarodnye Otnosheniia (MEiMO)*, no. 8 [1963]: 21–35). However, it is correct that before 1966 the accuracy and quality of *MEiMO* articles on Western strategy was very poor.

165. The article was by V. Larionov (who was actually a serving General Staff officer at this time), "Razvitie sredstv vooruzheniia i strategicheskie kontseptsii SShA," *MEiMO*, no. 6 (1966): 74–81.

166. Oded, *Mezhdunarodniki*, p. 251. Examples of *MEiMO* and *SShA* (the ISKAN journal) summary articles on Western military technical developments include V. Kulish, "Novaia voennaia doktrina NATO," *MEiMO*, no. 9 (1968): 27–37; V. Kulish and S. Fedorenko, "Po povodu diskussia v SShA o strategicheskikh vooruzheniiakh," *MEiMO*, no. 3 (1970): 41–49; M. V. Belousov, "Tekhnicheskie aspekty sistemy 'seifgard,' " *SShA*, no. 5 (1970): 118–23; M. Mil'shtein, "Amerikanskie voennye doktriny: preemstvemost' i modifikatsiia," *MEiMO*, no. 8 (1971): 30–41; and V. V. Larionov, "Transformatsiia kontseptsii 'strategicheskoi dostatochnosti,' " *SShA*, no. 11 (1971): 27–36.

167. Kulish, Larionov and Mil'shtein were all General Staff officers; at this time, probably only Larionov remained on active duty.

168. See, for example, early articles by G. A. Trofimenko, including "Nekotory aspekty voenno-politicheskoi strategii SShA," *SShA*, no. 10 (1970): 14–27, and "Politicheskaia realizm i strategiia 'realisticheskogo sderzhivaniia,' " *SShA*, no. 12 (1971): 3–15.

169. See Wolfe, *Soviet Power and Europe*, pp. 294–95, 326–28; and Jonathan Dean, *Watershed in Europe* (Lexington, Mass.: Lexington Books, 1987), pp. 99–102.

170. This is discussed in some detail by Harry Gelman in *The Brezhnev Politburo and the Decline of Détente* (Ithaca: Cornell University Press, 1984), chap. 3.

171. Ibid., p. 81, and note on p. 239.

172. Thomas W. Wolfe, *Soviet Power and Europe*, p. 464.

173. See John Erickson, *Soviet Military Power*, p. 18.

174. This is one of the themes of Tatu, *Power in the Kremlin*. The connection between civil-military debate and intra-Party debate under Khrushchev is also stressed by Christoph Bluth, "Defence and Security," in *Khrushchev and Khrushchevism*, ed. Martin McCauley (London: MacMillan, 1987), pp. 194–209.

175. This in fact includes all of those military writers that this chapter defines as conservatives whose biographies appear in the *Soviet Military Encyclopedia*: V. Margelov, who became Deputy Commander-in-Chief of the Ground Forces for Airborne Troops in 1956; P. Poluboiarov, who held the same position for Armored Troops beginning in 1957; I. Shavrov, who was in the group of World War II Front Commanders that Erickson defined as the old guard; and Malinovskii himself, who was also a World War II Front Commander.

Chapter 4
Soviet Reactions to the Schlesinger Doctrine

1. Recently, Western scholars have pointed out that there was another component of the Schlesinger Doctrine which did not receive much public attention: targeting under the massive strike, Assured Destruction option of the Single Integrated Operational Plan (SIOP) was changed to focus on destroying Soviet economic recovery capabilities. See Desmond Ball, "The Development of the SIOP, 1960–1983," in *Strategic Nuclear Targeting*, ed. Desmond Ball and Jeffrey Richelson (Ithaca: Cornell University Press, 1986), p. 73; and Scott Sagan, *Moving Targets* (Princeton: Princeton University Press, 1989), p. 44. My study will deal only with the limited war portion of the Schlesinger Doctrine, and not with the antirecovery component. This latter component augmented the efficiency of a massive countervalue, Assured Destruction nuclear strike on the Soviet Union, but was not a true innovation in doctrine. It did not involve a basic rethinking of what future war would look like, since the Assured Destruction mission had always been directed toward inflicting unacceptable damage on Soviet society.

2. The best summary of the Soviet military literature on this subject is provided by Notra Trulock, "Soviet Perspectives on Limited Nuclear Warfare," in *Swords and Shields*, ed. Fred S. Hoffman, Albert Wohlstetter, and David S. Yost (Lexington, Mass.: Lexington Books, 1987).

3. Jonathan Haslam notes that from the Soviet perspective, U.S. forward-based systems are a "strategic" threat to Soviet territory, even though the U.S. officially has not considered them part of the "central forces." See *The Soviet Union and the Politics of Nuclear Weapons in Europe, 1969–1987* (Ithaca: Cornell University Press, 1990).

4. See Robert McNamara, Appendix 1, "Recommended Long Range Nuclear Delivery Forces 1963–1967," to the Draft Presidential Memorandum, September 23, 1961, DOD/OSD FOIA, no page numbers on available copy; statement by McNamara before the Senate Armed Services Committee, FY 1963–67 Defense Program and 1963 Defense Budget, January 19, 1962, p. 15, DOD Dir. 5200.10 FOIA; Draft Presidential Memorandum (DPM) on Recommended FY 1965–1969 Strategic Retaliatory Forces, December 6, 1963, DOD/OSD FOIA, pp. I-5, I-6; Statement Before a Joint Session of the Senate Armed Services Committee and the Senate Subcommittee on DOD Appropriations on FY 1965–1969 and 1965 Defense Budget, February 3, 1964, DOD/OSD FOIA pp. 35–36; DPM on Recommended FY 1966–1970 Programs for Strategic Offensive Forces, Continental Air and Missile Defense Forces, and Civil Defense, December 3, 1964, DOD/OSD FOIA, pp. 2–3; Statement before a Joint Session of the Senate Armed Services Committee and the Senate Subcommittee on DOD Appropriations on the FY

1966–1970 Defense Program and 1966 Defense Budget, January/February 1965, DOD/OSD FOIA, p. 48; and DPM on Recommended FY 1967–1971 Strategic Offensive and Defensive Forces, November 1, 1965, DOD/OSD FOIA, no page numbers on available copy; DPM on Recommended FY 1968–1972 Strategic Offensive and Defense Forces, November 9, 1966, DOD/OSD FOIA, pp. 5, 12. All FOIA citations appearing in this chapter refer to documents contained in the collection of the National Security Archive in Washington, D.C.

5. DPM on Strategic Offensive and Defensive Forces, January 15, 1968, DOD/OSD FOIA, p. 6.

6. DPM on Strategic Offensive and Defensive Forces, January 9, 1969, DOD/OSD FOIA, pp. 5, 12.

7. A thorough description of the early phase of this project is provided by Fred Kaplan, *The Wizards of Armageddon* (New York: Touchstone, 1983), pp. 356–58.

8. Ibid., pp. 366–67.

9. Desmond Ball, "The Development of the SIOP," p. 71, notes Secretary of State Henry Kissinger's account of this problem, in *White House Years* (Boston: Little, Brown and Co., 1979), pp. 216–17.

10. Kaplan, *Wizards of Armageddon*, p. 368.

11. This according to Janne E. Nolan, *Guardians of the Arsenal* (New York: Basic Books, 1989), pp. 107–8.

12. Kaplan, *Wizards of Armageddon*, p. 369.

13. Nolan, *Guardians of the Arsenal*, p. 118.

14. Ibid., pp. 108–9.

15. Ball, "Development of the SIOP," pp. 72–73; Kaplan, *Wizards of Armageddon*, p. 369.

16. Ball, "Development of the SIOP," p. 74.

17. Ibid.

18. Lynn Etheridge Davis, *Limited Nuclear Options*, Adelphi Paper 121 (London: International Institute for Strategic Studies, 1976), p. 3.

19. Schlesinger provided evidence of this continuing line in his testimony before the Subcommitee on Arms Control, International Law and Organization of the Senate Foreign Relations Committee, in hearings on "U.S.-USSR Strategic Policies," March 4, 1974; sanitized and released April 4, 1974, pp. 26–27. He cited a number of quotations from McNamara, Clark Clifford, Melvin Laird, and Elliot Richardson which mentioned the need for alternatives to all-out attack and in some cases the desirability of controlled escalation capabilities, but which never directly said that targeting policy needed revision.

20. According to Lynn Etheridge Davis, the three most significant of Schlesinger's first statements were made to the Overseas Writers Association on January 10; at a press conference on January 24; and in the Annual Defense Department Report to Congress on the Defense Budget for Fiscal Year 1975, on March 4. Davis, *Limited Nuclear Options*, p. 1.

21. Kaplan, *Wizards of Armageddon*, p. 373.

22. Schlesinger, testimony, "U.S.-USSR Strategic Policies," pp. 9, 11.

23. James R. Schlesinger, prepared report to the Congress on the FY 1975 Defense Budget, March 4, 1974, p. 5.

24. Ibid., p. 40.

25. Hearings, "U.S.-USSR Strategic Policies," p. 16.

26. A clear explanation of the relative importance of warhead yield and missile accuracy is provided in *Strategic Survey 1969* (London: Institute for Strategic Studies, 1970), pp. 30–33.

27. It should be noted that at the Schlesinger Doctrine hearings, Schlesinger did not seem to defend his plan by arguing that strategic nuclear-armed submarines and bombers could be used to ensure the preservation of a retaliatory capability, even if the land-based strategic nuclear missiles were destroyed in a first strike attack. Some theorists have used such an argument to maintain that accurate strategic land-based missiles do not threaten Mutual Assured Destruction.

28. Hearings, "U.S.-USSR Strategic Policies," pp. 16–17.

29. Schlesinger report, p. 4.

30. Hearings, "U.S.-USSR Strategic Policies," pp. 12–13.

31. Some analysts have since suggested that this limited use of strategic weapons could serve military goals, for example, by blunting Soviet conventional force capabilities located outside of major population centers. See Paul Bracken, *The Command and Control of Nuclear Forces* (New Haven: Yale University Press, 1983), p. 86. This does not appear to have been among Schlesinger's original goals, however.

32. Raymond L. Garthoff notes these strains and particularly Secretary of State Kissinger's contributions to them, in *Détente and Confrontation* (Washington, D.C.: Brookings, 1985), pp. 109, 321–22.

33. Schlesinger's prepared statement, p. 4.

34. Ibid., p. 5.

35. This argument is made forcefully by Terry Terriff, based on evidence from interviews with policymakers, in "The Innovation of U.S. Strategic Nuclear Policy in the Nixon Administration, 1969–1974: Objectives, Process and Politics," Nuclear History Program Working Paper 4 (College Park, Md.: Center for International Security Studies at Maryland, 1990), p. 92.

36. Ibid., p. 55.

37. See *Strategic Survey 1974* (London: International Institute of Strategic Studies, 1975), p. 47.

38. Hearings, "U.S.-USSR Strategic Policies," p. 29.

39. Ibid.

40. Ibid.

41. Davis, *Limited Nuclear Options*, p. 10.

42. Schlesinger claimed that "The reaction in Europe to change in targeting doctrine has been uniformly welcoming, even joyous. . . ." Hearings, "U.S.-USSR Strategic Policies," p. 8.

43. Davis, *Limited Nuclear Options*, p. 11.

44. These are chronicled by Davis, ibid., p. 10.

45. Hearings, "U.S.-USSR Strategic Policies," p. 36.

46. Davis, *Limited Nuclear Options*, p. 12.

47. This trend is among those chronicled by Sagan, *Moving Targets*, pp. 48–54.

48. Richard Lee Walker, *Strategic Target Planning: Bridging the Gap between Theory and Practice*, National Security Affairs Monograph Series 83–9 (Wash-

ington, D.C.: National Defense University Press, 1983), p. 33. I am grateful to Lynn Eden for bringing this source to my attention.

49. Ibid., p. 34.

50. Ibid., pp. 26–29. For an additional statement about poor intelligence leading to a tendency toward overestimation of the amount of destructive power needed, see Theodore A. Postol, "Targeting," in *Managing Nuclear Operations*, ed. Ashton B. Carter, John D. Steinbruner, and Charles A. Zracket (Washington, D.C.: Brookings, 1987), p. 392.

51. Nolan, *Guardians of the Arsenal*, p. 125.

52. Desmond Ball, "U.S. Strategic Forces: How Would They Be Used?" *International Security* 7 (Winter 1982/3): 37.

53. Kaplan, *Wizards of Armageddon*, pp. 370–71.

54. Terriff, "Innovation of U.S. Strategic Nuclear Policy," pp. 28–29.

55. Ibid., pp. 49–50.

56. Ibid., p. 93.

57. Ibid., p. 51.

58. The first mention of these topics in the General Staff's main strategy journal, *Voennaia Mysl'*, apparently was by Maj. Gen. V. Zemskov, "Kharakternye strategicheskie cherty mirovykh voin," *Voennaia Mysl'*, no. 7 (1974): 19–33, which was sent to the typesetter in May 1974. The topic seems not to have been mentioned at all in the semiclassified version of the journal which chronicled foreign military affairs, *Voennyi Zarubezhnik*, which ceased publication at the end of 1973. The first mention of these topics in the open journal which replaced *Voennyi Zarubezhnik* in 1974, *Zarubezhnoe Voennoe Obozrenie* (ZVO), was apparently not until an article by Maj. Gen. in the Reserves P. Sergeev and Col. in the Reserves V. Trusenkov, "Voennaia doktrina SShA," *ZVO*, no. 9 (1975): 3–10.

59. B. A. Baraniuk and V. I. Vorob'ev, *Avtomatizirovannye Sistemy Upravleniia Shtabov i Voennykh Uchrezhdenii* (Moscow: Voenizdat, 1974), sent to the typesetter on October 5, 1973 and to the printer on April 24, 1974; pp. 108–9.

60. "Vystuplenie ministra oborony SShA," *Krasnaia Zvezda*, January 26, 1974. See also William F. Scott and Harriet Fast Scott, "Soviet Perceptions of Limited Nuclear Options," section of an unpublished manuscript, sanitized by the authors, 1978, p. 38.

61. Ibid.

62. Scott and Scott, "Soviet Perceptions," pp. 37–39, 42.

63. Ibid., p. 39.

64. V. V. Larionov, "Ogranichenie vooruzhenii i ego protivniki," *Pravda*, April 7, 1974.

65. Ibid.

66. V. Larionov, "Razriadka napriazhennosti i printsip ravnoi bezopasnosti," *Krasnaia Zvezda* July 18, 1974.

67. This has been confirmed to the author by a number of civilian ISKAN scholars.

68. M. A. Mil'shtein and L. S. Semeiko, "Problema nedopustimosti iadernogo konflikta," *SShA*, no. 11 (1974): 8.

69. L. Semeiko, "Formy novye, sut' prezhniaia," *Krasnaia Zvezda* April 8, 1975.

70. R. G. Bogdanov, M. A. Mil'shtein, and L. S. Semeiko, *SShA: Voenno-Strategicheskie Kontseptsii* (Moscow: Nauka, 1980), pp. 203–4.

71. From an interview by the author in Moscow, October 1990.

72. "Briefing on Counterforce Attacks," September 11, 1974, included as an appendix to the Senate Foreign Relations Committee Print, *Analyses of the Effects of Limited Nuclear Warfare*, September 1975, pp. 142–43.

73. See Haslam, *Soviet Union and the Politics of Nuclear Weapons in Europe*, pp. 44–47.

74. The report is included in Scott and Scott, "Soviet Perceptions," pp. 43–45.

75. Maj. Gen. V. Zemskov, "Kharakternye strategicheskie cherty," p. 20; Col. A. Sergeev, "Krizis voennoi doktriny i strategii amerikanskogo imperializma," *Voennaia Mysl'*, no. 8 (1974): 90; Maj. Gen. A. Slobodenko, "Vozmozhnyi kharakter sovremennykh voin," *ZVO*, no. 11 (1975): 4; Maj. Gen. R. G. Simonian, "Klassifikatsiia sovremennykh voin," *Voennaia Mysl'*, no. 6 (1979): 69; and Lt. Gen. N. F. Petrov and Col. I. S. Popov, " 'Bol'shaia strategiia' SShA na 80-e gody," *Voennaia Mysl'*, no. 10 (1980): 32.

76. N. A. Chaldymov, "Burzhuaznye voenno-strategicheskie kontseptsii i kritika ikh ideologicheskikh osnov," *Voennaia Mysl'*, no. 6 (1978): 74.

77. Ibid., pp. 74, 77.

78. Sergeev and Trusenkov, "Voennaia doktrina SShA," pp. 8–9.

79. P. Sergeev and V. Trusenkov, "Amerikanskaia strategiia 'realisticheskogo ustrasheniia,' " *ZVO*, no. 11 (1977): 11.

80. U.S. Departments of State and Defense, *Soviet Strategic Defense Programs*, no identifying reference number, October 1985, pp. 9, 13; Stephen M. Meyer, "Soviet Nuclear Operations," in *Managing Nuclear Operations*, ed. Ashton B. Carter, John D. Steinbruner, and Charles A. Zraket (Washington, D.C.: Brookings, 1987), p. 482; and Sayre Stevens, "The Soviet BMD Program," in *Ballistic Missile Defense*, ed. Ashton B. Carter and David N. Schwartz (Washington, D.C.: Brookings, 1984), p. 197.

81. Engineer Maj. V. Kulikov, "Dal'nee obnaruzhenie tselei," *Tekhnika i Vooruzhenie*, no. 10 (1971): 18. Stephen Meyer cites this source in his analysis of this same point in "Soviet Nuclear Operations," p. 482.

82. A critique of Soviet ABM capabilities is provided by Stevens, "The Soviet BMD Program," pp. 182–220.

83. See Desmond Ball, "Soviet Strategic Planning and the Control of Nuclear War," in *The Soviet Calculus of Nuclear War*, ed. Roman Kolkowicz and Ellen Propper Mickiewicz (Lexington, Mass.: Lexington Books, 1986), pp. 49–67; Robert P. Berman and John C. Baker, *Soviet Strategic Forces* (Washington, D.C.: Brookings, 1982), pp. 30–34; Benjamin S. Lambeth, *Selective Nuclear Operations and Soviet Strategy*, P-5506 (Santa Monica: RAND, 1975); Meyer, "Soviet Nuclear Operations," in *Managing Nuclear Operations*.

84. For example, Colin S. Gray, *Nuclear Strategy and National Style* (Lanham, Md.: Hamilton Press, 1986).

85. Jack L. Snyder, *The Soviet Strategic Culture: Implications for Limited Nuclear Options*, R-2154 (Santa Monica: RAND, 1977).

86. Ibid., p. v.

87. Raymond L. Garthoff, "Conflict Termination in Soviet Military Thought and Strategy," reprinted in *Soviet C3*, ed. Stephen J. Cimbala (Washington, D.C.: AFCEA/Signal, 1987), pp. 404–5.

88. Ibid., p. 410. In conversation with the author, Garthoff has confirmed this interpretation of his statements.

89. See Col. B. Samorukov, "Combat Operations Involving Conventional Means of Destruction," *Voennaia Mysl'*, no. 8 (1967): 30; and Meyer, "Soviet Nuclear Operations," p. 482.

90. Trulock, "Soviet Perspectives on Limited Nuclear Warfare," pp. 77–78.

91. Ibid., p. 78.

92. From two interviews by the author in the United States in summer 1990 and three in Moscow in autumn 1990.

93. From an interview by the author in Moscow, November 1990.

94. From an interview by the author in the United States in summer 1990.

95. See, for example, Col. N. Voroshilov, "Problemy voiny i mira v sovremennuiu epokhu," *KVS*, no. 6 (1964): 9; Lt. Col. T. R. Kondratkov, in *Metodologicheskie Problemy Voennoi Teorii i Praktiki*, ed. N. Ya. Sushko and T. R. Kondratkov (Moscow: Voenizdat, 1966), p. 56; Kondratkov, in *Metodologicheskie Problemy Voennoi Teorii i Praktiki*, 2d ed., ed. A. S. Zheltov, Kondratkov, and Ye. A. Khomenko, (Moscow: Voenizdat, 1969), pp. 89–90; Marshal of the Soviet Union and Minister of Defense A. Grechko, "Torchestvo leninskikh idei o zashchite sotsialisticheskogo otechestva," *KVS*, no. 20 (1967): 37; and Col. P. Trifonenkov, "Voenno-teoreticheskoi nasledie V. I. Lenina i sovremennost'," *VIZh*, no. 11 (1967): 8.

96. See Lt. Col. Ye. Rybkin, "O sushchnosti mirovoi raketno-iadernoi voiny," recommended by the editors for study on the theme of "Nuclear Rocket War and Politics," *KVS*, no. 17 (1965): 54; and Col. A. Soshov, "Vooruzhennye sily SSSR v poslevoennyi period," identified by the editors for use in political classes, *KVS*, no. 15 (1970): 74.

97. See Col. Gen. N. Lomov, "Vliianie sovetskoi voennoi doktriny na razvitie voennogo iskusstva," *KVS*, no. 21 (1965): 19; Capt. 1st Rank M. Ruban, "Vooruzhennye sily SSSR v period stroitel'stva kommunizma," *KVS*, no. 13 (1968): 80–81; Col. S. Lipitskii, "M. V. Frunze—polkovodets novogo tipa," *VIZh*, no. 2 (1970): 122–23; I. I. Anureev, *Oruzhie Protivoraketnoi i Protivokosmicheskoi Oborony* (Moscow: Voenizdat, 1971), pp. 3–4; and N. A. Lomov, introduction, *Nauchno-tekhnicheskii Progress i Revoliutsiia v Voennom Dele* (Moscow: Voenizdat, 1973), p. 6.

98. See "Kharakter i osobennosti raketno-iadernoi voiny," instruction materials for political classes, *KVS*, no. 21 (1965): 70; M. Ruban, cited above, pp. 80–81; Col. S. A. Tiushkevich and Col. V. M. Bondarenko, "Nauchno-tekhnicheskii progress i ego vliianie na razvitie voennogo dela," in *Nauchno-tekhnicheskii Progress*, p. 37; and (somewhat of an anomaly because of its late date, in October 1974) Maj. Gen. A. Milovidov, "Marksizm-leninizm—teoreticheskaia osnova sovetskoi voennoi nauki," *KVS*, no. 19 (1974): 18.

99. Maj. Gen. N. Pavlenko, "Kharakternye cherty strategicheskogo nastupleniia Sovetskikh Vooruzhennykh Sil v Velikoi Otechestvennoi Voine," reported

to have been given at a Moscow conference of military historians in April 1965, *VIZh*, no. 3 (1966): 9–23.

100. Raymond L. Garthoff, "Introduction: U.S. Considerations of Soviet Military Thinking," in *The Voroshilov Lectures*, vol. 1 (Washington, D.C.: National Defense University Press, 1989), p. 8.

101. Ghulam Dastagir Wardak, *The Voroshilov Lectures*, vol. 1, ed. Graham Hall Turbiville, Jr. (Washington, D.C.: National Defense University Press, 1989), passim. See especially pp. 159, 234, 236, 252, 263, 271, 298–99.

102. Ibid., pp. 245, 247.

103. L. I. Brezhnev, speech, as printed in *Pravda*, May 9, 1975.

104. Ibid., March 31, 1971.

105. See, for example, Lt. Col. V. Serebriannikov, "Metodologiia voennogo dela," *KVS*, no. 9 (1970): 89–90; Vice Adm. V. Andreev, "V. I. Lenin o vzaimosviazi faktorov, opredeliaiushchikh khod i iskhod voiny," *KVS*, no. 8 (1971), especially p. 87; Col. T. Kondratkov, "Sotsial'nyi kharakter sovremennoi voiny," *KVS*, no. 21 (1972), especially p. 15; Col. D. Volkogonov, "Idei V. I. Lenina o moral'no-politicheskoi i psikhologicheskoi podgotovke voinov," *KVS*, no. 7 (1974), especially p. 17; Marshal of the Soviet Union and Minister of Defense A. A. Grechko, *Vooruzhennye Sily Sovetskogo Gosudarstva* (Moscow: Voenizdat, 1974), which mentions the importance of decisive action several times in passing but never directly links it to use of strategic nuclear weapons, as his earlier article did; Col. V. Izmailov, "Kharakter i osobennosti sovremennykh voin," *KVS*, no. 6 (1975): 67–75; Col. A. Dmitriev, "Marksistsko-Leninskoe uchenie o voine i armii," *KVS*, no. 13 (1975), especially pp. 13–14; and Kondratkov, "Eloveshchii kharakter militaristicheskikh dogm," *KVS*, 1978, no. 19 (1978): 78–83.

106. V. Zemskov, "Kharakternye strategicheskie cherty mirovykh voin," p. 29; and Col. Gen. A. Maiorov, "Kharakternye cherty sovetskoi voennoi strategii," *Voennaia Mysl'* no. 1 (1975): 17–18.

107. From an interview by the author in Moscow, October 1990.

108. "Doktrina Voennaia," in *Sovetskaia Voennaia Entsiklopedia*, vol. 3 (Moscow: Voenizdat, 1977), pp. 225–29.

109. Mil'shtein and Semeiko, "Problema nedopustimosti iadernogo konflikta," p. 10. [Italics not in the original.]

110. L. Semeiko, "Formy novye." [Italics not in the original.]

111. Bogdanov, Mil'shtein and Semeiko, *SShA: Voenno-Strategicheskie Kontsepsii*, p. 206. [Italics not in the original.]

112. R. Simonian, "Kontseptsiia 'vybora tselei,'" *Krasnaia Zvezda*, September 28, 1976. [Italics not in the original.]

113. R. Simonian, "Strategicheskie pozitsii Pentagona i bezopasnost' narodov," *Mirovaia Ekonomika i Mezhdunarodnye Otneshenie (MEiMO)*, no. 11 (1978): 22; and "Klassifikatsiia sovremennykh voin," *Voennaia Mysl'*, no. 6 (1979): 69.

114. R. Simonian, "Voennoe iskusstvo SShA posle vtoroi mirovoi voiny," *ZVO*, no. 2 (1976): 20.

115. Larionov, "Razriadka napriazhennosti i printsip ravnoi bezopasnosti," p. 3.

116. M. Mil'shtein, "Vopreki dukhu vremeni," *MEiMO*, no. 7 (1976): 106.

117. M.A. Mil'shtein, "Na opasnom perekrestke," *SShA*, no. 10 (1978): 6.

118. See Rep. Jonathan B. Bingham's remarks before the Subcommittee on National Security Policy and Scientific Development of the House Foreign Affairs Committee, hearings on "Diplomatic and Strategic Impact of Multiple Warhead Missiles," July 8, 1969, p. 4. Also note George B. Kistiakowsky's estimates of the effects that this had on the Soviet audience, p. 88.

119. This information is taken from table 5, "Intercontinental Ballistic Missiles," of John M. Collins, *U.S.-Soviet Military Balance, 1960–1980* (Washington, D.C.: McGraw-Hill, 1980), p. 446. These Soviet missiles deployed in 1974 and 1975 were so accurate because they included on-board digital computers and advanced guidance calibration; see Thomas B. Cochran et al., *Soviet Nuclear Weapons*, vol. 4 of the Nuclear Weapons Databook of the National Resources Defense Council (New York: Harper and Row [Ballinger], 1989), p. 104.

120. See, for example, Donald Mackenzie, "The Soviet Union and Strategic Missile Guidance," *International Security* 13 (Fall 1988): 28; his table on p. 52 indicates that the SS-9 was much more accurate than its Soviet contemporaries. See also John Erickson, *Soviet Military Power* (London: Royal United Services Institute, 1971), pp. 43–45. Others maintain that the early SS-9s had a countervalue mission, and that this mission was changed to respond to U.S. ICBM deployments. See Cochran et al., *Soviet Nuclear Weapons*, p. 101.

121. Cochran et al., *Soviet Nuclear Weapons*, point out (p. 104 n. 30) that by 1976 the Soviet launch control centers (LCCs) were hardened, although in the mid-1970s only a quarter of the silos and LCCs were considered "hard" by Western experts (the rest ranged from "soft" to "moderately hard").

122. This is detailed in chapter 5.

123. For example, see Harry Gelman, *The Brezhnev Politburo and the Decline of Détente* (Ithaca: Cornell University Press, 1984).

124. Dale R. Herspring, *The Soviet High Command 1967–1989* (Princeton: Princeton University Press, 1990), pp. 79–112.

125. See Lawrence T. Caldwell, *Soviet Attitudes to SALT*, Adelphi Paper 75 (London: Institute for Strategic Studies, 1971).

126. See Raymond Garthoff, "The Soviet Military and SALT," in *Soviet Decisionmaking for National Security* (London: George Allen and Unwin, 1984), pp. 145, 154; and Thomas Wolfe, *The SALT Experience* (Cambridge, Mass.: Ballinger, 1979), p. 61.

127. Ibid.

128. This procurement increase slowdown was first publicly postulated by the U.S. Central Intelligence Agency (CIA) in late 1984; see Robert Gates, statement before the Subcommittee on International Trade, Finance and Security Economics of the U.S. Congress Joint Economic Committee, hearings, *Allocation of Resources in the Soviet Union and China—1984*, part 10, November 21, 1984, pp. 2–118. Maj. Gen. Schuyler Bissell, Deputy Director of the U.S. Defense Intelligence Agency, concurred in the CIA's observation of a procurement increase slowdown, even though the two agencies described different reasons for its occurrence; see ibid., January 15, 1985, pp. 122–35.

129. See, for example, Col. N. Solntsev, "Znachenie reshenii XXV s'ezda KPSS dlia dal'neishego povysheniia tekhnicheskoi osnashchennosti armii i flota," *KVS*,

no. 22 (1977): 82–89; the article makes a strident plea for the strengthening of the state's defense capabilities in view of the aggressive behavior of the West.

130. V. Kulikov, "Sovetskaia voennaia nauka segodniia," *Kommunist*, no. 7 (1976): 38–48.

131. See Jeremy R. Azrael, *The Soviet Civilian Leadership and the Military High Command, 1976–1986*, R-3521 (Santa Monica: RAND, 1987), p. 10. Azrael does not cite Kulikov's article, but it does provide evidence for the argument he makes.

132. Ibid. See also Richard Kaufman, "Causes of the Slowdown in Soviet Defense," *Soviet Economy* 1 (1985): 9–31.

133. Azrael, *Soviet Civilian Leadership*, pp. 8–9.

134. *Pravda*, January 19, 1977.

135. N. Ponomarev and V. Zhuravlev, "xxv s'ezd KPSS i bor'ba SSSR za prekrashchenie gonki vooruzhenii i razoruzhenie," *Voenno-Istoricheskii Zhurnal* (*VIZh*), no. 5 (1977): 8–9.

136. Thomas N. Bjorkman and Thomas J. Zamostny, "Soviet Politics and Strategy Toward the West: Three Cases," *World Politics* 36 (January 1984): 206.

137. N. V. Ogarkov, "Strategiia Voennaia," in *Sovetskaia Voennaia Entsiklopediia*, vol. 7 (Moscow: Voenizdat, 1979), p. 564.

138. Bjorkman and Zamostny, "Soviet Politics and Strategy," pp. 199–201, and David Holloway, *The Soviet Union and the Arms Race* (New Haven: Yale University Press, 1983), pp. 164–67.

139. See Holloway, ibid., and Edward L. Warner III, *The Military in Contemporary Soviet Politics* (Westport, Conn.: Praeger, 1977), p. 128.

140. Bjorkman and Zamostny, "Soviet Politics and Strategy Toward the West," pp. 203–4.

141. In fact, Warner states that retired Soviet Col. V. M. Kulish of ISKAN told him that they did not. Warner, *The Military in Contemporary Soviet Politics*, p. 131.

142. Ibid., pp. 204–5.

143. See, for example, A. Kaliadin, "Bor'ba za razoruzhenie: novye perspektivy," *MEiMO*, no. 11 (1974): 3–14; and V. M. Berezhkov, "Perspektivy razriadki i sovetsko-amerikanskie otnosheniia," *SShA*, no. 9 (1975): 3–14.

144. G. A. Trofimenko, "Voprosy ukrepleniia mira i bezopasnosti v sovetsko-amerikanskikh otnosheniiakh," *SShA*, no. 9 (1974): 17.

145. G. A. Trofimenko, *SShA: Politika, Voina, Ideologiia* (Moscow: Mysl', 1976), p. 323.

146. Edward Warner III has noted that Trofimenko quoted Grechko as saying that the Soviet military would respond to a limited nuclear attack with "full defeat of any aggressor." A review of Grechko's original argument, however, reveals that Grechko's analysis of the Schlesinger Doctrine was in fact separated by several unrelated paragraphs from a rather standard statement about the basically offensive and decisive character of Soviet military operations. If Grechko meant this latter statement to apply to the Schlesinger Doctrine, he did not do a very good job of signaling his intentions. Trofimenko's quotation of the supposed Grechko statement is not repeated in any Soviet military sources. See Edward Warner III, *Soviet Concepts and Capabilities for Limited Nuclear War: What We Know*

and How We Know It, N-2769 (Santa Monica: RAND, 1989), p. 35; A. A. Grechko, *Vooruzhennye Sily Sovetskogo Gosudarstva*, 2d ed. (Moscow: Voenizdat, 1975), pp. 344–45.

147. For examples of this, see the definition of "Nuclear War" in *Voennyi Entsiklopedicheskii Slovar'* (the Soviet military encyclopedic dictionary) (Moscow: Voenizdat, 1984), p. 842; see also articles by Capt. 1st Rank of the Navy, Prof. A. Beliaev, "Nauchnye predstavleniia o sovremennoi voine—vazhnyi element soznaniia sovetskogo voina," *Kommunist Vooruzhennykh Sil*, no. 7 (1985): 28, and by then-Deputy Chief of the General Staff with doctrinal responsibilities, Col. Gen. Makhmut A. Gareev, "The revised Soviet military doctrine," *Bulletin of the Atomic Scientists* 44, no. 10 (December 1988): 30.

148. Speech of S. F. Akhromeev to the All-Union Conference of Scholars on Sparing Humanity from the Threat of Nuclear War, for Disarmament and Peace, May 17–19, 1983, as reported in *Vestnik Akademii Nauk SSSR* 1983, no. 9 (1983): 47–48. The quotation is from p. 48.

149. N. V. Ogarkov, "Strategiia Voennaia," in *Sovetskaia Voennaia Entsiklopediia*, vol. 7 (Moscow: Voenizdat, 1979), p. 564. A similarly worded statement appeared in the semiclassified literature that same year; Maj. Gen. V. V. Voznenko wrote, "Osnovnye etapy razvitiia sovetskoi voennoi strategii," *Voennaia Mysl'*, no. 4 (1979): 24.

150. See, for example, N. Ogarkov, "Pobeda i sovremennost'," *Izvestiia*, May 9, 1983; "Zashchita sotsializma: opyt istorii i sovremennost'," *Krasnaia Zvezda*, May 9, 1984; and "Nemerknushchaia slava sovetskogo oruzhiia," *KVS*, no. 21 (1984): 26.

151. Edgar Ulsamer, "The Soviet Juggernaut," *Air Force Magazine*, March 1976: 61–62. The article's conclusions were said to be based on the best unclassified assessments of Soviet capabilities available to the Air Force at that time.

152. Trulock, "Soviet Perspectives on Limited Nuclear Warfare," pp. 77–78.

153. For a thorough description and analysis of the early years of this debate, see David Holloway, *Technology, Management and the Soviet Military Establishment*, Adelphi Paper 76 (London: Institute for Strategic Studies, 1971).

154. See George Martin Weinberger, comp. and ed., *Soviet Cybernetic Technology: A Timeline, Researcher's Data Base and Guide to Professional Literature*, vol. 1 (New York: University Press of America, 1985).

155. M. M. Kozlov, ed. *Akademiia General'nogo Shtaba* (Moscow: Voenizdat, 1987), p. 165.

156. See, for example, "Nauchno-tekhnicheskii progress i ego rol' v povyshenii boevoi moshchi armii i flota," written for leaders of political classes, *KVS*, no. 21 (1974): 67–74; Engineer Col. A. Volkov, "Nauchnye osnovy upravlencheskoi deiatel'nosti voennykh kadrov," *KVS*, no. 15 (1976), especially p. 15; and Col. V. M. Bondarenko and Engineer Col. A. F. Volkov, ed., *Avtomatizatsiia Upravleniia Voiskami* (Moscow: Voenizdat, 1977), especially p. 21.

157. Notra Trulock III, "The Impact of World War II on Contemporary Soviet Military Theory," in *Contemporary Soviet Military Affairs*, ed. Jonathan R. Adelman and Cristan Lea Gibson (Boston: Unwin Hyman, 1989), p. 159.

158. John Erickson makes this point in "Soviet Cybermen," included in *Soviet C3*, ed. Stephen J. Cimbala (Washington, D.C.: AFCEA/Signal, 1987), p. 83.

159. A. Vasil'ev and N. Pimenov, "Perspektivy razvitiia raket strategi-cheskogo naznacheniia," *Voennaia Mysl'*, no. 1 (1970): 34.

160. One of his earliest articles on this subject is with Col. S. Tiushkevich, an author with whom he often collaborated; "Sovremennyi etap revoliutsii v voen-nom dele i trebovaniia k voennym kadram," *KVS*, no. 6 (1968): 18–25.

161. Bondarenko, "Nauchno-tekhnicheskii progress i ukreplenie oborono-sposobnosti strany," recommended for study by officers, *KVS*, no. 24 (1971): 9–16.

162. Bondarenko, "Nauchno-tekhnicheskii progress i upravlenie voiskami," *KVS*, no. 10 (1973): 27–33. See also Bondarenko, *Sovremennaia Nauka i Razvitie Voennogo Dela* (Moscow: Voenizdat, 1976), p. 131.

163. B. A. Baraniuk, V. I. Vorob'ev, *Avtomatizirovannye Sistemy Upravleniia Shtabov i Voennykh Uchrezhdenii*, especially pp. 108–9.

164. Ibid., pp. 209–11.

165. V. V. Borisov, *Opasnaia Stavka: Nauchno-tekhnicheskaia Revoliutsiia i Voennye Prigotovleniia SShA* (Moscow: Voenizdat, 1979), p. 122.

166. Ibid., pp. 63–65, 122.

167. V. G. Kulikov, ed. *Akademiia General'nogo Shtaba* (Moscow: Voe-nizdat, 1976), pp. 205–6.

168. Kozlov, *Akademiia General'nogo Shtaba* (1987).

169. Kulikov, *Akademiia General'nogo Shtaba*, p. 186.

170. Richard Woff, comments, in John Erickson, *Proceedings of a Conference on the Soviet Military and Future*, Stratech Studies Series SS85–1 (College Station, Tex.: Texas A and M University Center for Strategic Technology, 1985), pp. III-20–21.

171. A search of Erickson's table reveals that eighty promotion dates are pro-vided for the whole High Command membership; of these, sixty-one were listed as 1967 or later (and many were much more recent than 1967). Of promotion dates listed for the MPA, five out of seven were made before 1967; of those listed for the navy, six out of twelve were made before 1967. The remaining eight pre-1967 appointments were spread among the rest of the services. John Erickson, "The Soviet High Command," in *Soviet-Warsaw Pact Force Levels*, USSI Report 76–2 (Washington, D.C.: United States Strategic Institute, 1976), pp. 22–25.

172. For a discussion of Ogarkov's interests in C^3I, see Erickson, *Proceedings of a Conference*, p. I-13.

173. These fit two of the four definitions of "ambiguity" or opaqueness that are hypothesized to apply to all complex organizations, by James G. March and Johan P. Olsen, *Ambiguity and Choice in Organizations* (Bergen, Norway: Universitetsforlaget, 1979), p. 12.

Chapter 5
Soviet Reactions to Western Deep-Strike Doctrines

1. Mikhail Gorbachev, speech at Stanford University, according to the tran-script of the official translation, as reported in *The Stanford University Campus Report*, June 6, 1990, p. 14. The Russian word for "scientist" [*uchenyi*] is the same as the word for "scholar," and I made the substitution because "scholar" seems to fit better in the context here.

2. Condoleezza Rice, "The Party, the Military, and Decision Authority in the Soviet Union," *World Politics* 40 (October 1987): 78–80; and Stephen M. Meyer, "The Sources and Prospects of Gorbachev's New Political Thinking on Security," *International Security* 13 (Fall 1988): 130.

3. See Edward L. Warner III's and Jack Snyder's testimony before the Defense Policy Panel of the House Armed Services Committee, "The Impact of Gorbachev's Reform Movement on the Soviet Military," July 14, 1988, pp. 30–32, 62–66; Jack Snyder, "Limiting Offensive Conventional Forces: Soviet Proposals and Western Options," *International Security* 12 (Spring 1988): 48–77; Edward L. Warner III, "New Thinking and Old Realities in Soviet Defence Policy," *Survival* 31 (January/February 1989): 19; and Stephen M. Meyer and Jeffrey I. Sands, "Soviet Military Doubts Competence of the 'New Thinkers,' " *Soviet Defense Notes* 1 no. 6 (November/December 1989): 1–4.

4. From an interview by the author in the United States, spring 1990.

5. Jacob W. Kipp, Bruce W. Menning, David M.Glantz, Graham H. Turbiville, Jr., "Editorial: Marshal Akhromeev's Post-INF World," *Journal of Soviet Military Studies* 1 (June 1988): 168–69.

6. *The Soviet Military Under Gorbachev: Report on a RAND Workshop*, ed. Alexander Alexiev and Robert Nurick, R-3907 (Santa Monica: RAND, 1990), pp. 47–48.

7. Examples of this include Georgii Arbatov, "Armiia dlia strany ili strana dlia armii?" *Ogonek*, no. 4 (1990): 4, the reply by Maj. Gen. V. Medvedev, "Armiia strany, armiia naroda," *Ogonek*, no. 9 (1990): 30–31, and the rejoinder by G. Arbatov, "A esli bez lukavstva," *Ogonek*, no. 17 (1990): 8–11.

8. Aleksei Arbatov, "Skol'ko oborony dostatochno?" *Mezhdunarodnaia Zhizn'*, no. 3 (1989): 33–47. A Lieutenant General in the Reserves, two Colonels, and a Major General accused Aleksei Arbatov of incompetence and tendentiousness. F. I. Rybintsev, "Net problemy," *Mezhdunarodnaia Zhizn'*, no. 7 (1989): 157–58; A. P. Vasil'ev and V. K. Rudiuk, "Dostatochna li protivovozdushnaia oborona?" *Voennaia Mysl'*, no. 9 (1989): 59–68; and Yu. Liubimov, "O dostatochnosti oborony i nedostatke kompetentnosti," *Kommunist Vooruzhennykh Sil* (*KVS*), no. 16 (1989): 21. Aleksei Arbatov was allowed to respond in the General Staff journal itself ("K voprosu o dostatochnosti protivovozdushnoi oborony," *Voennaia Mysl'*, no. 12 [1989]: 41–45), as well as in the journal of the Main Political Administration of the military ("Poleznee razgovor po sushchestvu," *KVS*, no. 22 [1989]: 17–21).

9. See the article by Radomir Bogdanov and Andrei Kortunov, " 'Minimum Deterrent': Utopia or a Real Prospect?" *Moscow News*, no. 23 (1989): 6; and the responses by Col. Vladimir Dvorkin and Col. Valery Torbin, "On Real Sufficiency in Defense," *Moscow News*, no. 26 (1989): 6; Lt. Gen. in Reserves Ye. Volkov, "Ne raz'iasniaet, a zatumanivaet . . . ," *Krasnaia Zvezda*, September 28, 1989; and by a civilian Academy of Sciences specialist in the modeling of nuclear warfare, Nikita Moiseev, "Both Calculation and Common Sense," *Moscow News*, no. 28 (1989): 7. Several civilian scholars at ISKAN and IMEMO have, in private conversation, criticized Bogdanov and Kortunov's minimum deterrent proposal, saying that the analysis is simplistic and that it therefore gives the military excuses for doubting civilians' expertise.

10. See Vitaly Zhurkin, Sergei Karaganov, Andrei Kortunov, "Reasonable suf-

ficiency—or how to break the vicious circle," *New Times* (Moscow), no. 40 (1987): 13–15; V. V. Zhurkin, S. A. Karaganov, A. V. Kortunov, "O razumnoi dostatochnosti," *SShA*, 1987 no. 12 (1987): 11–21; V. Zhurkin, S. Karaganov, A. Kortunov, "Vyzovy bezopasnosti—starye i novye," *Kommunist*, no. 31 (1988): 42–50; and the apparent responses by Capt. O. Boltunov, "Bezotvetsvennye prizyvy," *KVS*, no. 1 (1989): 22, and Chief of the General Staff Mikhail Moiseev, "S pozitsii oboronitel'noi doktriny," *Krasnaia Zvezda*, February 10, 1989.

11. From a private conversation between the author and an IMEMO department head.

12. See *Foreign Broadcast Information Service Daily Report: Soviet Union (FBIS-SOV)*, June 18, 1986, p. AA5. See also the analysis in Alexiev and Nurick, eds., *The Soviet Military Under Gorbachev*, p. 10.

13. Stephen Shenfield, "Minimum Nuclear Deterrence: The Debate Among Soviet Civilian Analysts," Center for Foreign Policy Development, Brown University, November 1989, p. 5.

14. Alexiev and Nurick, eds., *The Soviet Military Under Gorbachev*, p. 11.

15. Pat Litherland, *Gorbachev and Arms Control: Civilian Experts and Soviet Policy*, Peace Research Report 12 (Bradford, England: University of Bradford School of Peace Studies, 1986), p. 5.

16. This is reported in "V diplomaticheskoi akademii," *Vestnik Ministerstva Inostrannykh Del SSSR*, no. 23 (1988): 21. The citation is from Shenfield, "Minimum Nuclear Deterrence," p. 3.

17. From an interview by the author in Moscow, fall 1991.

18. See the summary of Sergei Zamascikov's analysis on this point in Alexiev and Nurick, *The Soviet Military Under Gorbachev*, pp. vi, 10. Also, see the excellent analysis made by John Van Oudenaren, *The Role of Shevardnadze and the Ministry of Foreign Affairs in the Making of Soviet Defense and Arms Control Policy*, R-3898 (Santa Monica: RAND, 1990).

19. See John Van Oudenaren, *The Role of Shevardnadze*, pp. 38–46, 56–59.

20. For differing reports of Shevardnadze's motives, see Bill Keller, "Shevardnadze Asserts Possibility of a Crackdown Led Him to Quit," *New York Times*, January 3, 1991; Vernon V. Aspaturian, "Farewell to Soviet Foreign Policy," *Problems of Communism* 40 (November/December 1991): 53–62; and Eduard Shevardnadze, *The Future Belongs to Freedom*, trans. Catherine A. Fitzpatrick (New York: Free Press, 1991), p. xvi, especially.

21. Press reports to this effect are summarized by Stephen M. Meyer, "How the Threat (and the Coup) Collapsed: The Politicization of the Soviet Military," *International Security* 16 (Winter 1991/92): 5–38.

22. Litherland, *Gorbachev and Arms Control*, p. 5.

23. From an interview in the United States, spring 1990.

24. See Phillip A. Petersen, "A New Security Regime for Europe?" *Problems of Communism*, 39 (March/April 1990): 94.

25. The appointment was first reported by Moscow ITAR-TASS World Service in Russian, April 3, 1992, as reported in *FBIS-SOV*, April 6, 1992, p. 26. A few days later, Kokoshin reiterated many of the themes that follow here. Moscow Teleradiokompaniia Ostankino Television First Program Network in Russian, April 5, 1992, as reported in *FBIS-SOV*, April 7, 1992, pp. 19–20.

26. Kokoshin revealed this in an interview to Elena Agapova, "Nash chelovek v kongresse," *Krasnaia Zvezda*, September 15, 1989.

27. From interviews with members of ISKAN.

28. From an interview with an IMEMO scholar in the U.S., spring 1992.

29. From conversations with a variety of IMEMO and ISKAN scholars.

30. A. Arbatov, "Deistvitel'no, est'-li povod dlia spora?" *Mirovaia Ekonomika i Mezhdunarodnye Otnosheniia (MEiMO)*, no. 10 (1988): 131.

31. From an interview with one such scholar in the U.S., winter 1990.

32. Agapova, "Nash chelovek v kongresse."

33. From a private conversation with one of his ISKAN coworkers.

34. This has been confirmed to the author by several civilians at the institutes.

35. From interviews in Moscow, summer 1989 and fall 1990.

36. From interviews with ISKAN scholars.

37. From interviews with several institute civilian scholars.

38. Nikita Zholkver et al., reported on the Moscow meeting of the two groups in February 1987, in "For a Nuclear-Free World, for the Survival of Mankind," *New Times*, no. 8 (1987): 8; John H. Cushman, Jr., reported on their meeting in Washington, D.C., in April of that year, in "Old Soldiers of Two Camps Talk of Peace," *New York Times*, April 28, 1987.

39. Col. A. Popov, "Diskussiiu nado prodolzhit'," *KVS*, no. 3 (1990): 26–27.

40. Maj. Gen. N. A. Chaldymov and Lt. Col. B. V. Molostov, "Vseobshchaia bezopasnost' novye filosofsko-politicheskie podkhody," *Voennaia Mysl'*, no. 2 (1990): 73.

41. Maj. Gen. Yuri Kirshin, "Why military reform is needed?" *New Times*, no. 12 (1990): 30.

42. See Bill Keller, "Soviet Officers Pressing for Change and a Union," *New York Times*, October 22, 1989.

43. See "Officers, Deputies Discuss Professional Military," Moscow World Service in Russian, March 8, 1990, reported by *FBIS-SOV*, March 9, 1990, p. 61.

44. " 'My ne "lishnie liudi" v parlamente . . .' " *KVS*, no. 3 (1990): 37–49; see especially the comments by Maj. V. P. Zolotukhin, p. 38, and Col. A. V. Stalko, p. 49.

45. This is according to an interview with an ISKAN scholar in the United States, spring 1990.

46. This latter description is given by William and Jane Taubman, *Moscow Spring* (New York: Summit Books, 1989), p. 122.

47. From private conversations; see also Alexiev and Nurich, *The Soviet Military Under Gorbachev*, p. 46.

48. See the Committee's publications, *Space-Strike Arms and International Security*, abridged version (Moscow: Novosti, 1985), and *The Large-Scale Anti-Missile System and International Security* (Moscow: Novosti, 1986). See also the summary of the group's work by A. A. Vasil'ev, M. I. Gerasev, and A. A. Kokoshin, "Asimmetrichnyi otvet," *SShA*, no. 2 (1987): 26–35.

49. Kokoshin, testimony before the House Armed Services Committee, "Gorbachev's Force Reductions and the Restructuring of Soviet Forces," March 10, 1989, p. 27.

50. From a variety of interviews.

51. This according to Eberhard Schneider, "Soviet Foreign-Policy Think Tanks," *Washington Quarterly* 11 (Spring 1988): 153.

52. Andrei Kokoshin et al., "Problems of Ensuring Stability with Radical Cuts in Armed Forces and Conventional Armaments in Europe," Soviet Committee for European Security and Cooperation, Committee of Soviet Scientists for Peace, Against the Nuclear Threat, and ISKAN, 1989.

53. For a typical Soviet discussion of this, see Marshal of Armored Tank Forces O. Losik, Commandant of the Malinovskii Armored Tank Forces Academy, "Sposoby vedeniia vysokomanevrennykh boevykh deistvii bronetankovymi i mekhanizirovannymi voiskami po opytu Belorusskoi i Vislo-Oderskoi operatsii," *Voenno-Istoricheskii Zhurnal (VIZh)*, no. 9 (1980): 18–25.

54. The first public Western discussion of the OMG is Christopher N. Donnelly, "The Soviet Operational Manoeuvre Group: A New Challenge for NATO," *International Defense Review* 15 (September 1982): 1177–86. Westerners learned of the OMG's existence from Polish military journal articles; Soviet sources long denied that such forces existed, but finally admitted their existence in discussions with Western defense analyst Phillip A. Karber in early 1989. See John J. Fialka, "Soviets Outline Troop-Cut Plan in East Germany," *Wall Street Journal* March 14, 1989.

55. "Emerging Technologies: An Uncertain Future," *Strategic Survey 1983–1984* (London: International Institute for Strategic Studies, 1984), p. 12.

56. See, for example, the section on "New Conventional Weapons" in *Strategic Survey 1974* (London: International Institute for Strategic Studies, 1975), pp. 43–46.

57. FM 100–5, "Operations," U.S. Army, July 1, 1976, chap. 2.

58. Ibid., p. I-1.

59. Ibid., p. V-13.

60. Ibid., p. V-14.

61. Ibid., chap. 8.

62. Ibid., chap. 4, especially p. IV-5.

63. William S. Lind, "FM 100–5, Operations: Some Doctrinal Questions for the United States Army," *Military Review* 57 (March 1977): 54–65. This critique and others are summarized by John L. Romjue, *From Active Defense to AirLand Battle: The Development of Army Doctrine 1973–1982* (Ft. Monroe, Va.: U.S. Army Training and Doctrinal Command, 1984), pp. 14–18; and by Romjue, "The Evolution of the AirLand Battle Concept," *Air University Review*, 35 (May/June 1984): 6–7.

64. Romjue, *From Active Defense to AirLand Battle*, p. 25.

65. Ibid., pp. 37–38.

66. Ibid., p. 42.

67. Romjue, "The Evolution of the AirLand Battle Concept," p. 8.

68. Ibid.

69. Donn A. Starry, "Extending the Battlefield," *Military Review* 61 (March 1981): 31–50. This article is noted as being the first public mention of the new doctrine by William G. Hanne, "Airland Battle: Doctrine not Dogma," *International Defense Review* 16 (August 1983): 1036.

70. The summary is Romjue's, in *From Active Defense to AirLand Battle*, p. 45.

71. Romjue, "The Evolution of the AirLand Battle Concept," p. 10.

72. Ibid., pp. 8–9.

73. FM 100–5, "Operations," Headquarters, Department of the Army, Washington, D.C., August 20, 1982, p. i.

74. Ibid., p. VII-1.

75. Ibid., p. I-1.

76. Ibid., p. II-1.

77. Ibid., p. VIII-1.

78. Ibid., p. X-1.

79. Ibid., p. IX-16.

80. Ibid., p. IX-19.

81. "Emerging Technologies," *Strategic Survey 1983–1984*, p. 15.

82. On this latter point, see Bernard W. Rogers, "Follow-on Forces Attack (FOFA): Myths and Realities," *NATO Review* 32 (December 1984): 8.

83. Ibid., pp. 6–7.

84. Ibid., pp. 2, 7.

85. Ibid., p. 7.

86. Ibid.

87. FM 100–5, "Operations," 1982, p. XVII-2.

88. This is discussed in James C. Wendt and Nanette Brown, *Improving the NATO Force Planning Process*, R-3383 (Santa Monica: RAND, 1986), pp. 11–12.

89. Ibid., p. 14.

90. Ibid.

91. See Joyce P. Kaufman, "Conventional and Theater Nuclear Force Modernization: The Military Response," in *NATO in the 1980s*, ed. Linda P. Brady and Joyce P. Kaufman (New York: Praeger, 1985), pp. 127–28.

92. This explanation is provided by the U.S. Congress Office of Technology Assessment, *New Technologies for NATO: Implementing Follow-on Forces Attack*, OTA-ISC-309 (Washington, D.C.: Government Printing Office, 1987), p. 75.

93. Rogers, "Follow-on Forces Attack," p. 1.

94. Ibid.

95. Ibid., pp. 1–2.

96. Ibid., p. 6.

97. These are summarized by the Office of Technology Assessment (OTA), in *New Technologies for NATO*, pp. 119–20.

98. "Emerging Technologies," *Strategic Survey 1983–1984*, p. 16.

99. James C. Wendt and Nanette Brown, *Improving the NATO Force Planning Process*, p. 18.

100. David J. Stein, *The Development of NATO Tactical Air Doctrine, 1970–1985*, R-3385 (Santa Monica: RAND, 1987), p. 41.

101. Hans Gunter Brauch, "West German Alternatives for Reducing Reliance on Nuclear Weapons," in *Rethinking the Nuclear Weapons Dilemma in Europe*, ed. P. Terrence Hopmann and Frank Barnaby (London: Macmillan, 1988), p. 157.

102. "Conventional Defense Improvements in NATO," *Strategic Survey 1985–1986* (London: International Institute for Strategic Studies, 1986), p. 38–39.

103. This according to François Heisbourg, "The Three Ages of NATO Strategy," *NATO Review* 37 (February 1989): 27.

104. OTA, *New Technologies for NATO*, p. 123.

105. John R. Galvin, "Getting Better: Improving Capabilities for Deterrence and Defense," *NATO Review* 37 (April 1989): 12.

106. Ibid., p. 13.

107. Col. of Engineering I. Loshchilov, "Sredstva avtomatizatsii upravleniia voiskami v boiu," *Zarubezhnoe Voennoe Obozrenie (ZVO)*, no. 5 (1978): 35–40; and V. Filippov, "Soedinenie novogo tipa armii SShA," *ZVO*, no. 7 (1978): 29.

108. Maj. Gen. A. Solov'ev and Col. of Engineering L. Guliaev, "Radio-elektronnaia razvedka," *ZVO*, no. 7 (1978): 12–18; Col. of Engineering V. Afinov, "Sredstva REB sukhoputnykh voisk SShA," *ZVO*, no. 4 (1980): 34–39.

109. Afinov, "Amerikanskaia sistema PLSS," *ZVO*, no. 5 (1980): 55–57.

110. Col. S. Cherkov, "Lazery v voennom dele," *ZVO*, no. 11 (1984): 18–23.

111. Lt. Col. of Engineering N. Fomich, "Protivotankovye sredstva armii SShA," *ZVO*, no. 8 (1981): 35–40; Col. in Reserves P. Isaev, "Bor'ba s tankami," *ZVO*, no. 12 (1982): 37–42.

112. See Col. A. Bulatov, "Bor'ba s tankami na bol'shikh dal'nostiakh," *ZVO*, no. 8 (1979): 29; Col. Eng. V. Dmitriev, Lt. Col. Eng. N. Germanov, "Upravliaemye aviatsionnye bomby," *ZVO*, no. 3 (1981): 55–60; Lt. Col. Eng. B. Semenov, "Takticheskie upravliaemye rakety klassa 'vozdukh-poverkhnost,' " *ZVO*, no. 5 (1981): 50–57; and Col. Eng. V. Dmitriev, "Amerikanskaia sistema SOTAS," *ZVO*, no. 4 (1982): 40–42.

113. Col. in Reserves N. Dmitriev, "Vzaimodeistvie aviatsii s sukhoputnymi voiskami," *ZVO*, no. 6 (1980): 48; Col. N. Stapenko, "Batal'onnaia takticheskaia gruppa v 'aktivnoi oborone,' " *ZVO*, no. 2 (1981): 29–34; and Maj. Gen. R. Simonian, "Tendentsii v razvitii voennoi doktriny SShA," *ZVO*, no. 11 (1981): 12.

114. Col. in Reserves G. Semin, "Voennaia strategiia NATO," *ZVO*, no. 8 (1983): 15.

115. For example, an article in December gave a very faithful summary of the new FM 100–5 document. Lt. Col. G. Vasil'ev, "Voprosy operativnogo iskusstva v vooruzhennykh silakh SShA," *ZVO*, no. 12 (1983): 3–7.

116. Maj. Gen. V. Kozhin and Col. V. Trusin, "Voprosy primeneniia vooruzhennykh sil v operatsiiakh," *ZVO*, no. 10 (1983): 18.

117. Maj. Gen. N. Ivlev and Lt. Col. V. Viktorov, "Kompleksnoe uchenie voisk tsentral'noi gruppy armii NATO 'karbain fortress,' " *ZVO*, no. 9 (1983): 10.

118. Ibid., pp. 10–11.

119. Col. L. Levadov and Lt. Col. V. Viktorov, "Manevry i ucheniia NATO—ugroza miru," *ZVO*, no. 7 (1984): 8.

120. Documents recently retrieved from the former East German military headquarters suggest that Warsaw Pact plans for war in Europe in 1989 may have integrated nuclear weapons use into battle plans within the first few days of fight-

ing, given the speed of attack indicated. It is thus not clear that the Soviets would have allowed the conventional-only period to last for fifteen days. However, there is apparently a great deal of uncertainty about how the particular combat option found here fits into "real" Soviet war plans, since Warsaw Pact officers were apparently not allowed access to the most classified Soviet operational planning. See Timothy Aeppel, "East German Papers Yield War Scenario," *Wall Street Journal*, June 13, 1991.

121. See, for example, Lt. Col. S. Yegorov, "Mekhanizirovannaia diviziia SShA v nastuplenii," *ZVO*, no. 4 (1984): 23–28; Lt. Col. V. Lavkhin, "Vozhdushnaia nastupatel'naia operatsiia," *ZVO*, no. 11 (1984): 47–54; and Lt. Col. V. Sidorov, "Vedenie operatsii s primeneniem obychnykh sredstv porazheniia," *ZVO*, no. 1 (1986): 7–15.

122. Maj. Gen. I. N. Vorob'ev, "Sootnoshenie i vzaimosviaz' nastupleniia i oborony," *Voennaia Mysl'*, no. 4 (1980): 49–59.

123. Barry R. Posen, *The Sources of Military Doctrine* (Ithaca: Cornell University Press, 1984).

124. Stephen D. Shenfield, "Soviet Historiography and the Operational Art: Historical Coverage of the Great Patriotic War by Period As an Indicator of the Orientation of Soviet Military Art, 1959–88," *Soviet Military Studies* 2 (September 1989): 358.

125. In a sense, the doctrine and technology are not separable in this case. Deep-strike defensive doctrines depend on long-range, precision-guided weapons. However, long-range, precision-guided weapons are not necessarily deep-strike weapons; they can be used in stand-off missions aimed at the FEBA as well. Therefore, in terms of what it is that the Soviets were reacting to, it is the doctrinal shift which is determining.

126. See Ye. G. Yevgen'iev, "Novye napravleniia gonki vooruzhenii v stranakh NATO," *Voennaia Mysl'*, no. 1 (1977): 88–96; M. V. Ruban, *V. I. Lenin o Bditel'nosti i Boevoi Gotovnosti* (Moscow: Voenizdat, 1984), especially pp. 22 and 25; Marshal of the Soviet Union S. Akhromeev, Chief of the General Staff, "Na strazhe mira i sotsializma," *Krasnaia Zvezda*, February 2, 1985; and Maj. Gen. M. Yasiukov, "Voennaia politika KPSS: Sushchnost', soderzhanie," *KVS*, no. 20 (1985): 14–21.

127. Maj. Gen. Eng. in Reserves N. Maksimov, "Kontseptsiia 'vystrel-prorazhenie,' " *ZVO*, no. 11 (1979): 13–14.

128. Col. V. V. Afinov, "Razvitie v SShA vysokotochnogo oruzhiia i perspektivy sozdaniia razvedyvael'no-udarnykh kompleksov," *Voennaia Mysl'*, no. 4 (1983): 71.

129. N. V. Ogarkov, *Istoriia Uchit Bditel'nosti* (Moscow: Voenizdat, 1985), p. 52.

130. Ibid., p. 54. Rose Gottemoeller notes that earlier, while he was Chief of the General Staff, Ogarkov had used a similar analysis to argue that tanks had become obsolete in modern battle. See Gottemoeller, *Conflict and Consensus in the Soviet Armed Forces* (Santa Monica: RAND, 1989), pp. 10–21. I do not see any evidence of this debate spilling over into Soviet consideration of the consequences of FOFA and ALB. Several articles in the 1980s laud the role of the technologically

improved tank in current warfare, and discuss ways of using and camouflaging tanks in the presence of the new antitank weapons; see Col. A. Kol'tsov, "Novye sredstva vooruzhennoi bor'by armii stran NATO i ikh vliianie na razvitie voennogo iskusstva," *VIZh*, no. 10 (1980): 64–67 especially; Maj. Gen. of Tank Troops I. Krupchenko, "Sposoby razvitiia uspekha v operativnoi glubine silami tankovykh armii, tankovykh i mekhanizirovannykh korpusov," *VIZh*, no. 7 (1981): 12–20; and Krupchenko, "Tanki v boiu i operatsii," *VIZh*, no. 9 (1986): 57–63. However, there seems to be no evidence of anyone in the Soviet military countering this with claims that tanks are obsolete.

131. Col. N. Volkov, "Mirovaia kapitalisticheskaia systema," designed for leaders of political classes but without the standard recommendation of the editor, *KVS*, no. 5 (1978): 77.

132. Maj. Gen. I. N. Vorob'ev, "Novoe oruzhie i razvitie printsipov obshchevoiskogo boia," *Voennaia Mysl'*, no. 6 (1986): 40.

133. Ibid., p. 39.

134. Ibid., p. 40.

135. Maj. Gen. I. N. Manzhurin, "Otrazhenie kontraudarov protivnika v khode nastupatel'noi operatsii," *Voennaia Mysl'*, no. 10 (1986): 17, 18.

136. "Obsuzhdaem opyt obespecheniia voisk v nastupatel'nykh operatsiiakh," *VIZh*, no. 3 (1982): 27.

137. Lt. Gen. I. Korotchenko, "Razvedka," *VIZh*, no. 3 (1982): 27–34.

138. Col. Gen. P. Mel'nikov, Commandant of the Frunze Academy, "Operativnaia maskirovka," *VIZh*, no. 4 (1982): 18–26.

139. Maj. of Engineering A. Krupchenko, "Tekhnicheskoi obespechenie tankovykh i mekhanizirovannykh korpusov, deistvovavshchikh v kachestve podvizhnykh grupp," *VIZh*, no. 6 (1982): 27–33.

140. Col. Yu. Molostov, "Zashchita ot vysokotochnogo oruzhiia," *Voennyi Vestnik*, no. 2 (1987): 83–86.

141. Some examples from the 1970s include Col. V. Maramain, "Nekotorye voprosy organizatsii i vedeniia frontovykh oboronitel'nykh operatsii," *VIZh*, no. 5 (1974): 10–20; Maj. Gen. V. Cherniaev, "Razvitie taktiki oboronitel'nogo boia," *VIZh*, no. 6 (1976): 20–36; and Col. A. Strusevich and Col. O. Frantsev, "Primenenie aviatsii v oboronitel'nykh operatsiiakh pervogo perioda voiny," *VIZh*, no. 1 (1978): 39–47.

142. See the summary of Soviet doctrine in the 1970s, as revealed in lectures at the General Staff Academy, by Raymond Garthoff, "Introduction," in *The Voroshilov Lectures*, vol. 1, ed. Graham Hall Turbiville, Jr. (Washington, D.C.: National Defense University Press, 1989), p. 10.

143. Maj. Gen. V. V. Turchenko, "Tendentsii razvitiia teorii i praktiki strategicheskoi oborony," *Voennaia Mysl'*, no. 8 (1979): 13.

144. Ibid., p. 17.

145. Ibid., p. 13.

146. Ibid., p. 16.

147. Turchenko wrote again on a similar subject in 1982: "O strategicheskoi oborone," *Voennaia Mysl'*, no. 7 (1982): 16–27.

148. Vorob'ev, "Sootnoshenie i vzaimosviaz' nastupleniia i oborony," p. 53.

149. Ibid., pp. 55–56.

150. M. M. Kozlov, *Akademiia General'nogo Shtaba* (Moscow: Voenizdat, 1987), p. 185.

151. M. Kozlov, "Organizatsiia i vedenie strategicheskoi oborony po opytu Velikoi Otechestvennoi Voiny," *VIZh*, no. 12 (1980): 9–17.

152. Col. Gen. M. Gareev, "Ob opyte boevoi podgotovki voisk," *VIZh*, no. 4 (1983): 12.

153. His use of these terms is borrowed from Turchenko, "Tendentsii razvitiia teorii i praktiki strategicheskoi oborony," pp. 17–18.

154. Maj. Gen. A. P. Maryshev, "Nekotorye voprosy strategicheskoi oborony v Velikoi Otechestvennoi Voine," *VIZh*, no. 6 (1986): 16.

155. Lt. Col. V. Kuskov, "Nemetskii voennyi teoretik Karl Klausevits," *VIZh*, no. 8 (1980): 80–83.

156. Maj. Gen. of Tank Forces I. Krupchenko, "A. V. Suvorov i voennoe iskusstvo," *VIZh*, no. 10 (1980): 71–75.

157. Retired Col. V. Ivanov, "Voennoe iskusstva Petra I," *VIZh*, no. 8 (1981): 66–71.

158. Kuskov, "Nemetskii voennyi teoretik," p. 82.

159. Krupchenko, "A. V. Suvorov," p. 73.

160. Ivanov, "Voennoe iskusstva Petra I," p. 68.

161. Army Gen. G. Obaturov, "Proslavlennyi polkovodets leninskoi shkoly," *KVS*, no. 2 (1985): 25.

162. Col. Gen. M. A. Gareev, *M. V. Frunze: Voennyi Teoretik* (Moscow: Voenizdat, 1985), p. 174.

163. Ibid., p. 214.

164. Ibid., p. 171.

165. Ogarkov, *Istoriia Uchit Bditel'nost'*, p. 45.

166. Gareev, *M. V. Frunze*, p. 171.

167. Ibid.; see, for example, p. 230.

168. Col. Gen. A. A. Danilevich, "Voenno-teoreticheskoi nasledie M. V. Frunze i sovremennost'," *VIZh*, no. 6 (1985): 80–87, especially p. 86.

169. For standard analyses of Tukhachevskii, see John Erickson, *The Soviet High Command: A Military-Political History, 1918–1941* (New York: St. Martin's Press, 1962), pp. 128, 133–34; Malcolm Mackintosh, *Juggernaut: A History of the Soviet Armed Forces* (New York: Macmillan, 1967), p. 54; Vitaly Rapoport and Yuri Alexeev, *High Treason: Essays on the History of the Red Army, 1918–1938*, ed. Vladimir G. Treml, co-ed. and trans. Bruce Adams (Durham, N.C.: Duke University Press, 1985), pp. 136–37; and Condoleezza Rice, "The Making of Soviet Strategy," in *Makers of Modern Strategy from Machiavelli to the Nuclear Age*, ed. Peter Paret (Princeton: Princeton University Press, 1986), pp. 664, 668–69.

170. V. M. Ivanov, *Marshal M. N. Tukhachevskii* (Moscow: Voenizdat, 1985), p. 314.

171. Col. Gen. V. N. Lobov, "Aktual'nye voprosy razvitiia teorii sovetskoi voennoi strategii 20-x-serediny 30-x godov," *VIZh*, no. 2 (1989): 50.

172. Col. Gen. M. A. Gareev, "Tvorcheskii kharakter sovetskoi voennoi nauki v velikoi otechestvennoi voine," *VIZh*, no. 7 (1985): 22–30; Maj. Gen. V. Matsulenko, "Nekotorye vyvody iz opyta nachal'nogo perioda Velikoi Ote-

chestvennoi Voiny," *VIZh*, no. 3 (1984): 39–40; and Col. A. D. Borshchov, "Otrazhenie fashistskoi agressii; uroki i vyvody," *Voennaia Mysl'*, no. 3 (1990): 13–22.

173. Lt. Gen. M. M. Kir'ian, *Fronty Nastupali* (Moscow: Nauka, 1987), p. 28; and Chief Marshal of Artillery V. F. Tolubko, "Strategicheskoe vzaimo-deistvie po opytu Velikoi Otechestvennoi Voiny," *VIZh*, no. 2 (1987): 11–19.

174. Before Kokoshin wrote his article on the proper response to FOFA and ALB, two other Soviet academics wrote their own articles on the subject. However, neither was a significant departure from standard military viewpoints. See S. Karaganov, "Avantiurizm voennoi strategii SShA," *MEiMO*, no. 3 (1984): 52; and G. Vorontsov, "SShA, NATO i gonka obychnykh vooruzhenii," *MEiMO*, no. 5 (1985): 58.

175. Matthew Evangelista has discovered a range of paths by which defensive defense ideas may have been introduced to the top leadership by civilian scholars. For his excellent detective work, see "Transnational Alliances and Soviet Demilitarization," unpublished paper prepared for the Council on Economic Priorities Project on Military Expenditures and Economic Priorities, October 1990.

176. A. A. Kokoshin, " 'Plan Rodzhersa,' alternativnye kontseptsii oborony i bezopasnost' v evrope," *SShA*, no. 9 (1985): 3.

177. Ibid., pp. 4, 5.

178. Ibid., p. 8.

179. Ibid., p. 9.

180. Ibid.

181. Ibid., p. 10.

182. Ibid.

183. Ibid., p. 11.

184. The author has confirmed this interpretation of the article with a number of ISKAN scholars.

185. Kokoshin, " 'Plan Rodzhersa,' " p. 11.

186. Ibid., pp. 12–13.

187. Ibid.

188. For an article by another author which repeats Kokoshin's themes almost exactly, including the idea that these proposals are a reaction to FOFA and ALB, see Aleksei Arbatov, "Military Doctrines," in *Disarmament and Security*, the IMEMO Yearbook, 1987 (Moscow: Novosti, 1988), pp. 201–33.

189. A. Vasil'ev and M. Gerasev, "Nekotorye itogi voenno-politicheskogo kursa administratsii R. Reigana," *MEiMO*, no. 5 (1988): 50.

190. A. A. Kokoshin, *V Poiskakh Vykhoda* (Moscow: Politizdat, 1989), pp. 224–25.

191. Oleg Amirov et al., " 'Conventional War': Strategic Concepts," *Disarmament and Security*, 1987, p. 357. Vadim Makarevskii, one of the "bridge group" of retired generals identified above, participated in this collective of authors.

192. Aleksei Arbatov, "Skol'ko oborony dostatochno?" p. 37.

193. A. A. Kokoshin, *V Poiskakh Vykhoda*, pp. 28–29.

194. Ibid., p. 212.

195. Ibid., p. 214.

196. See, for example, Philip Karber's testimony before the House Armed Services Committee, "Gorbachev's Force Reductions and the Restructuring of Soviet Forces," March 14, 1989, pp. 86–89; the summary of the International Institute for Strategic Studies report on the subject, in "Report Says Soviet Cuts Would Delay Attack," *New York Times*, October 6, 1989, and IISS Director François Heisbourg's statement in "The Three Ages of NATO Strategy," p. 27; and the U.S. Department of Defense, *Soviet Military Power: Prospects for Change, 1989*, Washington, D.C., 1989, p. 61.

197. A. Kokoshin and V. Larionov, "Kurskaia bitva v svete sovremennoi oboronitel'noi doktriny," *MEiMO*, no. 8 (1987): 32–40.

198. Ibid., p. 38.

199. For example, Paula J. Dobriansky and David B. Rivkin, Jr., claim that the article "suffers from an overdose of historical revisionism" on this issue; see their "Changes in Soviet Military Thinking: How Do They Add Up and What Do They Mean for Western Security?" in *Gorbachev and His Generals*, ed. William C. Green and Theodore Karasik (Boulder, Colo.: Westview, 1990), p. 171.

200. Ibid., p. 39.

201. A. Kokoshin, "Razvitie voennogo dela i sokroshchenie vooruzhennykh sil i obychnykh vooruzhenii," *MEiMO*, no. 1 (1988): 30. R. Hyland Phillips and Jeffrey I. Sands, in their otherwise excellent article on Soviet conventional defense concepts, place this article in the category of civilian writings which call for unilateral Soviet moves in the direction of defensive defense. Phillips and Sands, "Reasonable Sufficiency and Soviet Conventional Defense: A Research Note," *International Security* 13 (Fall 1988): 174. In fact, Kokoshin makes clear throughout this article that he sees nonprovocative defense as a bilateral concept; whatever his private beliefs may be on the matter, and in spite of the logic of the concept, which argues that nonprovocative defense can stop any offensive, Kokoshin never appears to have published in the Gorbachev era an analysis which said that nonprovocative defense could be pursued by one side alone. He always called for mutual resolution of doctrinal problems. While more recently he has become interested in the idea of "reciprocal unilateral initiatives" pursued by both sides on military issues, he nonetheless sees the unilateral initiatives as occurring within a framework of bilateral cooperation.

202. Ibid., p. 24.

203. A. Kokoshin and V. Larionov, "Protivostoianie sil obshchego naznacheniia strategicheskoi stabil'nosti," *MEiMO*, no. 6 (1988): 24–25.

204. Ibid., p. 26.

205. Ibid., pp. 27–28.

206. Ibid., pp. 28–30.

207. See Andrei Kokoshin et al., "Problems of Ensuring Stability with Radical Cuts in Armed Forces and Conventional Armaments in Europe"; Kokoshin, testimony before the U.S. House of Representatives Armed Services Committee, "Gorbachev's Force Reductions and the Restructuring of Soviet Forces," March 10, 1989, pp. 2–50; and Kokoshin, "The Future of NATO and Warsaw Pact Strategy: Paper II," in *The Strategic Implications of Change in the Soviet Union, Part I*, Adelphi Paper 247 (London: International Institute for Strategic Studies, 1989/90), pp. 62–63.

208. See Kokoshin, "The Future of NATO and Warsaw Pact Strategy," p. 63; and Kokoshin, testimony, "Gorbachev's Force Reductions."

209. Kokoshin, "Gorbachev's Force Reductions," p. 49.

210. Ibid., p. 5.

211. A. Savel'ev, "Predotvrashchenie voiny i sderzhivanie: podkhody OVD i NATO," *MEiMO*, no. 6 (1989): 26.

212. Aleksei Arbatov and Aleksandr Savel'ev, "Military Doctrines: Discussions in the East," *Disarmament and Security, 1988–1989*, the IMEMO Yearbook (Moscow: Novosti, 1989), p. 204.

213. A. A. Kokoshin and V. N. Lobov, "Predvidenie," *Znamia*, no. 2 (1990): 181.

214. G. Kunadze, "Ob oboronnoi dostatochnosti voennogo potentsiala SSSR," *MEiMO*, no. 10 (1989): 63–83, particularly pp. 68–69.

215. From an interview in the United States, spring 1989. The text of the appeal appears in *Pravda*, June 12, 1986.

216. *Pravda*, June 12, 1986.

217. A. A. Konovalov, "Nauchno-tekhnicheskii progress i tendentsii razvitiia neiadernykh vooruzhenii dlia sil obshchego naznacheniia v 80-kh godakh," in *Voenno-tekhnicheskaia Politika SShA v 80-e gody*, ed. A. A. Kokoshin and A. A. Konovalov (Moscow: Nauka, 1989), p. 199.

218. Schneider, "Soviet Foreign-Policy Think Tanks," p. 154.

219. This starting point is identified by two military sources: Chief of the General Staff Moiseev in his speech as a Congress of People's Deputies candidate, "S pozitsii oboronitel'noi doktriny"; and former Chief of the General Staff Akhromeev, in his interview by Col. S. Pogrebenkov, "Novaia politika protiv arsenaly voiny," *KVS*, no. 1 (1990): 17.

220. Lt. Gen. of Aviation V. Serebriannikov, "Osnova osnov ukrepleniia oborony strany," *KVS*, no. 4 (1986): 22; received by the typesetter on January 16, 1986.

221. Roy Allison, "Reasonable Sufficiency and Changes in Soviet Security Thinking," to be published in *Soviet Military Doctrine from Lenin to Gorbachev*, ed. P. Gillette and W. Frank (New York: Greenwood, forthcoming); the citation is from p. 3 of Allison's preliminary manuscript.

222. Gerhard Wettig, "Sufficiency in Defense—A New Guideline for the Soviet Military Posture?" *Radio Liberty Research Bulletin*, no. 38 (September 23, 1987): 1.

223. "O voennoi doktrine gosudarstv-uchastnikov Varshavskogo Dogovora," *Pravda*, May 30, 1987.

224. Ibid.

225. This was reported by Bill Keller, "Gorbachev Vows Major Military Cutback and a 'Clearly Defensive' Stand in Europe," *New York Times* December 8, 1988.

226. On Karber's views, see Fialka, "Soviets Outline Troop-Cut Plan"; François Heisbourg outlines his views in "The Three Ages of NATO Strategy," p. 27.

227. Mikhail Mil'shtein, "New Concepts of a Safe World," in *Dialogue: Reflections on Security in the Nuclear Age*, a book written by Generals for Peace and Disarmament East and West (Moscow: Progress, 1988), pp. 91–92.

228. Ibid., pp. 57–58.

229. Vadim Makarevskii, "Military Détente in Europe," in ibid., p. 123.

230. Ibid., p. 130.

231. Andrei Kokoshin, "Defence Is Best for Stability," *New Times*, no. 33 (1988): 18–19.

232. Ibid., p. 18.

233. Col. V. Kosarev, "Doktrina sokhraneniia mira," *Krasnaia Zvezda*, September 25, 1987.

234. Stanislav Kosterin, "Armiia i perestroika," *Sovetskaia Rossiia*, January 14, 1989.

235. Col. O. Nikonov, "Kursom obnovleniia," *Krasnaia Zvezda*, December 28, 1988.

236. Col. Gen. M. A. Moiseev, "S pozitsii oboronitel'noi doktriny."

237. Maj. Gen. Yu. Liubimov, "O dostatochnosti oborony," p. 22.

238. "Doktrina novaia—problemy starye?" *KVS*, no. 16 (1989): 28.

239. Col. V. Davydikov, "Following Course of Military Reform," *Krasnaia Zvezda*, April 13, 1990, as reported in *FBIS-SOV*, April 18, 1990, p. 73.

240. See, for example, Army Gen. P. Lushev, Commander-in-Chief of the Warsaw Pact forces, "Na strazhe zavoevanii revoliutsii," *Mezhdunarodnaia Zhizn'*, no. 8 (1987): 69.

241. Sergei Akhromeev, "Doktrina predotvrashcheniia voiny, zashchity mira i sotsializma," *Problema Mira i Sotsializma*, no. 12 (1987): 26.

242. M. Moiseev, "Sovetskaia voennaia doktrina: realizatsiia ee oboronitel'noi napravlennosti," *Pravda*, March 13, 1989.

243. Maj. Gen. N. V. Meshcheriakov, "Ideologiia obnovleniia: sotsializm i ego vooruzhennaia zashchita," *Voennaia Mysl'*, no. 2 (1990): 60; emphasis added.

244. Ibid., p. 58.

245. For examples, see M. A. Gareev, *Sovetskaia Voennaia Nauka* (Moscow: Znanie, 1988), pp. 15–17; Lt. Gen. of Aviation V. Serebriannikov, "Predotvrashchenie voiny: vklad armii," *KVS*, no. 17 (1989): 22; and D. Yazov, "Novaia model' bezopasnosti i vooruzhennye sily," *Kommunist*, no. 18 (1989): 63.

246. Gareev, *Sovetskaia Voennaia Nauka*, p. 7; Serebriannikov, "Predotvrashchenie voiny," p. 27.

247. For example, see Col. Gen. Dmitrii Volkogonov, "The anti-war doctrine," *New Times*, no. 25 (1987): 15.

248. Capt. 1st Rank V. Alekseev, "Vnezapnost' v morskom boiu," *Morskoi Sbornik*, no. 10 (1988): 15–20. The issue was sent to the typesetter on August 19, even though it did not go into print until October 6.

249. See, for example, Col. M. Ponomarev, "V gotovnosti k otporu agressoru," *Krasnaia Zvezda*, June 17, 1987; "Povyshaia boevuiu gotovnost', uglubliaia perestroiku," book review, *KVS*, no. 3 (1988): 88; Army Gen. Ivan Tretiak, Commander-in-Chief of the PVO Strany, in an interview by Yuri Teplyakov, "Reliable defence first and foremost," *Moscow News*, no. 8 (1988): 12; Army Gen. S. I. Postnikov, "Razvitie sovetskogo voennogo iskusstva v kurskoi bitve," *VIZh*, no. 7 (1988): 18; and M. A. Gareev, *Sovetskaia Voennaia Nauka*, pp. 36–37.

250. See, for example, Sergei Akhromeev, "Doktrina predotvrashcheniia

voiny," p. 28; and Col. V. Strebkov, "Novaia model' bezopasnosti: voennyi aspekt," *KVS*, no. 2 (1990): 26.

251. M. A. Gareev, *Sovetskaia Voennaia Nauka*, pp. 36–37.

252. Makhmut Gareev, "The revised Soviet military doctrine," *Bulletin of the Atomic Scientists* 44 (December 1988): 31–32.

253. Army Gen. P. Lushev, "V interesakh prochnogo mira," *Krasnaia Zvezda*, March 3, 1989.

254. This is according to Moscow TASS in English, January 19, 1990, as reported in *FBIS-SOV*, January 22, 1990, p. 1.

255. M. Moiseev, "Sovetskaia voennaia doktrina," p. 5.

256. Brigitte Sauerwein and Matthias Plugge, "New Soviet Military Doctrine: The Voroshilov Academy's Interpretation," *International Defense Review* 23 (January 1990): 21.

257. Maj. Gen. A. S. Kulikov and Maj. Gen. A. D. Nefedov, "Pozitsionnye i manevrennye deistviia: pol' i mesto v oboronitel'noi operatsii," *Voennaia Mysl'*, no. 3 (1990): 24.

258. James F. Holcomb and Stephen R. Covington, "CSBM Seminar on Military Doctrine, Vienna, Austria, Week Three: Soviet and NSWP Training," unclassified version of an unpublished manuscript, February 8, 1990, p. 1.

259. See, for example, Col. Gen. V. Lobov, Chief of Staff of the Warsaw Pact, "Vysokoe kachestvo—glavnyi kriterii boevoi podgotovki," *KVS*, no. 1 (1989): 13–14; and Deputy Minister of Defense for Armaments Army Gen. V. M. Shabanov, interviewed by Col. V. Pogrebenkov, "Novaia politika protiv arsenalov voiny," *KVS*, no. 1 (1990): 21.

260. Stephen R. Covington and James F. Holcomb, "CSBM Seminar on Military Doctrine, Vienna, Austria, Week One: Soviet Military Doctrine," unclassified version of an unpublished manuscript, January 22, 1990, p. 2.

261. Holcomb and Covington, "CSBM Seminar on Military Doctrine, Vienna, Austria, Week Two: Soviet Force Structure," unclassified version of an unpublished manuscript, February 7, 1990, p. 2.

262. Galina Sidorova and Nikita Zholkver, interview with Shevardnadze, in "Losing Enemies: Notes from the Bonn Conference," *New Times*, no. 20 (1990): 6.

263. "O voennoi doktrine SSSR," in *Voennaia Mysl' Spetsial'nyi Vypusk* 1990 (given to the typesetter on November 20, 1990), pp. 24–28.

264. Ibid., p. 27.

265. Ibid.

266. David M. Glantz, "Soviet Military Strategy after CFE: Historical Models and Future Prospects," *Journal of Soviet Military Studies* 3 (June 1990): 259.

267. Mikhail Tsypkin, "The Soviet Military: Glasnost' Against Secrecy," *Problems of Communism* 40 (May/June 1991): 51–66.

268. O. Losik, "Gde granitsy razumnoi dostatochnosti," *Krasnaia Zvezda*, March 5, 1991.

269. Retired Lt. Gen. E. D. Grebish, "Evoliutsiia doktrinal'nykh ustanovok v Sovetskom voennom iskusstve v 80-x godakh," *Voennaia Mysl'*, no. 6 (1991): 31–37 (quotation is from p. 37).

270. See, for example, Col. R. M. Portugal'skii, "K voprosu o perekhode ot oborony k nastupleniiu," *Voennaia Mysl'*, no. 6 (1990): 15; Col. Gen. A. A.

Demidov, "Osobennosti boevoi podgotovki Sukhoputnykh voisk," *Voennaia Mysl'*, no. 7 (1990): 49; Retired Capt. 1st Rank N. S. Volgin, "Ne zabyli li my staroe . . ." *Voennaia Mysl'*, no. 8 (1991): 46–52, which argues that the best defense is a good offense; and Retired Maj. Gen. I. N. Vorob'ev, "Printisipy formirovaniia voennoi doktriny," *Voennaia Mysl'*, no. 11–12 (1991): 22–29, which provides another offensive-leaning critique of the draft doctrine statement.

271. Jacob W. Kipp, "General of the Army Vladimir Nikolayevich Lobov: One of Gorbachev's *Genshtabisty*," *Soviet Military Studies* 2 (September 1989): 403.

272. Alexander Rahr, "Gorbachev Discloses Details of Defense Council," *Radio Liberty Report on the USSR* 1, no. 36 (September 8, 1989): 12; Rahr cites his source as an unpublished stenographic record given to Supreme Soviet deputies after the hearings.

273. Dale R. Herspring, *The Soviet High Command, 1967–1989* (Princeton: Princeton University Press, 1990), p. 218.

274. Stanislav Kosterin, interview with Sergei Akhromeev, "Armii i perestroika," *Sovetskaia Rossiia*, January 14, 1989.

275. Christopher Wilkinson, "Perestroika: The Role of the Defence Sector," *NATO Review* 38 (February 1990): 22.

276. See the analysis by Herspring, *The Soviet High Command*, p. 218.

277. For example, see the interview with Deputy Chief of the General Staff V. Lobov, "Iskhodia iz printsipov oboronitel'noi doktriny," *Pravda*, December 17, 1988; Yuri Teplyakov's interview with Akhromeev, "General Staff Changes," *Moscow News*, no. 5 (1989): 5; and Chief of the General Staff Moiseev's response to a letter to the editor, "Eshche raz o prestizhe armii," *KVS*, no. 13 (1989): 7. See also Kokoshin's U.S. testimony, "Gorbachev's Force Reductions," pp. 20, 43.

278. Peter Schweizer, "The Soviet Military Goes High-Tech," *Orbis* 35 (Spring 1991): 202.

279. From an interview with a high-ranking Soviet military officer in the United States, summer 1990.

280. Stephen M. Meyer, "The Army Isn't Running Gorbachev," *New York Times*, May 8, 1990.

281. Defense Policy Panel Report, "The Fading Threat: Soviet Conventional Military Power in Decline," July 9, 1990, p. 10.

282. Ibid., pp. 10, 11.

283. This argument is made well by Evangelista, "Transnational Alliances and Soviet Demilitarization."

284. Konstantin Pleshakov, "The Zhukovsky Dilemma," *New Times*, no. 29 (1990): 36–39.

285. Ibid., p. 39.

Chapter 6
Doctrine, Innovation, and Competition

1. Barry Posen, *The Sources of Military Doctrine* (Ithaca: Cornell University Press), pp. 55–57.

2. L. Semeiko, "Formy novye, sut' prezhniaia," *Krasnaia Zvezda*, April 8, 1975.

3. Makhmut Akhmatovich Gareev, *M. V. Frunze, Military Theorist*, trans. from Russian by an unnamed source (Washington, D.C.: Pergamon-Brassey's, 1988), p. 64.

4. There is a growing body of political science literature, especially in the field of international political economy, which recognizes the importance of individuals and their ideas. See, for example, John S. Odell, *U.S. International Monetary Policy* (Princeton: Princeton University Press, 1982); Judith Goldstein, "The Impact of Ideas on Trade Policy," *International Organization* 43 (Winter 1989): 31–71; and Peter A. Hall, ed., *The Political Power of Economic Ideas* (Princeton: Princeton University Press, 1989).

5. This term is borrowed from Robert D. Putnam, "Diplomacy and Domestic Politics: The Logic of Two-Level Games," *International Organization* 42 (Summer 1988): 427–60.

6. Jack Snyder and Andrei Kortunov, "French Syndrome on Soviet Soil," *New Times*, no. 44 (1989): 18–20.

7. Jack Snyder, "France: Offensive Strategy as an Institutional Defense," and "France: Du Picq, Dreyfus, and the Errors of Plan 17," in his *The Ideology of the Offensive* (Ithaca: Cornell University Press, 1984), pp. 41–106.

8. Ibid., pp. 46–48, 50–53.

9. Ibid., pp. 54–56.

10. Ibid., pp. 53–54.

11. The example Snyder gives is of Gen. Victor Michel, vice-president of the Supreme War Council; ibid., p. 49.

12. Ibid.

13. Ibid., pp. 54–55, 62–96.

14. Ibid., p. 52.

Postscript
After the Cold War

1. Some of these efforts are summarized in "Documentation," *NATO Review* 40 (April 1992): 31–35.

2. One sign of this may be the Pentagon's February 1992 list of potential future threats to U.S. security interests. Of the seven threats predicted, two refer directly or indirectly to Russian expansionism. See Patrick E. Tyler, "Seven Hypothetical Conflicts Foreseen by the Pentagon," *New York Times*, February 17, 1992.

3. Stephen M. Meyer, "How the Threat (and the Coup) Collapsed: The Politicization of the Soviet Military," *International Security* 16 (Winter 1991/92): 5–38.

4. The following argument is largely based on Kimberly Marten Zisk, "Reciprocal Unilateral Measures and Military Doctrine in Europe in the Post-Cold War Era," paper prepared for delivery at the Conference on Reciprocal Unilateral Measures and the U.S. Soviet Security Relationship, Stanford University Center for International Security and Arms Control (CISAC), Stanford, Ca., December 1990.

5. These criteria are drawn, with some alterations, from the discussion about

definitions of NOD in Graeme Cheeseman, "The Application of the Principles of Non-Offensive Defense Beyond Europe: Some Preliminary Observations," Working Paper 78 of the Peace Research Center (Canberra: Australian National University, 1990).

6. For examples, see James F. Holcomb and Stephen R. Covington's description of General Markovskii's comment at the first Conference on Security Building Measures doctrine meeting, "CSBM Seminar on Military Doctrine, Vienna, Austria, Week Two: Soviet Force Structure," unclassified version of an unpublished manuscript, February 7, 1990, p. 2; N. F. Chervov, "Na puti k doveriiu i bezopasnosti," *Voennaia Mysl'*, no. 6 (1990): 9; and Col. I. Vladimirov, "NATO na poroge peremen?" *Zarubezhnoe Voennoe Obozrenie*, no. 9 (1990): 17–20.

7. "The Alliance's New Strategic Concept," signed by the Heads of State and Government of NATO, reprinted in *NATO Review* 39 (December 1991): 29.

8. William H. Taft IV, "European Security: Lessons Learned from the Gulf War," *NATO Review* 39 (June 1991): 10.

9. "Kontseptsiia voennoi reformy," *Voennaia Mysl' Spetsial'nyi Vypusk* 1990: 7–8.

10. Eckhard Lubkemeier, "The Political Upheaval in Europe and the Reform of NATO Strategy," *NATO Review* 39 (June 1991): 19.

11. Ibid., p. 21.

Bibliography

Achalov, V. "Vozdushno-desantnym voiskam—60 let." *Voennaia Mysl'*, no. 9 (1990): 31–38.

Aeppel, Timothy. "East German Papers Yield War Scenario." *Wall Street Journal*, June 13, 1991.

Afinov, V. V. "Amerikanskaia sistema PLSS." *Zarubezhnoe Voennoe Obozrenie*, no. 5 (1980): 55–57.

———. "Razvitie v SShA vysokotochnogo oruzhiia i perspektivy sozdaniia razvedyvael'no-udarnykh kompleksov." *Voennaia Mysl'*, no. 4 (1983): 63–71.

———. "Sredstva REB sukhoputnykh voisk SShA." *Zarubezhnoe Voennoe Obozrenie*, no. 4 (1980): 34–39.

Agapova, Elena. "Nash chelovek v kongresse." *Krasnaia Zvezda*, September 15, 1989.

Akhromeev, Sergei. "Doktrina predotvrashcheniia voiny, zashchity mira i sotsializma." *Problema Mira i Sotsializma*, no. 12 (1987): 23–28.

———. "Na strazhe mira i sotsializma." *Krasnaia Zvezda*, February 2, 1985.

Akimov, V., and A. Damor. "The Foreign Press on Military-Economic Preparations of the Chinese People's Republic." *Voennaia Mysl'*, no. 9 (1973): 99–108.

Albritton, Robert B. "Measuring Public Policy: Impacts of the Supplemental Security Income Program." *American Journal of Political Science* 23 (August 1979): 559–78.

Aldrich, Howard E. *Organizations and Environments*. Englewood Cliffs, N.J.: Prentice-Hall, 1979.

Alekseev, V. "Vnezapnost' v morskom boiu." *Morskoi Sbornik*, no. 10 (1988): 15–20.

Alexander, Arthur J. *Decision-Making in Soviet Weapons Procurement*. Adelphi Paper 147/8. London: International Institute for Strategic Studies, 1978.

Alexiev, Alexander, and Robert Nurick, eds. *The Soviet Military Under Gorbachev: Report on a RAND Workshop*, R-3907. Santa Monica: RAND, 1990.

Allen, R. "Polevaia armiia pri razvitii uspekha." *Voennyi Zarubezhnik*, no. 7 (1958): 12–23.

"The Alliance's New Strategic Concept." *NATO Review* 39 (December 1991): 25–32.

Allison, Graham T. *Essence of Decision*. Boston: Little, Brown and Co., 1971.

———. "Questions about the Arms Race." In *Contrasting Approaches to Strategic Arms Control*. Lexington, Mass.: Lexington Books, 1974.

Allison, Roy. "Reasonable Sufficiency and Changes in Soviet Security Thinking." In *Soviet Military Doctrine from Lenin to Gorbachev*, ed. P. Gillette and W. Frank. New York: Greenwood, forthcoming.

Amirov, Oleg, et al. " 'Conventional War': Strategic Concepts." In *Disarmament and Security, 1987*. Moscow: Novosti, 1988.

Andreev, N., and I. Aleksandrov, "Izmeneniia v organizatsii soedinenii sukho-putnykh voisk SShA." *Voennyi Zarubezhnik*, no. 10 (1961): 69–75.

Andreev, V. "V. I. Lenin o vzaimosviazi faktorov, opredeliaiushchikh khod i iskhod voiny." *Kommunist Vooruzhennykh Sil*, no. 8 (1971): 84–90.

Antonov, N. "The U.S. Military Budget." *Voennaia Mysl'*, no. 8 (1967): 69–81.

Anureev, I. I. *Oruzhie Protivoraketnoi i Protivokosmicheskoi Oborony*. Moscow: Voenizdat, 1971.

Anureev, I., et al. "The Aims and Content of the Theory of Operations Research." *Voennaia Mysl'*, no. 7 (1963): 20–34.

Arbatov, Aleksei G. "Deistvitel'no, est'-li povod dlia spora?" *Mirovaia Ekonomika i Mezhdunarodnye Otnosheniia*, no. 10 (1988): 130–34.

———. "How Much Defense Is Sufficient?" *International Affairs* (Moscow), 1989, no. 4: 31–44.

———. "K voprosu o dostatochnosti protivovozdushnoi oborony." *Voennaia Mysl'*, no. 12 (1989): 41–45.

———. "Military Doctrines." In *Disarmament and Security, 1987*. Moscow: Novosti, 1988.

———. "Poleznee razgovor po sushchestvu." *Kommunist Vooruzhennykh Sil*, no. 22 (1989): 17–21.

———. "Skol'ko oborony dostatochno?" *Mezhdunarodnaia Zhizn'*, no. 3 (1989): 33–47.

Arbatov, Aleksei, and Aleksandr Savel'ev. "Military Doctrines: Discussions in the East." In *Disarmament and Security, 1988–1989*. Moscow: Novosti, 1989.

Arbatov, Georgii. "Armiia dlia strany ili strana dlia armii?" *Ogonek*, 1990, no. 4: 4.

———. "A esli bez lukavstva." *Ogonek*, no. 17 (1990): 8–11.

Arushanian, B. "Combat Operations by Tank Units against Operational Defense Reserves." *Voennaia Mysl'*, no. 1, pt. 2 (1966): 29–35.

Aspaturian, Vernon V. "Farewell to Soviet Foreign Policy." *Problems of Communism* 40 (November/December 1991): 53–62.

Azrael, Jeremy R. *The Soviet Civilian Leadership and the Military High Command, 1976–1986*, R-3521. Santa Monica: RAND, 1987.

Babadzhanian, A. Kh., ed. *Tanki i Tankovye Voiska*. Moscow: Voenizdat, 1970.

Bacevich, A. J. *The Pentomic Era*. Washington, D.C.: National Defense University Press, 1986.

Balansov, L., and L. Sapozhnikov. "Troop Combat Operations under Conditions of Radioactive Contamination of Terrain." *Voennaia Mysl'*, no. 7 (1963): 48–61.

Balev, B. "Sea and Ocean Communications and Warfare on Them." *Voennaia Mysl'*, no. 10 (1971): 47–57.

Ball, Desmond. "The Development of the SIOP, 1960–1983." In *Strategic Nuclear Targeting*, ed. Ball and Jeffrey Richelson. Ithaca: Cornell University Press, 1986.

———. "Soviet Strategic Planning and the Control of Nuclear War." In *The Soviet Calculus of Nuclear War*, ed. Roman Kolkowicz and Ellen Propper Mickiewicz. Lexington, Mass.: Lexington Books, 1986.

———. "U.S. Strategic Forces: How Would They Be Used?" *International Security* 7 (Winter 1982/3): 31–60.

Baraniuk, B. A., and V. I. Vorob'ev. *Avtomatizirovannye Sistemy Upravleniia Shtabov i Voennykh Uchrezhdenii*. Moscow: Voenizdat, 1974.

Begunov, S. "The Maneuver of Forces and Materiel in an Offensive." *Voennaia Mysl'*, no. 5 (1968): 42–48.

Beliaev, A. "Nauchnye predstavleniia o sovremennoi voine—vazhnyi element soznaniia sovetskogo voina." *Kommunist Vooruzhennykh Sil*, no. 7 (1985): 24–31.

Belousov, L. "Konferentsiia o sovetskoi voennoi doktrine." *Voenno-Istoricheskii Zhurnal*, no. 10 (1963): 121–26.

Belousov, M. V. "Tekhnicheskie aspekty sistemy 'seifgard,' " *SShA*, no. 5 (1970): 118–23.

Berezhkov, V. M. "Perspektivy razriadki i sovetsko-amerikanskie otnosheniia." *SShA*, no. 9 (1975): 3–14.

Berger, Peter L., and Thomas Luckmann. *The Social Construction of Reality: A Treatise in the Sociology of Knowledge*. New York: Irvington, 1966.

Berman, Robert P., and John C. Baker. *Soviet Strategic Forces*. Washington, D.C.: Brookings, 1982.

Berry, Frances Stokes, and William D. Berry. "State Lottery Adoptions as Policy Innovations." *American Political Science Review* 84 (June 1990): 395–415.

Bjorkman, Thomas N., and Thomas J. Zamostny. "Soviet Politics and Strategy Toward the West: Three Cases." *World Politics* 36 (January 1984): 189–214.

Bloor, David. *Knowledge and Social Imagery*. Boston: Routledge and Kegan Paul, 1976.

Bluth, Christoph. "Defence and Security." In *Khrushchev and Khrushchevism*, ed. Martin McCauley. London: MacMillan, 1987.

Bochkarev, K. "An Evaluation of the Results of the June Plenum of the Central Committee of the Communist Party USSR [sic]." *Voennaia Mysl'*, no. 7 (1963): 1–19.

Bogdanov, Radomir, and Andrei Kortunov. " 'Minimum Deterrent': Utopia or a Real Prospect?" *Moscow News*, no. 23 (1989): 6.

Bogdanov, R. G., M. A. Mil'shtein, and L. S. Semeiko. *SShA: Voenno-Strategicheskie Kontseptsii*. Moscow: Nauka, 1980.

Boltunov, O. "Bezotvetsvennye prizyvy." *Kommunist Vooruzhennykh Sil*, no. 1 (1989): 20.

Bondarenko, V. M. "Nauchno-tekhnicheskii progress i ukreplenie oboronosposobnosti strany." *Kommunist Vooruzhennykh Sil*, no. 24 (1971): 9–16.

———. "Nauchno-tekhnicheskii progress i upravlenie voiskami." *Kommunist Vooruzhennykh Sil*, no. 10 (1973): 27–33.

———. *Sovremennaia Nauka i Razvitie Voennogo Dela*. Moscow: Voenizdat, 1976.

Bondarenko, V. M., and S. Tiushkevich. "Sovremennyi etap revoliutsii v voennom dele i trebovaniia k voennym kadram." *Kommunist Vooruzhennykh Sil*, no. 6 (1968): 18–25.

Bondarenko, V. M., and A. F. Volkov, eds. *Avtomatizatsiia Upravleniia Voiskami*. Moscow: Voenizdat, 1977.

Borisov, V. V. *Opasnaia Stavka: Nauchno-tekhnicheskaia Revoliutsiia i Voennye Prigotovleniia SShA*. Moscow: Voenizdat, 1979.

Borshchov, A. D. "Otrazhenie fashistskoi agressii; uroki i vyvody." *Voennaia Mysl'*, no. 3 (1990): 13–22.

Boulding, Kenneth E. "The World War Industry As an Economic Problem." In *Disarmament and the Economy*, ed. Emile Benoit and Kenneth E. Boulding. New York: Harper and Row, 1963.

Bracken, Paul. *The Command and Control of Nuclear Forces*. New Haven: Yale University Press, 1983.

Brauch, Hans Gunther. "West German Alternatives for Reducing Reliance on Nuclear Weapons." In *Rethinking the Nuclear Weapons Dilemma in Europe*, ed. P. Terrence Hopmann and Frank Barnaby. London: Macmillan, 1988.

"Briefing on Counterforce Attacks." Appendix to the Senate Foreign Relations Committee, *Analyses of the Effects of Limited Nuclear Warfare*. Print, September 1975.

Bronevskii, S. "The Factors of Space and Time in Military Operations." *Voennaia Mysl'*, no. 7 (1963): 35–47.

Bulatov, A. "Bor'ba s tankami na bol'shikh dal'nostiakh." *Zarubezhnoe Voennoe Obozrenie*, no. 8 (1979): 29–33.

Bunce, Valerie, and John M. Echols III. "Power and Policy in Communist Systems: The Problem of Incrementalism." *Journal of Politics* 40 (August 1978): 911–32.

Burns, John F. "Moscow Replaces Military Chief of Warsaw Pact." *New York Times*, February 3, 1989.

Caldwell, Lawrence T. *Soviet Attitudes to SALT*. Adelphi Paper 75. London: International Institute for Strategic Studies, 1971.

Chaldymov, N. A. "Burzhuaznye voenno-strategicheskie konstseptsii i kritika ikh ideologicheskikh osnov." *Voennaia Mysl'*, no. 6 (1978): 70–81.

Chaldymov, N. A., and B. V. Molostov. "Vseobshchaia bezopasnost' novye filosofsko-politicheskie podkhody." *Voennaia Mysl'*, no. 2 (1990): 69–77.

Cheeseman, Graeme. "The Application of the Principles of Non-Offensive Defense Beyond Europe: Some Preliminary Observations." Working Paper 78 of the Peace Research Center. Canberra: Australian National University, 1990.

Cherednichenko, M. "Military Strategy and Military Technology." *Voennaia Mysl'*, no. 4 (1973): 47–60.

Cherkov, S. "Lazery v voennom dele." *Zarubezhnoe Voennoe Obozrenie*, no. 11 (1984): 18–23.

Cherniaev, V. "Razvitie taktiki oboronitel'nogo boia." *Voenno-Istoricheskii Zhurnal*, no. 6 (1976): 20–36.

Chervov, N. F. "Na puti k doveriiu i bezopasnosti." *Voennaia Mysl'*, no. 6 (1990): 9–10.

Chirvin, V. A. "Oboronnaia dostatochnost' i problemy predotvrashcheniia voiny." *Voennaia Mysl'*, no. 7 (1990): 5–12.

Clifford, Clark. Draft Presidential Memorandum on Strategic Offensive and Defensive Forces. January 9, 1969. DOD/OSD FOIA. National Security Archive collection.

Cochran, Thomas B., et al. *Soviet Nuclear Weapons*, vol. 4 of the Nuclear Weapons Databook of the National Resources Defense Council. New York: Harper and Row (Ballinger), 1989.

Collins, John M. *U.S.-Soviet Military Balance, 1960–1980*. Washington, D.C.: McGraw-Hill, 1980.

Colton, Timothy P. *Commissars, Commanders and Civilian Authority*. Cambridge: Harvard University Press, 1979.

———. "Perspectives on Civil-Military Relations in the Soviet Union." In *Soldiers and the Soviet State: Civil-Military Relations from Brezhnev to Gorbachev*. Princeton: Princeton University Press, 1990.

Committee of Soviet Scientists for Peace, Against the Nuclear Threat. *The Large-Scale Anti-Missile System and International Security*. Moscow: Novosti, 1986.

———. *Space-Strike Arms and International Security*. Abridged ed. Moscow: Novosti, 1985.

"Conventional Defense Improvements in NATO." In *Strategic Survey 1985–1986*. London: International Institute for Strategic Studies, 1986.

Covington, Stephen R., and James F. Holcomb. "CSBM Seminar on Military Doctrine, Vienna, Austria, Week One: Soviet Military Doctrine." Unclassified version of an unpublished manuscript. January 22, 1990.

Cushman, John H. Jr. "Old Soldiers of Two Camps Talk of Peace." *New York Times*, April 28, 1987.

Danilevich, A. A. "Voenno-teoreticheskoi nasledie M. V. Frunze i sovremennost'." *Voenno-Istoricheskii Zhurnal*, no. 6 (1985): 80–87.

Danilov, V. D. "Kommentarii voennogo istorika." *Voennaia Mysl'*, no. 11 (1990): 51–56.

Davis, Lynn Etheridge. *Limited Nuclear Options*. Adelphi Paper 121. London: International Institute for Strategic Studies, 1976.

Davis, Vincent. "Defense Reorganization and National Security." *Annals of the American Academy of Political and Social Sciences* 517 (September 1991): 157–73.

———. *The Politics of Innovation: Patterns in Navy Cases*. Vol. 4, Monograph 3 of the Social Science Foundation and Graduate School of International Studies University of Denver Monograph Series in World Affairs. Denver, 1966–67.

Davydikov, V. "Following Course of Military Reform." *Krasnaia Zvezda*, April 13, 1990. As reported in *Foreign Broadcast Information Service Daily Report: Soviet Union*, April 18, 1990, p. 73.

Dean, Jonathan. *Watershed in Europe*. Lexington, Mass.: Lexington Books, 1987.

"Deistvie atomnogo oruzhiia." *Voennaia Mysl'*, no. 3 (1954): 69–78.

Demidov, A. A. "Doktrina novaia—problemy starye?" *Kommunist Vooruzhennykh Sil*, no. 16 (1989): 27–33.

———. "Osobennosti boevoi podgotovki Sukhoputnykh voisk." *Voennaia Mysl'*, no. 7 (1990): 44–50.

Demidov, B. "Zakony dialektiki i voennaia nauka." *Kommunist Vooruzhennykh Sil*, no. 9 (1964): 91–93.

Derevianko, P. "Nekotorye osobennosti sovremennoi revoliutsii v voennom dele." *Kommunist Vooruzhennykh Sil*, no. 1 (1964): 15–25.

DeWeerd, H. A. "Meniaiushchaiasia voennaia politika Velikobritanii." *Voennyi Zarubezhnik*, no. 2 (1956): 43–53.

Dinerstein, Herbert S. *War and the Soviet Union*. Rev. ed. New York: Praeger, 1962.

Dinerstein, Herbert S., Leon Gouré, and Thomas W. Wolfe, trans. and annotators. *Soviet Military Strategy*. Original (in Russian) ed. V. D. Sokolovskii. Santa Monica: RAND, 1963.

Dmitriev, A. "Marksistsko-Leninskoe uchenie o voine i armii." *Kommunist Vooruzhennykh Sil*, no. 13 (1975): 9–17.

Dmitriev, N. "Vzaimodeistvie aviatsii s sukhoputnymi voiskami." *Zarubezhnoe Voennoe Obozrenie*, no. 6 (1980): 43–50.

Dmitriev, V. "Amerikanskaia sistema SOTAS." *Zarubezhnoe Voennoe Obozrenie*, no. 4 (1982): 40–42.

Dmitriev, V., and N. Germanov. "Upravliaemye aviatsionnye bomby." *Zarubezhnoe Voennoe Obozrenie*, no. 3 (1981): 55–60.

Dobriansky, Paula J., and David B. Rivkin, Jr. "Changes in Soviet Military Thinking: How Do They Add Up and What Do They Mean for Western Security?" In *Gorbachev and His Generals*, ed. William C. Green and Theodore Karasik. Boulder, Colo.: Westview, 1990.

"Doktrina Voennaia." In *Sovetskaia Voennaia Entsiklopedia*, vol. 3. Moscow: Voenizdat, 1977: 225–29.

Donnelly, Christopher N. "Future Soviet Military Policy, Part I: Doctrine and Economics." *International Defense Review* 22 (January 1989): 19–22.

———. "The Soviet Operational Manoeuvre Group: A New Challenge for NATO." *International Defense Review* 15 (September 1982): 1177–86.

Douglass, Joseph D. Jr., and Amoretta M. Hoeber. *Conventional War and Escalation: The Soviet View*. New York: Crane, Russak and Co., 1981.

Dvorkin, Vladimir, and Valery Torbin. "On Real Sufficiency in Defense." *Moscow News*, no. 26 (1989): 6.

Dzhelaukhov, Kh. "The Evolution of U.S. Military Doctrine." *Voennaia Mysl'*, no. 9 (1967): 93–98.

———. "The Infliction of Deep Strikes." *Voennaia Mysl'*, no. 2 (1966): 39–49.

"Emerging Technologies: An Uncertain Future." In *Strategic Survey 1983–1984*. London: International Institute for Strategic Studies, 1984.

Erickson, John. *Proceedings of a Conference on the Soviet Military and Future*, Stratech Studies Series SS85–1. College Station, Tex.: Texas A and M University Center for Strategic Technology, 1985.

———. "Rejuvenating the Soviet High Command." *Military Review* 50 (July 1970): 83–94.

———. "Soviet Cybermen." In *Soviet C3*, ed. Stephen J. Cimbala. Washington, D.C.: AFCEA/Signal, 1987.

———. "The Soviet High Command." In *Soviet-Warsaw Pact Force Levels*, USSI Report 76–2. Washington, D.C.: United States Strategic Institute, 1976.

———. *The Soviet High Command: A Military-Political History, 1918–1941*. New York: St. Martin's Press, 1962.

———. *Soviet Military Power*. London: Royal United Services Institute, 1971.

Evangelista, Matthew. *Innovation and the Arms Race*. Ithaca: Cornell University Press, 1988.

———. "Sources of Moderation in Soviet Security Policy." In *Behavior, Society, and Nuclear War*, vol. 2, ed. Robert Jervis et al. New York: Oxford University Press, 1991.

———. "Transnational Alliances and Soviet Demilitarization." Unpublished paper prepared for the Council on Economic Priorities Project on Military Expenditures and Economic Priorities, October 1990.

Fedulaev, E. "Strategiia bezrassudnogo avantiurizma." *Kommunist Vooruzhennykh Sil*, no. 16 (1962): 83–87.

Fedulov, M. "Problems of Modern Combined-Arms Combat." *Voennaia Mysl'*, no. 10 (1964): 28–31.

Fialka, John J. "Soviets Outline Troop-Cut Plan in East Germany." *Wall Street Journal*, March 14, 1989.

Filippov, V. "Soedinenie novogo tipa armii SShA." *Zarubezhnoe Voennoe Obozrenie*, no. 7 (1978): 25–29.

Fomich, N. "Protivotankovye sresdstva armii SShA." *Zarubezhnoe Voennoe Obozrenie*, no. 8 (1981): 35–40.

Freedman, Lawrence. *The Evolution of Nuclear Strategy*. New York: St. Martin's Press, 1981.

———. *U.S. Intelligence and the Soviet Strategic Threat*. 2d ed. London: Macmillan, 1986.

Frunze, M. V. *Izbrannye Proizvedenniia*. Reissued. Moscow: Voenizdat, 1984.

Gabelic, Andro. "New Accent in Strategy." *Military Review* 48 (August 1968): 83–87.

Galitskii, Ye. "Restoration of Combat Effectiveness of Troops and Elimination of the Effects of Enemy Nuclear Strikes during an Offensive." *Voennaia Mysl'*, no. 8 (1967): 42–48.

Gallagher, Matthew P., and Karl F. Spielmann, Jr. *Soviet Decision-Making for Defense*. New York: Praeger, 1972.

Galvin, John R. "Getting Better: Improving Capabilities for Deterrence and Defense." *NATO Review* 37 (April 1989): 11–16.

Gareev, Makhmut A. *M. V. Frunze: Voennyi Teoretik*. Moscow: Voenizdat, 1985. English trans.: *M. V. Frunze: Military Theorist*. Trans. unidentified. Washington, D.C.: Pergamon-Brassey's, 1988.

———. "Ob opyte boevoi podgotovki voisk." *Voenno-Istoricheskii Zhurnal*, no. 4 (1983): 11–20.

———. "The Revised Soviet Military Doctrine." *Bulletin of the Atomic Scientists* 44 (December 1988): 31–32.

———. *Sovetskaia Voennaia Nauka*. Moscow: Znanie, 1988.

———. "Tvorcheskii kharakter sovetskoi voennoi nauki v velikoi otechestvennoi voine." *Voenno-Istoricheskii Zhurnal*, no. 7 (1985): 22–30.

Garthoff, Raymond L. "Conflict Termination in Soviet Military Thought and Strategy." In *Soviet C3*, ed. Stephen J. Cimbala. Washington, D.C.: AFCEA/Signal, 1987.

———. *Detente and Confrontation*. Washington, D.C.: Brookings, 1985.

Garthoff, Raymond L. "Introduction: U.S. Considerations of Soviet Military Thinking." In *The Voroshilov Lectures*, vol. 1, ed. Graham Turbiville, Jr. Washington, D.C.: National Defense University Press, 1989.

———. "The Soviet Military and SALT." In *Soviet Decisionmaking for National Security*, ed. William Potter and Jiri Valenta. London: George Allen and Unwin, 1984.

———. *Soviet Military Policy*. New York: Praeger, 1966.

———. *Soviet Strategy in the Nuclear Age*. New York: Praeger, 1958.

Gates, Robert. Statement before the U.S. Congress Joint Economic Committee, Subcommittee on International Trade, Finance and Security Economics. *Allocation of Resources in the Soviet Union and China—1984*, pt. 10. Hearings, November 21, 1984.

Gelman, Harry. *The Brezhnev Politburo and the Decline of Detente*. Ithaca: Cornell University Press, 1984.

George, Alexander L. "Case Studies and Theory Development." In *Diplomacy*, ed. Paul Gordon Lauren. New York: Free Press, 1979.

———. *Presidential Decisionmaking in Foreign Policy: The Effective Use of Information and Advice*. Boulder, Colo.: Westview, 1980.

Glantz, David M. "Soviet Military Strategy after CFE: Historical Models and Future Prospects." *Journal of Soviet Military Studies* 3 (June 1990): 254–95.

Glazov, V. "O nekotorykh osobennostiakh vedeniia boevykh deistvii v iadernoi voine." *Kommunist Vooruzhennykh Sil*, no. 3 (1964): 41–46.

Glazunov, N. "The Bundeswehr—Weapon of Aggression and Revenge." *Voennaia Mysl'*, no. 1 (1969): 75–81.

Goffman, Erving. *Strategic Interaction*. Philadelphia: University of Pennsylvania Press, 1969.

Goldberg, Andrew C. *New Developments in Soviet Military Strategy*, CSIS Significant Issues Series, vol. 9, no. 7. Washington, D.C.: Center for Strategic and International Studies, 1987.

Goldstein, Judith. "The Impact of Ideas on Trade Policy." *International Organization* 43 (Winter 1989): 31–71.

Golovchiner, B. "Counterattack and Repulse of Counterattacks." *Voennaia Mysl'*, no. 6 (1959): 13–24.

———. "Encirclements and Annihilation of Groupings of Defending Troops." *Voennaia Mysl'*, no. 8 (1964): 42–52.

Gorbachev, Mikhail. Speech at Stanford University, June 5, 1990, official translation. *The Stanford University Campus Report*, June 6, 1990.

Gorelick, Ya. M. "Trud neprekhodiashchei tsennosti." *Voennaia Mysl'*, no. 7 (1989): 77–78.

Gottemoeller, Rose. *Conflict and Consensus in the Soviet Armed Forces*. Santa Monica: RAND, 1989.

Gouré, Leon. *Notes on the Second Edition of Marshal V. D. Sokolovskii's "Military Strategy"*, RM-3972. Santa Monica: RAND, 1964.

Grandori, Anna. *Perspectives on Organization Theory*. Cambridge, Mass.: Ballinger, 1987.

Gray, Colin S. *Nuclear Strategy and National Style*. Lanham, Md.: Hamilton Press, 1986.

————. *The Soviet-American Arms Race*. Lexington, Mass.: Lexington Books, 1976.

Grebish, Ye. D. "Evoliutsiia doktrinal'nykh ustanovok v sovetskom voennom iskusstve v 80-x godakh." *Voennaia Mysl'*, no. 6 (1991): 31–37.

Grechko, A. A. "Torchestvo leninskikh idei o zashchite sotsialisticheskogo otechestva." *Kommunist Vooruzhennykh Sil*, no. 20 (1967): 31–39.

————. *Vooruzhennye Sily Sovetskogo Gosudarstva*. Moscow: Voenizdat, 1974.

————. *Vooruzhennye Sily Sovetskogo Gosudarstva*. 2d ed. Moscow: Voenizdat, 1975.

Griffiths, Franklyn. "A Tendency Analysis of Soviet Policy-Making." In *Interest Groups in Soviet Politics*, ed. H. Gordon Skilling and Franklyn Griffiths. Princeton: Princeton University Press, 1971.

Haas, Ernst B. *When Knowledge Is Power: Three Models of Change in International Organizations*. Berkeley: University of California Press, 1990.

Haas, Peter M. "Do Regimes Matter? Epistemic Communities and Mediterranean Pollution Control." *International Organization* 43 (Summer 1989): 378–403.

————, ed. "Knowledge, Power, and International Policy Coordination." *International Organization* (special issue) 46 (Winter 1992).

————. *Saving the Mediterranean: The Politics of International Environmental Cooperation*. New York: Columbia University Press, 1990.

Hall, Peter A., ed. *The Political Power of Economic Ideas*. Princeton: Princeton University Press, 1989.

Halperin, Morton H. *Bureaucratic Politics and Foreign Policy*. Washington, D.C.: Brookings, 1974.

Halpern, Nina P. "Policy Communities in a Leninist State." *Governance* 2 (January 1989): 23–41.

Hanne, William G. "Airland Battle: Doctrine not Dogma." *International Defense Review* 16 (1983): 1035–40.

Hasegawa, Tsuyoshi. "Soviets on Nuclear-War-Fighting." *Problems of Communism* 35 (July/August 1986): 68–79.

Haslam, Jonathan. *The Soviet Union and the Politics of Nuclear Weapons in Europe, 1969–1987*. Ithaca: Cornell University Press, 1990.

Heisbourg, François. "The Three Ages of NATO Strategy." *NATO Review* 37 (February 1989): 24–29.

Herspring, Dale R. *The Soviet High Command, 1967–1989*. Princeton: Princeton University Press, 1990.

Hickson, David J., et al. *Top Decisions: Strategic Decision-Making in Organizations*. San Francisco: Jossey-Bass, 1986.

Holcomb, James F., and Stephen R. Covington. "CSBM Seminar on Military Doctrine, Vienna, Austria, Week Three: Soviet and NSWP Training." Unclassified version of an unpublished manuscript. February 8, 1990.

————. "CSBM Seminar on Military Doctrine, Vienna, Austria, Week Two: Soviet Force Structure." Unclassified version of an unpublished manuscript. February 7, 1990.

Holloway, David. *The Soviet Union and the Arms Race*. 2d ed. New Haven: Yale University Press, 1984.

Holloway, David. *Technology, Management and the Soviet Military Establishment*. Adelphi Paper 76. London: International Institute for Strategic Studies, 1971.

Holzner, Burkart, and John H. Marx. *Knowledge Application: The Knowledge System in Society*. Boston: Allyn and Bacon, 1979.

Huntington, Samuel. *The Soldier and the State*. Cambridge, Mass.: Harvard University Press, 1957.

Iofin, G. Book review. *Voennyi Zarubezhnik*, no. 10 (1960): 81–88.

Iolev, A. "Trebovaniia xxii s'ezda partii i programmy kpss k voennym kadram." *Kommunist Vooruzhennykh Sil*, no. 15 (1963): 42–50.

Ionin, G., and K. Kushch-Zharko. "Defense in the Past and the Present." *Voennaia Mysl'*, no. 7 (1971): 62–75.

Iovlev, A. "On Mass Armies in Modern War." *Voennaia Mysl'*, no. 10, pt. 2 (1963): 1–12.

Isaev, P. "Bor'ba s tankami." *Zarubezhnoe Voennoe Obozrenie*, no. 12 (1982): 37–42.

Ivanov, D. "The Hotbed of Militarism and Tension in Europe." *Voennaia Mysl'*, no. 7 (1967): 73–83.

Ivanov, K. "Izmeneniia v voennoi politike: strategiia SShA." *Voennaia Mysl'*, no. 7 (1962): 46–56.

Ivanov, S. "Soviet Military Doctrine and Strategy." *Voennaia Mysl'*, no. 5 (1969): 40–51.

Ivanov, V. "Voennoe iskusstva Petra I." *Voenno-Istoricheskii Zhurnal*, no. 8 (1981): 66–71.

Ivanov, V. M. *Marshal M. N. Tukhachevskii*. Moscow: Voenizdat, 1985.

Ivlev, N., and V. Viktorov. "Kompleksnoe uchenie voisk tsentral'noi gruppy armii nato 'karbain fortress.' " *Zarubezhnoe Voennoe Obozrenie*, no. 9 (1983): 7–12.

Izmailov, V. "Kharakter i osobennosti sovremennykh voin." *Kommunist Vooruzhennykh Sil*, no. 6 (1975): 67–75.

Janowitz, Morris. *The Professional Soldier*. New York: Free Press, 1960.

Jones, Ellen. *Red Army and Society*. Boston: Allen and Unwin, 1985.

Kalashnik, M. "Actual Questions of Ideological Work in the Armed Forces." *Voennaia Mysl'*, no. 8 (1966): 1–16.

Kaliadin, A. "Bor'ba za razoruzhenie: novye perspektivy." *Mirovaia Ekonomika i Mezhdunarodnye Otnosheniia*, no. 11 (1974): 3–14.

Kaplan, Fred. *The Wizards of Armageddon*. New York: Touchstone, 1983.

Karaganov, S. "Avantiurizm voennoi strategii SShA." *Mirovaia Ekonomika i Mezhdunarodnye Otnosheniia*, no. 3 (1984): 45–53.

Karber, Philip. Testimony before the House Armed Services Committee. *Gorbachev's Force Reductions and the Restructuring of Soviet Forces*. Hearings, March 14, 1989.

Kaufman, Daniel J. "National Security: Organizing the Armed Forces." *Armed Forces and Society* 14 (Fall 1987): 85–112.

Kaufman, Joyce P. "Conventional and Theater Nuclear Force Modernization: The Military Response." In *NATO in the 1980s*, ed. Linda P. Brady and Joyce P. Kaufman. New York: Praeger, 1985.

Kaufman, Richard. "Causes of the Slowdown in Soviet Defense." *Soviet Economy* 1 (1985): 9–31.

Kazakov, D. "Teoreticheskaia i metodologicheskaia osnova sovetskoi voennoi nauki." *Kommunist Vooruzhennykh Sil*, no. 10 (1963): 7–15.

Kelleher, Catherine McArdle. *Germany and the Politics of Nuclear Weapons*. New York: Columbia University Press, 1975.

Keller, Bill. "Gorbachev Vows Major Military Cutback and a 'Clearly Defensive' Stand in Europe." *New York Times*, December 8, 1988.

————. "Shevardnadze Asserts Possibility of a Crackdown Led Him to Quit." *New York Times*, January 3, 1991.

————. "Soviet Officers Pressing for Change and a Union." *New York Times*, October 22, 1989.

Khabarov, B. "Nekotorye voprosy upravleniia voiskami v nastupatel'noi operatsii." *Voennaia Mysl'*, no. 7 (1959): 80–87.

"Kharakter i osobennosti raketno-iadernoi voiny." *Kommunist Vooruzhennykh Sil*, no. 21 (1965): 69–74.

Khor'kov, A. G. "Istoricheskii opyt v razvitii voennoi nauki." *Voennaia Mysl'*, no. 6 (1990): 28–36.

Khrisanfov, A. "Nachalnyi period sovremennoi voiny po vzgliadam burzhuazhnykh voennykh ideologov." *Voennyi Zarubezhnik*, no. 10 (1960): 61–71.

————. "Vzgliady komandovanniia armii SShA na primenenie raketno-iadernogo oruzhiia." *Voennyi Zarubezhnik*, no. 5 (1961): 66–75.

Khrushchev, Nikita. *Khrushchev Remembers: The Last Testament*. Trans. and ed. Strobe Talbott. Boston: Little, Brown and Co., 1974.

Kingdon, John W. *Agendas, Alternatives, and Public Policies*. Boston: Little, Brown and Co., 1984.

Kipp, Jacob W. "General of the Army Vladimir Nikolayevich Lobov: One of Gorbachev's *Genshtabisty*." *Soviet Military Studies* 2 (September 1989): 403–16.

Kipp, Jacob W., Bruce W. Menning, David M. Glantz, and Graham H. Turbiville, Jr. "Editorial: Marshal Akhromeev's Post-INF World." *Journal of Soviet Military Studies* 1 (June 1988): 168–69.

Kir'ian, M. M. *Fronty Nastupali*. Moscow: Nauka, 1987.

————. "Weapons of Mass Destruction in the Aggressive Plans of NATO." *Voennaia Mysl'*, no. 12 (1971): 108–19.

Kirshin, Yurii. "Politika i voennaia strategiia v iadernyi vek." *Mirovaia Ekonomika i Mezhdunarodnye Otnosheniia*, no. 11 (1988): 35–45.

————. "Why Military Reform Is Needed?" *New Times*, no. 12 (1990): 30.

Kissinger, Henry. *White House Years*. Boston: Little, Brown and Co., 1979.

Kistiakowsky, George B. *A Scientist at the White House*. Cambridge, Mass.: Harvard University Press, 1976.

Knight, Amy. "The KGB and Civil-Military Relations." In *Soldiers and the Soviet State: Civil-Military Relations from Brezhnev to Gorbachev*, ed. Timothy J. Colton and Thane Gustafson. Princeton: Princeton University Press, 1990.

Kohl, Wilfrid L. *French Nuclear Diplomacy*. Princeton: Princeton University Press, 1971.

Kokoshin, Andrei A. "Defense Is Best for Stability." *New Times*, no. 333 (1988): 18–19.

————. "The Future of NATO and Warsaw Pact Strategy: Paper II." In *The Strate-*

gic Implications of Change in the Soviet Union, Part I. Adelphi Paper 247. London: International Institute for Strategic Studies, 1989/90.

———. " 'Plan Rodzhersa,' alternativnye kontseptsii oborony i bezopasnost' v evrope." *SShA*, no. 9 (1985): 3–14.

———. "Razvitie voennogo dela i sokrashchenie vooruzhennykh sil i obychnykh vooruzhenii." *Mirovaia Ekonomika i Mezhdunarodnye Otnosheniia*, no. 1 (1988): 20–32.

———. Testimony before the House Armed Services Committee. *Gorbachev's Force Reductions and the Restructuring of Soviet Forces.* Hearings, March 10, 1989.

———. *V Poiskakh Vykhoda.* Moscow: Politizdat, 1989.

Kokoshin, A., and V. Larionov. "Kurskaia bitva v svete sovremennoi oboro-nitel'noi doktriny." *Mirovaia Ekonomika i Mezhdunarodnye Otnosheniia*, no. 8 (1987): 32–40.

———. "Protivostoianie sil obshchego naznacheniia strategicheskoi sta-bil'nosti." *Mirovaia Ekonomika i Mezhdunarodnye Otnosheniia*, no. 6 (1988): 23–30.

Kokoshin, A. A., and V. N. Lobov. "Predvidenie." *Znamia*, no. 2 (1990): 170–82.

Kokoshin, Andrei, et al. "Problems of Ensuring Stability with Radical Cuts in Armed Forces and Conventional Armaments in Europe." Moscow: Soviet Committee for European Security and Cooperation, Committee of Soviet Scientists for Peace, Against the Nuclear Threat, and Institute for U.S. and Canada Studies, 1989.

Kolkowicz, Roman. *The Soviet Military and the Communist Party.* Princeton: Princeton University Press, 1967.

Kol'tsov, A. "Novye sredstva vooruzhennoi bor'by armii stran NATO i ikh vliianie na razvitie voennogo iskusstva." *Voenno-Istoricheskii Zhurnal*, no. 10 (1980): 64–70.

Kondratkov, T. R. "Eloveshchii kharakter militaristicheskikh dogm." *Kommunist Vooruzhennykh Sil*, no. 19 (1978): 78–83.

———. "Sotsial'nyi kharakter sovremennoi voiny." *Kommunist Vooruzhennykh Sil*, no. 21 (1972): 9–16.

Konovalov, A. A. "Nauchno-tekhnicheskii progress i tendentsii razvitiia neia-dernykh vooruzhenii dlia sil obshchego naznacheniia v 80-kh godakh." In *Voenno-tekhnicheskaia Politika SShA v 80-e gody*, ed. A. A. Kokoshin and A. A. Konovalov. Moscow: Nauka, 1989.

Konstantinov, S. "Voennaia doktrina amerikanskogo imperializma." *Kommunist Vooruzhennykh Sil*, no. 23 (1962): 79–85.

"Kontseptsiia voennoi reformy." *Voennaia Mysl' Spetsial'nyi Vypusk*, 1990: 3–23.

Korotchenko, I. "Razvedka." *Voenno-Istoricheskii Zhurnal*, no. 3 (1982): 27–34.

Korotkov, I. "On the Development of Soviet Military Theory in the Post-war Years." *Voenno-Istoricheskii Zhurnal*, no. 4 (1964): 39–50.

———. "Some Questions on the History of Soviet Military Science." *Voennaia Mysl'*, no. 11 (1973): 101–13.

Kosarev, V. "Doktrina sokhraneniia mira." *Krasnaia Zvezda*, September 25, 1987.

Kosterin, Stanislav. "Armiia i perestroika." *Sovetskaia Rossiia*, January 14, 1989.

Kozhin, V., and V. Trusin. "Voprosy primeneniia vooruzhennykh sil v operatsiiakh." *Zarubezhnoe Voennoe Obozrenie*, no. 10 (1983): 16–22.

Kozlov, M. M., ed. *Akademiia General'nogo Shtaba*. 2d ed. Moscow: Voenizdat, 1987.

———. "Organizatsiia i vedenie strategicheskoi oborony po opytu Velikoi Otechestvennoi Voiny." *Voenno-Istoricheskii Zhurnal*, no. 12 (1980): 9–17.

Kozlov, S. "The Development of Soviet Military Science after World War II." *Voennaia Mysl'*, no. 2 (1964): 9–16.

———. "The Formulation and Development of Soviet Military Doctrine." *Voennaia Mysl'*, no. 7 (1966): 47–65.

———. "Voennia doktrina i voennaia nauka." *Kommunist Vooruzhennykh Sil*, no. 5 (1964): 9–16.

———. "Voennaia nauka i voennye doktriny v pervoi mirovoi voine." *Voenno-Istoricheskii Zhurnal*, no. 11 (1964): 31–41.

Kruglov, V., and M. Yegorov. "The Military Doctrines of the NATO Countries." *Voennaia Mysl'*, no. 8 (1966): 88–99.

Krupchenko, A. "Tekhnicheskoi obespechenie tankovykh i mekhanizirovannykh korpusov, deistvovavshchikh v kachestve podvizhnykh grupp." *Voenno-Istoricheskii Zhurnal*, no. 6 (1982): 27–33.

Krupchenko, I. "A. V. Suvorov i voennoe iskusstvo." *Voenno-Istoricheskii Zhurnal*, no. 10 (1980): 71–75.

———. "Sposoby razvitiia uspekha v operativnoi glubine silami tankovykh armii, tankovykh i mekhanizirovannykh korpusov." *Voenno-Istoricheskii Zhurnal*, no. 7 (1981): 12–20.

———. "Tanki v boiu i operatsii." *Voenno-Istoricheskii Zhurnal*, no. 9 (1986): 57–63.

Kulakov, V. "Problems of Military-Technical Superiority." *Voennaia Mysl'*, no. 1 (1964): 1–14.

Kulikov, A. S., and A. D. Nefedov. "Pozitsionnye i manevrennye deistviia: pol' i mesto v oboronitel'noi operatsii." *Voennaia Mysl'*, no. 3 (1990): 23–31.

Kulikov, V. "Dal'nee obnaruzhenie tselei." *Tekhnika i Vooruzhenie*, no. 10 (1971): 18–21.

Kulikov, V. G., ed. *Akademiia General'nogo Shtaba*. Moscow: Voenizdat, 1976.

———. "General'nyi Shtab." In *Sovetskaia Voennaia Entsiklopediia*. Vol. 2. Moscow: Voenizdat, 1976.

———. "Sovetskaia voennaia nauka segodniia." *Kommunist*, no. 7 (1976): 38–48.

Kulish, V. "Novaia voennaia doktrina NATO." *Mirovaia Ekonomika i Mezhdunarodnye Otnosheniia*, no. 9 (1968): 27–37.

Kulish, V., and S. Fedorenko. "Po povodu diskussia v SShA o strategicheskikh vooruzheniiakh." *Mirovaia Ekonomika i Mezhdunarodnye Otnosheniia*, no. 3 (1970): 41–49.

Kunadze, G. "Ob oboronnoi dostatochnosti voennogo potentsiala SSSR." *Mirovaia Ekonomika i Mezhdunarodnye Otnosheniia*, no. 10 (1989): 63–83.

Kurochkin, P. "A Chronicle of Heroism and Victories." *Voennaia Mysl'*, no. 5 (1968): 83–93.

Kuskov, V. "Nemetskii voennyi teoretik Karl Klausevits." *Voenno-Istoricheskii Zhurnal*, no. 8 (1980): 80–83.

Kuvshinnikov, V. "Nekotorye voprosy sovremennogo vstrechnogo boia." *Voennaia Mysl'*, no. 5 (1959): 17–27.

Kuz'min, I. "Bor'ba novogo so starym v razvitii voennogo dela." *Kommunist Vooruzhennykh Sil*, no. 8 (1964): 40–45.

Lambeth, Benjamin S. "On Thresholds in Soviet Military Thought." *Washington Quarterly* 7 (Spring 1984): 69–76.

———. *Selective Nuclear Operations and Soviet Strategy*, P-5506. Santa Monica: RAND, 1975.

Lapshin, K. "Surmounting Obstacles and Zones of Destruction and Radioactive Contamination of the Offense." *Voennaia Mysl'*, no. 10, pt. 1 (1963): 15–27.

Larionov, V. V. "Ogranichenie vooruzhenii i ego protivniki." *Pravda*, April 7, 1974.

———. "Razriadka napriazhennosti i printsip ravnoi bezopasnosti." *Krasnaia Zvezda*, July 18, 1974.

———. "Razvitie sredstv vooruzheniia i strategicheskie kontseptsii SShA." *Mirovaia Ekonomika i Mezhdunarodnye Otnosheniia*, no. 6 (1966): 74–81.

———. "Za tvorcheskoe razvitie sovetskoi voennoi nauki." *Voennaia Mysl'*, no. 10 (1962): 17–24.

Larson, Deborah Welch. *The Origins of Containment*. Princeton: Princeton University Press, 1985.

Lavkhin, V. "Vozhdushnaia nastupatel'naia operatsiia." *Zarubezhnoe Voennoe Obozrenie*, no. 11 (1984): 47–54.

"Leninizm—nashe vsepobezhdaiushchee znamia." *Voennaia Mysl'*, no. 1 (1954): 3–16.

"Let's Raise Military-Scientific Work to the Level of Party Demands." *Voennaia Mysl'*, no. 3 (1966): 1–12.

Lebow, Richard Ned. "The Soviet Offensive in Europe: The Schlieffen Plan Revisited?" *International Security* 9 (Spring 1985): 44–78.

Levadov, L., and V. Viktorov. "Manevry i ucheniia NATO—ugroza miru." *Zarubezhnoe Voennoe Obozrenie*, no. 7 (1984): 3–9.

Lind, William S. "FM 100-5 Operations: Some Doctrinal Questions for the United States Army." *Military Review* 57 (March 1977): 54–65.

Lindblom, Charles E. "The Science of 'Muddling Through.' " *Public Administration Review* 19 (Spring 1959): 79–88.

Lipitskii, S. "M. V. Frunze—polkovodets novogo tipa." *Voenno-Istoricheskii Zhurnal*, no. 2 (1970): 118–124.

Litherland, Pat. *Gorbachev and Arms Control: Civilian Experts and Soviet Policy*. Peace Research Report 12. Bradford, England: University of Bradford School of Peace Studies, 1986.

Liubimov, Yu. "O dostatochnosti oborony i nedostatke kompetentnosti." *Kommunist Vooruzhennykh Sil*, no. 16 (1989): 21–26.

Liutov, I. "Some Problems of Defense without the Use of Nuclear Weapons." *Voennaia Mysl'*, no. 7 (1966): 36–46.

Liutov, N. Comment, *Voennaia Mysl'*, no. 10 (1964): 41.

Lobov, V. N. "Aktual'nye voprosy razvitiia teorii sovetskoi voennoi strategii 20-x-serediny 30-x godov." *Voenno-Istoricheskii Zhurnal*, no. 2 (1989): 41–50.

———. "Iskhodia iz printsipov oboronitel'noi doktriny." *Pravda*, December 17, 1988.

———. "Vysokoe kachestvo—glavnyi kriterii boivoi podgotovki." *Kommunist Vooruzhennykh Sil*, no. 1 (1989): 12–18.

Lomov, N. A. Introduction and Conclusion. In *Nauchno-tekhnicheskii Progress i Revoliutsiia v Voennom Dele*. Moscow: Voenizdat, 1973.

———. "Vliianie sovetskoi voennoi doktriny na razvitie voennogo iskusstva." *Kommunist Vooruzhennykh Sil*, no. 21 (1965): 15–24.

Loshchilov, I. "Sredstva avtomatizatsii upravleniia voiskami v boiu." *Zarbuezhnoe Voennoe Obozrenie*, no. 5 (1978): 35–40.

Losik, O. "Gde granitsy razumnoi dostatochnosti." *Krasnaia Zvezda*, March 5, 1991.

———. "Sposoby vedeniia vysokomanevrennykh boevykh deistvii bronetankovymi i mekhanizirovannymi voiskami po opytu Belorusskoi i Vislo-Oderskoi operatsii." *Voenno-Istoricheskii Zhurnal*, no. 9 (1980): 18–25.

Lubkemeier, Eckhard. "The Political Upheaval in Europe and the Reform of NATO Strategy." *NATO Review* 39 (June 1991): 16–21.

Lushev, P. "Na strazhe zavoevanii revoliutsii." *Mezhdunarodnaia Zhizn'*, no. 8 (1987): 60–70.

———. "V interesakh prochnogo mira." *Krasnaia Zvezda*, March 3, 1989.

L'vov, N. "Iadernaia politika NATO—protivorechiia i razgory." *Mirovaia Ekonomika i Mezhdunarodnye Otnosheniia*, no. 8 (1963): 21–35.

Machalov, V. "Voennaia programma SShA." *Voennaia Mysl'*, no. 1 (1962): 49–58.

Mackenzie, Donald. *Inventing Accuracy: A Historical Sociology of Nuclear Missile Guidance*. Cambridge, Mass.: MIT Press, 1990.

———. "The Soviet Union and Strategic Missile Guidance." *International Security* 13 (Fall 1988): 5–54.

Mackintosh, J. M. "The Red Army, 1920–1936." In *The Red Army*, ed. B. M. Lidell Hart. New York: Harcourt, Brace and Co., 1956.

Mackintosh, Malcolm. *The Evolution of the Warsaw Pact*, Adelphi Paper 58. London: International Institute for Strategic Studies, 1969.

———. *Juggernaut: A History of the Soviet Armed Forces*. New York: Macmillan, 1967.

Maiorov, A. "Kharakternyi cherty sovetskoi voennoi strategii." *Voennaia Mysl'*, no. 1 (1975): 12–26.

Makarevskii, Vadim. "Military Detente in Europe." In *Dialogue: Reflections on Security in the Nuclear Age*. Moscow: Progress Publishers, 1988.

Mako, William P. *U.S. Ground Forces and the Defense of Central Europe*. Washington, D.C.: Brookings, 1983.

Maksimov, N. "Kontseptsiia 'vystrel-prorazhenie.'" *Zarubezhnoe Voennoe Obozrenie*, no. 11 (1979): 10–14.

Malinovskii, R. Ya. *Bditel'no Stoiat' na Strazhe Mira.* Moscow: Voenizdat, 1962.

————. "Historical Exploits of the Soviet People and their Armed Forces in the Great Patriotic War." *Voennaia Mysl'*, no. 5 (1965): 1–29.

————. "Revoliutsiia v voennom dele i zadachi voennoi pechati." *Kommunist Vooruzhennykh Sil*, no. 21 (1963): 8–10.

————. "Znachenie pobedy Rossii v Otechestvennoi voine 1812 goda." *Voenno-Istoricheskii Zhurnal*, no. 9 (1962): 3–12.

Manzhurin, I. N. "Otrazhenie kontraudarov protivnika v khode nastupatel'noi operatsii." *Voennaia Mysl'*, no. 10 (1986): 14–22.

Maramain, V. "Nekotorye voprosy organizatsii i vedeniia frontovykh oboronitel'nykh operatsii." *Voenno-Istoricheskii Zhurnal*, no. 5 (1974): 10–20.

March, James G. "The Business Firm as a Political Coalition." *Journal of Politics* 24 (1962): 662–78.

————. *Decisions and Organizations.* Cambridge, Mass.: Basil Blackwell, 1988.

————. "Footnotes to Organizational Change." *Administrative Science Quarterly* 26 (1981): 563–77.

March, James G., and John P. Olsen. *Ambiguity and Choice in Organizations.* Bergen, Norway: Universitetsforlaget, 1979.

————. *Rediscovering Institutions: The Organizational Basis of Politics.* New York: The Free Press, 1989.

March, James G., and Herbert A. Simon. *Organizations.* New York: John Wiley and Sons, 1958.

Mares, David R., and Walter W. Powell. "Cooperative Security Regimes: Preventing International Conflicts." In *Organizations and Nation-States: New Perspectives on Conflict and Cooperation*, ed. Robert L. Kahn and Mayer N. Zald. San Francisco: Jossey-Bass, 1990.

Margelov, V. "Airborne Troops of the Soviet Army." *Voennaia Mysl'*, no. 8 (1967): 12–19.

Marionov, A. "On a Dangerous Path." *Voennaia Mysl'*, no. 1 (1968): 81–90.

Maryshev, A. P. "Nekotorye voprosy strategicheskoi oborony v Velikoi Otechestvennoi Voine." *Voenno-Istoricheskii Zhurnal*, no. 6 (1986): 9–16.

Matsulenko, V. "Nekotorye vyvody iz opyta nachal'nogo perioda Velikoi Otechestvennoi Voiny." *Voenno-Istoricheskii Zhurnal*, no. 3 (1984): 35–43.

MccGwire, Michael. *Military Objectives in Soviet Foreign Policy.* Washington, D.C.: Brookings, 1987.

McConnell, James M. *The Soviet Shift in Emphasis from Nuclear to Conventional*, vols. 1 and 2, Center for Naval Analyses Research Contribution 490. Alexandria, Va.: Center for Naval Analyses, 1983.

McNamara, Robert. Draft Presidential Memorandum on Recommended FY 1965–1969 Strategic Retaliatory Forces. December 6, 1963. DOD/OSD FOIA. National Security Archive collection.

————. Draft Presidential Memorandum on Recommended FY 1966–1970 Programs for Strategic Offensive Forces, Continental Air and Missile Defense Forces, and Civil Defense. December 3, 1964. DOD/OSD FOIA. National Security Archive collection.

————. Draft Presidential Memorandum on Recommended FY 1967–1971 Strategic Offensive and Defensive Forces. November 1, 1965. DOD/OSD FOIA. National Security Archive collection.

———. Draft Presidential Memorandum on Recommended FY 1968–1972 Strategic Offensive and Defense Forces. November 9, 1966. DOD/OSD FOIA. National Security Archive collection.

———. Draft Presidential Memorandum on Strategic Offensive and Defensive Forces. January 15, 1968. DOD/OSD FOIA. National Security Archive collection.

———. "Recommended Long Range Nuclear Delivery Forces 1963–1967." Appendix 1 to the Draft Presidential Memorandum, September 23, 1961. National Security Archive collection.

———. Remarks at NATO Ministerial Meeting, May 5, 1962, Restricted Session. OSD/FOIA. National Security Archive collection.

———. Statement before a Joint Session of the Senate Armed Services Committee and the Senate Subcommittee on DOD Appropriations on the FY 1965–1969 Defense Program and 1965 Defense Budget. Hearings, Feb. 3, 1964. DOD/OSD FOIA. National Security Archive Collection.

———. Statement before a Joint Session of the Senate Armed Services Committee and the Senate Subcommittee on DOD Appropriations on the FY 1966–1970 Defense Program and 1966 Defense Budget. Hearings, January/February 1965. DOD/OSD FOIA. National Security Archive collection.

———. Statement before the Senate Armed Services Committee, FY 1963–67 Defense Program and 1963 Defense Budget. Hearings, January 19, 1962. DOD Dir. 5200.10 FOIA. National Security Archive collection.

Mearsheimer, John J. "Back to the Future: Instability in Europe after the Cold War." *International Security* 15 (Summer 1990): 5–56.

Medvedev, V. "Armiia strany, armiia naroda." *Ogonek*, no. 9 (1990): 30–31.

Mel'nikov, P. "Operativnaia maskirovka." *Voenno-Istoricheskii Zhurnal*, no. 4 (1982): 18–26.

Meshcheriakov, N. V. "Ideologiia obnovleniia: sotsializm i ego vooruzhennaia zashchita." *Voennaia Mysl'*, no. 2 (1990): 52–60.

Meyer, Stephen M. "The Army Isn't Running Gorbachev." *New York Times*, May 8, 1990.

———. "Civilian and Military Influence in Managing the Arms Race in the USSR." In *Reorganizing America's Defense*, ed. Robert J. Art, Vincent Davis, and Samuel P. Huntington. Washington, D.C.: Pergamon-Brassey's, 1985.

———. "Cracks in the Soviet Military-Industrial Complex?" *Soviet Defense Notes* 2 (February/March 1990): 7–8.

———. "How the Threat (and the Coup) Collapsed: The Politicization of the Soviet Military." *International Security* 16 (Winter 1991/92): 5–38.

———. "The Sources and Prospects of Gorbachev's New Political Thinking on Security." *International Security* 13 (Fall 1988): 124–63.

———. "Soviet National Security Decisionmaking: What Do We Know and What Do We Understand?" In *Soviet Decisionmaking for National Security*, ed. William Potter and Jiri Valenta. London: Allen and Unwin, 1984.

———. "Soviet Nuclear Operations." In *Managing Nuclear Operations*, ed. Ashton B. Carter, John D. Steinbruner, and Charles A. Zracket. Washington, D.C.: Brookings, 1987.

———. *Soviet Theatre Nuclear Forces*, parts 1 and 2, Adelphi Papers 187 and 188. London: International Institute for Strategic Studies, 1984.

Meyer, Stephen M., and Jeffrey I. Sands. "Soviet Military Doubts Competence of the 'New Thinkers.' " *Soviet Defense Notes* 1 (November/December 1989): 1–4.

Mikhailov, M. "Sukhoputnye voiska v ogranichennoi voine." *Voennyi Zarubezhnik*, no. 10 (1958): 82–87.

Miksche, F. "Soobrazheniia po organizatsii budushchikh sukhoputnykh voisk." *Voennyi Zarubezhnik*, no. 6 (1956): 3–14.

Milovidov, A. "Marksizm-leninizm—teoreticheskaia osnova sovetskoi voennoi nauki." *Kommunist Vooruzhennykh Sil*, no. 19 (1974): 11–19.

Mil'shtein, Mikhail A. "Amerikanskie voennye doktriny: preemstvemost' i modifikatsiia." *Mirovaia Ekonomika i Mezhdunarodnye Otnosheniia*, no. 8 (1971): 30–41.

———. "Na opasnom perekrestke." *SShA*, no. 10 (1978): 3–13.

———. "New Concepts of a Safe World." In *Dialogue: Reflections on Security in the Nuclear Age*. Moscow: Progress Publishers, 1988.

———. "Vopreki dukhu vremeni." *Mirovaia Ekonomika i Mezhdunarodnye Otnosheniia*, no. 7 (1976): 103–8.

Mil'shtein, M. A., and L. S. Semeiko. "Problema nedopustimosti iadernogo konflikta." *SShA*, no. 11 (1974): 3–12.

Mochalov, V. "Osobennosti nastupatel'nykh deistvii polevoi armii v sovremennykh usloviiakh." *Voennaia Mysl'*, no. 7 (1954): 74–84.

Mohr, Lawrence B. "Determinants of Innovation in Organizations." *American Political Science Review* 63 (January 1969): 111–26.

Moiseev, M. A. "Eshche raz o prestizhe armii." *Kommunist Vooruzhennykh Sil*, no. 13 (1989): 3–14.

———. "Ob avtore i ego knige." In M. V. Zakharov, *General'nyi Shtab v Predvoennye Gody*. Moscow: Voenizdat, 1989.

———. "S pozitsii oboronitel'noi doktriny," *Krasnaia Zvezda*, February 10, 1989.

———. "Sovetskaia voennaia doktrina: realizatsiia ee oboronitel'noi napravlennosti." *Pravda*, March 13, 1989.

Moiseev, Nikita. "Both Calculation and Common Sense." *Moscow News*, no. 28 (1989): 7.

Molino, Michael A. "Division Defensive Operations for Nuclear and Nonnuclear Environments." *Military Review* 53 (December 1973): 13.

Molostov, Yu. "Zashchita ot vysokotochnogo oruzhiia." *Voennyi Vestnik*, no. 2 (1987): 83–86.

" 'My ne "lishnie liudi" v parlamente . . .' " *Kommunist Vooruzhennykh Sil*, no. 3 (1990): 37–49.

Murav'ev, R. "O sisteme boevoi podgotovki amerikanskoi armii." *Voennia Mysl'*, no. 5 (1954): 58–65.

———. "Osobennosti vedeniia boevykh deistvii v pustyne." *Voennaia Mysl'*, no. 2 (1955): 77–84.

"Nauchno-tekhnicheskii progress i ego rol' v povyshenii boevoi moshchi armii i flota." *Kommunist Vooruzhennykh Sil*, no. 21 (1974): 67–74.

"New Conventional Weapons." In *Strategic Survey 1974*. London: International Institute for Strategic Studies, 1975.

Nikonov, O. "Kursom obnovleniia." *Krasnaia Zvezda*, December 28, 1988.

Nolan, Janne E. *Guardians of the Arsenal*. New York: Basic Books, 1989.

Novokhatko, M. "Voennye voprosy v proizbedeniiakh V. I. Lenin." *Voennaia Mysl'*, no. 4 (1955): 3–15.

"Novyi voennyi biudzhet SShA—usilenie gonki vooruzhenii." *Voennyi Zarubezhnik*, no. 8 (1961): 16–17.

"O voennoi doktrine SSSR." *Voennaia Mysl' Spetsial'nyi Vypusk* 1990: 24–28.

Obaturov, G. "Proslavlennyi polkovodets leninskoi shkoly." *Kommunist Vooruzhennykh Sil*, no. 2 (1985): 18–25.

"Obsuzhdaem opyt obespecheniia voisk v nastupatel'nykh operatsiiakh." *Voenno-Istoricheskii Zhurnal*, no. 3 (1982): 27.

Oded, Eran. *Mezhdunarodniki*. Ranat Gan, Israel: Turtledove Publishers, 1979.

Odell, John S. *U.S. International Monetary Policy*. Princeton: Princeton University Press, 1982.

Ogarkov, N. V. *Istoriia Uchit Bditel'nosti*. Moscow: Voenizdat, 1985.

―――. "Nemerknushchaia slava sovetskogo oruzhiia." *Kommunist Vooruzhennykh Sil*, no. 21 (1984): 16–26.

―――. "Pobeda i sovremennost'." *Izvestiia*, May 9, 1983.

―――. "Strategiia Voennaia." In *Sovetskaia Voennaia Entsiklopediia*, vol. 7. Moscow: Voenizdat, 1979: 555–65.

―――. "Zashchita sotsializma: opyt istoriia i sovremennost'." *Krasnaia Zvezda*, May 9, 1984.

Osgood, Robert. *NATO: The Entangling Alliance*. Chicago: University of Chicago Press, 1962.

Pavlenko, N. "Kharakternye cherty strategicheskogo nastupleniia Sovetskikh Vooruzhennykh Sil v Velikoi Otechestvennoi Voine." *Voenno-Istoricheskii Zhurnal*, no. 3 (1966): 9–23.

Pedlow, Gregory M. "Multinational Contingency Planning During the Second Berlin Crisis: The Live Oak Organization, 1959–1963." Presented at the Third Study and Review Conference of the Nuclear History Program, Ebenhausen, Germany, June 1991.

Penkovskii, V. "Combat Training of Troops at the Present Stage." *Voennaia Mysl'*, no. 11 (1967): 52–61.

Penkovskiy, Oleg. *The Penkovskiy Papers*. New York: Doubleday and Co., 1965.

Peredel'skii, G. "Artillery in the Struggle to Attain Fire Superiority." *Voennaia Mysl'*, no. 10 (1973): 57–67.

―――. "Evolution of Forms and Methods of Artillery Control." *Voennaia Mysl'*, no. 3 (1972): 90–102.

Perlmutter, Amos. *The Military and Politics in Modern Times*. New Haven: Yale University Press, 1977.

Perrow, Charles. *Complex Organizations: A Critical Essay*. 2d ed. Glenview, Ill.: Scott, Foresman and Company, 1979.

Petersen, Phillip A. "A New Security Regime for Europe?" *Problems of Communism* 39 (March/April 1990): 91–97.

Petrov, N. F., and I. S. Popov. " 'Bol'shaia strategiia' SShA na 80-e gody." *Voennaia Mysl'*, no. 10 (1980): 24–34.

Petrov, V. "Gotovit' podchinennykh k aktivnym boevym destviiam v usloviiakh primeneniia raketno-iadernogo oruzhiia." *Kommunist Vooruzhennykh Sil*, no. 12 (1963): 70–77.

Pfeffer, Jeffrey, and Gerald R. Salancik. *The External Control of Organizations: A Resource Dependence Perspective.* New York: Harper and Row, 1978.

Phillips, R. Hyland, and Jeffrey I. Sands. "Reasonable Sufficiency and Soviet Conventional Defense: A Research Note." *International Security* 13 (Fall 1988): 164–78.

Pierre, Andrew J. *Nuclear Politics.* London: Oxford University Press, 1972.

Pleshakov, Konstantin. "The Zhukovsky Dilemma." *New Times*, no. 29 (1990): 36–39.

Pogrebenkov, V. "Novaia politika protiv arsenalov voiny." *Kommunist Vooruzhennykh Sil*, no. 1 (1990): 15–21.

"Polozhenie o sluzhbe General'nogo shtaba Raboche-Krest'ianskoi Krasnoi Armii." Reprinted in *Voennaia Mysl'*, no. 11 (1990): 49–51.

Poluboiarov, P. "The Armored Troops of the Soviet Army." *Voennaia Mysl'*, no. 9 (1967): 16–27.

Ponomarev, M. "V gotovnosti k otporu agressoru." *Krasnaia Zvezda*, June 17, 1987.

Ponomarev, N., and V. Zhuravlev. "xxv s'ezd KPSS i bor'ba SSSR za prekrashchenie gonki vooruzhenii i razoruzhenie." *Voenno-Istoricheskii Zhurnal*, no. 5 (1977): 3–9.

Popov, A. "Diskussiiu nado prodolzhit." *Kommunist Vooruzhennykh Sil*, no. 3 (1990): 26–27.

Portugal'skii, R. M. "K voprosu o perekhode ot oborony k nastupleniiu." *Voennaia Mysl'*, no. 6 (1990): 15–22.

Posen, Barry R. *The Sources of Military Doctrine.* Ithaca: Cornell University Press, 1984.

Postnikov, S. I. "Razvitie sovetskogo voennogo iskusstva v kurskoi bitve." *Voenno-Istoricheskii Zhurnal*, no. 7 (1988): 10–18.

Postol, Theodore A. "Targeting." In *Managing Nuclear Operations*, ed. Ashton B. Carter, John D. Steinbruner, and Charles A. Zraket. Washington, D.C.: Brookings, 1987.

Povalyi, M. "Development of Soviet Military Strategy." *Voennaia Mysl'*, no. 2 (1967): 61–72.

"Povyshaia boevuiu gotovnost', uglubliaia perestroiku." *Kommunist Vooruzhennykh Sil*, no. 3 (1988): 87–92.

Prusanov, I. "Deiatel'nost' partii po ukrepleniiu vooruzhennykh sil v usloviiakh revoliutsii v voennom dele." *Kommunist Vooruzhennykh Sil*, no. 3 (1966): 8–16.

Putnam, Robert D. "Diplomacy and Domestic Politics: The Logic of Two-Level Games." *International Organization* 42 (Summer 1988): 427–60.

Ra'anan, Uri, and Igor Lukes, eds. *Inside the Apparat: Perspectives on the*

Soviet System from Former Functionaries. Lexington, Mass.: Lexington Books, 1990.

Rahr, Alexander. "Gorbachev Discloses Details of Defense Council." *Radio Liberty Report on the USSR* 1, no. 36 (1989): 11–12.

Rapoport, Vitaly, and Yuri Alexeev. *High Treason: Essays on the History of the Red Army, 1918–1938,* ed. Vladimir G. Treml; Bruce Adams, co-ed. and trans. Durham, N.C.: Duke University Press, 1985.

Reed, Laura. "The Rise and Fall of a Divided Europe: What Do Organizational Models Tell Us About Changes in the Security Agenda After World War II and at the End of the Cold War?" presented at the 1990 Annual Meeting of the American Political Science Association.

Reznichenko, V., and E. Bob. "Consolidating a Gain in an Offensive Operation." *Voennaia Mysl',* no. 3 (1966): 45–51.

Riabov, V. S., ed. *Dvina.* Moscow: Voenizdat, 1970.

Rice, Condoleezza. "The Impact of Institutional Norms and Development on the Evolution of the Central Staff Systems of the United States and the Soviet Union," presented at the 1987 Annual Meeting of the American Political Science Association.

———. "The Making of Soviet Strategy." In *Makers of Modern Strategy from Machiavelli to the Nuclear Age,* ed. Peter Paret. Princeton: Princeton University Press, 1986.

———. "The Party, the Military and Decision Authority in the Soviet Union." *World Politics* 40 (October 1987): 55–81.

———. "Soviet Staff Structure and Planning in World War II." In *Contemporary Soviet Military Affairs: The Legacy of World War II,* ed. Jonathan R. Adelman and Christann Lea Gibson. Boston: Unwin Hyman, 1989.

Rodin, A. "Increasing Antitank Stability—A Trend of Modern Defense." *Voennaia Mysl',* no. 8 (1972), as excerpted by Joseph D. Douglass, Jr., and Amoretta M. Hoeber, in *Index to and Extracts from Voyennaya Mysl', 1971–1973.* Alexandria, Va.: Systems Planning Corporation, 1980.

Rogers, Bernard W. "Follow-on Forces Attack (FOFA): Myths and Realities." *NATO Review* 32 (December 1984): 1–9.

Rogers, Everett M. *Diffusion of Innovations.* 3d ed. New York: Free Press, 1983.

Romjue, John L. *From Active Defense to AirLand Battle: The Development of Army Doctrine 1973–1982.* Ft. Monroe, Va.: U.S. Army Training and Doctrinal Command, 1984.

———. "The Evolution of the AirLand Battle Concept." *Air University Review* 35 (May/June 1984): 4–15.

Rose, John P. *The Evolution of U.S. Army Nuclear Doctrine.* Boulder, Colo.: Westview Press, 1980.

Rosen, Stephen Peter. "New Ways of War." *International Security* 13 (Summer 1988): 134–68.

———. *Winning the Next War: Innovation and the Modern Military.* Ithaca: Cornell University Press, 1991.

Rosenau, James N. "Before Cooperation: Hegemons, Regimes, and Habit-Driven Actors in World Politics." *International Organization* 40 (Autumn 1986): 849–94.

Rosenberg, David Alan. "The Origins of Overkill." *International Security* 7 (Spring 1983): 3–71.

———. "Reality and Responsibility: Power and Process in the Making of United States Nuclear Strategy, 1945–1968." *Journal of Strategic Studies* 9 (March 1986): 35–52.

Rotmistrov, P. "O roli vnezapostni v sovremennoi voine." *Voennaia Mysl'*, no. 2 (1955): 14–26.

Ruban, M. "Vooruzhennye sily sssr v period stroitel'stva kommunizma." *Kommunist Vooruzhennykh Sil*, no. 13 (1968): 77–83.

Ruban, M. V. *V. I. Lenin o Bditel'nosti i Boevoi Gotovnosti*. Moscow: Voenizdat, 1984.

Rubtsov, O. "West Germany: Politics and the Bundeswehr." *Voennaia Mysl'*, no. 3 (1971): 106–16.

Rybintsev, F. I. "Net problemy." *Mezhdunarodnaia Zhizn'*, no. 7 (1989): 157–58.

Rybkin, Ye. "O sushchnosti mirovoi raketno-iadernoi voiny." *Kommunist Vooruzhennykh Sil*, no. 17 (1965): 50–56.

———. "Zakony materialisticheskoi dialektiki i ikh proiavlenie v voennom dele." *Kommunist Vooruzhennykh Sil*, no. 7 (1964): 45–51.

Sagan, Scott D. "1914 Revisited." *International Security* 11 (Fall 1986): 151–75.

———. *Moving Targets*. Princeton: Princeton University Press, 1989.

Samurokov, B. "Combat Operations Involving Conventional Means of Destruction." *Voennaia Mysl'*, no. 8 (1967): 29–41.

Samurokov, D. "On the Question of Foresight." *Voennaia Mysl'*, no. 9 (1971): 27–40.

Sauerwein, Brigitte, and Matthias Plugge. "New Soviet Military Doctrine: The Voroshilov Academy's Interpretation." *International Defense Review* 23 (1990): 21.

Savel'ev, A. "Predotvrashchenie voiny i sderzhivanie: podkhody ovd i nato." *Mirovaia Ekonomika i Mezhdunarodnye Otnosheniia*, no. 6 (1989): 19–29.

Schapiro, Leonard. "The Great Purge." In *The Red Army*, ed. B. M. Lidell Hart. New York: Harcourt, Brace and Co., 1956.

Schick, Jack M. *The Berlin Crisis, 1958–1962*. Philadelphia: University of Pennsylvania Press, 1971.

Schlesinger, James R. Prepared report to the Congress on the FY 1975 Defense Budget. March 4, 1974.

———. Testimony before the Senate Foreign Relations Committee Subcommittee on Arms Control, International Law and Organization. *U.S.-USSR Strategic Policies*. Hearings, March 4, 1974; sanitized and released April 4, 1974.

Schmemann, Serge. "Soviets Say Their Weapons Were Not Iraqis' Weak Spot." *New York Times*, March 1, 1991.

Schneider, Eberhard. "Soviet Foreign-Policy Think Tanks." *Washington Quarterly* 11 (Spring 1988): 145–55.

Schwartz, David N. *NATO's Nuclear Dilemmas*. Washington, D.C.: Brookings, 1983.

Schweizer, Peter. "The Soviet Military Goes High-Tech." *Orbis* 35 (Spring 1991): 195–205.

Scott, Richard W. *Organizations: Rational, Natural, and Open Systems.* 2d ed. Englewood Cliffs, N.J.: Prentice-Hall, 1987.

Scott, William F. "Changes in Tactical Concepts within the Soviet Forces." In *The Future of Soviet Military Power*, ed. Lawrence L. Whetten. New York: Crane, Russak and Co., 1976.

Scott, William F., and Harriet Fast Scott. "Soviet Perceptions of Limited Nuclear Options." Section of an unpublished manuscript, sanitized by the authors, 1978.

Seaton, Albert. *Stalin as Warlord.* London: B. T. Batsford, 1976.

Semeiko, L. "Formy novye, sut' prezhniaia." *Krasnaia Zvezda* April 8, 1975.

Semenov, B. "Takticheskie upravliaemye rakety klassa 'vozdukh-poverkhnost.' " *Zarubezhnoe Voennoe Obozrenie*, no. 5 (1981): 50–57.

Semenov, G. "The Content of the Concept of an Operation." *Voennaia Mysl'*, no. 1 (1968): 91–94.

Semin, G. "Voennaia Strategiia NATO." *Zarubezhnoe Voennoe Obozrenie*, no. 8 (1983): 11–17.

Senghaas, Dieter. "Arms Race Dynamics and Arms Control in Europe." *Bulletin of Peace Proposals* 10 (1979): 8–19.

Serebriannikov, V. "Metodologiia voennogo dela." *Kommunist Vooruzhennykh Sil*, no. 9 (1970): 188–192.

———. "Osnova osnov ukrepleniia oborony strany." *Kommunist Vooruzhennykh Sil*, no. 4 (1986): 21–28.

———. "Predotvrashchenie voiny: vklad armii," *Kommunist Vooruzhennykh Sil*, no. 17 (1989): 21–27.

Sergeev, A. "Krizis voennoi doktriny i strategii amerikanskogo imperializma." *Voennaia Mysl'*, no. 8 (1974): 78–90.

Sergeev, P., and V. Trusenkov. "Amerikanskaia strategiia 'realisticheskogo ustrasheniia.' " *Zarubezhnoe Voennoe Obozrenia*, no. 11 (1977): 9–15.

———. "Voennaia doktrina SShA." *Zarubezhnoe Voennoe Obozrenie*, no. 9 (1975): 3–10.

Sergeev, V. "Partiinost' voennoi nauki." *Kommunist Vooruzhennykh Sil*, no. 1 (1963): 20–27.

Shakarubskii, P. "The Artillery in Modern Combat Operations." *Voennaia Mysl'*, no. 6 (1968): 61–66.

Shaposhnikov, B. M. *Vospominaniia/Voenno-nauchnye Trudy.* Reissued. Moscow: Voenizdat, 1974.

Shavrov, I. "Sorok let voennoi akademii General'nogo Shtaba." *Voennaia Mysl'*, no. 11 (1976): 3–14.

———. "Soviet Operational Art." *Voennaia Mysl'*, no. 10 (1973): 1–16.

Shchedrov, V. "Camouflaging Troops during Regrouping and Maneuver." *Voennaia Mysl'*, no. 6 (1966): 61–69.

Shenfield, Stephen D. "Minimum Nuclear Deterrence: The Debate Among Soviet Civilian Analysts." Center for Foreign Policy Development, Brown University, November 1989.

———. *The Nuclear Predicament.* Chatham House Papers no. 37. New York: Routledge and Kegan Paul Ltd., 1987.

———. "Soviet Historiography and the Operational Art: Historical Coverage of the Great Patriotic War by Period As an Indicator of the Orientation of Soviet Military Art 1959–88." *Soviet Military Studies* 2 (September 1989): 346–60.

Shevardnadze, Eduard. *The Future Belongs to Freedom*, ed. Catherine A. Fitzpatrick. New York: Free Press, 1991.

Shkadov, I. "Contemporary Art of Warfare and Some Questions on the Training of Military Personnel." *Voennaia Mysl'*, no. 11 (1973): 17–30.

Shkarubskii, S. "Artillery Before and Now." *Voennaia Mysl'*, no. 2 (1966): 50–57.

Shliapkin, A. "Air Support of Ground Troops." *Voennaia Mysl'*, no. 8 (1968): 33–41.

Shmelev, M., and A. Sinaev. Comment, *Voennaia Mysl'*, no. 10 (1964): 32.

Shtrik, S. "The Encirclement and Destruction of the Enemy during Combat Operations Not Involving the Use of Nuclear Weapons." *Voennaia Mysl'*, no. 1 (1968): 53–61.

Shulman, Marshall D. "SALT and the Soviet Union." In *SALT: The Moscow Agreements and Beyond*, ed. Mason Willrich and John B. Rhinelander. New York: Free Press, 1974.

Sidorova, Galina, and Nikita Zholkver. "Losing Enemies: Notes from the Bonn Conference." *New Times*, no. 20 (1990): 6–7.

Sidorov, P. "The Leninist Methodology of Soviet Military Science." *Voennaia Mysl'*, no. 4 (1969): 14–29.

Sidorov, V. "Vedenie operatsii s primeneniem obychnykh sredstv porazheniia." *Zarubezhnoe Voennoe Obozrenie*, no. 1 (1986): 7–15.

Simon, Herbert A. *Administrative Behavior*. 2d ed. New York: Macmillan, 1961.

Simon, Jeffrey. "Evaluation and Integration of Non-Soviet Warsaw Pact Forces into the Combined Armed Forces." *Signal* 40 (December 1985): 45–65.

Simonian, R. G. "The Development of Military Intelligence." *Voennaia Mysl'*, no. 8 (1972), as excerpted by Joseph D. Douglass, Jr., and Amoretta M. Hoeber, in *Index to and Extracts from Voyennaya Mysl', 1971–1973*. Alexandria, Va.: Systems Planning Corporation, 1980.

———. "Klassifikatsiia sovremennykh voin." *Voennaia Mysl'*, no. 6 (1979): 66–73.

———. "Kontseptsiia 'vybora tselei.' " *Krasnaia Zvezda*, September 28, 1976.

———. "Strategicheskie pozitsii Pentagona i bezopasnost' narodov." *Mirovaia Ekonomika i Mezhdunarodnye Otneshenie*, no. 11 (1978): 16–26.

———. "Tendentsii v razvitii voennoi doktriny SShA." *Zarubezhnoe Voennoe Obozrenie*, no. 11 (1981): 7–14.

———. "Voennoe iskusstvo SShA posle vtoroi mirovoi voiny." *Zarubezhnoe Voennoe Obozrenia* no. 2 (1976): 13–21.

Skovorodkin, M. "Some Questions on Coordination of Branches of Armed Forces in Major Operations." *Voennaia Mysl'*, no. 2 (1967): 36–44.

Sliunin, N. "Nuclear Resistance of Ground Troops." *Voennaia Mysl'*, no. 12 (1967): 37–44.

Slobodenko, A. "Vozmozhnyi kharakter sovremennykh voin." *Zarubezhnoe Voennoe Obozrenie*, no. 11 (1975): 3–10.

Smirnov, M., et al. "K voprosu o kharaktere sovetskoi voennoi nauke, ee predmete i soderzhannii." *Voennaia Mysl'*, no. 7 (1959): 3–30.

Smirnov, N. "A Meeting Engagement in Nuclear Warfare." *Voennaia Mysl'*, no. 9 (1967): 48–54.

Snyder, Jack L. "Averting Anarchy in the New Europe." *International Security* 14 (Spring 1990): 5–41.

———. "Civil-Military Relations and the Cult of the Offensive, 1914 and 1984." *International Security* 9 (Summer 1984): 108–46.

———. "The Gorbachev Revolution." *International Security* 12 (Winter 1987/88): 93–131.

———. *The Ideology of the Offensive*. Ithaca: Cornell University Press, 1984.

———. "Limiting Offensive Conventional Forces: Soviet Proposals and Western Options." *International Security* 12 (Spring 1988): 48–77.

———. *The Soviet Strategic Culture: Implications for Limited Nuclear Options*, R-2154. Santa Monica: RAND, 1977.

———. Testimony before the House Armed Services Committee Defense Policy Panel. *The Impact of Gorbachev's Reform Movement on the Soviet Military*. Hearings, July 14, 1988.

Snyder, Jack, and Andrei Kortunov. "French Syndrome on Soviet Soil." *New Times*, no. 44 (1989): 18–20.

Sokolovskii, V. D., ed. *Voennaia Strategiia*. Moscow: Voenizdat, 1962; rev. ed., 1963; 3d ed., 1967.

Solntsev, N. "Znachenie reshenii XXV s'ezda KPSS dlia dal'neishego povysheniia tekhnicheskoi osnashchennosti armii i flota." *Kommunist Vooruzhennykh Sil*, no. 22 (1977): 82–89.

Solov'ev, A., and L. Guliaev. "Radioelektronnaia razvedka." *Zarubezhnoe Voennoe Obozrenie*, no. 7 (1978): 12–18.

Soshov, A. "Vooruzhennye sily SSSR v poslevoennyi period." *Kommunist Vooruzhennykh Sil*, no. 15 (1970): 70–76.

Spirov, K. "Criticism of the Philosophical Foundations of the Imperialist Military Ideology." *Voennaia Mysl'*, no. 3 (1966): 28–44.

Stapenko, N. "Batal'onnaia takticheskaia gruppa v 'aktivnoi oborone.' " *Zarubezhnoe Voennoe Obozrenie*, no. 2 (1981): 29–34.

Starry, Donn A. "Extending the Battlefield." *Military Review* 61 (March 1981): 31–50.

Stein, David J. *The Development of NATO Tactical Air Doctrine, 1970–1985*, R-3385. Santa Monica: RAND, 1987.

Steinbruner, John D. *The Cybernetic Theory of Decision*. Princeton: Princeton University Press, 1974.

Stepan, Alfred. "The New Professionalism of Internal Warfare and Military Role Expansion." In *Authoritarian Brazil*, ed. Alfred Stepan. New Haven: Yale University Press, 1973.

Stevens, Sayre. "The Soviet BMD Program." In *Ballistic Missile Defense*, ed. Ashton B. Carter and David N. Schwartz. Washington, D.C.: Brookings, 1984.

Stockton, Paul N. "Services and Civilians." Ph.D. diss., Harvard University, 1986.

Strebkov, V. "Novaia model' bezopasnosti: voennyi aspekt." *Kommunist Vooruzhennykh Sil*, no. 2 (1990): 21–27.

Stromseth, Jane E. *The Origins of Flexible Response*. New York: St. Martin's Press, 1988.

Strusevich, A., and O. Frantsev. "Primenenie aviatsii v oboronitel'nykh operatsiiakh pervogo perioda voiny." *Voenno-Istoricheskii Zhurnal*, no. 1 (1978): 39–47.

Sulimov, Ye., and A. Timorin. "Osnovye cherty sovremennogo etapa v razvitii vooruzhennykh sil SSSR." *Kommunist Vooruzhennykh Sil*, no. 24 (1962): 38–44.

Taft, William H. IV. "European Security: Lessons Learned from the Gulf War." *NATO Review* 39 (June 1991): 7–11.

"The Tasks of Soviet Military Science in Light of the Decisions of the 24th CPSU Congress." *Voennaia Mysl'*, no. 8 (1971): 1–9.

Tatu, Michel. *Power in the Kremlin*. London: Collins, 1969.

Taubman, William, and Jane Taubman. *Moscow Spring*. New York: Summit Books, 1989.

Teplyakov, Yuri. "General Staff Changes." *Moscow News*, no. 5 (1989): 5.

———. "Reliable Defence First and Foremost." *Moscow News*, no. 8 (1988): 12.

Terriff, Terry. "The Innovation of U.S. Strategic Nuclear Policy in the Nixon Administration, 1969–1974: Objectives, Process and Politics." Nuclear History Program Working Paper 4. College Park, Md.: Center for International Security Studies at Maryland, 1990.

Tiushkevich, S. A., and V. M. Bondarenko. "Nauchno-tekhnicheskii progress i ego vliianie na razvitie voennogo dela." In *Nauchno-tekhnicheskii Progress i Revoliutsiia v Voennom Dele*. Moscow: Voenizdat, 1973.

Tolubko, V. F. "Strategicheskoe vzaimodeistvie po opytu Velikoi Otechestvennoi Voiny." *Voenno-Istoricheskii Zhurnal*, no. 2 (1987): 11–19.

Tolubko, V. I. *Nedelin*. Moscow: Molodaia Gvardiia, 1979.

Tonkikh, A. "Voenno-nauchnye konferentsii—vazhnaia forma voenno-nauchnoi raboty." *Voennaia Mysl'*, no. 12 (1971): 35–39.

Trifonenkov, P. "Voenno-teoreticheskoi nasledie V. I. Lenina i sovremennost'." *Voenno-Istoricheskii Zhurnal*, no. 11 (1967): 3–13.

"Triumphal Step of Leninism." *Voennaia Mysl'*, no. 4 (1967): 1–10.

Trofimenko, G. A. "Nekotory aspekty voenno-politicheskoi strategii SShA." *SShA*, no. 10 (1970): 14–27.

———. "Politicheskii realizm i strategiia 'realisticheskogo sderzhivaniia,' " *SShA*, no. 12 (1971): 3–15.

———. *SShA: Politika, Voina, Ideologiia*. Moscow: Mysl', 1976.

———. "Voprosy ukrepleniia mira i bezopasnosti v sovetsko-amerikanskikh otnosheniiakh." *SShA*, no. 9 (1974): 7–18.

Trulock, Notra III. "The Impact of World War II on Contemporary Soviet Military Theory." In *Contemporary Soviet Military Affairs*, ed. Jonathan R. Adelman and Christann Lea Gibson. Boston: Unwin Hyman, 1989.

———. "Soviet Perspectives on Limited Nuclear Warfare." In *Swords and Shields*, ed. Fred S. Hoffman, Albert Wohlstetter, and David S. Yost. Lexington, Mass.: Lexington Books, 1987.

Tsvetkov, V. "Vydaiushchiisia voennyi myslitel' XIX veka." *Voenno-Istoricheskii Zhurnal*, no. 1 (1964): 47–59.

Tsypkin, Mikhail. "The Soviet Military: Glasnost' Against Secrecy." *Problems of Communism* 40 (May/June 1991): 51–66.

Tumas, V., and N. Sergeev. "The West German Army Corps in Basic Types of Combat." *Voennaia Mysl'*, no. 1 (1972): 97–108.

Turchenko, V. V. "O strategicheskoi oborone." *Voennaia Mysl'*, no. 7 (1982): 16–27.

———. "Tendentsii razvitiia teorii i praktiki strategicheskoi oborony." *Voennaia Mysl'*, no. 8 (1979): 13–24.

Tyler, Patrick E. "Seven Hypothetical Conflicts Foreseen by the Pentagon." *New York Times*, February 17, 1992.

Ulsamer, Edgar. "The Soviet Juggernaut." *Air Force Magazine*, March 1976: 36–65.

U.S. Army. FM 100–5, "Operations." February 19, 1962.

———. FM 100–5, "Operations." July 1, 1976.

———. FM 100–5, "Operations." August 20, 1982.

U.S. Congress Office of Technology Assessment. *New Technologies for NATO: Implementing Follow-on Forces Attack*, OTA-ISC-309. Washington, D.C.: Government Printing Office, 1987.

U.S. Department of Defense. *Soviet Military Power: Prospects for Change, 1989.* Washington, D.C.: GPO, 1989.

U.S. Departments of State and Defense. *Soviet Strategic Defense Programs.* Washington, D.C.: GPO, October 1985.

"V diplomaticheskoi akademii." *Vestnik Ministerstva Inostrannykh Del SSSR*, no. 23 (1988): 21.

Van Evera, Stephen. "Causes of War." Ph.D. diss., University of California at Berkeley, 1984.

———. "The Cult of the Offensive and the Origins of the First World War." *International Security* 9 (Summer 1984): 58–107.

Van Oudenaren, John. *The Role of Shevardnadze and the Ministry of Foreign Affairs in the Making of Soviet Defense and Arms Control Policy.* R-3898. Santa Monica: RAND, 1990.

Vasendin, N., and N. Kuznetsov. "Modern Warfare and Surprise Attack." *Voennaia Mysl'*, no. 6 (1968): 42–48.

Vasil'ev, A., and N. Pimenov. "Perspektivy razvitiia raket strategicheskogo naznacheniia." *Voennaia Mysl'*, no. 1 (1970): 26–35.

Vasil'ev, A. A., and M. I. Gerasev. "Nekotorye itogi voenno-politicheskogo kursa administratsii R. Reigana." *Mirovaia Ekonomika i Mezhdunarodnye Otnosheniia*, no. 5 (1988): 43–56.

Vasil'ev, A. A., M. I. Gerasev, and A. A. Kokoshin. "Asimmetrichnyi otvet." *SShA*, no. 2 (1987): 26–35.

Vasil'ev, A. P., and V. K. Rudiuk. "Dostatochna li protivovozdushnaia oborona?" *Voennaia Mysl'*, no. 9 (1989): 59–68.

Vasil'ev, G. "Voprosy operativnogo iskusstva v vooruzhennykh silakh SShA." *Zarubezhnoe Voennoe Obozrenie*, no. 12 (1983): 3–7.

Vasil'ev, P. "O roli vnezapnosti v sovremennoi voine i sposobakh ee dostizheniia." *Voennyi Zarubezhnik*, no. 3 (1961): 50–59.

Vilinov, M. "An Object Lesson of History." *Voennaia Mysl'*, no. 5 (1969): 79–85.

Vishnevskii, Ernest, and Zdzislav Golomb. "Voennye deistviia bez primeneniia iadernogo oruzhiia." *Voennia Mysl'*, no. 2 (1970): 62–70.

Vladimirov, D. Book review. *Voennyi Zarubezhnik*, no. 12 (1959): 73–76.

Vladimirov, I. "NATO na poroge peremen?" *Zarubezhnoe Voennoe Obozrenie*, no. 9 (1990): 17–20.

Voennyi Entsiklopedicheskii Slovar'. Moscow: Voenizdat, 1984.

Volgin, N. S. "Ne zabyli li my staroe . . ." *Voennaia Mysl'*, no. 12 (1991): 20–31.

Volkogonov, Dmitry. "The anti-war doctrine." *New Times*, no. 25 (1987): 15.

———. "Idei V. I. Lenina o moral'no-politicheskoi i psikhologicheskoi podgotovke voinov." *Kommunist Vooruzhennykh Sil*, no. 7 (1974): 15–25.

Volkov, A. "Nauchnye osnovy upravlencheskoi deiatel'nosti voennykh kadrov." *Kommunist Vooruzhennykh Sil*, no. 15 (1976): 9–16.

Volkov, A., and N. Zapara, "Nauchno-tekhnicheskaia revoliutsiia i voennoe delo." *Kommunist Vooruzhennykh Sil*, no. 2 (1971): 8–15.

Volkov, N. "Mirovaia kapitalisticheskaia systema." *Kommunist Vooruzhennykh Sil*, 1978, no. 5: 75–82.

Volkov, S., and A. Zaletnyi, "Vozrozhdeniie fashistskoi voennoi ideologii v Zapadnoi Germanii." *Voennaia Mysl'*, no. 5 (1954): 65–76.

Volkov, Ye. "Ne raz'iasniaet, a zatumanivaet . . ." *Krasnaia Zvezda*, September 28, 1989.

Vorob'ev, I. "Maneuver in Operations and in Combat." *Voennaia Mysl'*, no. 9 (1963): 19–30.

Vorob'ev, I. N. "Novoe oruzhie i razvitie printsipov obshchevoiskogo boia." *Voennaia Mysl'*, no. 6 (1986): 35–45.

———. "Printsipy formirovaniia voennoi doktriny." *Voennaia Mysl'*, no. 11–12 (1991): 22–29.

———. "Sootnoshenie i vzaimosviaz' nastupleniia i oborony." *Voennaia Mysl'*, no. 4 (1980): 49–59.

Vorontsov, G. "SShA, NATO i gonka obychnykh vooruzhenii." *Mirovaia Ekonomika i Mezhdunarodnye Otnosheniia*, no. 5 (1985): 49–60.

The Voroshilov Lectures, vol. 1, Ghulam Dastagir Wardak, comp.; ed. Graham Hall Turbiville, Jr. Washington, D.C.: National Defense University Press, 1989.

Voroshilov, N. "Problemy voiny i mira v sovremennuiu epokhu." *Kommunist Vooruzhennykh Sil*, no. 6 (1964): 9–17.

Voznenko, V. V. "Osnovye etapy razvitiia sovetskoi voennoi strategii." *Voennaia Mysl'*, no. 4 (1979): 15–26.

"Vystuplenie ministra oborony SShA." *Krasnaia Zvezda*, January 26, 1974.

Walker, Jack L. "The Diffusion of Innovation among the American States." *American Political Science Review* 63 (September 1969): 880–99.

———. "The Diffusion of Knowledge, Policy Communities and Agenda Setting." In *New Strategic Perspectives on Social Policy*, ed. John E. Tropman, Milan J. Dluhy, and Roger M. Lind. New York: Pergamon, 1981.

Walker, Richard Lee. *Strategic Target Planning: Bridging the Gap between Theory and Practice*. National Security Affairs Monograph Series 83–9. Washington, D.C.: National Defense University Press, 1983.

Walt, Stephen M. "The Search for a Science of Strategy." *International Security* 12 (Summer 1987): 140–65.

Waltz, Kenneth N. *Theory of International Politics*. New York: Random House, 1979.

Wampler, Robert A. *NATO Strategic Planning and Nuclear Weapons, 1950–1957*. Nuclear History Program Occasional Paper 6. College Park, Md.: Center for International Security Studies at Maryland, 1990.

Wanty, Emile. "Vliianie atomnogo oruzhiia na organizatsiiu i taktiki voisk." *Voennyi Zarubezhnik*, no. 2 (1956): 3–12.

Warner, Edward L. III. *The Military in Contemporary Soviet Politics*. Westport, Conn.: Praeger, 1977.

———. "New Thinking and Old Realities in Soviet Defence Policy." *Survival* 31 (January/February 1989): 13–33.

———. *Soviet Concepts and Capabilities for Limited Nuclear War: What We Know and How We Know It*, N-2769. Santa Monica: RAND, 1989.

———. Testimony before the House Armed Services Committee Defense Policy Panel. *The Impact of Gorbachev's Reform Movement on the Soviet Military*. Hearings, July 14, 1988.

Weick, Karl E. *The Social Psychology of Organizing*. 2d ed. Reading, Mass.: Addison-Wesley, 1979.

Weinberger, George Martin, comp. and ed. *Soviet Cybernetic Technology: A Timeline, Researcher's Data Base and Guide to Professional Literature*, vol. 1. New York: University Press of America, 1985.

Wendt, James C., and Nanette Brown. *Improving the NATO Force Planning Process*, R-3383. Santa Monica: RAND, 1986.

Wettig, Gerhard. "Sufficiency in Defense—A New Guideline for the Soviet Military Posture?" *Radio Liberty Research Bulletin*, no. 38 (1987): 1.

Wildavsky, Aaron. *The Politics of the Budgetary Process*. 4th ed. Boston: Little, Brown and Co., 1984.

Wilkinson, Christopher. "Perestroika: The Role of the Defence Sector." *NATO Review* 38 (February 1990): 20–25.

Wilson, James Q. *Bureaucracy: What Government Agencies Do and Why They Do It*. New York: Basic Books, 1989.

Wolfe, Thomas W. "The Convergence Issue and Soviet Strategic Policy." In *The RAND 25th Anniversary Volume*. Santa Monica: RAND, 1973.

———. *A First Reaction to the New Soviet Book "Military Strategy"*, RM-3495. Santa Monica: RAND, 1963.

———. *The SALT Experience*. Cambridge, Mass.: Ballinger, 1979.

———. *The Soviet Military Scene: Institutional and Defense Policy Considerations*, RM-4913. Santa Monica: RAND, 1966.

———. *Soviet Power and Europe, 1945–1970*. Baltimore: Johns Hopkins University Press, 1970.

Wyman, Willard G. "Osnovnye printsipy doktriny Armii." *Voennyi Zarubezhnik*, no. 7 (1958): 3–12.

Yakubovskii, I. "50 Years of the USSR Armed Forces." *Voennaia Mysl'*, no. 2 (1968): 15–35.

Yasiukov, M. "Voennaia politika KPSS: Sushchnost', soderzhanie." *Kommunist Vooruzhennykh Sil*, no. 20 (1985): 14–21.

Yazov, D. "Novaia model' bezopasnosti i vooruzhennye sily." *Kommunist*, no. 18 (1989): 61–72.

Yegorov, S. "Mekhanizirovannaia diviziia SShA V nastuplenii." *Zarubezhnoe Voennoe Obozrenie*, no. 4 (1984): 23–28.

Yemelin, V. "Zametki o literature po protivoatomnoi zashchite." *Voennaia Mysl'*, no. 6 (1959): 83–89.

Yepishev, A. "The Question of Moral-Political and Psychological Training of Troops." *Voennaia Mysl'*, no. 12 (1968): 1–22.

Yevgen'iev, Ye. G. "Novye napravleniia gonki vooruzhenii v stranakh NATO." *Voennaia Mysl'*, no. 1 (1977): 88–96.

Zakharov, M. V. *General'nyi Shtab v Predvoennye Gody*. Moscow: Voenizdat, 1989.

———. "New Horizons of the Military Press." *Voennaia Mysl'*, no. 9 (1966): 1–13.

———. "Soviet Military Science over Fifty Years." *Voennaia Mysl'*, no. 2 (1968): 36–52.

Zaltman, Gerald, Robert Duncan, and Jonny Holbek. *Innovations and Organizations*. New York: John Wiley and Sons, 1973.

Zav'ialov, I. "Evolution in the Correlation of Strategy, Operational Art and Tactics." *Voennaia Mysl'*, no. 11 (1971): 30–41.

Zemskov, V. "Kharakternye strategicheskie cherty mirovykh voin." *Voennaia Mysl'*, no. 7 (1974): 19–33.

———. "Wars of the Modern Era." *Voennaia Mysl'*, no. 5 (1969): 52–63.

Zhelnov, A. "O deistvii zakona otritsaniia otritsaniia v voennom dele." *Voennaia Mysl'*, no. 3 (1962): 18–32.

Zheltov, A. S., T. R. Kondratkov, and Ye. A. Khomenko, eds. *Metodologicheskie Problemy Voennoi Teorii i Praktiki*. 2d ed. Moscow: Voenizdat, 1969.

Zhilin, A. "Some Questions of Meeting Engagements of Large Tank Groupings." *Voennaia Mysl'*, no. 2 (1964): 1–8.

Zhilin, P. "Polkovodcheskaia deiatel'nost' M. I. Kutuzova v Otechestvennoi voine 1812 goda." *Voenno-Istoricheskii Zhurnal*, no. 7 (1962): 29–41.

Zholkver, Nikita, et al. "For a Nuclear-Free World, for the Survival of Mankind." *New Times*, no. 8 (1987): 4–8.

Zhurkin, Vitaly V., Sergei A. Karaganov, and Andrei V. Kortunov. "O razumnoi dostatochnosti." *SShA*, no. 12 (1987): 11–21.

———. "Reasonable sufficiency—or how to break the vicious circle." *New Times*, no. 40 (1987): 13–15.

———. "Vyzovy bezopasnosti—starye i novye." *Kommunist*, no. 31 (1988): 42–50.

Zisk, Kimberly Marten. "Reciprocal Unilateral Measures and Military Doctrine in the Post-Cold War Era." Paper prepared for delivery at the Conference on Reciprocal Unilateral Measures and the U.S.-Soviet Security Relationship, Stanford University Center for International Security and Arms Control (CISAC), December 1990.

Index

interests of military organizations, 3, 4,
11–14, 174, 176, 180–81, 184, 185–
86, 187
Intermediate-range Nuclear Force (INF)
negotiations, 123–24
International Department, Communist
Party Central Committee, 124
Ionin, G., 71–72
Iran, 92. *See also* nuclear strikes: on non-
Soviet periphery
Iraq. *See* Operation Desert Storm
ISKAN. *See* Institute of USA and Canada
Studies
Ivanov, S., 73
Ivanov, V. M., 150
Ivlev, N., 139

Janowitz, Morris, 12
Joint Chiefs of Staff system, U.S., 8–9, 21.
See also general staff systems
Jones, Ellen, 35

Karber, Phillip A., 163–64, 236n.54
Karpov, Viktor, 124
Kazakov, D., 59
Kennedy, John F., 52
KGB, 34, 43–44, 209n.44
Khalkhin-Gol, Battle of, 158, 159, 170
Khrushchev, Nikita S., 7, 41, 48–49,
55, 58–59, 79, 121, 123, 177, 214–
15n.76; civil-military relations under,
62–69, 174, 184; nuclear bluffing of,
61
Kingdon, John W., 23, 205n.47
Kipp, Jacob W., 122, 173
Kirshin, Sergei, 127
Kirshin, Yurii, 127, 128–29
Kissinger, Henry, 85, 92
Knight, Amy, 209n.44
Kokoshin, Andrei A., 125–27, 129–30,
152–62, 175, 189, 243n.201
Kommunist Vooruzhennykh Sil, 44
Konev, I. S., 66
Konovalov, A. A., 161
Korean War Model. *See* Khalkhin-Gol,
Battle of
Korotkov, I., 80
Kortunov, Andrei, 185–87
Kozhin, V., 139
Kozlov, M. M., 147
Kozlov, S., 60–62
Krasnaia Zvezda, 44

Kulikov, A. S., 170
Kulikov, Viktor G., 33, 109, 219n.142
Kunadze, G., 160
Kurochkin, P., 72
Kursk, Battle of, 148, 156–57, 158, 172
Kushch-Zharko, K., 72
Kutuzov, Mikhail I., 65
Kuz'min, I., 66
Kuznetsov, N., 70

Laird, Melvin, 107
Larionov, Valentin V., 78, 94, 106–7, 108,
127, 156
Larson, Deborah Welch, 24, 205–6n.57
launch-on-warning, Soviet, 115–16
Levadov, V., 139
limited nuclear war, Soviet interest in, 98–
101
limited strategic strikes. *See* nuclear strikes:
limited strategic
Lindblom, Charles E., 16
Litherland, Pat, 125
Liubimov, Yu., 128, 166
Liutov, N., 61–62
LIVE OAK, 52, 54
Lobov, Vladimir N., 39, 150–51, 160
local war, 218n.127
Lomov, N. A., 72
Losik, O., 172
Lubkemeier, Eckhard, 196
Lukes, Igor, 35
Lushev, P., 168–69

Mackenzie, Donald, 204n.28
Main Intelligence Directorate, Soviet. *See*
GRU
Makarevskii, Vadim, 127, 164–65
Maksimov, N., 143
Malinovskii, R. Ya., 54, 64–65, 68,
222n.175
Manzhurin, I. N., 145
March, James G., 15–16, 20, 203n.24
Margelov, V., 222n.175
Marx, John H., 31
Maryshev, A. P., 148
Massive Retaliation, 47, 49–51
MccGwire, Michael, 219n.143
McConnell, James M., 218n.127
McNamara, Robert, 84, 86
Meshcheriakov, N. V., 167
Meyer, Stephen M., 34, 73, 122, 174,
175